— ROSEMARY DESJARDINS —

THE RATIONAL ENTERPRISE

LOGOS IN PLATO'S *THEAETETUS*

STATE UNIVERSITY OF NEW YORK

PRESS

Published by
State University of New York Press, Albany

© 1990 State University of New York

For information, address State University of New York
Press, State University Plaza, Albany, N.Y., 12246

Library of Congress Cataloging in Publication Data

CIP to come

Desjardins, Rosemary, 1936—
    The rational enterprise : logos in Plato's Theaeteus / Rosemary
Desjardins.
        p.   cm. — (SUNY series in ancient Greek philosophy)
    Bibliography: p.
    Includes index.
    ISBN 0-88706-837-5.   ISBN 0-88706-838-3 (pbk.)
    1. Plato.   Theaetetus.   2. Knowledge, Theory of.   3. Logos.
    I. Title.   II. Series.
    B386.D45   1990
    121—dc19

                                                                88-20001
                                                                CIP

10   9   8   7   6   5   4   3   2   1

Cover art courtesy of the American Numismatic Society, New York.

To the memory of my parents
in celebration
of all the St. Hilary years

CONTENTS

ACKNOWLEDGMENTS

To those who have encouraged this venture, I am grateful—especially to Richard Bernstein, James Ross, Alasdair MacIntyre, David Gallop, Reginald Allen, Abraham Edel, and Ronald Polanski. For confronting me with hard questions I am indebted to Charles Kahn, with whom I originally tried out some of these hypotheses, and particularly to the anonymous publishing house readers who forced me to think through some of the tougher issues. For their indefatigable patience (with the text and with me) I would like to thank my SUNY editors, Bernadine Dawes and Susan Zorn—as also I thank Jan Richard and David Gontrum for their help in getting this manuscript through the intricacies of computer technology. Above all, I am grateful to Paul Desjardins, who first introduced me to Plato and taught me how to read a dialogue.

PROLOGUE

Any discourse ought to be constructed like a living
creature, with its own body as it were; it must not
lack either head or feet; it must have a middle
and extremities so composed as to suit each other
and the whole work.

(Phaedr. 264c2-5)

Plato's words ring in my ears as I face the task of writing about the *Theaetetus*, for as a piece of philosophical literature, this dialogue meets with stunning success his own criteria for an organically structured logos. There are, nevertheless, difficulties that confront the would-be analyst, since there are various ways in which the divisions may be drawn.[1] What follows is one possible—and I hope fruitful—proposal.

There is a story that Plato had a dream in which, turned into a swan, he flew from tree to tree to escape the bonds of those who would ensnare him.[2] Like the swan, Plato will escape capture in the net of this or any other interpretation. For in the long run, any adequate response to the living logos of the dialogue will involve, not merely this kind of analytic dissection, but a heady participation in the dynamic and multidimensional flow of the work itself.

INTRODUCTION

OVERVIEW OF THE *THEAETETUS*

Plato sometimes talks of philosophical inquiry as the challenge to battle the waves and currents of the sea as, like Odysseus, we strive for the distant shore and rocky crags of truth.[1] Throughout the mainstream of Western philosophy, there have flowed two persistent currents of concern which, despite (or perhaps because of) new twists and turns, challenge us today no less than they did our philosophical forebears. The sometimes subtle, sometimes seething, intersection of both currents in Plato's *Theaetetus* makes it not only one of the more difficult, but also one of the most intriguingly contemporary of Plato's dialogues.

The first turbulence, catching us between the extremes of a Cartesian approach on the one hand and a postmodernist and feminist critique on the other, eddies around the very notion of reason and rationality. The second (epistemological when viewed from one angle, ontological when viewed from another) snags us on the question of a "given"—whether such "givenness" be interpreted in terms of the specific objects of an external world, of discrete impressions or sense data of perceptual experience, or of our conceptual categories themselves. The myth of a sheer objective "given" tends to evoke in turn a counterstress on a subjective "taken"—variations on which lie at the heart of a number of current debates, not only in philosophy, but also in anthropology, linguistics, cognitive psychology, the philosophy of science, and the sociology of knowledge. In the best of the tradition there occurs a skillful maneuvering between the Scylla of an unqualified "given" and the Charybdis of an unqualified "taken". The present study will explore one classical experiment in mediation between "given" and "taken," for in the reciprocity of its discursive and dramatic dimensions, Plato's *Theaetetus* simultaneously exhibits, and reflects on, a peculiarly fruitful "taking" of a "given." Ironically, the inquiry thus leads him into the thick of our own current debate about reason and rationality,[2] since, on the proposed interpretation, it is this activity of "taking" that characterizes *nous* as creative intelligence, ultimately defines what it is to be rational, and in its most comprehensive and self-conscious realization constitutes the exercise of philosophic wisdom.

1

APPARENT FAILURE OF THE *THEAETETUS*

On his way to the Porch of the King Archon to face arraignment on the charge that would lead to his condemnation and death, Socrates apparently stopped to talk with two distinguished mathematicians. Plato's reconstruction of this conversation has come down to us as the dialogue known as the *Theaetetus*.[3]

Perhaps the most conspicuous and well-known feature of the *Theaetetus* is its apparent failure to provide a satisfactory account of knowledge—in spite of the pivotal role that knowledge seems to play in Plato's philosophy. Thus, looking back at the long discussion that constitutes the dialogue, Socrates seems driven to the conclusion that "all the offspring that have been born [their attempts at definition] are mere windeggs and not worth rearing" (210b8-9), for "neither perception. . . nor true opinion, nor logos[4] combined with true opinion could be knowledge [*epistēmē*]" (210a9-b2).[5] For several reasons, this apparently negative conclusion is problematic.

First, and most obviously, it seems on the face of it to be seriously inconsistent with what Plato has to say about knowledge in other dialogues—not only earlier, but also later than the *Theaetetus*. Second, it raises difficulties with respect to the educational role of *aporia* (confusion, perplexity) as this role is considered elsewhere in the dialogues. Finally, it is not clear how such a conclusion is to be interpreted in light of Plato's reservations about language and his own writing of the dialogues. These difficulties are serious enough to warrant closer examination.

Knowledge as involving true opinion and logos

Within the larger picture of the dialogues as a whole, true opinion is usually approached from two rather different angles. On the one hand, its importance is emphasized with reference to, and in direct association with, knowledge. Thus, from the *Meno* (97e6-98a6) to the *Republic* (IX, 585b14-cl), and on through dialogues like the *Timeaus* (77b4-5),[6] *Statesman* (309c5-8), and *Philebus* (38a6-8), true opinion is consistently (though sometimes vaguely) linked with knowledge. On the other hand, at least from the *Meno* through those same later dialogues, it is made equally clear that true opinion by itself will not suffice, that even if true opinion should prove to be necessary, it can not constitute a sufficient condition of knowledge in its full sense as *epistēmē*. Socrates' conviction on this point is in fact one of the most emphatic he allows himself:

> I speak as one who does not know but only conjectures; yet that there is a difference between true opinion and knowledge is not at all a conjecture

with me, but something I would particularly assert that I knew; there are not many things of which I would say that, but this one at any rate I will include among those that I do know. (*Meno* 98b1-5)

The claim is at various points backed up by argument. As the senses are distinguished by the difference in their objects, so opinion (whether true or false) is differentiated from knowledge in being set over different objects (*Rep. V*, 477b3-8); cf. *Tim.* 37b3-c3; 51e6-52a7); again, opinion (whether true or false) comes through persuasion, whereas knowledge comes through teaching (*Tim.* 51e2-4); opinion can *happen* to be true, whereas knowledge properly claims infallibility (*Rep. V*, 477e4-478a1; cf. *Gorg.* 454d1-8; even *Theaet.* 152c5-6; and for reiteration of the contrast in general, compare *Phaedr.* 247d1-e2; 262c1-3; *Phil.* 58e5-59b8).

It is this distinction, of course, that leads us to the role of logos, for not only is logos in a general way necessary for knowledge, since "if we are deprived of logos we should be deprived of philosophy" (*Soph.* 260a6-7), but even more emphatically, "no worse evil can befall a man than to come to hate logoi," for in such a case he should be "deprived of the truth and knowledge of reality" (*Phaedo* 90d6-7). On the contrary, one who is able to produce logoi—seeking through definition to organize multiplicity in terms of unifying structures—may properly be said to be a dialectician, and to be divine (*Phaedr.* 265d3-266c1). For, as Socrates asks in a well-known passage, "Do you not give the name *dialectician* to the man who is able to exact a logos of each thing? And will you not say that the one unable to do this, insofar as he is incapable of rendering an account [*logon didonai*] to himself and others, does not possess full reason and intelligence?" (*Rep.* VII, 534b3-6; cf. *Phaedr.* 278c4-d6). In the middle dialogues it is logos, especially when interpreted as discrimination according to nature and function, that Socrates endorses as defining the pursuit of knowledge (e.g., *Phaedr.* 270c10-d7)—and it is not clear that the claim is ever really relinquished. Although the later period sees an enlargement of focus (from an earlier concern with collecting a plurality of particulars under a single form and then dividing that form into subforms [*Phaedr.* 265d3-266b2], to a later concern with division and combination in the context of formal classification as such), the underlying continuity of structure will (so this study will argue) prove to be significant. As a result, the later dialogues echo the earlier demand for logos, and the later version of structural discrimination is correspondingly exalted both in the *Sophist,* as "the method of logos . . . pursued for the sake of *nous*" (*Soph.* 227a7-c6), and in the *Statesman,* as the method whose goal is "the making of the hearers better dialecticians and quicker to discover through logos the truth of realities" (*Stat.* 286d8-287a4). In whatever terms knowledge is finally to be understood, it seems indubitably evident that—at least from the *Meno* to the *Statesman*—logos (whatever that turns out exactly to be) is crucial for the kind of knowledge that qualifies as philosophic, dialectical, or true *epistēmē*.

In case it were not already suggested in all this that knowledge is to be sought in some combination of true opinion and logos, there are those well-known passages in which Socrates explicitly reminds us that "to have true opinion, if you can provide no logos for it, is not full knowledge, for how can an unreasoned (*alogon*) thing be knowledge?" (*Symp.* 202a5-7)—or, as he yet more specifically explains:

> True opinions run away out of the human soul, and thus are of no great value until one makes them fast with causal reasoning [*aitias logismō*] ...But when once they are fastened, in the first place they turn into *epistēmē*, and in the second, are abiding. And this is why *epistēmē* is more prized than true opinion: the one transcends the other by its bond. (*Meno* 98a2-8)

Finally, just in case one were to suppose that in the *Theaetetus* Plato temporarily changes his mind and is no longer convinced that true opinion and logos together constitute knowledge, he seems to go out of his way to make it clear that no, these and these only—true opinion and logos—must provide the conditions of *epistēmē*, "for [as Socrates observes to Theaetetus] what knowledge could there still be apart from logos and true opinion?" (*Theaet.* 202d6-7). In other words, even here, in the midst of his challenge to just that definition, he seems at the same time to be warning us that true opinion and logos are still to be understood as providing the necessary, and even in some elusive sense the sufficient, conditions of knowledge. But then, if this be so, what does it do to our understanding of the apparently negative conclusion? At the very least, it would surely seem, one might be just a little wary of accepting the ostensible conclusion at face value.

This consideration leads to the second reason one ought perhaps to look more carefully at the apparent "failure" of the dialogue. For, whatever the status or function of Socratic refutation (elenchus) in the early dialogues, at least by the time of the *Theaetetus* Plato seems to be quite deliberate in his educational use of *aporia* (confusion, puzzlement).

Positive role of *aporia*

Whether the *Theaetetus* is to be read as a "failed" inquiry or not, either way there remains the question of Why? What is the educational point of a dialogue whose conclusion is aporetic? Is it self-critique that leads to rejection of earlier Platonic doctrine? Is it the humbling of a reason that seeks answers where there are none? To what degree, in other words, is *aporia* purely negative?

That there might be more to Theaetetus' *aporia* than the merely negative aspect that at first sight meets the eye seems to be suggested by the fact that, in the continued conversation of the next day (i.e., in the *Sophist*), Theaetetus' reaction to *aporia* does quite clearly play a positive role in the inquiry, for it is his *aporia* at the heart of the discussion (e.g., *Soph.* 236e3; 238a2, d5; 241b6; 243b10; 249d10; 250d8-e6) that precipitates the resolution of the central paradoxes of the dialogue.[7] Lest, however, we miss the import of the argument (as—so this study will argue—it was missed by both Theaetetus and Theodorus in the earlier conversation), on this occasion Theaetetus—and we the readers with him—are carefully led beyond *aporia* and the stalemate of the dilemma to seize both horns together, and so "push a way through between both of them at once" (*Soph.* 251a2-3).

It should not really be surprising that *aporia*—meaning literally "no passage," "no way out," "no exit"—should function positively within Plato's educational framework. After all, no matter how perplexed the participants in any dialogue, "storm-tossed [as Protarchus later puts it] in the puzzling crosscurrents of discussion," Plato's intention in writing dialogues is surely not mere perplexity, but rather the kind of critique that will foster knowledge and wisdom. "Let us not imagine [as, again, Protarchus puts it to Socrates] that the end of our discussion is a mere puzzling of us all" (*Phil.* 29b1-2; 20a2-4). That the goal of *aporia* is more than merely negative seems, moreover, to be attested to from the early through the late dialogues.

Already back in the *Meno*, it will be recalled, we were warned to see a positive purpose to this sort of reduction to perplexity. Socrates' response when Meno sought to blame him for his own confusion (*Meno* 80a2-b7) was to take the slave boy through a series of moves that exactly parallel Meno's conversation up to that point. When, like Meno, the boy is reduced to perplexity, Socrates pauses to point out that, not only has he now been negatively helped by discovering that "besides not knowing, he does not think he knows," but more importantly, he has actually been directed towards a positive result. In other words, he has been "given assistance towards finding out the truth of the matter . . . and will discover by seeking the truth" (*Meno* 84a7-c11). And so indeed it turns out, for the boy proceeds to discover the diagonal. But how did the boy's *aporia* prove to be a positive help? Socrates goes on to explain: "He who does not *know* about something or other may yet have *true opinion* about that same thing about which he knows nothing"; for, as the *Statesman* puts it in only slightly different language, "It would seem that each of us knows everything that he knows as if in

a dream [*hoion onar*]" (*Stat.* 277d2-3). So too Socrates will say in the case
of the slave boy, "At this moment those opinions have just been stirred
up in him, like a dream [*hosper onar*]" (*Meno* 85c9-10). It is—as he
elaborates later in the *Sophist*—a question of "removing obstructions"
(*Soph.* 230c4-d2) to allow those true opinions to reveal their presence
through what in the *Meno* he calls "recollection."[8]

But once again, if this is truly how Plato would have us understand
aporia, then perhaps it will help us better understand the aporetic
conclusion of the *Theaetetus.* After all, the conversation with Theaetetus
on the one hand closely parallels the negative purification of the slave
boy (e.g., *Theaet.* 210b11-c4), yet on the other hand and at the same time,
it seems to be echoing the *Meno's* talk of "remembering" and of
opinions stirred up as in "a dream" (Socrates uses the same word *onar*:
Theaet. 201c8-d8).[9] If this were indeed Plato's intention, then one result
would be that the riddle of the *Theaetetus* would no longer be a riddle.[10]
The final definition of knowledge as "true opinion with logos" (*Theaet.*
201c9-d1) would then be understood as recollected or "dreaming" *true*
opinion, requiring only that it be "made fast" in order to "turn into
epistēmē" (*Meno* 98a3-6). Viewed in this light, Socrates' response to this
final effort at definition (which on the "failure" theory is incomprehensible) is exactly what one might expect. As a statement, he
observes, it is probably fair enough (*Theaet.* 202d4-6); as is so often the
case, the problem will be that of really *understanding* what the formula
means. Such understanding, this study will argue, is the real goal of the
apparent "refutation of the dream"; if effective, that cross-examination
will transform Theaetetus' "dreaming" true opinion into "waking"
knowledge (*Stat.* 278e10). It is, however, in this, the subsequent effort to
"make the true opinion fast with causal reasoning" (*Meno* 98a3-4) that
Theaetetus is unsuccessful; but the recollected definition as such, the
dialogue seems to be saying, is not only unexceptionable, but is solid
Platonic doctrine. And this brings me to one last point about the
apparent failure of the dialogue.

Language and ambiguity

Seen in sufficiently large perspective, this movement in the *Theaetetus* is
hardly unique. In fact, as I see it, the problem involved in understanding
just what any given statement or formula means is one that is
absolutely central to Plato's whole philosophical enterprise. All philosophical formulas—and most particularly those representing hard-
core Platonic doctrine—are one and all subject to inadequate or false, as
well as adequate or true, interpretations. Thus—whether it is Critias'
understanding of *sōphrosynē* as "minding one's own business" (*Charm.*
162e6ff.), Meno's understanding of "virtue is knowledge" (*Meno*

87c5ff.), Polemarchus' understanding of justice as "giving to each his due" (*Rep.* I, 331e1ff.), Theaetetus' understanding of traditional pre-Socratic formulas about "being" and "nonbeing" (*Soph.* 243d3ff.), even Socrates' own understanding of the Delphic oracle (*Apol.* 21b2ff.)—each is in turn subjected to crossexamination in order to purify it of false or inadequate interpretation.[11] Sometimes Plato communicates a sense of the basic ambiguity inherent in such statements by referring to them as "riddles" (*ainigmata, ainittomai*: e.g., *Apol.* 21b4; *Charm.* 161c9; 162a10, b4; *Rep.* I, 332b9). In one form or another, as he puts it to Theaetetus, the problem is that, in quoting a statement or citing a formula, "we may think that it is plain sailing and that we understand when an expression is used, though we may be in difficulties elsewhere, whereas really we understand equally little of both" (*Soph.* 243c3-5). It is not that such statements, accounts, or definitions are not necessary; it should be perfectly clear that they are. It is simply that to think we ever have, or ever could have, the truth literally and unambiguously wrapped up in any logos is, to use Platonic imagery, to be in the cave; for "he who thinks . . . that anything in writing will be clear and certain would be an utterly simple person" (*Phaedr.* 275c5-7)—and there seems reason to believe that Plato's reservations hold not only for writing, but for all purely verbal expression.[12] It is, I believe, in Plato's preoccupation with this "weakness inherent in language" (*Seventh Epistle* 343a1)[13] that we must look for his clue to interpreting the *Theaetetus*; for "logos, inasmuch as it is compounded of nouns and verbs, is in no case established with sufficient stability" (*Seventh Epistle* 343b4-6). That we are meant to understand Theaetetus' efforts in this light seems to be reinforced by further remarks in the *Sophist* which pick up this same problem of language and logoi exactly as it was originally raised in Plato's famous attack on writing in the *Phaedrus*. The threat is still that of deception, and ultimately perhaps of self-deception—the danger that the glib appearance of wisdom be passed off as the real thing (*Soph.* 233a8-c11; cf. *Phaedr.* 275a6-b2).

And so we are brought back once more to the problem of appearance and reality as it relates to the quest of the *Theaetetus*—the appearance of knowledge without the reality, and the appearance of failure without the reality. The challenge now will be to show exactly how the account of knowledge in the *Theaetetus*—and especially the final definition—simultaneously succeeds (because it is an objectively true definition) and yet fails (because it is not subjectively understood by Theaetetus); why, in other words, their dreaming true opinion fails to become waking, or real, *epistēmē* of *epistēmē* (cf. *Charm.* 166e5ff.).

It will be my argument that the *Theaetetus* is not inconclusive, nor a "failure"; that, on the contrary, it offers a carefully developed account of knowledge consistent with that found in other dialogues, both earlier and later; that this account is, moreover, both anticipated from the beginning of the dialogue and at the end encapsulated in Socrates' "dream"; and that, far from being rejected, the "dream" theory is actually reconfirmed by the supposed refutation, and the reader led to the point at which such "dreaming" can be transformed into waking knowledge (cf. *Stat.* 278e10).

INTERPRETATION OF THE *THEAETETUS*

In light of this proposed interpretation, it is puzzling if not disconcerting, to read the literature on the *Theaetetus*. In the first place, far from seeing Socrates' "dream" as a case of true opinion that needs the binding of the logos to establish it as waking or certain knowledge, it seems (almost without exception) to be taken for granted that the "dream" has been conclusively refuted.[14] Some of the commentators are explicit in their assertion that "the theory here put forward was certainly not held by Plato himself";[15] it is presumably this conviction that motivated the detective work as to authorship—Aristotle having apparently set off a hue and cry after Antisthenes.[16] Meanwhile, Campbell's suggestion that the author must be "some Pythagorean"[17] is narrowed down by Burnet and Taylor to Ecphantus of Syracuse (whose dates are uncertainly fixed between the fifth and fourth centuries B.C.)[18]—although this proposal is rejected by Cornford on grounds of insufficient evidence.[19] One solution to the puzzlement over the theory's being expressed in a "dream" is to read it as Plato's oblique way of telling us that the theory was advanced after Socrates' death,[20] and since there is supposedly no place for any reference to recollection in the *Theaetetus*,[21] Plato's calling it a "dream" is assumed to mean that "it is a post-Socratic theory, and Plato's historical conscience is pricking him."[22]

In the second place, it seems generally to be accepted without much question that the dialogue is indeed a failure as far as an account of knowledge is concerned.[23] Perhaps even more puzzling is the wide variety of reasons offered for this supposed failure. At one extreme are those who hold that Plato himself is here at a loss as far as any theory of knowledge is concerned—finding, for example, with Shorey, that although "the *Theaetetus* . . . makes a serious effort to solve the epistemological problem, here the Socratic avowal of perplexity expresses Plato's own state of mind."[24] At the other extreme are those who read the "failure" of the dialogue as deliberate evidence of a shift in Plato's epistemology—but again, the interpretations differ. According to Lutoslawski, the *Theaetetus* should be seen as effecting a "transition from selfexisting ideas to categories of reason," thus introducing so radically new an approach to knowledge that it qualifies as "a new philosophical movement."[25] Although Burnet basically agrees with Lutoslawski as far as the change evinced in the *Theaetetus* is concerned, he sees it as marking, not a development within Plato's own thinking, but rather a transition from Socratic to Platonic doctrine,[26] the first signs of which he detects in the *Republic* and the *Phaedrus*.[27] He likewise draws attention to the shift away from the (Socratic) doctrine of Forms, pointing out that "instead, we have the beginning of a theory of what were afterwards called categories"—which is developed in the *Sophist* as the basis of the science of combination. These Burnet is prepared to accept as "the Platonic forms, as distinct from the Pythagorean or Socratic."[28] From this point of view, the account of knowledge as true opinion with logos is something already outgrown, and the purpose of the dialogue is intentionally negative on that score, being simply "to clear the ground by showing that knowledge cannot be identified either with sensation or with thought."[29] In line, however, with the shift towards logic, he sees the dialogue as providing some significant pointers, for "we have incidentally made several discoveries as to the nature of knowledge...in the first place, that it implies certain 'common' or generic predicates, *ta koina*; secondly, that to know a thing we must know its *differentia*."[30] All in all, however, Burnet seems to be in agreement with Lutoslawski that the significance of the *Theaetetus* lies in its shift from a relatively empirical to a logical interest,[31] the chief evidence for which is the introduction of *ta koina* as "categories" which then (indirectly) provide "the foundation of Plato's logic." This view of the *Theaetetus* as marking a watershed between a Socratic and a more truly Platonic phase is echoed by A.E. Taylor. Again, the major significance of the dialogue is thought to involve a shift from the concern in the *Phaedrus* with the relation of the sensible particulars to a variety of forms (the only relation between the forms being their simultaneous "presence" in the object) to a new concern with "a different issue"— the interrelation of the forms themselves as that which makes predication possible.[32] Viewed as transitional between an earlier concern with the relation between knowledge and opinion on the one hand, and on the other a new method that reflects logical concerns growing out of the justification of predication, the apparently negative result of the dialogue seems of little interest. By contrast, the introduction of what Plato calls *"ta koina"* takes on a significance far greater than any ostensible conclusion of the dialogue. Hence, "the most important positive result of the discussion" is seen as barely bearing on the proposed accounts of knowledge, but rather to be "the recognition that the discovery of the great categories, both of existence and value, is the work of thought, 'the soul by herself without any instrument.'"[33]

Within this line of interpretation, there are yet further variations.

Stenzel, for example, gives it a slightly different twist by interpreting the supposed shift towards logical concerns as a rejection of the moral and theological overtones that had marked the *Republic*.[34] Again, seen as primarily negative (posing problems, the solutions to which are provided only in the *Sophist*), the significance of the *Theaetetus* is found to lie in the fact that it shifts the focus of inquiry to logical definition; for it is towards the introduction of this purportedly new method of division for the sake of definition that the *Theaetetus* is seen to point.[35]

Although a large body of criticism emphasizes this shift away from an empirical concern with sensibles (and their relation to the forms) and towards a logical concern with abstract definition, a number of commentators at the same time discern quite a different kind of change in almost the opposite direction: a growing openness to, and provision for, the empirical dimension of practical experience. For Campbell, this awareness of the empirical role of appearance and becoming seems to be more a question of degree than a really radical change.[36] Others find the *Theaetetus* to be effecting a sharper transition to the practical and empirical. Thus, elaborating on the change from an earlier to a later phase, Burnet explains that "the point of view is no longer Socratic. Plato is now as much impressed by the dangers of a one-sided intellectualism as by those of a one-sided sensationalism."[37] Even in the introduction of the so-called categories, since they involve questions not only of being but also of value, he can observe that "the practical is becoming more prominent than it was in the earlier dialogues."[38] This second stress on a supposed shift in Plato's epistemology has been picked up and developed by several commentators— although there seems to have been little serious effort to relate this shift to the one in the opposite direction (i.e., towards logic and more abstract classification). Stenzel goes so far as to talk of the *Theaetetus* as thus signaling "a complete change," introducing an openness to *kinēsis* which he finds "foreign to Plato's earlier works."[39] Meanwhile Malcolm Brown sees the *Theaetetus* as initiating a new empirical awareness to "the fluid whole of sensed and judged phenomena" that propels him to "a new stage in his thinking."[40] Richard Robinson, however, wonders whether this "new" possibility of knowledge in the world of becoming is "a slip or an unnoticed implication on Plato's part."[41]

In between these two extremes—of those, on the one hand, who find Plato himself at a loss or confused and, on the other, those who see the "failure" of the dialogue as a deliberate indication of a new development in his thought—fall various explanations of why the formula *doxa alēthēs meta logou* does in fact (but actually need not) fail.

One such line of approach focuses on Plato's failure to offer an interpretation of logos in its sense of providing *grounds*. Already Lutoslawski had found this strange,[42] and some of the more recent

literature follows him in continuing to find such disregard puzzling—
especially if, as is sometimes thought likely, it is deliberate on Plato's
part.[43] Perhaps this concern with "grounds" reflects our own contemporary passion for an analysis of knowledge as justified true
belief;[44] so too, perhaps, it is contemporary concern which dictates a
different line of criticism. This is one which stresses the distinction
between "knowledge by acquaintance" (in which the object is apprehended as relatively simple), and "knowledge that" (propositional
knowledge of complexes or states of affairs). Whereas (according to the
argument for this position) an interpretation of logos as involving
propositional content might have yielded an adequate definition of
epistēmē, in fact the limitation of the discussion to knowledge by
acquaintance is seen to undercut the possibility of any adequate
account of knowledge. Failure of the final formula is thus attributed to
Plato's confusion—either deliberate or inadvertent—between the two.
If deliberate, it is concluded either that Plato is offering a critique of his
own earlier conception of knowledge as primarily, if not exclusively, by
acquaintance,[45] or that it simply reflects his continuing conviction that
real knowledge is indeed of simples and therefore by acquaintance,[46]
or, more subtly still, that he is attributing the failure of the definition to
Theaetetus' confusion between the two—thus preparing the reader for
the distinction on which later dialogues will build a more logically
sophisticated epistemology.[47] If inadvertent, it substantiates
Runciman's claim that "the confusion between knowledge-that and
knowledge by acquaintance" underlies both the problems raised and
the manner of dealing with them.[48]

It is not possible to take account of all the ingenious responses to
this question of the inconclusiveness of the Theaetetus; among them,
however, is one that is too important to overlook. Cornford is perhaps
the best-known spokesman for the theory that the solution to the
problem of knowledge as posed in the Theaetetus lies in a recognition of
the forms—which, he argues, have been expressly banished from the
discussion in order to underline the epistemological failure consequent
upon their denial or absence.[49] Cherniss follows Cornford in this
respect[50] as does Hackforth,[51] and already Shorey, although not sharing
Cornford's view concerning the total absence of the forms from the
Theaetetus[52]—nor, on this point, that of Burnet[53] or Taylor[54]—had,
nevertheless, "concede [d] that the Theaetetus may be, not an introduction to the Ideas, but an indirect argument in support of the familiar
doctrine."[55] Even earlier, Jackson had proposed that the inquiry of the
Theaetetus "is thus intended to prepare the way for, and to lead up to,
the theory of ideas, or, to speak more precisely, the fundamental
proposition of that theory, 'besides sensibles, there are eternal and
immutable existences called ideas'", whereas Ross finds that, although

the forms are never mentioned, it is here in the *Theaetetus* that "Plato most fully states the grounds on which his theory of Forms rest, because it argues that sensation is different from knowledge."[56] Unfortunately, however, as pointed out by Robinson, followed by Morrow and others, it is not completely clear just how such recourse to the doctrine of forms might actually solve the problem of the *Theaetetus*.[57] Moreover, any indirect reference to forms may turn out to be tricky in its own right. It will be recalled that the relation of the *Theaetetus* to the theory of forms has already been obliquely raised— first in connection with those who see in the *Theaetetus* a transition from an earlier conception of "forms" to a new theory of "categories" involving *ta koina*, and second in connection with those who suggest a transition from an earlier conception of *epistēmē* as knowledge by acquaintance to a later understanding involving knowledge that the various kinds do or do not combine. Arising in part out of this argument over knowledge of propositions versus knowledge of simples, an even more acute difficulty has been brought against this position—and indeed against one version of the theory of forms altogether. It hinges, in a nutshell, on the knowability or unknowability of the forms, following the criticism of Socrates' "dream." For it would seem that either some irrational (*alogon*) things are knowable (as Robinson suggests),[58] or the forms themselves—whether simple or complex—are unknowable. In originally drawing attention to this problem, Ryle explains that the criticism applies "whether Plato realized it or not."[59] But since even the language used in the crossexamination of Socrates' "dream" echoes language previously used to describe the forms, one might seriously doubt that Plato was unaware of what he was doing.[60]

Finally, there is the assertion that the quest of the *Theaetetus* for a definition of knowledge was misconceived, and therefore had to fail,[61] the lesson to be learned being one of humility.[62]

How then, after all, shall we read the *Theaetetus*? As confusion on Plato's part, or as deliberate notification of a change in doctrine? As defense of the theory of forms, or as devastating criticism of that same theory? As offering a definition that embodies Plato's own belief about knowledge, or as only a formula shown to be empty and indefensible? Reading the literature, one becomes increasingly fascinated by the range and mutual inconsistency of responses to the dialogue, for even the superficial survey of critical response that has been sketched here evidences something of the wild variety of explanations and interpretations.

Of all these introductions to the puzzle and challenge of the *Theaetetus*, Glenn Morrow's is probably as pointed as any. First, warning us against taking too gullibly "the apparent frustration with which the dialogue ends," he reminds us that "few commentators have believed that Plato himself was stymied at the end of the dialogue."[63] This, of course, is the irony of the piece. No wonder that contemporary readers—and I among them—continue to be intrigued and tantalized by the almost teasing character of the dialogue. Again, as Morrow puts it, "We all tend to suppose there is some positive doctrine to which he is pointing, and of which we could get glimpses if we examined carefully the preceding pages."[64]

It is on just such a careful examination of the preceding pages that we must now embark, for the glimpses they provide do indeed point to a fully positive, entirely coherent, and not at all insignificant theory of knowledge. I am far from confident that I can properly separate the various strands of the dialogue, and even less optimistic about being able to weave them together again, but (as Plato's Socrates would say) calling on Zeus, the Savior, let me try.

— ONE —

AMBIGUITY

The ostensible subject of the *Theaetetus* is introduced by what must surely be one of the most lightheartedly ironic of all Plato's understatements: "I am puzzled about one small matter . . . this is what I am perplexed about and cannot fully grasp by my own efforts: what knowledge is" (145d6-e9). To all appearances, the question is never answered. In reality, so this study will argue, we are provided with a carefully worked-out answer—an answer recognized as explicit, however, only if the dialogue is taken self-referentially. The project of this study is therefore relatively straightforward. It consists, quite simply, of an effort to read the *Theaetetus* as a whole, in the hope (and promise) that if we do so, the parts—especially the conclusion of the dialogue— will fall into place.[1]

AMBIGUITY OF THEAETETUS' LOGOS

By the time Theaetetus comes through with the first effort at real definition, several points have already been established—both as to the content of the inquiry, and as to its form.

In the first place, the nature of the inquiry has been defined—on the one hand, as being a quest after that peculiar kind of knowledge (*epistēmē*) which is properly identified as wisdom (145d11-e7), and on the other, as seeking to grasp what essentially defines that knowledge: "what *epistēmē* really is" (146e9-10). A notion of the denotative range of *epistēmē* has also been provided, indicating dimensions both theoretic and practical: "Geometry and all the things you spoke of just now [i.e., astronomy, arithmetic, and music: 145a7-8], and also cobblery and the other craftsmen's arts; each and all of these are nothing else but knowledge" (146c8-d2). In the second place, the nature of logos, as definition, has been clarified, for although on the one hand Plato has made a point of having Theaetetus first enumerate a multiplicity of instances (146c7-d2), on the other he has Socrates go on to demand an account that will justify that enumeration in terms of the essentially differentiating characteristics of *epistēmē* (146d3-e10). Moreover, an

15

example of just such a logos has been provided in Theaetetus' own definition of surd—where he too first indicates the denotative range by enumerating 3, 5 and so on up to 17, as instances of measures involving incommensurable roots, and then goes on to focus on the essentially differentiating characteristic of irrational radicals as being in fact the square roots of oblong numbers (147c7-148b2). This interpretation of logos at the beginning of the inquiry will prove to be significant, not only as a model for their own search, but also as matter for the reflexive critique of logos at the end of the dialogue. Urged therefore by Socrates to "take your answer about the roots as a model, and just as you embraced them all in one class, though they were many, try to designate the many forms of knowledge in one logos" (148d4-7), Theaetetus produces his first definition: "knowledge is nothing other than perception [*ouk allo ti estin epistēmē ē aisthēsis*] " (151e2-3).

Before tackling specific problems with Theaetetus' proposal, this is perhaps the place to register what for the reader must be an overriding question: Why on earth will Plato (or at least the Platonic Socrates) become so caught up in what is obviously an unpromising proposal? It turns out that more than half the dialogue is devoted to discussion of this first definition. Why, in a search for knowledge, do we find such a disproportionate preoccupation with perception—especially since, as any student of Plato could surely have anticipated—it will in the long run be shown to be inadequate? This is one of the *Theaetetus'* many puzzles which we must eventually address. In the meantime, however, let us return to the definition itself.

The vagueness and even ambiguity of Theaetetus' proposal should be immediately evident. In the first place, we need to know exactly what he means by "perception," since Socrates has just asked him, "Does anyone, do you think, understand the name of anything when he does not know what that thing is?" (147b2). Pursuit of this first question—the meaning of "perception"—will thus occupy a substantial section of the dialogue. Second, we want to know exactly what is meant by the expression *is nothing other than*. After all, Theaetetus has just said of geometry, cobblery, and the rest, that they are "nothing other than knowledge [*ouk allo ti ē epistēmē*] " (146d2). Thus, we have the following:

1. Geometry, cobblery, etc., are nothing other than *epistēmē*. (146d2)
2. *Epistēmē* is nothing other than perception. (151e2-3)

Hence, by implication:

3. Geometry, cobblery, etc., are nothing other than perception.

Clearly, it needs some further explanation to enable us to see in exactly what sense geometry, cobblery, and the rest are to be understood as "nothing other than" perception. As I read him, one of Plato's major concerns in the dialogue is to focus precisely on the ambiguity of this expression, *is nothing other than*, demonstrating on the one hand a sense of the expression according to which Theaetetus' proposed definition is entirely unacceptable, and on the other unfolding a different sense of *is nothing other than* according to which the definition becomes both accurate and illuminating.

Echoing this initial ambiguity, therefore, Socrates' first response to the proposed definition is the wry assessment that "it is not a bad logos of knowledge [*logos ou phaulon*]" (151e8). At first hearing, *ou phaulon* should bring the reader up with a jerk. On the face of it—at least if it is read in the sense of *reducing epistēmē* to perception—Theaetetus' proposal is in Platonic terms preposterous, and hence utterly *phaulos*. Read in light of the ambiguity for which I am arguing, however, there will be a sense in which (if *is nothing other than* is understood in a certain way) the statement will be quite acceptable. How is Plato to communicate this double-edged assessment that, although on the surface Theaetetus' definition is patently false, nevertheless if understood at a more sophisticated level (on which, of course, Theaetetus himself is not at the moment operating), it will turn out to be true? As I read him, this double-edged assessment is carried in the slightly ironic overtones of *ou phaulon*. (Actually, *phaulos* proves to be even more ambiguous than this, for Diogenes Laertius tells us that Plato used the term *phaulos* with a variety of meanings, ranging from *kakos* [bad] to *haploos* [whose meaning in turn ranges from "honestly simple" to "foolishly simple"] [*Lives of Eminent Philosophers*, III, 63-64]).

Socrates' second observation in response to this first effort at definition is to suggest that this logos of Theaetetus is in substance the same as that of Protagoras (152a1-2). Since this assimilation of Theaetetus' definition to Protagorean doctrine is not at first sight evident either to Theaetetus or to the reader, Socrates will now proceed to demonstrate the sense in which he finds this to be the case.

AMBIGUITY OF PROTAGORAS' LOGOS

Protagoras' doctrine, to which this first definition of Theaetetus is now assimilated, is quoted as the assertion that "Man is the measure of all things: of those that are, that they are, and of those that are not, that they are not" (152a2-4). Interpreting this doctrine in a more specific sense—" Is not this about what he means, that each thing is for me such as it appears to me, and for you in turn such as it appears to you—you and I being 'man'?" (152a6-8)—Socrates now proceeds to argue that this interpretation of Protagorean doctrine is "the same as" Theaetetus' definition. Once again, however, we are confronted with one of Plato's weasel expressions; what does he mean by the expression *is the same as (ta auta tauta*: 152a2)? And how does *is the same as* relate to the earlier expression, *is nothing other than?* These questions concerning sameness and difference, together with the parallel questions of reducibility and irreducibility of things to one another, seem to underlie the entire inquiry into knowledge and being as it is initiated by this first definition of Theaetetus, and then pursued into the *Sophist.*[2] In the present context, an initial distinction between form and content reminds us that "the same thing" may be said in different ways, even though the meaning is not always immediately evident, since "Protagoras has said the same thing [i.e., the same content] in a different way [i.e., in a different form]" (152a1-2). The question therefore confronts us: In what sense can it be said that Theaetetus' first definition and Protagoras' doctrine are "the same" in content?

The moves are sufficiently condensed that there is room for different readings here. One reading would suggest a fairly straight-forward claim: (a) knowledge is infallible; (b) perception is of one's own experience; (c) awareness of one's own experience is infallible.[3] But at most that would show simply that knowledge and perception are alike in both being infallible, not that the statements of Theaetetus and Protagoras are the same. A more roundabout reading suggests that the two statements are "the same" insofar as the same conclusions may be drawn independently from Protagoras' doctrine and from Theaetetus' definition —and this seems to be the route they will take. It is not clear that there are really two distinct conclusions, but at least there seems to be an objective as well as a subjective dimension to the argument developed.[4] What might be called the objective dimension (because it focuses on what is apprehended) points up to the relativity of perceptual reality in the sense that, according to either thesis, one does not talk of objective reality (e.g., the wind itself[5]), but rather of a subjectively relative reality in that to be is to be *for someone* (152b6-7), and to be for someone is to be, period (152c1-5).[6] Socrates' claim here, according to this reading, is that the same conclusion about this relative character of perceptual reality[7] may be drawn independently from Protagoras' doctrine and from Theaetetus' proposed definition.[8] By contrast, what I am calling the subjective dimension of the conclusion, focusing on the character of perception itself, asserts the infallibility of perception.[9] For not only is infallibility of perception clearly implied by Protagoras' claim, but so too is it implied by Theaetetus' definition.[10] Having established, apparently to Theaetetus' satisfaction, this sense in which his first definition is the same as the doctrine of Protagoras—i.e., in the sense that they each yield the same conclusions with respect to both the relative character of reality and the infallible character of perception—Socrates now proceeds to the next stage of the argument. This epistemological doctrine, attributed jointly to Theaetetus and Protagoras, is now shown to yield the ontological implication that "nothing is of itself any one thing"[11]—and this conclusion is now in turn attributed jointly to Theaetetus and Protagoras (151e8-152a1; 152c8-d3). This critical claim will, however, also turn out to be ambiguous. The resulting challenge to find an adequate interpretation of this formula—an endeavor which at first sight seems to occupy a disproportionate amount of the discussion—will lead them step by step into the heart of the inquiry, and will actually develop the conditions for understanding the dialogue's elusive conclusion.

Socrates' first response to this ontological thesis, couched in exactly the same words as his earlier response to Theaetetus' logos above, presents us with a parallel that is difficult to dismiss, for the Protagorean statement he also finds to be "not a bad logos" (*ou phaulon logon:* 152d2). This repetition of the same phrase with its ironic overtones seems designed to reinforce the reader's earlier awareness of underlying ambiguity. Just as Theaetetus' definition will prove to be false on his own interpretation of its terms, but nevertheless (so this study will argue) susceptible of a true interpretation, so too, it is now being hinted, Protagorean doctrine might likewise prove to be false on a conventional interpretation, but nevertheless susceptible of a different, and true, interpretation. As Plato subtly suggests, not only Theaetetus, but maybe Protagoras too, was wiser than he knew—"a really wise man" (*passophos tis:* 152c8)—and Plato's almost wry suggestion is that in spite of himself, "it is likely that a wise man is not talking nonsense" (152b1). To sort out sense from nonsense will, once again, call for interpretation, and first of all for the recognition that the same logos might be susceptible of a more elusive and perhaps truer interpretation as well as of a more obvious and perhaps foolish one. Thus we are warned to see it as a puzzling or riddling expression, "a dark saying hinted to the common crowd like ourselves, the truth of which Protagoras might have revealed in secret to his pupils" (152c9-10). It is this "hidden truth" (155d10)—the full import of which was, conceivably, hidden even from the "really wise" Protagoras himself[12]—that the subsequent discussion will now seek to unfold.

This first response on the part of Socrates, hinting at ambiguity in the expression of Protagorean doctrine, parallels fairly clearly his previous response to Theaetetus' initial definition of knowledge. So too, the second part of Socrates' response to Theaetetus—assimilating his particular definition to the broader doctrine of Protagoras—will now be paralleled by assimilating the Protagorean doctrine in turn to a broader strand of philosophical thought within the tradition as a whole:

> On this subject all the philosophers except Parmenides may be marshalled in one line—Protagoras and Heracleitus and Empedocles—and the chief poets in the two kinds of poetry, Epicharmis in comedy, and in tragedy Homer, who in the line
>> Oceanus, the origin of the gods,
>> and Tethys, their mother
> has said that all things are the offspring of flow and motion [*panta. . .ekgona rhoēs te kai kinēseōs*]. (152e2-8)

This now leads to the next phase of the argument, in which fundamental ambiguity—first hinted at in the case of Theaetetus' definition, then more broadly suggested with the formulation of Protagorean doctrine—is now even more explicitly spelled out in the case of the ontological doctrine being attributed not only to Theaetetus and Protagoras, but also to Heracleitus and major figures in the tradition. What follows is a complex section whose intricate twists and turns will lay the foundations of the theory, both epistemological and ontological, that is embodied in the *Theaetetus-Sophist* sequence.

AMBIGUITY OF HERACLEITUS' LOGOS[13]

Having been restated in the form of an ontological proposition, "Nothing is of itself any one thing [*hen men auto kath' auto ouden estin*]" (152d2-3), Theaetetan-Protagorean-Heracleitean doctrine is now shown to be not only ambiguous in a general kind of way, but actually susceptible of three related, but different, interpretations.

1. *Weak interpretation:* It could be interpreted simply to mean that nothing is of itself of any particular (sensible) quality—that is to say, independently of any perceiver, or until a perceiver perceives it. Of itself, however, this interpretation would not necessarily be inconsistent with the view that an object really is of *some* quality, but just does not become of some *perceptual* quality until perceived.

It seems certainly to mean at least this.[14]

2. *Neutral interpretation:* It could mean interpretation 1 *plus* the claim that since things are as they appear to each person, therefore anything may be both of some particular quality and not of that

particular quality, and therefore in this sense "nothing is of itself
any one thing"—meaning "nothing is of itself of any particular
quality"—since it may appear, and therefore be, equally of the
opposite quality.

On their account of Protagorean doctrine, it does mean this:

> Nothing is of itself any one thing, and you could not rightly ascribe any
> quality whatsoever to anything, but if you call it large it will also appear to
> be small, and light if you call it heavy, and everything else in the same way,
> since nothing whatever is... of any particular quality. (152d2-6)

If, however, it meant only this, then we would have a world of real
objects having no particular perceptual qualities—which certainly
raises a question as to what might be the ontological status of a
physical object having no specific sensible properties. (Both interpretations 1 and 2 suggest an ontology in which first there are physical
objects, and then there are sensible properties of those objects.) There
is also the question of the status and function of qualitative predicates
in light of the apparent invalidation of qualitative language.

3. *Strong interpretation:* It could mean interpretation 1 plus interpretation 2 *plus* the claim that the reason "nothing is of itself any
   one thing," in the sense of nothing being of any one particular
   quality rather than its opposite, is that "nothing is of itself any
   one thing" in the prior sense of there really being no strictly
   identifiable stable object there in the first place to which any
   particular quality could be fixedly attributed.

This is indeed what Socrates now goes on to propose as the underlying
meaning of Protagorean doctrine revealed in secret to his pupils:

> Nothing is of itself any one thing... since nothing whatever is one, *either a
> particular thing* or of a particular quality; but it is out of movement and
> motion and mixture with one another that all those things become which
> we wrongly say "are"—wrongly because nothing ever is, but is always
> becoming. (152d2-e1)

This strong proposal has now raised three questions: (a) What is the
relation between the weaker versions of the secret doctrine (i.e.,
interpretations 1 and 2) and this strong version (i.e. interpretation 3)?
(b) Insofar as interpretation 3 is presenting itself as neutral with regard
to the priority of physical objects or their sensible qualities, it has (for
the time being) dissolved the problem of physical objects having no
sensible properties; but this question of the relation between objects

and their sensible (and physical) properties is left dangling—and will certainly require of Plato some answer in the sequel. (c) Since interpretation 3 would seem to invalidate not only quality-language but also thing-language, it raises the whole question of the status and function of linguistic differentiation.[15]

This strong interpretation 3 of Protagorean doctrine is now attributed, not only to Protagoras' secret circle of pupils but also to the philosophical tradition as a whole, with the exception of Parmenides (152e2-5). To disagree with so great a host, on this point agreeing among themselves, would be to run the risk of being ridiculous.

In originally introducing this ontological doctrine (interpretation 3: that neither qualities *nor objects themselves* really exist as discrete stable entities), Socrates immediately adds, as a kind of explanatory gloss, that "it is out of movement and motion and mixture with one another that all these things become [*ek de dē phoras te kai kinēseōs kai kraseōs pros allēla gignetai panta*]" (152d7-8)—which is now restated as "All things are the offspring of flow and motion [*panta eirēken ekgona rhoēs te kai kinēseō s*]" (152e8). This is to pose two problems: one is the question of exactly how either or both objects and their sensible qualities arise as "offspring" of flow (*rhoē*), or mixture (*krasis*), or motion (*phora* or *kinēsis*); this in turn reiterates the question already raised as to the epistemo-logical and ontological relation of objects and their sensible qualities (that is to say, whether or in what sense objects or qualities are epistemologically or ontologically prior). These, too, will require some clear answer in the sequel.

Since it is not at first sight evident either to Theaetetus or to the reader just why the Theaetetan-Protagorean thesis should be assimi-lated to Heracleitean doctrine, it would seem that two things must now be done: (a) the Heracleitean logos must be shown to be, if not actually reasonable, then at least initially plausible; (b) it must be argued that what Theaetetus has now accepted as Protagorean doctrine (i.e., interpretation 2 of "nothing is of itself any one thing") is in fact to be assimilated to the more radical doctrine of Heracleitus (i.e., interpre-tation 3 of "nothing is of itself any one thing"). This would be in effect, of course, to argue not only the plausibility but also the acceptability of the Heracleitean doctrine. These two things Socrates now proceeds to do.

First, by way of initial support from common experience for the Heracleitean doctrine that all things arise out of motion, Socrates points to (a) inanimate nature, in which heat, the source of everything, arises out of motion (153a7-10); (b) animate nature, in which life arises from the same source (153b2-3); (c) healthy habits of body which are promoted by motion and activity but impeded by rest (153b5-7); (d) healthy habits of soul for which the same is true (153b9-c1); and (e)

general, it requires some space to spell these out for a twentieth-century reader. Second, it does not in any way alter, but only strongly reinforces, the interpretation of that theory here being offered. For both these reasons it has seemed wiser not to interrupt the main thread of the argument here, and therefore to refer the reader to appendix A for the more integral and sophisticated reading of this section dealing with the dice illustration.

Taking this entire section, therefore (154b1-155d5), simply as positive and negative argumentation for the truth of interpretation 2, one sees that "nothing is of itself of any particular quality," because qualities exist neither in subjects nor in objects, but are rather events that occur uniquely between a particular object and a particular subject on a particular occasion (153e5-154a8); to speak as though this were not the case leads to confusion and contradiction (154b1-155d5). In other words, there has been no serious difficulty in moving from the weak version of interpretation 1 (that objects do not of themselves possess sensible qualities independently of being perceived) to the stronger claim of interpretation 2—since this latter provides the proper grounds for the Protagorean-Theaetetan claim that "as each person perceives things, such they are to each person" (152c2-3). What Plato is proposing now, however, in introducing the theory of the sophisti-cates—*hoi kompsoteroi*—is the provision of still prior grounds on which, in turn, this account of perception might rest—"the starting-point [*archē*] upon which all that we were just now speaking of depends" (156a3-4). But what is meant here? What exactly is it, first of all, that these things are depending on? Then, which of the things they have been discussing are thus dependent? And how, finally, are we to conceive of that dependence?

The text does make it clear that the dependence in question is dependence on "the hidden truth" underlying, not only the inner-circle doctrine taught by one man, Protagoras, but likewise the doctrine attributed to all those famous men already listed (155d9-10; cf. 152e2-9). This secret doctrine (the mere hearing of which, in contrast to understanding its hidden significance, required no special initiation) is, of course, the doctrine that "nothing is of itself any one thing"—this time under interpretation 3; hence it will be back to this formula that Socrates' initiation of Theaetetus will selfconsciously refer (e.g., 156e8-157a1; 157a8). What Plato is forcing us to confront is the fact that a formula of this kind is susceptible of layers of interpretation, layers of meaning involving successively sophisticated interpretation.[19] In the previous section, we had tried out interpretation 2, that "nothing is of itself of any particular quality"—and found ourselves with physical objects having no sensible properties. And in case we thought we could solve it by shifting from (what one might call) secondary qualities like colors, tastes, etc., to (what one might call) primary qualities of mathematically measurable qualities like number or size, the discussion of 154c1-155c5 suggests that such primary qualities are no less perceiver-dependent than the secondary qualities of sense. In short, nothing is of itself of any particular quality with respect to either secondary or primary qualities—which still leaves us with the problem of physical objects having no sensible qualities. Once we understand, however (on initiation into the hidden meaning of the doctrine), that there really are no physical objects either, then the anomaly vanishes. For if we accept interpretation 3, "nothing is of itself any one determinate thing—because there are no things in the first place, but only the indeterminacy of motion"—then interpretation 2 will follow without inconsistency: "nothing is of itself of any particular quality— either secondary or primary." As Socrates puts it at the end of the initiation, "And so it *results* from all this, as we said at the beginning, that nothing is of itself any one thing" (157a7-8). This is the first and most obvious sense in which Socrates argues for the dependence of the Theaetetan-Protagorean claim on the theory of the *kompsoteroi*. In the course of spelling out this dependence, moreover, he has resolved one of the central puzzles bequeathed by interpretation 2: the apparent existence of sensible objects having no sensible properties. There are, however, other "things we were just now speaking of" whose dependence on interpretation 3 will now be clarified, and in the course of which other puzzles raised by interpretation 2 will likewise be resolved.

First of all, there is the question of generation. The earlier account of interpretation 2, as constituting inner-circle Protagorean doctrine, had referred without explanation to a doctrine of generation according to which

> it is out of movement and motion and mixture with one another that all those things become which we wrongly say "are"—wrongly because nothing ever is, but is always becoming...[which in turn was identified with the doctrine that] all things are the offspring of flow and motion. (152d7-e8)

At the time, this statement left unanswered questions as to how and why things are "always becoming," and if they are, then in what sense do they become "out of movement and motion and mixture with one another," and in what sense can they be said to be "the offspring of flow and motion"? Now with the fuller elaboration, we see a dependence between that simpler summary statement of a theory of generation out of flux, and the more complex theory of the *kompsoteroi*—a dependence that seems to be analogous to the dependence between a single theorem and the comprehensive theory within which it receives whatever meaning and whatever truth it carries.

Kompsoteros theory likewise accounts for the further claim of inner-circle Protagorean doctrine that language speaks, not of some actual given but, on the contrary, of "those things which we wrongly say 'are'—wrongly, because nothing ever is, but is always becoming" (152e1). This claim, too, is now seen to be a derivation from the more comprehensive theory, for of course if nothing is of itself any determinate thing, but apparent things are only indeterminate motion, then it is obvious that the verb *to be* of thing-language is less accurate than the verb *to become* of event-language. Hence

> It *results from all this,* as we said at the beginning, that nothing is of itself any one thing, but everything is always becoming in relation to something, and "being" should be altogether abolished...but in accordance with nature we should speak of things as "becoming" and "being made" and "being destroyed" and "changing." (157a7-b7)

Finally, the theory of the *kompsoteroi* will further develop the earlier account of sensation, according to which qualities are to be understood as events occurring on impact between a subject and object (153d8-154a2). In light of the more comprehensive ontological theory, these propositions concerning the nature of sensible properties are now likewise seen as derived from, or "dependent on," the encompassing theory (156a5-157a3).

In short, the status of this hidden truth of the *kompsoteroi* seems to be in this sense that of explanatory theory within which functions assigned to terms like *sense-organ, color,* etc., will define a relatively precise meaning for these concepts, and the truth of derived theorems will be judged in terms of the adequacy of the theory as a whole. Such adequacy will in turn depend on internal consistency (coherence on the abstract level of theory) and external completeness (correspondence at the concrete level of practice). Internal consistency requires that the body of axioms and theorems be such that contradiction may not be deduced; external completeness requires that the theory be able to account for all relevant data. Hence the insistence on the explanatory role of *kompsoteros* theory vis-á-vis what they have already accepted, both factually and theoretically:

> Do you begin to see why these things are so? (155d5-6)

> What does this account mean for us, Theaetetus, with reference to what was said before? (156c3-4)

> And so it results from all this, as we said at the beginning...(157a7-8)

Having thus teased Theaetetus on with the promise of initiation into mysteries that will not only nourish his sense of philosophic wonder, but actually provide grounds for his holding what he has in fact committed himself to holding, Plato now proceeds to unfold the doctrine of the *kompsoteroi*.[20]

TRANSITION
Ambiguity and Initiation

Plato's image of initiation (155d9-156a3) seems deliberate and well chosen. Initiation into hidden levels of meaning is, after all, what he has been doing all along. Thus, just as Theaetetus' logos, on closer analysis, proves to be susceptible of further meaning of which he was not initially aware, and so comes to be assimilated to the doctrine of Protagoras, and just as, in turn, Protagoras' logos, on closer analysis, yields hidden meaning revealed only to an inner circle of disciples, and so comes to be assimilated to the doctrine of Heracleitus, so too now again does this likewise prove to be the case with the logos of Heracleitus, for, on closer analysis it too turns out to contain "hidden truth" to be assimilated to the doctrine of the *kompsoteroi,* and revealed only through initiation into the appropriate "mysteries." Significantly, we too along with Theaetetus, were—throughout this movement of penetration into successive levels of meaning—apparently being initiated into the realization that language is pregnant with ambiguity.

As I see it, this reiteration of studied ambiguity in verbal formulation establishes one of the major themes of the dialogue. Played on and replayed through the introductory argument, now even more clearly articulated through the imagery of initiation into mysteries, it will gradually be enriched with variations until we are catapulted with breathless anticipation into the carefully controlled and climactic ambiguity of the dialogue's conclusion. In this sense, Theaetetus' (and the reader's) initiation into the mysteries of the *kompsoteroi* will comprise not only the immediately ensuing account, but in fact the remainder of the entire dialogue. Moreover, just as recognition of this element of basic ambiguity seems to be a condition of Theaetetus' initiation into the "mysteries" of generation and sensation, so too will it be a condition—for the reader as well as for Theaetetus—of initiation into the "mysteries" of knowledge that constitute the enigmatic conclusion of the dialogue.

In line with this approach, it will be important to recognize that the inner doctrine into which Theaetetus is now initiated, involves much more than just a theory of sensation: ranging in concern from cosmology to language, it offers a complex vision of the cosmos as a whole. It will therefore be fruitful to identify in the account of doctrine at 156a3-157c2 three distinct, though intertwined, dimensions or levels:

Level Alpha: An ontological dimension. Consideration of this level will be taken up in chapter 2; its focus is the *kompsoteros* account of generation of the physical world.

Level Beta: An epistemological dimension. Consideration of this level will be taken up in chapter 3; its focus is the *kompsoteros* account of perception.

Level Gamma: A reflective dimension. Recognition of this level requires a degree of abstraction which permits one to view both levels Alpha and Beta as special cases of a more general method. This will be taken up in chapter 4 (although by that time it will no longer be necessary to think of it as level Gamma, but simply as *kompsoteros* method).

—— PART TWO ——

THE "MYSTERIES" OF *EPISTĒMĒ*

—— TWO ——

KOMPSOTEROS THEORY OF GENERATION

Although ostensibly introduced as an account of sensation, the theory into which Theaetetus is now initiated will actually propose a far-reaching ontology, with repercussions not only for perception, but for language, knowledge, and the very conception of rationality itself.[1]

Working carefully through the account that Socrates proceeds to lay out for Theaetetus, a quite extraordinary recognition begins to impose itself upon the reader. For, on reflection, a pattern is seen to emerge which opens up unexpected connections to a number of other dialogues—doing so, moreover, in a way that suggests even more surprising links *between* those dialogues. The "mysteries" into which we are being initiated turn out, in other words, to offer an overall vision whose account of generation is consistent with the cosmology of the *Timaeus,* and whose account of cognitive structure is reminiscent of the epistemology of both the *Meno* and *Republic;* meanwhile, the entire approach finds clear echo in the *Philebus'* account of that method which, characterizing reason (logos) itself, Socrates tells us he has always loved and sought to follow (*Phil.* 15d1-16c3). Although full justification for such a claim obviously requires larger compass than the present work, it will nevertheless be this line of argument that enables us to develop a consistently fruitful interpretation of the *Theaetetus,* locating it, moreover, within a larger scheme that ranges across much of Plato's work.

Perhaps the first point to make in this connection is that, as will become increasingly clear, the model for "the mysteries" that Socrates will somewhat cryptically reveal has already been provided by Theaetetus' own work in geometry, and specifically by his earlier report on the treatment of surds. My reading of the dice illustration immediately preceding Theaetetus' initiation suggests that it too is designed to reiterate for Theaetetus the mathematical paradigm that will illumine what follows (see appendix A). It will, accordingly, be fruitful to distinguish within the *kompsoteros* account three phases which can best be understood in light of that mathematical model. These stages will consist of (1) apprehension of an original *continuum* (corresponding to the flow of Theaetetus' linear and planar magnitude; see appendix A); (2) *division* of the continuum (corresponding to Theaetetus' determination of line segments, where linear flow is literally segmented or "cut" into rational or irrational lengths— similarly to his determination of plane areas bounded by equal or unequal sides to yield squares or oblongs); and (3) non-additive, interactive *combination* (corresponding to Theaetetus' squaring and cubing of the roots to generate figures in two, and later three, dimensions [147e5-148b2]).

STAGE 1: CONTINUUM

As its first axiom and starting point (*archē* : 156a3), *kompsoteros* theory now directs our focus to the primary matrix out of which everything originally arises—that is to say, a matrix encompassing both knower and known *and* the knowledge that arises in the relation between them, for "there is nothing else besides" (156a5). Undercutting from the outset the very notion of a percipient standing over and against a "given" (whether naively realistic or phenomenalistic), the *kompsoteroi* see the sensitive apparatus of percipients as part and parcel of whatever it is that constitutes the fundamental reality of the universe. That is to say, they take as basic the occurrence of an interaction between a subjective aspect and an objective aspect of the real, the sort of impact and mutual modification that might stir echoes of Hobbes and later empiricists—except that people like Hobbes have been excluded along with other uninitiates: for the *kompsoteros* model is not, as we shall see, that of particles in collision, but rather the continuum of mathematics. To talk of atoms, or elements, or even elementary particles is, for the *kompsoteroi,* to talk of a world already measured out into discrete entities, a world already structured by thought and theory.[2] As starting point, therefore, what is required is that we try to conceptualize a state prior to, or at least independent of, organizing intelligence[3]—knowing at the same time, of course, that for the mind to focus on a state defined as preceding just such advent of mind can never be more than what we would call a "thought experiment": for the mind to apprehend is already to organize, and so in that very act to change what it apprehends. Therefore such a state—radically prior to the intrusion of organizing mind—will be by definition inherently mindless or irrational; that is to say, it will be as yet undifferentiated, as yet without ratio, as yet indeterminate, as yet uncut by the measuring of mind.[4] Thus, in the strictest sense of the original nature of reality, "nothing is of itself any one thing." Here at last, according to this hidden truth, we are face to face with the basic material "stuff" of the universe, which, despite the paradox involved in trying to give a rational account of that which is essentially irrational (thus anticipating the later problem of Socrates' "dream"), seems nevertheless to be characterized in three ways. These characteristics are, moreover, just those that may be attributed to the kind of geometrical "flow" presupposed by Theaetetus in his earlier discussion of surds.[5] Thus, straining to describe this indescribable stuff of the universe, *kompsoteros* theory tells us the following:

  a. It is continuous, consisting of ceaseless motion: "For them the starting-point upon which all these things depend, is that everything is really motion and that there is nothing else besides this [*to pan kinēsis ēn kai allo para touto ouden*]" (156a3-5).
  b. Corollary of (a): Since this original state is prior to any introduction of discreteness through determinations of fixed quantity or measure (as, in linear dimensionality, a ray is prior to the specificity of any particular measured line), it is to be understood as internally indeterminate.
  c. It is fundamentally relative in that (echoing once again the concept of a ray) it may be identified simply in terms of the polar extremes of activity and passivity: "Of the motion there are two forms...one having an active, the other a passive force [*dynamin*]" (156a5-7). On the other hand, even these active and passive aspects must not be taken as in any strict sense determinate, but only as relative to each other (157a3-4).

In our language this would seem to say that the ontological "given" is not to be understood as discrete or particulate matter, but rather, on analogy with the notion of magnitude in geometry, as an as-yet-undifferentiated continuum in which an indeterminate flow of energy or "power" awaits the measuring and structuring activity of mind.[6]

This affirmation of a continuum constitutes the first stage of *kompsoteros* ontological theory (i.e., of what I am calling "level Alpha" of the mysteries). Its corollary, the denial of ultimate discreteness, is embodied in the extreme form of interpretation 3 of inner-circle Protagorean doctrine, that "nothing is of itself any one thing." This denial of particulate material discreteness, which marks the first phase of initiation, is, moreover, set in contrast to the first belief attributed to the uninitiated, "who think nothing is except what they can grasp firmly with their hands (155e4-5).[7]

What this first stage does, in effect, is to confront us with a kind of brute givenness in the continuum of motion, the inherent irrationality of which resists, or at least challenges, rational organization and structure. It is the achievement of rational structure that Socrates now goes on succinctly to describe in the next two stages of the theory. Stage 2 will introduce the notion of measure whereby the continuum, now cut into relatively determinate units, can be treated as though it were discrete; stage 3 will explore ways in which these units may interact.

STAGE 2: DIVISION OF THE CONTINUUM

The model for the activity that marks stage 2 of the theory is, once again, to be found in mathematics. Resorting to language that echoes Theaetetus' own mathematical terminology, Socrates now seems deliberately to play up the analogy with Theaetetus' earlier measuring off of determinate quantities representing rational and irrational roots.[8] (a) Theaetetus' term for "root" was *power* (*dynamis*) (e.g., 147d3, d8); Socrates now points out that the determinate active and passive motions similarly have "power" (*dynamis*) (156a6).[9] (b) Theaetetus had recognized that the number of roots "appear to be infinite" (*apeiroi to plēthos*) (147d7-8); Socrates now echoes this too in noting that the number of active and passive motions "are infinite in number" (*plēthei men apeira*) (156a8-b1). (c) One of the points made in the dice illustration had been the recognition that quantities are always relative. First, they are relative in the sense that there is strictly speaking no large or small as such, but rather in any given instance, what is larger is so only relative to what is in that instance smaller, and vice versa. Hence they are second, also relative in the sense that the same quantity will from one angle appear as larger, from another as smaller. Socrates now picks up this same point in the context of active and passive motions, which are presented as relative in the same two ways. First, they are relative in the sense that there is strictly speaking no active or passive as such, but rather, in any given instance, what is active is so only relative to what is in that instance passive, and vice versa: "It is impossible to form a firm conception of the active or the passive element as being anything separately; for there is no active element until there is a union with the passive element, nor is there a passive element until there is a union with the active" (157a3-6). Hence they are, second, also relative in the sense that these differentiated motions will from one angle appear as active, from another as passive: "that which unites with one thing is active and appears again as passive when it comes in contact with something else" (157a6-7).[10]

In affirming the continuum of motion, stage 1 of *kompsoteros* theory had focused on an original *archē*, as it were, "given" independently of organizing intelligence. By contrast, stage 2 has marked a positive move on the part of organizing mind which now imposes differentiation and division on this "given" of undifferentiated flux. This second stage of *kompsoteros* theory thus attributes the discreteness of our world, not to some original "given", but to a discriminating act of mind that imposes measure on the measureless, determinacy on the indeterminate, discreteness on the continuum. This second stage, moreover, Socrates seems to set in deliberate contrast to the second position he attributes to the uninitiated: the uninitiated take the world of discrete experience at face value; supposing it to be a pre-packaged "given" simply awaiting our passive response, they fail to recognize the action (*praxis*) of intelligence which imposes discreteness on an original flow. Socrates therefore specifically excludes "the uninitiated, who deny the existence of actions [*praxeis*]" (155e3-6).[11] With the *kompsoteros* stance thus clearly contrasted for a second time with that of the uninitiated, we are forthwith led into stage 3, where, taking these determinate units furnished under stage 2, the theory will now consider ways in which they may interact.

STAGE 3: GENERATIVE COMBINATION

The problem now confronting the *kompsoteroi* is that whereas, on the one hand, they want to assert that "everything is really motion," on the other they want equally to assert the reality of a sensible world.[12] Their solution to this dilemma will involve a process of generative combination as ingenious as Theaetetus' geometry—or sex. As the account unfolds, it begins to dawn on the reader that this is just what we have been cleverly prepared for from the outset of the dialogue. For there in the introduction, with what we now recognize to have been deliberate intent, Plato has made a point of providing us with Theaetetus' theory of irrationals on the one hand, and the image of Socrates as midwife assessing the product of intercourse on the other, so that both can function for us as pervasive and pointed models. In this third stage, therefore, not only is much of the theory couched in the language of sexual intercourse, but the analogy with Theaetetus' work in geometry becomes increasingly significant. The question of genuineness of pregnancy and viability of offspring will be resumed shortly; for the moment it is still the analogy with his discussion of surds that seems to be commanding Theaetetus' attention.

As we pick up the analogy with Theaetetus' discussion of roots, we are reminded that it was reflection on the "power" of roots (in the sense that we too talk of taking a given quantity to some exponential "power")[13] which had, on my reading of the dice illustration, "filled him with wonder" (see appendix A). How could there be a source of something's coming into being other than straightforward addition (154c3-155c10)? How could there be any other source of generation? He had to recognize, of course, that his own illustration of roots had demonstrated just such a source, but a deeply puzzling one at that. For it is not addition, but a uniquely interactive operation between the linear units (i.e., the roots as "powers") that now generates a product that did not exist before—and with the coming into being of two-dimensionality, we are projected into an entirely different order of things. It is this phase of Theaetetus' mathematical illustration that Socrates now points up. For analogously, in the next stage of *kompsoteros* theory, a correspondingly unique interactive operation between the active and passive units (i.e., those motions having "power") now similarly generates a product that did not exist before—and with the coming into being of sensibility, we are likewise projected into an entirely different order of things. It is this interactive and generative combination that constitutes the third stage of *kompsoteros* theory and now calls for analysis. To begin with, in response to the first and obvious question concerning criteria of combinability, Socrates returns once again to Theaetetus' discussion, drawing this time on the concepts of commensurability and incommensurability to illumine the issue.

With the introduction of division, in stage 2, a new factor has entered the picture, just as it did with the introduction of determinate quantities in the mathematical context. For in thus cutting or measuring off discrete units of activity and passivity within the flow of motion, it will become possible, on analogy with Theaetetus' distinction between lengths and surds, to recognize such units as being commensurable or incommensurable. As a result, the multitude of motions may now be grouped, now only according to difference (being either active or passive) but also, cutting across that classification, according to likeness, with some active and passive motions being mutually commensurable, and others not. Out of the infinite number, therefore, factors present themselves in pairs, first according to a criterion of difference that distinguishes them as relatively active and relatively passive,[14] and second, according to a criterion of sameness that relates them as mutually commensurable. Thus, for example, when we come shortly to sensation, vision will be said to occur "when the eye and some commensurable object which approaches beget [color] and the corresponding perception" (156d3-5). In other words, the motion that we call an "eye" and the motion that we say is "seeable" are commensurable,[15] whereas the motion that we call an "eye" and the motion that we say is "hearable" are incommensurable—or, as Socrates puts it at a later point in the discussion, "It is impossible to perceive through one sense what you perceive through another; for instance, to perceive through sight what you perceive through hearing, or through hearing what you perceive through sight" (184e8-185a2). This is why the occurrence of sensation will be said to depend on a kind of mutual "measuring off" of active and passive against each other, so that Socrates can talk of the object that appears light or white or hot as "that against which I measure myself, or that which I touch" (154b1), and the organ which does the sensing is viewed as "that which did the measuring off, or the touching" (154b3-4).

Factors eligible for interaction, then, must meet these two criteria, first of difference (one being active, the other passive), and second of sameness (the two being mutually commensurable). With these preliminaries understood, we are now in a better position to follow the *kompsoteros* account of generative combination—which will prove to be important, for it holds the clue, not only to perception, but ultimately to knowledge itself.

Sometimes (as for example with the account of the Good or the allegory of the Cave in the *Republic*) Plato has Socrates suggest that a central concept is best communicated indirectly by resorting to analogy (cf. *Stat.* 277d1-2; also Aristotle, *Met.* θ 1048a86-88). This seems clearly to be the case here, where this pivotal concept of generative combination is introduced. Thus, following quick reference to an analogy with fire produced by friction (156a8),[16] the account of generative combination is elaborated through the more fully developed analogy with a child begotten of sexual intercourse. Thus, just as friction yields a new product—the flame—through effecting a mutual modification in the two interacting firesticks (fire being generated in that very interaction in which each becomes redhot and fiery), and just as intercourse yields a new product—the child—through effecting a mutual transformation in the two interacting mates (offspring being generated in that very interaction in which one mate becomes father, the other childbearer and mother), so too, Socrates now asserts, there is a unique type of interaction between commensurable active and passive motions which likewise yields a new product, through effecting a mutual transformation in the two interacting factors. The relatively passive motion that in terms of its physiology we identify, for example, as an eye and the relatively active motion that we identify as a physical object interact in such a way that, on the one hand, the motion that in terms of its physiology we call an "eye" becomes no longer simply motion but actually an organ of *sense,* and on the other, the motion that we call the "physical thing" becomes no longer simply motion but actually a *sensible* object. The transformation is mutual in that the operation—in fact the very concept—of sense requires both subjective and objective sensibility, for it would be meaningless to talk of an organ of *sense* unless there were also things *sensible.* The *kompsoteros* way of expressing this idea is to talk of "twin" offspring generated in the interaction of active and passive motions: "From the union [*homilias*: literally, sexual intercourse] and friction of these two are born offspring...always twins, the object of sense and the sense which is always born and brought forth together with the object of sense" (156a7-b2). Relative to the original active and passive parent motions, which may be said to be "slow," these twin offspring of sense and sensible are said to be "swift," streaming forth to make spatio-temporal connection with each other, for "the things begotten in this way are quicker; for they move from one place to another, and their motion is naturally from one place to another" (156d1-3). By way of example, we are given the case of eye and object interacting so that "when the eye and some commensurable object which approaches beget whiteness [in the object] and the corresponding sense [i.e., sense of sight in the subject]" then the begotten twins of sight (as subjective sensibility) and coloredness (as objective sensibility) constitute swift motions in which "sight from the eye and whiteness [from the object]...move between the two" (156d3-e1). This generative combination, involving an interaction and mutual transformation of factors, is perhaps most readily understood when contrasted (as Socrates has in the dice illustration) with simple conjunction or addition. First of all, unlike intercourse and sensation, simple addition leaves the would-be factors unaffected (as would be the case, for example, with the mere juxta-position of, say, an eye and something only hearable); second, again unlike intercourse and sensation, simple addition yields nothing new (in the example above, mere juxtaposition yields neither sight nor heard sound).

This insistence on a peculiarly *generative* interaction as character-izing the third stage of *kompsoteros* theory is therefore now set over against the third position attributed to those uninitiates whose beliefs stand in the way of their understanding the *kompsoteros* mysteries, for "the uninitiated deny the existence of...generation [*geneseis*]" (155e5).[17]

THE GENERATED PRODUCT

Focusing now more closely on the actual product of this peculiarly generative combination, it begins to seem that what Socrates is talking about here is the arising of radical novelty out of previously present elements—in other words, what we might ourselves recognize as an assertion of emergence.[18] Thus, on the one hand, *kompsoteros* theory wants to insist that the original elements are simply active and passive motions, non-sensible and non-sensitive (156a5-7); on the other hand, the products of this special kind of transforming interaction between such elements represent a radically different dimension of reality from the interacting motions that produce them. Hence, both senses (e.g., sight) and sensibles (e.g., coloredness) are qualitatively different from either or both the active and passive motions that generate them. One way of marking this difference is, as the *kompsoteros* account explains, to classify the generative interacting motions of subject and object as "slow" motions, and the generated motions of senses and sensibles as "swift" motions (156c8-d2); this terminology, although marking a slow-swift distinction, does nevertheless call them both "motions," thereby at the same time stressing the continuity or similarity between the original elements and the generated product. Another way is to talk of new entities, or offspring brought newly into existence (e.g., 156a8, d1, d4, e4); this kind of terminology stresses the fact that interaction between those elements generates radical novelty that is somehow "more than" a reality exhaustively defined in terms of just active and passive motions. This simultaneous insistence *both* that there is nothing else besides the elemental motion, *and* that there is indeed much else besides, stands as an apparent paradox which harks back to Theaetetus' wonder confronting the problem of the dice, a paradox resolved only through the *kompsoteros* concept of what we might call "emergence." Thus, the theory asserts, it is in the first place true that insofar as nothing has been actually added to those primary elements of active and passive motions, just so far is it true to say that the sensibility that is begotten of their interaction is itself nothing else besides the interacting motions—and in this sense, then, sensibility may be viewed as indeed "nothing other than" those active and passive elements. In the second place, however, insofar as sensibility arises as a begetting of offspring that were not actually present or "real" prior to that interaction of active and passive motions, just so far must sensibility be viewed as indeed "other than" simply those original active and passive elements. It is, however, only in light of this subtler elaboration of *kompsoteros* theory that it becomes possible to understand the paradoxical nuances of meaning hidden beneath the superficially simple proposition "Everything is motion, and there is nothing else besides this" (156a5).

By contrast, there is, of course, a simplistic way of reading that statement which would be blind to the calculated ambiguity. Taken thus at face value (that is, without the counterbalancing insistence on the emergence of radical novelty), the doctrine would appear to mark a one-sided emphasis on the original motions as elemental material without recognition of anything beyond that. But, *kompsoteros* theory seems to be arguing, to concentrate in this way on the constituent matter of things, in the sense of their component elements, without recognizing the radical transformation effected in emergent generation would be to deny the power and reality of whatever it is, admittedly neither tangible nor visible, that is somehow different from and able to transform these elements—and without which the elements would never amount to more than mere elements. The point of view of the kompsoteroi is therefore contrasted with just such an unenlightened approach, which Socrates now lists as the fourth and final position to be attributed to the uninitiated: with their exclusive emphasis on the constitutive material, they naturally go on to "deny the existence of. . .all that is invisible" (155e5-6).[19]

This preliminary contrast between the position of the uninitiated on the one hand, that is to say, of those who (to summarize) "think nothing is except what they can grasp with their hands, and who deny the existence of actions and generation and all that is invisible" (155e4-6), and on the other, that represented by the kompsoteros theory of emergence, has now effectively prepared the ground for initiation into the next phase, the kompsoteros theory of perception and, eventually, knowledge. For, having now established that there "really" are no sensible qualities of things (nor determinate objects in which such qualities could in any case inhere), but only swifter motions generated on impact between slower motions, we are now prepared for the central question as to how it comes about that we should ever have come to think that there are either objects or qualities in the first place. This is, of course, to move from the ontological to the epistemological question. It will propel us from an initial occurrence of brute sensation, through perception, true opinion, and finally logos, to an anticipation of that ultimate goal which qualifies as knowledge proper (epistēmē). As I see it, this initiation—not only of Theaetetus and Theodorus, but most especially of the reader—into the mysteries of the kompsoteros theory of knowledge will lead us to the dialogue's conclusion, and the answer to its original and final question: What really is knowledge? (146e9-10; cf. 146c3; 151d4; 210a3-b9).

Before turning to the epistemological phase of the inquiry, however, it were well to review our understanding of what I have been calling "level Alpha" of the mysteries. For, in analyzing the kompsoteros theory of generation, what we have come to recognize is a structuring process which, on close analogy with Theaetetus' mathematical illustration, has operated according to three relatively clear-cut principles of organization.

1. There is an initial focusing on a continuum (an indeterminate, or apeiron), defined simply in terms of the duality of opposing extremes.

2. Through the introduction of measure that determines or cuts the flow, the continuum is divided into an innumerable number of discrete elements.
3. By requiring a special kind of combination, the theory describes a generative interaction between certain elements—thus yielding a radically novel product which is analyzable into, but not reducible to, its constitutive elements.

This will now provide the framework for our coming to understand the epistemological level of the mysteries.

———— THREE ————

KOMPSOTEROS THEORY OF PERCEPTION

Turning now from the *kompsoteros* theory of generation to the account of perception similarly attributed by Socrates to the *kompsoteroi*, one is suddenly struck by a remarkable discovery: for between the structure of their theory of generation as they apply it at level Alpha, and their account of sensation as now presented at level Beta, there seems to emerge a clearly articulated analogy. But thus to talk simply of a theory of sensation is already misleading; for despite the existence in Greek of a single word, *aisthēsis*, to cover all forms of sense-apprehension, what Socrates immediately focuses on is what we might describe as the move from sensation to perception—that is to say, the shift from a merely physical event to an epistemological act.

Picking up, therefore, where the account of generation left off, the epistemological approach of level Beta now requires a closer look at those swift motions generated in the interaction between passive/subjective and active/objective "twins" now themselves in turn become parent motions. These, as just explained above, consist of dual currents of activity conceived of, on the one hand, as swift motions streaming out from subject to object and thereby constituting the power to sense (as in the case of sight, hearing, etc.: 156b2-7), and on the other, as swift motions streaming out from object to subject and thereby constituting sensibles (such as whiteness and other colors, sounds, etc." 156b7-c3, d1-e1). Since the original active and passive motions that generate these twin currents of sensibility are ceaseless, it would seem that (short of shutting one's eyes, etc.) this kind of swift motion radiating out and mutually impinging on subjects and objects must be occurring all the time. Since, however, these are simply physical occurrences, not unlike those that we might today talk of at the physical and neuro-physiological level, what the theory has thus far described is the occurrence of brute sensation only, not perception—and to that extent is as yet hardly relevant in any significant way to our overall interest in knowledge. Clearly, in order to function as *cognitive* base, this input must amount to more than merely material impact. It would seem that the first phase of the cognitive enterprise must therefore involve some move from a state of sheer material occurrence that might be called "sensation" to a relatively conscious state of awareness that might more properly be called "perception." After all, if, as Socrates points out, the slower centers of passive motion that we call our "sense organs" (159d2-5; 182a6-b2) are being incessantly bombarded by the active motions in which we are immersed (at least in the sense that both the receptive power of our sense organs and the active power of the motions outside us are infinite in their manifestations: 156a6), then clearly only a small fraction of these ever reach to the conscious level. Elsewhere, Plato has Socrates draw a sharp distinction between those occurrences that do reach to the level of consciousness and so qualify as perception on the one hand, and on the other those innumerable occurrences that, on the level of sheer impact, constitute mere internal changes of which we never become aware. He suggests that, in its strict sense, the term *aisthēsis* (as "perception") might best be reserved for that peculiarly conscious sensation which penetrates beyond the bodily organs to the soul,[1] since, in the case of such conscious response, as Socrates now similarly suggests to Theaetetus, "it is soul...that perceives the objects of perception, through the organs as instruments" (184d4-5).

The question, of course, at once arises: What does it mean to talk of "soul perceiving through the senses"? In other words, how is this shift from brute sensation to conscious perception actually effected? I should like to suggest that in light of our earlier analysis of *kompsoteros* theory, we are now in a better position to answer this question, systematically unpacking the laconic account provided here in the *Theaetetus*; for it is at this point that soul first embarks on its peculiarly characteristic activity, thereby initiating that cognitive process which will finally culminate in *epistēmē*, the knowledge whose logos they are seeking.

It is the thesis of this section that this cognitive activity of soul proceeds along precisely those lines, and through precisely those steps, that were already laid down in the *kompsoteros* theory of generation. It will therefore argue first, that this "given" of brute sensation will now itself, at a further level, function as a continuum analogous to that which constituted the first stage of *kompsoteros* theory at level Alpha; second, that, paralleling the second stage of division effected at level Alpha, so too here, differentiation through division imposes discreteness on the flow of this continuum; and third, that interaction between the differentiated units now yields (from the epistemological as well as from the ontological point of view) a radically novel complex which will be analyzable into, but not reducible to, its motion-elements. A closer reading of the *kompsoteros* account of sensation now reveals the details of this structure.

STAGE 1: CONTINUUM

On analogy with flux or motion as the starting point (*archē*: 156a3) of generation, the starting point for perception is now provided by that ceaseless flow of "swift motions" (156d1-2) generated in active-passive interaction—twin currents streaming forth, on the one side, as the objective sensibility of coloredness, hearability, etc., and on the other, as the subjective sensibility of sight, ability to hear, etc. (156b1-2, d4-e1). Located between the original active-passive interaction and the subsequent occurrence of particular seeings-of-color, hearings-of-sound, etc., this stage of the theory is easy to overlook.[2] But having already highlighted the analogy with Theaetetus' own treatment of magnitude in geometry, Socrates seems to think that this part of the detail can be telescoped, and accordingly gives us an account that is tautly succinct. Even so, the somewhat sketchy characterization of these currents of sensibility, now themselves in turn understood as an epistemological continuum, seems clearly to echo the earlier character-ization of the original motion as an ontological continuum.

Sensibility is thus, in the first place, introduced simply as two-fold motion, streaming swiftly between the slower parent motions in whose interaction they are generated (156d1-3). Second, these flowing currents of sensibility, subjective and objective, can now be seen, within the perspective of this further level, as infinite in quantity (*plēthei men apeira*: 156a7-b1 can mean both infinite in number and infinite, or indeterminate, in quantity). Third, although these stream-ings of sensibility are as yet indeterminate in the sense that they are "not any one thing" but simply streaming effluences[3]—thus further elucidating and vindicating interpretation 3 of the secret doctrine—they may nevertheless be characterized in terms of polar extremes, this time of subjective sensibility (the senses) and objective sensibility (the sensible) (156b1-2; 156d4-e1). On the other hand, even these may not be taken as strictly determinate, but only as relative to each other; for as at level Alpha it was pointed out that the very conceptions of active and passive were meaningless except with reference to each other (157a3-4), so also is it true that the very conceptions of sense and sensible are meaningless except with reference to each other, so that "when I become a percipient, I must necessarily become percipient *of* some-thing, for it is impossible to become percipient and perceive nothing; and that which is perceived must become so *to* someone" (160a8-b1).

Summary of *kompsoteros* theory
at Stage 1: Continuum

Comparison of the ontological and epistemological "given". Summarizing, therefore, and comparing the first stage of *kompsoteros* theory at levels Alpha and Beta respectively, we can now line up their account of the basic material stuff of the world (the *ontological* starting point, or "given") on the one hand, and their account of the basic material stuff of perception (the *epistemological* starting point, or "given") on the other. In both cases, we recognize the following:

1. It consists of continuous motion.
2. It is infinite in quantity.
3. It is fundamentally relative in that it may be identified simply in terms of opposition between mutually relative extremes.

In our language, this would be to say that neither the ontological nor the epistemological "given" is to be understood as particulate or discrete (neither particulate matter nor discrete sense-impressions), but rather as a continuum on the model of magnitude in geometry. In other words, "nothing is of itself any one thing." Insofar as these three characteristics represent indeterminacy of place, quantity, and quality, it suggests that what is given to soul "by nature" is best understood negatively—as without determination (*apeiron*), without rational structure (*alogon*), without measure (*ametros*), and without any intelligent component (*anous*)—awaiting the measuring and structuring activity of soul or mind.

The problem of language. Perhaps the most significant result of this combined indeterminacy of quality, quantity, and even place is that, at this primary level of sheer interaction that constitutes raw sensation, language with its implication of determinacy is, strictly speaking, inapplicable.[4] This point, crucial to the theory, is made with increasing insistence: "It is out of movement and motion and mixture with one another that all those things become which we wrongly say 'are'— wrongly, because nothing ever is, but is always becoming" (152d7-e1). Again, after the detailed exposition, it is reaffirmed that

> it results from all this, that..."being" should be altogether abolished, though we have often—and even just now—been compelled by custom and ignorance to use the word. But we ought not, the wise men say, to permit the use of "something" or "somebody's" or "mine" or "this" or "that" or any other word that implies making things stand still, but, *in accordance with nature [kata physin]* we should speak of things as "becoming" and "being made" and "being destroyed" and "changing." (157a7-b7)

Recognition of these linguistic implications of *kompsoteros* theory, that is to say, the inapplicability of language *at this level of original flux,* is as basic to my argument here as it is to Socrates' argument in the *Theaetetus* itself. Socrates' reiteration of the point has the effect of sharpening the contrast between what is thus given "by nature" and subsequent stages that will bear the stamp of soul's organizing activity.

What this first stage has done is to confront us—exactly as in the ontological context of level Alpha—with a kind of brute givenness in the flow of sensibility, the inherent irrationality of which calls for the kind of organization characteristic of linguistic or epistemological structuring. On this irrational indeterminacy, soul will now proceed to impose an order of rational determinacy. Once again, following the pattern established in the account of generation, this is achieved in the next two stages of the theory: stage 2 will introduce measure, thereby cutting the continuum into relatively determinate units—which will permit us to treat sensibility as though it were discrete; stage 3 will concern itself with interaction between these units.

STAGE 2: DIVISION OF THE CONTINUUM

Faced simply with these undifferentiated currents of sensibility, then, how does soul make that initial move from sensibility to perception? What, in short, constitutes the primary act of cognition, marking the first advent of mind?[4] It is at this point that Plato has Socrates turn to a familiar contrast. Playing on the traditional tension between nature and convention, he suggests that we escape from the indeterminacy of flux as given "by nature" (*kata physin:* 157b6) by resorting to the relative determinacy of fixedness as provided "by convention" (*hypo synētheias:* 157b2). As already intimated, this escape is effected through the device of language (cf. 157b5-7).

At first sight, however, any assertion of a cognitive function for language seems to pose a paradoxical problem. If, on the one hand, language is to be accurate in reporting or reflecting the way things "really" are, then not only would determinate verbs (like *being:* 152d8; 157b1) and nouns and pronouns (like Socrates' *something, this, that:* 157b4-5) have to be replaced by less determinate expressions in order to describe things (like, for example, *becoming, being destroyed, or changing:* 157b6-7),[5] but, in the long run, from one sentence to the next, or even from one breath to the next, any kind of consistent reference would be impossible—and language, far from playing a cognitive role, would be reduced to indeterminate sound. If, on the other hand (since both thought and discourse require—as in this very presentation of doctrine [157b2-3]—that we be able to refer, compare, and in general use words consistently), we do go ahead and ensure the possibility of consistent reference by using language to "make things stand still" (157b7), then, in apparent denial of the theory, we imply, not the continuity of motion, but rather the discreteness of rest. In short, if we opt for language that would be in accordance with nature, and thus accurately reflective of the radical indeterminacy of flux as given in nature, then consistent reference becomes impossible; if, on the other hand, we opt for language in accordance with custom or convention, then we seem to deny the very theory we are supporting and so are forced into contradiction:

> We ought not, the wise men say, to permit the use of "something" or "somebody's" or "mine" or "this" or "that" or any other word that implies making things stand still . . . for anyone who by this mode of speech makes things stand still is easily refuted. (157b3-8)

At first sight, therefore, this constitutes a formidable attack, threatening to reduce to contradiction any *kompsoteros* claim about the cognitive function of language.

Faced with this attack, however, *kompsoteros* theory refuses to be caught on the horns of any such nature-versus-convention dilemma— and indeed undercuts the argument entirely by simply denying the proposed interpretation of what language is about. In contrast to their uninitiated critics, the *kompsoteroi* seem to envision the cognitive function of language as other than straightforward reflecting or mirroring.

According to this approach, then, a better way to understand language is to see it as introducing into the indeterminacy of a flowing reality such determinate distinctions as will "*give* things fixity" (183a7) by "*making* them stand still" (157b7)—so that it becomes strictly true to talk of language as the primary "tool" of mind or soul in determining reality.[6] In the case of geometry, the measuring off of the mathematical continuum yielded lines of determinate measure. So now, using language as the cutting instrument for similarly measuring off and so dividing up the continuum of reality, soul proceeds, at this second stage of level Beta, to distinguish within the dual flow of sensibility, on the one hand, distinct kinds of subjective sensibility so that "we have for the senses names [*onomata*] like these: sight and hearing and smell, and the sense of cold and of heat, and pleasures and pains and desires and fears and so forth" (156b2-5), and, on the other hand, different kinds of objective sensibility, each kind being linked to a corresponding sensation so that

> the class of objects of sense is akin to each of these; all sorts of colors are akin to all sorts of acts of vision, and in the same way, sounds to acts of

hearing, and the other objects of sense spring forth akin to the other senses. (156b7-c3)

In neither case, however, are these discriminations "given" by nature. What is given in nature is motion and flux, whereas the determinate divisions introduced through language are the work of mind or soul.[7]

As the *kompsoteros* pattern emerges here, we begin to recognize with increasing clarity the details of their ontological-epistemological parallel, for the account goes on to characterize these divisions that have been introduced into the swift streamings of sensibility: (1) Almost in passing, we find that, like Theaetetus' roots, these determinations introduced through division are referred to as "powers" (*dynameis*) (e.g., 184e8-185a1; 185c3)[8]—through which bodily "powers" soul itself perceives (185e6-7). (2) As with rational and irrational lines in geometry, so too with the divisions now introduced here: there are an unlimited number of different modes of sensibility which might be measured off as distinct determinations in these currents of sensibility—although, of course, those we actually name are numerous but limited: "Those that have names are very numerous; those that are unnamed are unlimited in number [*aperantoi*]" (156b6-7). (3) Like mathematical quantities, which as we saw are always relative, so too these divisions into senses and sensibilities are relative in the two familiar senses—first, in that they are mutually dependent or "related in their generation" (156b7-c1), for, as already noted, there could be no such thing as a sense of sight without the corresponding sensible of coloredness, and so on (160a8-b1); and second, in the sense with which we ourselves are familiar in taking about "determinables," for each of these divisions represents a range of determinability identified in terms of relative extremes. Thus, like Theaetetus' mathematically measurable magnitude of the relatively great-and-small (see discussion of 154c1-4 in appendix A), so too we find the visible to be that which is relatively light-and-dark (184b8-9; d8-e1), the hearable that which is relatively high-and-low (184b9), the tastable that which is relatively bitter-and-sweet (178c9), and the tactile that which is relatively hard-and-soft (186b2-4).

Summary of *kompsoteros* theory at Stage 2: Division

Comparison of ontological and epistemological elements. Summarizing, therefore, and comparing the second stage of *kompsoteros* theory at levels Alpha and Beta, we can now line up the two accounts—the determinate measuring off of the ontological continuum into active and passive motions (i.e., into discrete ontological elements) on the one hand, and the determinate measuring off of the epistemological continuum into subjective senses and objective sensibles (i.e., into discrete epistemological elements) on the other. In each case, we recognize the following:

1. The elements are said either to be, or to have, "power" (*dynamis*).
2. The elements are said to be "infinite in number."
3. The elements are said to be relative in a twofold sense.

In each case, the cutting of the continuum into discrete elements introduces fixity into the flow of motion by imposing determinate quantity or measure on flux that is by nature unmeasured and indeterminate.

STAGE 3: GENERATIVE COMBINATION

At this point, what we have in hand as the elements of perception are, first, a number of "subjective" powers (or senses) which, as swift motions, stream out from those slower motions that we call eyes, ears, etc., and second, a number of "objective" powers (or sensibles) which, as swift motions, stream out from those slower motions that we call visible, audible, tactile, etc., objects. This state of dual streaming sensibility, however, still does not add up to perception. In fact, the theory asserts, no amount of "adding up" will yield perception, any more than any mere "adding" of Theaetetus' lines could ever yield two-dimensionality. On the contrary, just as at the corresponding stage at level Alpha, so too here, the coming together of sense and sensible requires, not mere juxtaposition or addition, but rather a peculiarly generative kind of interactive combination. Insisting that what is involved here is analogous, not only to the generation of figure in geometry but also to the generation of living offspring, the discussion is heavy with metaphors of sexual intercourse, and of the coming into being of a child as something new and other than the parents (*pros allēla homilia . . . synapotiktontos . . . syggennēsan . . . pros allēla syggignomenōn . . . apotiktonta*: 157a1-2; 156e2, e4; 182b5-6).

Once again, moreover, as in the ontological context of level Alpha, eligibility for mating requires on the one hand, *dissimilarity*—a criterion met in Theaetetus' illustration by the lines being perpendicular to each other, met here by one partner being objective, the other subjective; on the other, *similarity*—here expressed as the recognition that both must be "akin" (156b7-c1) (which is another way the commensurability requirement from geometry is translated into the context of intercourse at level Beta). Similarity is represented in the reciprocity characteristic of perception; dissimilarity is represented in the subjective-objective opposition. Once again, finally, exactly as at level Alpha, it is in the very transformation of the two interacting elements themselves that the generated product emerges. In Theaetetus' illustration the two lines become the sides of a rectangular figure. So too, for example, in the generative interaction between the stream of sight and the stream of, say, whiteness, the eye becomes no longer simply the power of a sighted eye, but now an actually seeing eye, and the object in its turn becomes, no longer simply a power of overflowing whiteness, but now an actually white object. On the transforming character of this interaction the theory is quite explicit:

> When the eye and some commensurate object which approaches [i.e., two slower motions, passive and active, which constitute the mating partners at level Alpha] beget whiteness and the corresponding sense [i.e., two swifter motions, which constitute the twins generated at level Alpha] ... then, while sight from the eye and whiteness from that which joins to produce the color are moving from one to the other [i.e., subjective and objective sensibility, which constitute the mating partners at level Beta], then the eye becomes full of sight and so begins at that moment to see, and becomes, certainly not sight [which had been the product at level Alpha] but a seeing eye [which actual occurrence of white-seeing is the subjective product here at level Beta], and the object which joined in begetting the color is filled with whiteness and becomes in its turn, not whiteness [which had been the product at level Alpha], but white [which actual occurrence of seen-white is the objective product here at level Beta]. (156d3-e5)

And lest Theaetetus (or the reader) be still uncertain, Socrates reminds us again a little later that

> heat or whiteness [i.e., the active twin generated at level Alpha, which will become objective mating partner at level Beta] moves simultaneously with perception [i.e., the passive twin generated at level Alpha, which will become subjective mating partner at level Beta] between the active and passive elements [i.e., the mating partners at level Alpha], and the passive becomes percipient [which occurrence is the subjective product at level Beta], but not perception [which was the product at level Alpha], and the active becomes, not a quality [which was the product at level Alpha], but endowed with a quality [which occurrence is the objective product at level Beta].

He continues:

> Now perhaps quality [*poiotes*] seems an extraordinary word, and you do not understand it when used as a general expression, so let me give particular examples. For the active element becomes neither heat nor

whiteness [which state, generated at level Alpha, is already one of the partners here at level Beta], but hot or white [which occurrence is actually generated now at level Beta], and other things in the same way. (182a8-b2)

Should this verbal account still seem confusing, then the overall picture of generative combination becomes immediately clear in a diagram (fig. 1).

THE GENERATED PRODUCT

Having focused in some detail at level Alpha on the *kompsoteros* view of the generated product, we can now immediately recognize the analogy here. For there is clearly a sense in which, insofar as nothing has been added to those prior elements of sensibility, perception may be said to be "nothing other than" the interacting elements (for example, sight and visibility)—as, in turn, these too are of course "nothing other than" the prior interacting elements of active and passive motion, and Theaetetus' figure is "nothing other than" the lines that define it. It is in this sense that the overall account of perception concludes by reiterating, "We must take it that nothing is of itself anyone thing, but all things of all sorts arise out of motion and intercourse with each other" (156e8-157a3). On the other hand, any particular occurrence of perception begotten of that interaction of elements is qualitatively different from either, or both, the sense and sensible elements that generate it—and in this sense, perception must be said to be indeed "other than" its interacting elements (for example, sight and visibility)—just as these in turn, in one sense, proved likewise to be "other than" the prior elements of active and passive motion, and a two-dimensional figure is indeed "other than" just the one-dimensional lines that define it. From this angle, perception represents, in short, a radically different dimension of reality. Here again, however, it is only in light of this subtler elaboration of *kompsoteros* theory that it becomes possible to understand the deliberate ambiguity of meaning hidden beneath that original, and superficially simple, proposition that "everything is motion and *there is nothing else besides this*" (156a5).

RETROSPECTIVE

As we stand back now to put the account of *kompsoteros* theory into perspective, several things fall into place—enabling us, moreover, to answer some of the questions that originally puzzled us.

First of all, and most conspicuously, we can see how skillfully, from the very beginning, Plato has prepared the reader, along with

Figure 1.
Successive Generation at Ontological and Epistemological Levels

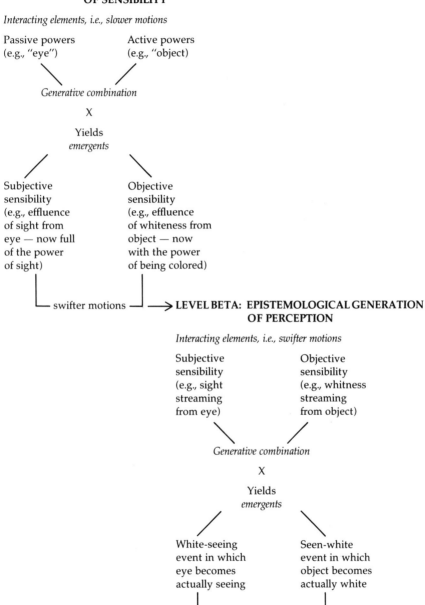

**LEVEL ALPHA: ONTOLOGICAL GENERATION
                     OF SENSIBILITY**

Interacting elements, i.e., slower motions

Passive powers   Active powers
(e.g., "eye")   (e.g., "object)

                    Generative combination

                              X

                           Yields
                         emergents

Subjective   Objective
sensibility   sensibility
(e.g., effluence   (e.g., effluence
of sight from   of whiteness from
eye — now full   object — now
of the power   with the power
of sight)   of being colored)

           swifter motions ⟶ **LEVEL BETA: EPISTEMOLOGICAL GENERATION
                                               OF PERCEPTION**

                         Interacting elements, i.e., swifter motions

                         Subjective   Objective
                         sensibility   sensibility
                         (e.g., sight   (e.g., whitness
                         streaming   streaming
                         from eye)   from object)

                              Generative combination

                                        X

                                     Yields
                                   emergents

                         White-seeing   Seen-white
                         event in which   event in which
                         eye becomes   object becomes
                         actually seeing   actually white

                              Unique occurrences

Theaetetus, for initiation into these mysteries of the *kompsoteroi*. The obvious level of introductory dialogue between Socrates and Theaetetus now peels back to reveal a subtler level; for "the hidden truth" here (cf. 155d10) is that Plato is bringing together Theaetetus *as mathematician* and Socrates *as midwife*, drawing on the language and imagery of both geometry and sexual intercourse in order to illumine the *kompsoteros* account of generative emergence.

Second, in watching Socrates assimilate Theaetetus' original definition of knowledge as perception first to Protagorean, then to Heracleitean doctrine, and now finally to that of the *kompsoteroi*, we can begin to glimpse a sense in which, on the kind of sophisticated reading he is proposing, there is (surprisingly) truth to be found in Theaetetus' statement. This is what we have been gently led to understand through the analogy between the ontological account of *kompsoteros* theory at level Alpha and the epistemological account at level Beta. Thus, ontologically, according to the theory of generative emergence, it is true to say "everything is motion" so long as this statement is interpreted to mean that, although nothing else is actually *added* (anymore than anything was *added* to Theaetetus' linear elements), nevertheless new dimensions of reality can be generated through productively interactive combination—so that the structured beauty of the entire cosmos is to be understood as both the same as, and yet different from, the original flux of motion out of which it emerges. So too, epistemologically (the discussion suggests), it will be true to say that "knowledge is perception" so long as this statement is interpreted to mean that, although nothing else is actually added, nevertheless new epistemological dimensions can be generated, so that the complex structure we call "knowledge" is similarly to be understood as both the same as and yet different from the perceptual flux out of which it emerges. For this reason Socrates was carefully accurate in his original assessment that it was *ou phaulon*—"not a bad (or 'not a simple') definition" (151e8). Fresh from these nuances of ambiguity, we therefore find ourselves listening with new understanding as Socrates helps Theaetetus to understand the significance of his own definition:

> So you were quite right in saying that knowledge is nothing other than perception, and there is complete identity between the doctrine of Homer and Heracleitus and all their followers—that all things are in motion, like streams; the doctrine of the great philosopher Protagoras—that man is the measure of all things; and the doctrine of Theaetetus—that, since these things are true, perception comes to be knowledge. (160d5-e2)

For, attuned now to subtleties of sameness and difference, we have come to understand that Theaetetus is after all right in saying that "knowledge is nothing other than perception"—so long as we take it under the interpretation that has been offered in the *kompsoteros* theory of perception. In this respect, Socrates seems to be suggesting that, like Protagoras' dictim, which was found to contain "hidden truth" (155d10), so too Theaetetus' proposed definition may prove to contain truth not initially or superficially evident.

Third, as we saw at the beginning of our inquiry, one of the questions that challenges any reader of the *Theaetetus* revolves around the role (within the dialogue as a whole) of the apparent obsession with this issue of perception, and consequently of what seems at first sight to be a disproportionate preoccupation with Theaetetus' first definition. After all, discussion of his initial proposal occupies more than half the entire dialogue. One reason has just been suggested (the definition is not to be rejected but *interpreted*), but there seems to be another reason as well. And this reason relates specifically to what, for want of a better term, I am going to call the "method" of the *kompsoteroi*, the method which, as we have seen in these two chapters, Socrates has been spelling out in such detail. It seems to me that the structure of argument and analysis into which Theaetetus has been initiated embodies a method which holds the key, not only to the *Theaetetus'* quest for knowledge, but to Plato's philosophy as a whole. It is this method I should now like to explore. By approaching it from a significantly different angle, through another dialogue altogether, it will, I believe, become overwhelmingly evident that what in the *Theaetetus* Socrates is calling the "mysteries of the *kompsoteroi*" will turn out to be central to an overall philosophical vision which becomes increasingly explicit through the later dialogues.

—— FOUR ——

KOMPSOTEROS METHOD

Since there is always the danger that one will fail to see the wood for the trees, what I have tried to do in the previous two chapters is to move constantly between a close scrutiny of the trees of the text to an overview of the wood as a whole. It is through this double awareness that we have found isolated features taking form as components of reiterated patterns. Now, however, an even larger perspective opens up.

Harking back to both Theaetetus' work in geometry and Socrates' work as a midwife, the articulation of *kompsoteros* ontological theory at level Alpha and the operation of perceiving soul at level Beta now begin to come into focus as special cases of a more generalized formula. What comes as something of a jolt, however, is the recognition that this structure seems remarkably, and unexpectedly, close to what Plato has Socrates elsewhere describe as the pattern par excellence of specifically rational activity. But let me take this step by step. First, it will be helpful to lay out in diagram form the comparison between the structure of the *kompsoteros* theory of generation (at level Alpha) and their theory of perception (at level Beta) (fig. 2).

What I should now like to explore is a hypothesis which, though it might initially appear reckless, will nevertheless (I believe) turn out to be true. It will be my thesis that the parallel between the method of the *kompsoteroi* in the *Theaetetus* and the method that in the *Philebus* Socrates tells us he has "always loved" (*Phil.* 16b6) is not only striking, but shows these two to be in fact the same method. If I am right, then this method will turn out to hold a key, not only to the *Theaetetus*, but to Plato's philosophy as a whole.

As here in the *Theaetetus*, where Socrates lays out a complex theory of generation and perception, so in the *Philebus* we find him offering a correspondingly dense analysis of generation—an account of "the things which are generated and the things out of which they are generated" (27a11-12). In the *Theaetetus*, he attributes his theory to the wise men of the past (152e2-153a3; 155d9-e1) whom he calls "subtle thinkers" (*kompsoteroi:* 156a3); in the *Philebus,* he similarly attributes the

Figure 2.
Comparison of *kompsoteros* Theories of Generation and Perception

LEVEL ALPHA: STRUCTURE OF PHYSICAL THEORY (Chapter 2)		
Stage	Operation	Characterization
1. Continuum: indeterminate flow	Focusing on an original flow of active-passive motion	Indeterminacy defined simply in terms of duality
2. Division of the continuum: imposes discreteness	Differentiation into active and passive elements e.g., physical objects, and subjects with eyes, etc.	i. Powers (*dynameis*) ii. Infinite in number iii. Relative in character
3. Combination: generates novelty	Slow motion Slow motion [e.g., eye] x [e.g., object] ↙ ↘ Begetting of twin swift motions a) senses, e.g., sight b) sensibles, e.g., visibility	i. Unlike: active-passive ii. Like: commensurable radical novelty: { analyzable into } { not reducible to } its elements

Figure 2.
Comparison of *kompsoteros* Theories of Generation and Perception

LEVEL BETA: STRUCTURE OF PERCEPTION (Chapter 3)		
Stage	Operation	Characterization
1. Continuum: indeterminate flow	Focusing on an original flow of objective-subjective sensibility	Indeterminacy defined simply in terms of duality
2. Division of the continuum: imposes discreteness	Differentiation into subjective and objective elements e.g., stream of sight, and stream of visibility	i. Powers (*dynameis*) ii. Infinite in number iii. Relative in character
3. Combination: generates novelty	e.g., stream stream of of sight x visibility ↙ ↘ Begetting of perceptual occurrences; (subjective white-seeing) (objective seen-white)	i. Unlike: subjective objective ii. Like: "akin" radical novelty: { analyzable into } { not reducible to } its elements

theory to "the wise men of the past" (16c7-8). In the *Theaetetus,* Socrates then sets out from a starting point (*archē*: 156a3) said to be disclosed in a kind of religious initiation (155d10-156a3); in the *Philebus,* he proposes a starting point (*archē*: 23c1) similarly said to be given in a kind of divine revelation (16c5-6, e3-4; 23c9-10). In the *Theaetetus,* Socrates then unfolds an account structured in terms of a three-fold process which involves (1) recognition of an indeterminate, or *apeiron,* ceaselessly in motion, which then (2) comes to be determined by the introduction of measure, in order (3) to generate products new and fair (see chapters 2 and 3). In the *Philebus,* Socrates goes on to develop an account similarly structured in terms of a three-fold process which also involves (1) an *apeiron,* an indeterminate ever in motion (24c3-d5), which then (2) is limited by the introduction of measure (25a6-b2), in order (3) to generate products new and fair (26b5-d9). Could it be that this method which in the *Philebus* Socrates calls the method of "dialectic"—and which, it has been argued, accords with Aristotle's otherwise puzzling account of Plato's philosophy,[1]—is really at the same time an account of the *kompsoteros* theory of the *Theaetetus*? Could it be, finally, that Plato's elusive "esoteric doctrine," thought to be the teaching to which Aristotle refers, is actually related to "the hidden truth" that Plato finds in the long intellectual tradition of his predecessors (*Theaet.* 155d9-10; 152e2-8), and into the mysteries of which Socrates initiates Theaetetus?[2]

A first reaction to such a comparison between the "way" (*hodos*: *Phil.* 16a8, b5) recommended in the *Philebus* and the method of the *kompsoteroi* in the *Theaetetus* must surely be a healthy skepticism lest one be taken in by too facile a fit. One the other hand, like Socrates, we should perhaps be challenged to subject the suggestion to cross-examination to determine whether this is indeed appearance only, or actual reality.

TRIPARTITE THEORY: *PHILEBUS*

What needs to be done for a start, therefore, is carefully to examine the tripartite structure that Socrates elaborates in the *Philebus*—rigor demanding that we look at enough of the text to furnish real testable evidence.

To Apeiron:
The Unlimited, or Indeterminate

In order to illustrate denotative range, Plato provides a series of examples of what he means by an "unlimited" or "indeterminate": hotter and colder, more and less, gentle and emphatic, drier and wetter, many and fewer, quicker and slower, greater and smaller, acute and grave, pleasant and painful (*Phil.* 24a6-d7; 25c5-11; 26a2-3; 27e5-9). He then goes on to suggest a common characterization which brings them all under a single description: a continuum whose flow may be characterized in terms of the duality of mutually relative extremes; it is indeterminate, not only in the absence of endpoints, but equally in the absence of any discrete (i.e., measurable or quantitative) divisions:

> What I ask you is difficult and debatable; but consider it all the same. In the first place, take hotter and colder and see whether the more and less which dwell in their very nature do not...preclude the possibility of any end...and, being endless,they are of course in-finite [*apeiro*]...
>
> Wherever more and less are present, they do not allow any definite quantity to exist; they always introduce in every case a comparison...and thus they create the relation of more and less, thereby doing away with fixed quantity...hotter and colder are always progressing and never stay still...
>
> To avoid waste of time in discussing all the individual examples, see if we can accept this as a designation [*semeion*] of the unlimited:...all things which appear to us to become more or less...[i.e., the class] which unites more and less. (24a6-25c11)

When we check this account of the unlimited against the *kompsoteros* account of the continuum as basic "given" (whether the flow of active and passive motion at level Alpha, or the swift streaming of objective and subjective sensibility at level Beta), the characterization seems clearly to be consistent: both are continuous, both are infinite, and both are to be characterized in relative terms of polar extremes.

To Peras:
Limit or Determination

Less space is devoted to an explanation of *to peras,* but the *Philebus* does present it as that which determines the indeterminate, or limits the unlimited, through the introduction of determinate quantity or measure—as, presumably, in the introduction of the quantitative measurement of degrees into the continuum of temperature, or the introduction of the quantitative measurement of number into the continuum of magnitude—thus for the first time marking discrete or fixed divisions that make the flow stand still. In this sense, *to peras* ends the tension between the opposites that characterize *to apeiron,* and introduces the possibility of commensurability and harmony between discriminated elements.

The things which do not admit of the more and less and the like, but do admit of all that is opposed to them—first, equality and the equal, then the double, and anything which is a definite number relative to number, or a definite measure relative to measure—all these might properly be assigned to the class of the limit, or the determinate [*to peras*]. (25a6-b2)

The class of the equal and the double and everything which puts an end to the differences between opposites, and makes them commensurable and harmonious by the introduction of number. (25d11-e2)

In allowing quantity and measure to make their appearance in the abode of the more and less . . . those latter would be banished from their own proper place . . . for quantity is at rest and does not move. (24c6-d5)

This characterization of limit as measuring determinate quantity, thereby introducing rest or fixity into the indeterminate, seems similarly to echo the *kompsoteros* account of division at the second stage of their theory (whether the measuring off of determinate objects at level Alpha, or the measuring off of determinate sensibility at level Beta).

To Mikton:
The Product Generated through Combination or Mixture (*Phil.* 25b5)

When limit or measure is applied to the span of polar duality provided by the unlimited or *apeiron*, then the continuum yields determinately discrete elements. In this sense, the combination of limit and unlimited is the source of the discrete things of this world—as, in the *kompsoteros* account, it is the source both of discriminated subjects and objects (at level Alpha) and of discriminated senses and sensibles (at level Beta). But it soon becomes evident that here in the *Philebus*, no less than in the *Theaetetus*, Socrates is concerned with more than simply the fact that innumerable such elements may be measured off in the determination of a polar span. Beyond this general kind of application of limit to unlimited that yields the multitude of discreteness (*to plēthos: Phil.* 26c8), we are now required to focus on the product generated through an appropriate combination or communion (*koinōnia*) of the discriminated opposites (e.g., 25e7). Although in one sense this product is hard to distinguish from the limit and unlimited from which it derives, it is nevertheless different enough to warrant identification as a distinct "third thing, generated from a mixture of these two" (27b8-9; cf. 23c12-13).

Once again, this third category seems to correspond to the product of generative combination that constituted the third stage in the *kompsoteros* theory. Further emphasizing the parallel, the *Philebus* even follows the *kompsoteroi* in comparing the product here with a child generated in intercourse (e.g., *to toutōn ekgonon*: 26d8; cf. 25e3-4). The challenge (echoing Theaetetus' search for the right factors needed to generate his squares) will now focus on determining exactly the appropriate elements out of which such a product will be generated. As Socrates puts it:

> All the things which are ever said to exist are sprung from the one and many and have inherent in them the limit [*peras*] and the unlimited [*apeirian*]. . . and we must see not only that the original entity is *one* [i.e., a single thing, the product, or *to mikton*] and *many* [i.e., a plurality of elements measured off by *to peras*,], and *infinite* [i.e., originally derived from the indeterminate duality of *to apeiron*] but *just how many it is* . . . The wise men of the present day make the one and the many too quickly or too slowly, in haphazard fashion, and they put infinity immediately after unity, disregarding all that lies between—and this it is which distinguishes dialectic from eristic. (16c9-17a5)

As we have by now come to expect, the full meaning of this statement is not immediately or transparently clear. On the other hand, we do recall that *kompsoteros* theory also asserted that any "one" thing should be understood as emerging from a generative combination of "many" factors—which factors have themselves been measured out from a prior indeterminate, or "infinite" continuum. When, therefore, Socrates proceeds to explain what he means by this method that he calls "dialectic," we are not surprised to find him articulating the familiar threefold structure of *kompsoteros* theory. Since the interests of Philebus and Protarchus are not those of a mathematician like Theaetetus, Socrates draws his examples instead from music (*Phil.* 17b11-e1)and language (*Phil.* 17a8-b9; 18b3-d2), in order to spell out the corresponding three stages of continuum, division, and generative combination.

In the first place (he explains), sound—a continuum conceived of as an indeterminate flow, or high-low polar duality (an *apeiron*)—constitutes the material stuff of both language and music. It is the differentiation of this continuum which, in the second place, provides plurality: in the case of language, the division cuts or limits the flow so as to discriminate determinate, and to that extent discrete, phonemic letters or sounds; in the case of music, division similarly cuts or limits the flow so as to differentiate analogously discrete and determinate intervals. In both cases, the third phase involves a certain combination of selected elements such that a piece of music, or intelligible discourse, emerges as a new whole—something that is at once an infinite flow of sound, a plurality of distinct elements, and comprehensive unified whole:

> Sound, which passes out through the mouth... is one, and yet again it is infinite in quantity. And no one of us is wiser than the other merely for knowing that it is infinite or that it is one; but that which makes each of us a grammarian is the knowledge of the number and nature of sounds...
>
> When someone, whether god or godlike man... observed that sound was infinite, he was the first to notice that there were vowel sounds in that infinite, not one but many, and again that there were other elements which were not vowels but did have a kind of sound, and that these also had a definite number; and he distinguished a third kind of letter which we now call mutes. Then he divided [*diērei*] the mutes until he distinguished each individual one, and he treated the vowels and semivowels in the same way, until he knew the number of them and gave to each and all the name of a letter [*stoicheion*] (*Phil.* 17b3-9; 18b6-c6)

Not only are the interval-elements of music then combined to produce a systematic whole (*systēma*) (17d1-2), but we also know that in the case of language the dialogues consistently conceive of a third stage which corresponds to that generative combination that we have come to expect as the final phase of structure. Thus, in the *Cratylus*, after going through the same series of divisions and subdivisions of vowels, consonants, and mutes, Socrates continues:

> And when we have made all these divisions properly... we must know how to apply each letter with reference to its fitness, whether one letter is to be applied to one thing or many are to be combined [*sygkerannunta*] ...many letters together forming syllables, as they are called, and in turn combining syllables, and by their combination forming nouns and verbs. And from nouns and verbs again we shall construct something great and fair, a systematic whole [*holon systēsomen*] (*Crat.* 424d4-425a3)

According to these accounts, the coming into being of a new whole seems to parallel in striking fashion the generated product of combination at stage 3 of *kompsoteros* theory—whether we are talking about the *systēmata* of language or music, or all "the beauties of our world" (*Phil.* 26b1): in every case a "one" generated from a combination of "many" elements discriminated out from an original "infinite." Again in line with *kompsoteros* theory, we recognize that whether it is a question of a song or a speech, there is on the one hand a sense in which each is still just (i.e., the same as) sound, and on the other a sense in which, just because they *are* what they are (i.e., a song or a speech), each is at the same time also an emergent entity and to that extent indeed something other than (i.e., different from) mere sound.

This threefold structuring of things as at once one, many, and infinite, is (Socrates suggests) like the original Promethean fire, a gift of gods to men (*Phil.* 16c5-6). It is in fact the operation par excellence of reason itself (*Phil.* 15d7-8) and, as the method of inquiry and teaching that characterizes dialectic (e.g., *Phil.* 17a3-5), can lead to understanding and wisdom in any area of inquiry (*Phil.* 16c5-e4, d6-e3).[3] On my reading of the *Theaetetus,* it is through his initiation into these mysteries that Theaetetus enters on the "pathway" toward that true knowledge and wisdom that the dialogue is seeking.

TRIPARTITE PRACTICE: *SOPHIST* AND *STATESMAN* *THEAETETUS*

If however, these *kompsoteros* mysteries really do constitute the method of dialectic and the enterprise of reason itself, then should we not expect to find it pursued in other dialogues as well? The question should offer a healthy challenge by which to test my hypothesis. Although I believe this is indeed the method that Socrates has consistently tried to follow despite its difficulty (*Phil* 16b5-c2), here let me concentrate on those two dialogues which, with the *Theaetetus,* form an obvious trilogy. For both the *Sophist* and the *Statesman* culminate in a discussion of just the kind of generative combination that lies at the heart of *kompsoteros* theory.

Thus, for example, the account of being that the *Sophist* gives us closely follows the same three stages delineated both in the *Philebus* and in Socrates' account of *kompsoteros* theory:

1. focusing on being as an indeterminate continuum (i.e., an "infinite") of activity-passivity, they first recognize it as "nothing other than power" (*ouk allo ti plēn dynamis*) (*Soph.* 247d8-e4);
2. they discriminate, as discretely different elements (i.e., a "many"), being at rest (*ousia*) and being in motion (*genesis*) (*Soph.* 248a7-13);
3. they acknowledge that although, on the one hand, being must indeed be composed of, and to that extent be the same as, these and only these elements (for there are no others: *Soph.* 250c9-d2) nevertheless, on the other hand, they seem driven to acknowledge being as an emergent entity (i.e., a "one") over and above, and to that extent different from, those elements: "The philosopher...must say that being and the universe consists of both...Being is something else, a third thing over and above these two, inasmuch as you think rest and motion are embraced by it...We find that being has emerged outside of both these [*ektos toutōn amphoterōn anapephantai*]" (*Soph.* 249c10-250d3).

It is the difficulty of understanding how there can be such a thing as an emergent encompassing within itself two elements which are obviously opposites (*Soph.* 250a8-9) and even contradictories (250c12-d4) that leads into the discussion of the possibility, and later the conditions (*Soph.* 251d5-260a3), of precisely the kind of generative "combination" that *kompsoteros* emergence requires. The model for emergence is here the same one we already noted in the context of both the *Philebus* and the *Cratylus*—the arising of linguistic meaning from mere sounds through their combination into syllables. (It will also, of course, be the same model to which Socrates will turn towards the end of the *Theaetetus.*)

In the *Statesman* we are first offered a paradigm of statecraft, and then the analogy is spelled out in political terms. The paradigm (which also carries overtones of the *Cratylus*) is drawn from weaving, an art which

1. takes the fibrous mass of fleece (an "infinite") as providing the material stuff out of which the web will be formed—for the final fabric will in one sense be "nothing other than" this original fleece;
2. divides or separates out the elements of warp and woof (the "many"); and
3. combines, or weaves together, these elements so as to create or produce a third thing (a "one") over and above warp and woof as such—a product on the one hand composed of, and to that extent the same as, its elements, and on the other an emergent entity, and to that extent different from those elements: "The process of weaving is a kind of combining together...But the first part is a separation of what is massed and matted together" (*Stat.* 281a3-6).

Then, almost as a reference back to the two operations in the *kompsoteros* process, the Stranger reminds us that "we have found two great arts, that of combination and division [*sygkritikē te kai diakritikē*]" (*Stat.* 282b7). If both the elements and the combining process itself are right, then we can expect a truly emergent product: "When that part of the art of combination which is included in the art of weaving forms a web by the right intertwining of woof and warp, we call the entire web a woolen garment" (*Stat.* 283a4-7). So the ground is prepared for an account of statecraft on the same model, the remainder of the dialogue explaining how the kingly political art

1. takes as its basic stuff or material the mass of the population capable of being educated (the "infinite")—for in this sense the polis will always be "nothing other than" the citizens who constitute it (*Stat.* 308d6-309b1);
2. divides the population, separating out as distinct elements, on the model of warp and woof, those who are by nature aggressive or courageous and those who are more restrained or stable (the "many") (*Stat.* 309b2-6); and

3. proceeds to combine and weave together these different elements so as to create a new and beautiful third thing (a "one") which on the one hand is composed of, and to that extent is the same as its elements, and which on the other is something else over and above, and to that extent is different from those elements: "Indeed the whole business of the kingly weaving is comprised in this and this alone...in weaving together the self-restrained and courageous characters...thus making of them a smooth and well-woven fabric" (*Stat.* 310e7-311a1).

But, one might ask, although it is true that all this does seem to point up an unsuspected seriousness and significance behind Socrates' initiation of Theaetetus into the mysteries and method of the *kompsoteroi*, what interest or relevance does it have with respect to the discussion at hand? In other words: However interesting this version of dialectical method might be in its own right, why—in the midst of an inquiry into knowledge—does Plato have Socrates go off on this tangent? This question leads to the next part of my thesis.

If Plato (or at least the Platonic Socrates) does believe that the mysteries open up reason's own dialectical route to understanding (*hodos* as road, way, method), then is it not possible that the point of the initiation is to invite us (i.e., the reader along with Theaetetus) to pursue that same *kompsoteros* route which, at pivotal points, we will rejoin in the *Sophist* and the *Statesman?* Might it not be, in other words, that we are being led to search for knowledge itself as a third thing (a "one") generated out of a right mixture of elements (a "many"), these in turn differentiated out from, and to that extent "nothing other than," an original continuum (an "infinite")? Could it be that we are being offered a threefold account of knowledge which

1. focuses on an original indeterminate, or continuum, that provides the basic material or stuff of knowledge (an "infinite")—by, for example, proposing that "knowledge is nothing other than perception" (*ouk allo ti estin epistēmē ē aisthēsis: Theat.* 151e2-3). This is, of course, Theaetetus' first definition (which, we recall, Socrates found to be "not a bad one" to begin with: 151e8);
2. discriminates out the constituent elements of knowledge (a "many")—as, for example, in the proposition that knowledge is true opinion (187b5-6) or true opinion and logos (201c9-d1). These are, of course, Theaetetus' second and third definitions (and again we recall that Socrates apparently agrees that those will be the elements needed: 202d6-7); and
3. anticipates and points the reader toward a recognition that knowledge must be a generated product (a "one"), which on the one hand must be composed of, and to that extent be the same as, those elements, and yet on the other hand must be an emergent entity, a third thing over and above, and to that extent different from, those elements?

IMPLICATIONS OF THE TRIPARTITE METHOD

If, however, the *kompsoteroi* are serious in pointing up these two operations as crucial—first, the separation out of elements, and second, their combination in generative emergence—then they must confront some very important questions, questions which, although present throughout Theaetetus' discussion that follows, are nevertheless larger than any single dialogue. The first relates, in a rather special use of the term, to the *cause* responsible for the operation. The answer to this question (which will in turn raise a host of further questions) is expressed in only slightly different terms in the different contexts, and points in a consistent direction. As the generative combination of limit and unlimited is effected only through the productive causality of mind (*Phil.* 26e2-30c10), as the generative combination of the warp and woof of the political fabric is achieved only through the productive act of the statesman (*Stat.* 310e7-311c6), as the generative combination of forms is realized only through the dialectic of the philosopher (*Soph.* 253b8-e6), and as the generative act of primordial creation is achieved only through the creative work of divine intelligence (*Soph.* 265b8-e3; *Stat.* 273b6-7; *Tim.* passim), so too the generative combination that starts with perception and culminates in the emergence of knowledge will be achieved through the operation of soul as generative, productive, or what we might even think of as creative, intelligence.[4] In characteristic fashion, however, the way to understand something as tricky as "soul" turns out to be through analysis of the way it functions (cf. *Phaedr.* 270c9-d7).

As I see it, it is the concern to understand this operation par excellence of mind or soul that in the *Theaetetus* leads us to concentrate on the two distinct aspects of the process. For, in the first place, the phase of division must select out elements that will prove to be appropriate or "fitting"; in the second, the phase of combination must itself prove to be genuinely productive (cf. *Soph.* 265b9-10). We are, of course, already familiar with both these conditions of successful generation. After all, the *Statesman* laid considerable stress on the whole notion of "fitness" (*to prepon*: e.g., 286d1-2), and in particular on the fact that "any constructive knowledge [*tis . . . tōn synthetikōn epistēmōn*] . . . takes only the materials which are appropriate and fitting [*ta d'epitēdeia kai ta chrēsta*], out of which it gathers all together, matching them to produce a single power and idea" (*Stat.* 308c1-7). In the *Sophist*, likewise, the Eleatic Stranger devotes a great deal of attention to just this question of whether, and if so what kinds of, elements can combine (*Soph.* 251d5-9); he and Theaetetus conclude, of course, that some will fit and others will not—falling back for illustration on the same cases of combination in grammar and music with which we are now familiar. It is in precisely this context of generative combination that they come to recognize the importance of "the knowledge of dialectic"—which turns out to be precisely "the knowledge and ability to distinguish by kinds how things can or cannot combine with one another" (*Soph.* 252e9-253e2).

This ability to distinguish which elements will best combine with one another constitutes, then, the first requirement for this operation of reason which the Stranger calls "dialectic"; a second requirement will involve the product, as such, of that combination. For, from the point of view of production, the question at stake is in the long run whether or not the generation is effective and the product really an emergent entity rather than a mere addition or juxtaposition of elements in conglomeration that—as the *Philebus* put is—results in simply "an uncompounded jumble" (*Phil.* 64d11-e1).

What is especially illuminating now, from the point of view of the *Theaetetus*, is the care with which, throughout these various discussions, Plato seems to have chosen the kinds of words he uses to express this notion of being appropriate (*chrēstos*), being fitting (*epitēdeios*), matching (*sunagō*), fitting together (*harmottō*), inter-weaving (*symplokē*), sharing (*koinōneō;*), and communion (*koinōnia*). For each of these words, while bearing the general meaning used in the translation above, also carries specifically sexual connotations. Thus:

chrēstos. "useful, serviceable, good for some purpose"—is also used of a man, to mean strong in body, or able for sexual intercourse (e.g., Hippocrates, *Genit., peri gones* 2; Liddell and Scott)

epitēdeios. "made for some end or purpose, fit, adapted for"—is also used of a person fit to live with (e.g., Euripides, *Andromache*, 206).

synagō. "bring together, match up"—is also used of the contracting of marriages (e.g., Xenophon, *Symposium*, 4. 64; cf. *Theaet.* 150a2)

harmottō (Attic for *harmozō*). "fit together, join, tune musical instruments"—is also used in the middle voice to mean taking to wife, betrothing oneself (e.g., Herodotus, 5. 32, 47), and in the passive to mean have someone betrothed or married to one (e.g., Herodotus, 3. 137)

sympokē. "interweaving, embrace"—is also used of sexual intercourse (e.g., *Symp.* 191c4)

koinōneō. "to share in, form a community"—is also used of sexual intercourse (e.g., *Laws* 784e3)

koinōnia. "partnership, community"—is also used of sexual intercourse (e.g., Euripides, *Bacchae*, 1276)

Recognizing, then, the overtonal ambiguity of these terms, it should perhaps come as no surprise that, in the *Theaetetus*, these same dimensions of the productive operation—on the one hand, determining the fitness of the interacting or mating partners, and, on the other, judging the success or failure of the interaction in terms of actual generation—

should be represented in terms that are consonant with the sexual analogy employed in all these discussions, and specifically in the *kompsoteros* account of the mysteries. Thus, in the universal sexual symbolism of the *Theaetetus*, it is likewise asserted that those who can determine which elements will best enter into communion with one another will also prove to be the best to supervise the emergence of the generated offspring. That is why

> midwives are also the most skillful of matchmakers, since they are very wise in knowing what union of man and woman will produce the best possible children... [Although] there is a wrongful and unscientific way of bringing men and women together [*synagōgēn*] nevertheless the true midwife is the only proper matchmaker. (149d5-150a6)

As one whose concern is the generation and emergence of knowledge, Socrates believes it a task imposed on him by the god that in this sense he should act both as matchmaker (151b3-5) and (in an adapted meaning of the term) as midwife, for "women do not, like my patients, bring forth at one time real children and at another mere images... but the greatest thing about my art is this, that it can test whether the mind of a young man is bringing forth a mere image and imposture, or real and genuine offspring" (150a9-c3). In other words, the whole thrust of the dialogue will be towards the success or failure of the combination that Theaetetus is being called upon to effect. If not for Theaetetus himself, then at least for the reader—who has also been initiated into the *kompsoteros* mysteries of generation and emergence—it must be made perfectly clear why, by the end of the dialogue, Socrates' art of midwifery has to judge that "all the offspring that have been born are mere windeggs, and not worth rearing" (210b8-9).

PRESUPPOSITIONS OF THE TRIPARTITE METHOD

If it is true that the task of soul or mind involves, on the one hand, discrimination (*diakritikē*) that will determine those elements genuinely "fit" for combination, and on the other, composition (*sygkritikē*) that will determine the genuinely, over and against only apparently, successful outcome of the combination (cf. *Stat.* 282b7)—then what does Plato propose as relevant criteria for genuine versus only apparent, with respect to both elements and product? Unless he provides an analysis more rigorous than these simple assertions, then this much-touted operation of reason, and the *kompsoteros* method of dialectic itself, will not amount to much. Interestingly enough, he does have Socrates suggest a list of things that soul needs to be able to do

(*Theaet.* 185c4-d1); the challenge will be to understand what he really means by them. To arrive at the criteria for selecting authentic elements on the one hand, and for generating a genuine product on the other, will therefore require a little more sleuthing than has so far been necessary, for these conditions must, I believe, be inferred as much from what actually goes on in the dialogues as from any explicit verbal account that is provided.

Criteria by Which to Determine "Real" Elements

Perhaps the best way to proceed here is to look first at some of the cases of successfully combined, and therefore "fitting," elements that Plato has lined up for us. A partial list, running from the least to the most abstract, might read as follows:

Statesman *Cratylus*	fabric may be analyzed into warp and woof as its elements.
Sophist *Cratylus*	A word may be analyzed into consonants and vowels as its elements.
Sophist *Theaetetus*	A statement may be analyzed into verbs and nouns as its elements.
Theaetetus *Timaeus*	Perception may be analyzed into swift motions which we call "sensings" and "sensibles" as its elements.
Theaetetus *Sophist*	Everything may be analyzed into active and passive motion or power as its elements.
Theaeteus *Timaeus*	Offspring may be analyzed into male and female components as its elements.
Sophist *Timaeus*	Being may be analyzed into rest and motion as its elements.
Philebus	Everything may be analyzed into limit and unlimited as its elements.

Seeking to articulate, not simply the characteristics these elements have in common, but especially the conditions they apparently meet in order to function *as* elements, we can now recognize the following:

1. There must be a certain likeness between the elements. The *Theaetetus*, on analogy with Theaetetus' example of linear elements, talks of this as "commensurability" (*symmetria*: e.g., 156d3-4; cf. *Tim.* 67c7; *Meno* 76d4; *Phil.* 25e1), or as a state of being "akin" (*homogonon*: 156b7-c1). Just as sight and the audible are

not in this sense alike and so cannot "fit" as elements (*Theaet.* 184e8-185a2), so obviously is this the case with, say, warp on the loom and a verb. In order to generate a child, the mating elements must be of the same species; to generate a sentence, the interwoven elements must both be words, and so on. Soul must therefore be able, as Socrates tells Theaetetus, to grasp, and judge of, *likeness* (*Theaet.* 185b4-5; c9-10).

2. Within this context of similarity, there must however be also unlikeness—even to the point of opposition between elements that can "fittingly" or fruitfully combine. Thus, for example, warp and woof must not only lie in opposite directions, but the warp must tightly twisted and hard, the woof loosely twisted and soft (*Stat.* 282e7-14; 309b3-6); so too with activity and passivity, rest and motion, and the others. Soul must therefore be able to judge of *unlikeness* (*Theaet.* 185b4, c9-10).

3. These similar but dissimilar elements, are, moreover, in each case mutually relative in the sense that the identification of each under this description is radically contingent on the other. Thus, for example, if there were no such notion as that of male, neither could there be of female; for nouns to be nouns at all involves a contrast with non-noun words such as verbs (*Soph.* 261e4-262c4); the *Theaetetus* finds the active and passive elements to be mutually dependent (157a4-7); again, the existence of vowels and consonants are such that "none of us could learn any one of them without learning them all" (*Phil.* 18c7-8).

4. Taken in isolation, each element as polar extreme is in an important sense useless (as it were, powerless) ever to become anything more. In interaction with its opposite, however, each becomes mutually transformed. Thus, for example,

- What in isolation presents itself as simply tightly twisted thread becomes, in interaction with its opposite, something more, i.e., warp, and

- What in isolation presents itself as simply loosely twisted thread becomes, in interaction with its opposite, something more, i.e., woof;

- What in isolation presents itself simply as unrestrained violence and brutality (*Stat.* 307b9-c1; 308a4-9; 310d6-8) becomes, in interaction with its opposite, the virtue of courage (*Stat.* 309d10-e3; 311b1-5), and

- What in isolation presents itself simply as weakness and cowardice (*Stat.* 307c1-2; 307e2-308a2) becomes, in interaction with its opposite, the virtue of restraint (*sōphrosyne*): (*Stat.* 309e6; 311b8-9).

The same holds for the other examples. In short, the kind of element that is "fit" for interaction will in one sense continue to remain the same—for warp is still tightly twisted thread, courage is still aggressive, etc.—but in another sense, will become something different—i.e., warp (which is now no longer simply twisted thread) and courage (which is now not simply aggression). Soul, Socrates points out, must therefore be able to grasp and judge *sameness* and *difference* (*Theaet.* 185a11-12, c10).

5. This follows immediately from what has just gone before, for it is now evident that insofar as something is an *element*, it must be said to have—even to *be*—a "power" to become something other than it is in isolation. Thus, the original motion-elements of the physical word are identified in terms of "power" (*dynamis: Theaet.* 156a6); earth, air, fire, and water, as elements combined to form the cosmos, are similarly regarded as "powers" (*Tim.* 32c8); in the context of perception, the subjective elements (i.e., the senses) are to be understood as "powers" (e.g., *Theaet.* 184e8; 185c3, e7; cf. *Rep.* VII, 532a3; VI, 507c7-8); but so too are the objective elements (i.e., those streamings of sensibility such as visibility, audibility, etc.: e.g., *Rep.* VI, 507c7-8; 507e6-508a1; 509b2-3). This I understand to be why, in discussing the combining of elements in general, the *Sophist* emphasizes the "power" to combine (e.g., *Soph.* 251e8) and the consequent need in philosophical analysis to consider first the nature of a thing, and then its "power" of combining (*Soph.* 254c4-5; cf. *Phaedr.* 270d3-4).

6. Once one grants all the above, there arises however something of a problem. For how could one ever recognize, for example, that letters have this "power" to combine to form a word— unless one first had some notion or idea of what a word might be? By implication, it would therefore seem that in order for there ever to be letters (a "many") rather than mere sounds in a sea of sound (an "infinite"), there has to be in the mind in the first place some idea of a word (a "one"). In order for there ever to be warp or woof, rather than chance twistings of fibers in a fibrous mass, there has to be in the first place in the mind of the weaver an idea of woven fabric; in order for there to be subjective senses and objective sensibles, rather than mere streamings of motion within the continuum of motion, there has to be in the first place in the mind of the perceiver the idea of physical objects.

I think this is what Plato is getting at when he has the Stranger talk of being—that third thing conceived of as a whole that encompasses both rest and motion—as "something *in the soul*" (*Soph.* 250b7), or when the *Theaetetus* talks of "the mind . . . bringing forth offspring" (150c2-3), or again as Socrates puts it so powerfully in the *Philebus*, "We say that one and many are identified by reason [*logos*]. . .it [is an operation that] belongs to reason as such" (*Phil.* 15d4-8).

This seems, in other words, to be crucial to the way mind functions—whether it is the idea of woven fabric that enables the weaver to pick out appropriate elements from an "infinite" fibrous mass, or the idea of a word that enables the grammarian or even a user of language to pick out the appropriate elements from an "infinite" flow of sound, and so for all the cases.[5] It is, in short, the way mind operates, whether on our small human scale or the great scale of the universe (cf. *Phil.* 29b6-30c7), for it is in this way that there arise "all the beauties of our world. . .and the many glorious beauties of the soul" (*Phil.* 26b1-7).

This brings us to the second aspect of soul's characteristic activity: the act of combination, or "making the mixture" (*Phil.* 59d10-e5; 61b11-c8), and the determination of real or genuine emergence over and against the "uncompounded jumble of elements" (*Phil.* 64d3-e3) that the *Theaetetus* discards as a windegg (150c2; 160e8-161a1; 210b8-9).

Criteria by Which to Determine "Real" Offspring

How can one tell if the combination is successful and the generated product a real, emergent being? For example, given that some letters will fit and others will not (*Soph.* 252e9-253a2), how can one tell if a particular combination of letters has generated a genuine word, or simply that "jumble" of the *Philebus*?[6] To find an answer, I believe we have to recall the assimilation of being to power (*dynamis: Soph.* 247d8-e4)—and this in two ways. If we consider a word, for example a noun, we realize that it can have referring "power"—which no mere piling up of letters could ever claim. Second, as a real or genuine word, it can now in turn itself function as an element or "power" within a larger context. Thus, if the letters *m, n, d,* and *i* (although appropriate as elements) are combined in that order, the product is not a genuine word: it has no power to refer or communicate. By contrast, combined as *mind,* it is a real word, and can now function as an element in a more complex combination, such as a sentence. So, what about a word now in its turn? How can one tell if a combination of words has generated a genuine sentence, or simply noise like "the beating of a bronze gong" (*Crat.* 430a5)? Once again, the answer seems to be the same. Thus if the words *is, mortal,* and *Socrates* (although appropriate elements to form a sentence, from the point of view of grammar or syntax) are combined in that order, the product proves to be only an apparent but not a real sentence. As the Stranger puts it to Theaetetus, "Those words which are spoken in order and mean something do unite, but those that mean nothing in their sequence do not unite" (*Soph.* 261d8-e2). Hence, when by contrast they are combined as *Socrates is mortal,* then the product is real, and for the same kinds of reasons that just now distinguished a real from a merely apparent word. First, it exhibits "power" in actually saying something, or "reaching a conclusion" (*Soph.* 262d3-4; cf. 263e12), whether true or false (*Soph.* 263a11-d4)—and to exercise "power" is a mark of genuine being (*Soph.* 247d8-e3). Second, as a real sentence, it can itself be in turn a "power" or element by functioning within a yet larger complex such as an argument or discourse—for discourse is generated in an act of interweaving (*symplokē*): a weaving of words (*Theaet.* 202b4) that images an interweaving of forms (*Soph.* 259e5-6). It is this reference to the imaging of forms or ideas that brings us to the last point in determining the success or failure of generative combination.

Just as, in the discrimination of appropriate or "fitting" elements, the starting point of the whole process was the mind's glimpse of some paradigmatic idea, so the final phase of the process returns to that idea in order to compare the generated product with the original paradigm (*Rep.* VI, 484c6-d3; cf. *Phaedr.* 247d2-4; *Crat.* 389b1-3). In this task of determining, first, the fitness of the elements, and second, the success of the generated complex, it is clear that these paradigmatic ideas—of words and language, physical objects and the natural universe, indeed anything at all—must be seen as exercising a very real power. And exercise of such power is evidence of real being, since "everything which possesses any power of any kind, either to produce a change in anything of any nature, or to be affected even in the least degree by the slightest cause...has real existence" (*Soph.* 247d8-e4). The kind of power exercised by such an idea or paradigm is, moreover, that of directing the activity of mind toward itself as goal to be sought and realized. In Plato's vocabulary, that which possesses power of this kind he calls "good." The most comprehensive and therefore the most powerful such goal, the glimpse of which powers this entire separating and combining operation of reason, is consequently the ultimate "good"—that which "embraces and hold together all things" (*Phaed.* 99c5-6), that which is most comprehensive, most complete, and most to be desired (*Phil.* 20d3-10), that which surpasses even being in power (*Rep.* VI, 509b9-10).

MATHEMATICAL INTERLUDE:
Kompsoteros Method and
"Playing the Geometer"[1]

Having taken seriously Socrates' account of "the mysteries" of the *kompsoteroi*, it has now turned out that their method corresponds in striking fashion to that "mode of investigation, learning, and teaching one another" that the *Philebus* identifies as the method of dialectic (*Phil.* 17a3-5), and which Socrates recommends as "the roadway...I have always loved" (*Phil.* 16b5-6). Through those mysteries, moreover, we have been initiated into a vision of ordered reality that becomes increasingly explicit through later dialogues like the *Sophist, Statesman,* and *Philebus.* For, whether viewed ontologically in terms of generation or epistemologically in terms of the rational operation of mind, the pattern of this ordering leads from primordial elements differentiated out as a "many" from an original continuum or "infinite," up through successive combinations, each of which marks the emergence of an ever more complex whole or "one."

In order to illustrate and illumine this vision of increasingly complex order and beauty, Plato frequently resorts to the model of language, where primary letters (*stoicheia*), differentiated out from an original continuum of sound, are successively combined to generate words, sentences, argument, and finally discourse as a whole—"a systematically constructed whole, great and fair" (*Crat.* 425a2-3; cf. *Soph.* 252e9-253a2; 261d1-262e1; *Phil.* 17a8-b1; 18b3-d2). Sometimes, again, the analogy is found in music, where the distinct intervals of the notes as elements (also *stoicheia: Theaet.* 206a10-b3) are likewise separated out from the continuum of sound and successively combined to generate the systematic wholes that we call "harmonies" (*Phil.* 17c1-d3; cf. *Soph.* 253b1-3; *Phaedr.* 268d7-e6). But in the inquiry into knowledge that we know as the *Theaetetus,* Socrates is talking, not with literary men, nor with musicians, but rather with distinguished mathematicians.[2] Since we know that the Platonic Socrates took pains to "adapt his discourse to the nature of each soul" (*Phaedr.* 277b8-c3), we might expect that in looking for an apt analogy for generative emergence he should in this case turn, not to the elements of language, but rather to those of mathematics. As I understand it, therefore, this is why (as already argued in chapters 2 and 3, and as further elaborated in appendix A) the entire inquiry is deliberately and carefully framed within a relatively detailed reference to Theaetetus' own work in geometry.[3] There seem to be at least two advantages to working, as Theaetetus does, in geometry rather than in straightforward arithmetic—both of which I see as relevant to Plato's discussion of generation, and eventually of knowledge.

In the first place, whereas arithmetic views number as basically discrete—the arithmetical primitive being the unit—in geometry, by contrast, number is viewed as continuous magnitude—the geometrical primitive being the line.[4] In light of this, we can more readily recognize that what Theaetetus' account here in the dialogue describes is a process by which line segments representing quantities, *either rational or irrational*, are measured out from an original continuum of magnitude (an "infinite") as the primitive elements (a "many") of mathematics. As already suggested, Plato seems to be drawing a direct analogy between this process on the one hand, and on the other the differentiating out of letters (a "many") from an original continuum of sound (an "infinite"), or the *kompsoteros* differentiation out of passive and active powers (a "many") from an original continuum of motion (an "infinite"), or soul's differentiation out of senses and sensibles (a "many") from an original continuum of sensibility (an "infinite"). This ability to deal with irrational as well as rational quantities constitutes, then, a first advantage of working in geometry.

The second kind of advantage that geometry can claim over arithmetic concerns the way in which it can deal with dimensionality—which becomes, for Greek mathematicians, a mode of exponential algebra permitting them to provide geometrical solutions to problems even with irrational roots.[5] Theaetetus' renowned work with solids thus involved dimensionality at least to the third degree, and is briefly but significantly referred to here in the dialogue (*Theaet.* 148b1-2). In an arithmetic where number is viewed as discrete, the only method of increase or decrease is by the addition or subtraction of units;[6] in a geometry that deals with magnitude, the mode of increase may be by "production"[7] or "flow" that can generate a higher dimension.[8] As already suggested, it is this issue that is at stake in the earlier illustration about the dice, and why Socrates' questions about increase and decrease are so challenging (154c7-155c10).[9] For what Theaetetus illustrates for us here in the dialogue is an account of non-additive increase—that is to say, the production of successively higher-dimensional entities through the generative interaction of factors—which seems to be exactly analogous to what the *kompsoteroi* are talking about as the process of generative combination. Having, for example, differentiated out a segment of length $\sqrt{a}$, the geometrician proceeds to a further step. Taking two line segments of length $\sqrt{a}$ as "fitting" interactive elements, multiplicative combination effectively generates, not simply a new segment of greater magnitude, but a radically new product: a two-dimensional figure, in this case a square of area a. And here two important observations seem in order.

First, the radicals Theaetetus is talking about qualify as "real" or "fitting" elements, meeting all the criteria or conditions elaborated above (see chapter 4): (1) they are similar in being mutually commensurable; (2) they are dissimilar in being (like warp and woof) positioned perpendicularly; (3) they are mutually relative in that the identification of each under that description is radically contingent on the other—because the very notion of perpendicularity involves mutual relativity; (4) taken in isolation, each is useless or powerless to become anything more than a mere linear segment; (5) on the other hand, insofar as each is an element, it is to be identified as a root or power (*dynamis:* 147d3, e1; 148b1-2), that is to say, a power to become something more—as the segment, remaining itself, yet becomes something more when it becomes the side of a square.[10] Second observation: the square, as product of the multiplicative/generative combination, is a "real" emergent entity, meeting all the criteria or conditions listed above: (1) it exhibits an emergent property, i.e., surface occupation of two-dimensional space, which no mere addition of one-dimensional line segments could ever achieve; (2) as a surface, it can itself in turn function as an element within a yet larger complex, such as a three-dimensional solid (*sterea:* 148b2). This would permit the kind of diagram in figure 3.

There is, finally, one more—and, ultimately (I believe) the most significant—reason why this mathematical operation which Theaetetus describes might be taken as paradigmatic for the operation of reason. It brings together the other two reasons above (ability to deal with irrationals, and the ability to generate higher levels of dimensionality). For, as Theaetetus explains, what appears in linear dimension as incommensurable or irrational may, when raised to the second dimension, be rendered rational—and so on for subsequent dimensions (148b1-2).[11] This successive emergence of the mathematically rational becomes a powerful model for the successive emergence of the cognitively rational. In extraordinary detail—as will become even more evident in the later discussion of the proportionality inherent in Theaetetus' account of his derivation of irrationals (see Epilogue)—Theaetetus' structuring of mathematical reality seems intended to serve as a paradigm for that analogous structuring of total reality by mind or soul which for Plato constitutes the enterprise of reason.[12]

Figure 3.
Parallelism between Generation in Language, Mathematics, Sensation, and Perception

	Language	Mathematics	Sensation	Perception
Original continuum or "infinite"	Sound	Magnitude	Motion/flow	Sensibility
Division of the continuum to yield elements or "many"	Letters vowels consonants	Line segments Mutually perpendicular	Slow motions active and passive	Senses (e.g., sight) sensibles (e.g., whiteness)
Generative combination of elements producing emergent entity or "one"	Words	Two-dimensional surface	Sensibility (senses and sensibles)	Perceptions (e.g, white: i.e., white-seeing of seen-white)

THE "MYSTERIES" OF *EPISTĒMĒ*

FIVE

"KNOWLEDGE IS...PERCEPTION (*AISTHĒSIS*)":
151e2-3

The starting point for this inquiry has been confrontation with our own *aporia* (literally, "no passage," or "im-passe") as we seek escape from the notorious labyrinth of questions raised by the *Theaetetus*. Why is the dialogue inconclusive in its search for a definition of knowledge? Why are we provided such a detailed account of Theaetetus' work with ⅃ surds? Why all the fanfare about midwifery and matchmaking? Why such disproportionate concern with Theaetetus' first definition? Why should such naive questions about the dice illustration cause a subtle mathematician like Theaetetus to be overcome with amazement? Why the uncharacteristically elaborate theory of sensation? Why the images of wax and aviary, since both will be rejected? Why the gratuitous introduction, then deliberate refutation, of Socrates' "dream"? But already we have learned that, far from ending inquiry, *aporia*, like wonder, can be instead the beginning of philosophy (*Theaet.* 155d3-4). Would you like me to show you a secret way? asks Socrates (in effect), when Theaetetus is stymied; shall I uncover for you the hidden truth (155d10)?

Following the thread that winds like Ariadne's "clew" from their first puzzling exchange about midwives and surds, through the twists and turns and apparent dead ends of his argument, we begin at last to see where Socrates is leading us. For this uncovering of what he calls the "secret doctrine" will provide the clue we need for finding answers to those questions, and in particular for coming to understand why the dialogue proposes these particular definitions of knowledge, why Socrates introduces his otherwise incomprehensible "dream," and finally why the dialogue ends as it does. Our task is now to trace that thread through the intricacies of argument that go to make up the complex design of the rest of the dialogue. For, although this next section may at first sight look like a long meandering conversation, it has in fact a carefully calculated structure.

Socrates' unfolding of successive layers of meaning has so far led us from Theaetetus' first definition of knowledge as "nothing other than perception," to Protagoras' doctrine of "man as the measure," to Heracleitus' doctrine that "everything is the offspring of flow and motion," and finally to the subtleties of the *kompsoteros* doctrine of perception. It is now time to cross-examine each of these versions of the first definition. As already indicated, I shall be arguing that this cross-examination leads not to rejection, but rather to the kind of purification that the *Sophist* advocates.[1] The examination that follows will therefore provide the occasion for clarifying each of the previous formulations of doctrine to reveal senses in which each may and may not be held. From an initial challenge addressed specifically to the *kompsoteros* account of perception, the discussion will zero in on the core issues, epistemological and ontological, implied in any version of the first definition.

An initial objection, based on the occurrence of various sense illusions due to "dreams and disease, including insanity" (157e2-3), allows Socrates to make clear the force, as well as the limits, of the *kompsoteros* claim. For although it is true that in dreams and illness men do indeed often hold false opinions (158b2), this fact turns out to be irrelevant to the *kompsoteros* account, which—both epistemologically on the side of the subject, and ontologically on the side of the object— restricts itself to perception only.

Epistemologically: on the side of the subject. Since each occurrence of perception is unique to each subject on that particular occasion (159c4-160a6), it follows that any perception at all must be simply "to me" and "peculiar to each individual" (154a2)—in other words, perception is first of all radically private in the sense that "since that which acts on me is to me and me only, it is also the case that I perceive it, and I only" (160c4-5). "False perception" is therefore, in terms of the theory, impossible, since perception is simply the interaction between swift motions from an organ of sense (such as taste) on the one hand, and some sensible (such as the flavor of wine) on the other. It follows that any perception that actually occurs must to that extent be infallibly "true" (i.e., truly occurrent) *for* the subject that helps to generate it (160c7). (This hold equally for after-images, illusions, or whatever: so long as the perception occurs, then the generating parent infallibly "has" it.) Hence, "to me my perception is true; for in each case it is part of my being; and I am . . . the judge of the existence of the things [i.e., the perceptions] that are to me and of the nonexistence of those that are not to me [and in this sense] I am an infallible judge" (160c7-d1).

Ontologically: on the side of the object. The other side of the foregoing claim requires that perception as such make no judgment about any independent existent; for how could the mere having of a perception legitimate any objective judgment—for example, about whether or not there might in fact be some corresponding existent, or about whether such a supposed existent might be the same or different from the perceived appearance? This is why the perception of the wine as sweet (to the subject in health) and bitter (to the subject in illness) causes no problem for the theory (159b3-160d3). In the occurrence of perception pure and simple, the most one is strictly justified in doing is to identify the experience by giving it a name, as, for example, *red-seeing* or *sweet-tasting.*

Having now spelled out a theory within which the meaning of the term *perception* is fairly carefully delineated, Socrates can proceed to the cross-examination of Theaetetus' first definition, "Knowledge is nothing other than perception." The detailed cross-examination that occupies most of the next twenty Stephanus pages (roughly, 161-186) is compared by Socrates to the rite in which the father determines whether or not his offspring is worth rearing (159e6-8). At least Protagoras' version is apparently not a windegg, but a real "child"; what is at stake now is its viability.

The examination will pursue two lines of development. The first will concentrate on the subjective, and hence epistemological, aspect in order to clarify the ambiguities in Protagorean doctrine, and so will develop the privacy-infallibility issue. Through elenchus we will be able to discard the worse interpretation (in which the essentially non-judgmental character of perception is confused with the judgmental character of opinion) in order to retain the better (in which perception is recognized as simply an event, an event, moreover, the occurrence of which can be infallibly experienced). We will thus be brought to see in exactly what sense it is to be denied, and in exactly what rigorously "purified" sense it is to be affirmed, that "man is the measure of all things" (160d9). The second line of development may be viewed as concentrating on the objective, hence ontological, aspect of perception in order to clarify the ambiguities in that doctrine, held by many in the tradition but attributed primarily to Heracleitus. Again, through elenchus, we will be brought to the point of discarding the worse interpretation and retaining the better. This will require hewing a fine line between motion that denies language and language that denies motion, but finally we will again come to see in exactly what sense it is to be denied, and in exactly what "purified" sense it is to be affirmed that "everything is in motion, flowing like streams" (160d7-8).

EPISTEMOLOGICAL DIMENSION: CROSS-EXAMINATION OF PROTAGOREAN DOCTRINE

Although the bout with Protagoras starts off boldly to involve his old friend Theodorus, since the latter does not pick up the ball, the game starts over with Theaetetus, opening with some light skirmishing.

Phase 1: Skirmishing

In this initial warm-up they consider a series of contradictions derived from a literal identification of perceiving and knowing:

> 163b1-c5:
> If to perceive is to know,
> then to perceive shapes or sounds of a foreign language (i.e., a language that is unknown) is to know a language that is unknown. (Theaetetus dodges this by sticking to the identification.)

> 163d1-164b12:
> If to perceive is to know,
> and not to perceive is not to know,
> and if to remember is to know,
> then to remember what is no longer perceived is at the same time both to know and not to know.

> 165b2-e4:
> If to perceive is to know,
> then various statements that can be true of perceiving should be able to be true of knowing, but prove instead to be absurd, for example:
>
> > seeing with one eye but not the other
> > seeing the same thing both sharply and dully
> > seeing close at hand but not at a distance.

With Socrates standing in for Protagoras, the response here follows two Humean-type lines. First, with regard to the experience itself, since the difference between actual perceiving and remembered perceiving is one of intensity of feeling (166b2-4), there need be no contradiction in asserting that one knows (i.e., is experiencing a less vivid, because remembered, perception) and at the same time does not know (i.e., is not experiencing a more vivid, because not current, perception: 166b4-5). Second, with regard to the perceiving subject, since, from one perception to another, a perceiver is constantly changing (i.e., is changed precisely in the perceiving), one can avoid contradiction by regarding the subject, not as a single self but rather as a series (bundle?) of perceptions, for "why admit that a person is one at all, and not many who become infinite in number if the process of becoming different continues?" (166b7-c1).

This question of the unity of the self will be picked up a little later. Meanwhile, lest Theaetetus (or the reader) forget that the task here is to sort out ambiguities inherent in the Protagorean formula, the exchange in this section is interspersed throughout with reminders to that effect. In what surely looks like deliberate reiteration of the *Phaedrus'* metaphor—which, highlighting the need for interpretation, had compared written words to a bereft and abused child who "needs its father to help it, for it has no power to protect or help itself" (*Phaedr.* 275e3-5)— Socrates here compares the formulation of Protagorean doctrine with "an orphan who needs its dead father to protect it against the abuse [of their misinterpretations]" (164e2-6). Speaking therefore in the person of Protagoras, Socrates rejects too literal a reading of the doctrine, insisting instead on intelligent interpretation: "Do not lay too much stress on the words of my doctrine, but get a clearer understanding of my *meaning* from what I am going to say" (166d8-e1). And again, emphasizing the distinction between merely "making points" and "carrying on a real dialogue" (167e4-5), the Socratean Protagoras insists that the real challenge is to "enter the lists with me and inquire *what we really mean* when we declare that all things are in motion and that whatever seems is to each individual, whether man or state" (168b3-6). Bearing in mind, then, that the point of the cross-examination is to discard unacceptable interpretations of Protagorean doctrine in the hope of finding hidden truth that will be worth retaining, Socrates proposes to take up that challenge, and we move in to the second phase.

Phase 2: Attack

This phase involves the *reductio* of the doctrine *if* it attributes to perception the judgmental character of opinion (*doxa*) (161b8-171c7; 177c6-179d1). The mistake rests, in Greek as in English, on the confusion deriving from the term *seems* or *appears (dokei)*.[2] The ambiguity of the term permits a fuzzy slide from the "seeming" of *perception,* according to which, for example, "x appears/seems red" (which in *kompsoteros* theory is an infallible appearance in the sense that, if it occurs, then it does infallibly occur), to the "seeming" of *opinion,* according to which, for example, "it appears/seems that x is red" (which, according to *kompsoteros* doctrine, can make no claim whatever to infallibility but, as simple opinion, may be true or false).

   If the kind of infallibility that in the Protagorean account is asserted of seemings is understood as applying beyond the non-judgmental seemings of perception to the judgmental seemings of opinion, then all opinions prove to be equally true—whether of tadpole or sage—which makes mock of the very possibility of that wisdom or knowledge which Protagoras himself claims to teach, and which is the quest of the entire conversation (161c2-162a3).

Phase 3: Riposte

In this section, the Protagorean response will (a) deny the possibility of false opinion and (b) shift the interpretation of wisdom from knowing-what-is-true to doing-what-is-good. The fact that in his reply the Socratean Protagoras continues to confuse the "seemings" of perception and opinion (e.g., 167a2, a6, a7, a8, b1, b2) leads him into two difficulties.

(a) Just as it is impossible to perceive nothing (160a8-b1), so his confusion between perception and opinion leads him to suppose that "it is impossible to opine that which is not" (167a7-8)—and correspondingly, since all perceptions are infallible, so he supposes all opinions must be true (167a8-b1). This confusion of falsity with nonbeing, and the consequent denial of the possibility of false opinion, is taken up at great length, both in the second half of the *Theaetetus*, and later in the *Sophist*.

(b) Since his earlier confusion of perception with opinion led to a denial of the possibility of wisdom or wise people (including himself), he is forced to shift ground from the question of being "true" to that of being "good," so that, while it is true that each man is a measure of what is and is not, nevertheless some of the things that appear are good, others not. Thus, "I do not by any means say that wisdom and the wise man do not exist; on the contrary, I say that if bad things appear and are to any one of us, precisely that man is wise who causes a change and makes good things appear and be to him" (166d5-8).

Phase 4: Attack

Socrates' reaction is to zero in on those two lines of Protagoras' defense: first, his claim about the impossibility of false opinion, and second, his shift from true to good.

(a) The force of this attack will be to challenge the very possibility of asserting Protagorean theory in the first place. For any occasion on which anyone thinks another person to hold a false opinion, this version of Protagorean theory turns out to be self-contradictory—since the same propositional content will, at one and the same time, be held to be both true (because "seeming" so to the first person) and false (because "seeming" so to the second person). Turned against Protagoras' own doctrine, its denial by others becomes, in terms of that very doctrine, true—and hence the theory itself, false (169d3-171c7).

(b) In shifting from "true" to "good," Protagoras has argued that wisdom involves, not the knowing of what is true—for this is supposedly the possession of all men—but rather (on analogy with medicine) the bringing about of what is good. In reply, Socrates insists that, even in Protagoras' own terms, the wise man who brings about good—whether the physician diagnosing a disease to bring about its cure, or Protagoras himself prescribing the pleasurable life for the individual, or other analogous cases—in every case depends upon a true or false judgment about the future: for example, what will bring health to the patient (178c2-8), pleasure to Protagoras' follower (178e2-179a4), or whatever. All of this again reduces Protagoras himself to self-contradiction in that, on the one hand, he denies the possibility of any special wisdom or knowledge of what is true and, on the other, he claims just such special wisdom and knowledge with regard to future pleasure (178e7-179a3). If, therefore, the infallibility of perception is taken in this judgmental sense that makes all opinions equally true so that "whatever seems to each man really *is* to him to whom it seems" (177c7-8), then even Protagoras himself must acknowledge that, *on this interpretation*, the doctrine that "man is the measure of all things" is manifestly absurd (179a10-c2).

Phase 5: Reinstatement

By contrast, of course, there is an interpretation which, *if limited to perception*, will withstand objections. This is, not surprisingly, the interpretation consonant with *kompsoteros* theory. Thus, picking up his earlier acknowledgment that

> His doctrine might stand most firmly in the form in which we sketched it when defending Protagoras: that most things—hot, dry, sweet, and everything of *that* sort—are to each person as they appear to him (171d9-e3),

Socrates now concludes his cross examination of Protagorean doctrine on that same note of ambiguity with which he first began (see chapter 1). For,

> with regard to what the individual experiences at the moment—the source of his sensations and the judgments in accordance with them—it is harder to assail the truth of these. Perhaps it is wrong to say "harder"; maybe they are unassailable, and those who assert they are transparently clear and are instances of knowledge may be in the right, and Theaetetus was not beside the mark when he said perception and knowledge were the same. (179c2-d1)

The reader will remember that, according to *kompsoteros* theory, it is in the act in which "I measure myself against" something (154b1)—i.e., "some commensurable object" (156d3-4)—that perception is generated (156e2, e4). Since it is the subjective organ of perception which is understood to be "that which does the measuring" (154b3-4), there is a real sense in which, on the *kompsoteros* interpretation, the Protagorean formula will hold. In this carefully delineated sense, therefore, Socrates will actually be able to agree that "Man is the measure of all things, as your school says, Protagoras, of the white, the heavy, the light, everything of *that* sort without exception" (178b3-5). What all this means is that Socrates has shown us the exact sense in which Protagorean doctrine must be rejected, and at the same time the exact sense in which it should be retained (cf. *Soph.* 226d5-7). Having undergone that "cross-questioning which is the greatest of all purifications" (*Soph.* 230d7-8), Protagoras' doctrine—thus sifted, tested, and tried—may be taken as a succinct statement of a far-reaching theory of perception; for *in terms of kompsoteros theory, and under its carefully controlled interpretation of the formula,* we can, with Socrates, recognize a sense in which it is true that "man is the measure of all things" (178b3).

ONTOLOGICAL DIMENSION:
CROSS-EXAMINATION OF HERACLEITEAN DOCTRINE

On examination, it will be recalled, Theaetetus' definition of knowledge as "nothing other than perception" was assimilated first to Protagorean, then to Heracleitean, doctrine (152e3; 160d7). The cross-examination of Protagorean doctrine has now discovered a core of truth hidden in the ambiguities of its formulation—which sets a precedent that will be significant for the rest of the dialogue. We are hardly surprised, therefore, when, turning to the docrtrine of Heracleitus, Socrates calls upon us similarly to "come up closer and examine this doctrine of motion as fundamental being, rapping on it to see whether it rings sound or unsound" (179d2-4).

The doctrine has been propounded, we are told, by ancients and moderns (180c8, d3), by poets in hidden metaphor and sophists in literal speech (180c8-d8). But, as we are well aware, it most recently and most pertinently was also proposed by Socrates himself when he introduced us to the *kompsoteros* claim that "everything is really motion and there is nothing else besides" (156a5). The form of our question will therefore be exactly analogous to that pursued in connection with the Protagorean doctrine of "man as the measure." For there we had asked in what sense, if any, is Protagorean doctrine to be rejected? in what sense, if any, to be retained? and how, if at all, does it relate to the *kompsoteros* doctrine concerning the role of measure in perception? Here now, we must ask the same questions of the Heracleitean doctrine of flow and motion: in what sense, if any, is it to be rejected? in what sense, if any, to be retained? and how, if at all, does it relate to the *kompsoteros* doctrine that "everything is really motion"? As Socrates puts it, "Exactly what do they *mean,* after all, when they say that all things are in motion?" (181c1-2).

Elenchus and Ambiguity in
Kompsoteros Argument

In differentiating *kompsoteros* from conventional Heracleitean doctrine, Socrates will resort to a type of argument which, while occurring frequently in other dialogues as well, proves to be absolutely pivotal here in the *Theaetetus*. It is not new: we have in fact, already encountered it embedded in our discussion of the *kompsoteros* theory of emergence. For when (in both its ontological and epistemological dimensions) *kompsoteros* theory asserted the generation of something new from prior components, it successfully skirted an apparent *reductio*: although sameness and difference might appear to be exhaustive disjuncts, the theory of emergent generation in effect challenged that simple disjunction. For if the *kompsoteros* account is correct, then (as we have already seen) the emergent product is in important respects *both* the same as *and* different from its elements: the same as, in the sense that nothing has been added or subtracted from the elements (fabric is nothing but threads of warp and woof; words are nothing but letters; perceptions are nothing but swift motions, etc.), and yet different, in the sense that the product has in each case a "power" that the elements do not (fabric can cover and clothe; words can mean; perceptions can be experienced phenomenally, etc.).

In appendix A I argue that it is just this paradoxical claim that was the source of Theaetetus' "amazement" over the apparent contradiction implied in Socrates' dice illustration (154c7-155b2). Thus, looking more closely at the would-be dice argument that introduced the *kompsoteros* account, we see that it too can be cast in the form of a *reductio*:

1. *Either a:*	a thing remains the same	
or b:	a thing becomes different	
2. *If a:*	then it cannot become more	
	(because to remain the same is interpreted as "to remain equal to itself")	
then not-c:	generation is impossible	
	(Because it involves becoming more)	
3. *If b:*	then it cannot remain equal to itself	
	(because "to become different" is interpreted as able to take place "only through addition or subtraction")	
then not-c:	generation is impossible	
	(because there is no addition or subtraction)	
4. *Therefore not-c:*	generation is impossible	

But that, of course, is exactly the reason for Theaetetus' wonder: he knows that non-additive generation does in fact occur: in particular, two-dimensional figures are generated from the one-dimensional lines, as demonstrated in his own earlier report on surds.[3] Since he is committed to the acceptance of generation in his mathematics, and at the same time to its rejection in the present argument about the dice, he finds himself holding mutually contradictory propositions (155a2-b6; cf. 154c10-d2; 154e3-5)—and therefore in a state of *aporia* (155c8-10). The solution to his wonder, Socrates suggests, lies through the hidden truth of *kompsoteros* emergence: "Do you begin to understand why these things are so, according to the doctrine we attribute to Protagoras, or do you not as yet? And will you be grateful to me if I help you to search out the hidden truth?" (155d5-10).

To reveal that hidden truth, Socrates will now approach the problem from the *kompsoteros* angle and thereby give the dice argument a subtle twist. Instead of the apparent *reductio,* mounted by uninitiates who "deny generation" (cf. 155e5-6), Socrates' account implies a different kind of argument represented by the *kompsoteroi* who affirm generation (156a2ff.).

ARGUMENT OF UNINITIATED	ARGUMENT OF KOMPSOTEROI
	1. *c*
1. *Either a or b*	2. *Either a or b*
2. *If a then not-c*	3. *If a then not-c*
	4. *Therefore not-a*
3. *If b then not-c*	5. *If b then not-c*
	6. *Therefore not-b*
4. *Therefore not-c*	7. *Therefore not-(a or b)*

Affirmation of *kompsoteros* theory can thus indeed, just as Socrates predicted, resolve Theaetetus' wonder. By developing "the hidden truth" within the Protagorean-Heracleitean formula, Socrates has in effect revealed "the hidden truth" within the apparent *reductio.* The *kompsoteros* reading of the dice argument may therefore be put as follows:

1. *c:*	there is generation.
2. *Either a:*	a thing remains the same,
or b:	it becomes different.
3. *If a:*	it remains the same ("equal to itself"),
	then it cannot become more;
then not-c:	generation is impossible.
4. *Therefore not-a.*	

5. *If b:*   it becomes different ("through addition"),
                          then it cannot be equal to itself;
    then not-c: generation is impossible.

6. *Therefore not-b.*

7. *Therefore not-(a or b):* it is *not* the case that
                               either a thing remains the same and equal to itself,
                               or a thing becomes different only by addition.

This, of course, now makes room for the possibility of generation, according to which the emergent product *both* remains the same *and* becomes different, while *neither* remaining equal to itself *nor* undergoing addition. In short, I am proposing that, like the other formulations of doctrine that Socrates has so far examined, so too is this formulation of argument also ambiguous. In "helping us search out hidden truth" beneath the ambiguity of this subtle argument, Socrates has opened up the "way" (*hodos*) that will lead Theaetetus out of his impasse—not only the present impasse deriving from Socrates' dice illustration, but eventually out of the impasse that is the labyrinth of the dialogue as a whole.

This use of an apparently negative argument in order precisely to make room for a positive affirmation proves, on reflection, to be a demonstration of elenchus in one of its subtler versions. Two things about this strike me as interesting. First, it illustrates the kind of elenchus which the Eleatic Stranger will describe for Theaetetus the following day when, in the *Sophist*, he extols it as a form of purification which rejects the worse in order to retain the better (*Soph.* 226d5-10). Second, it echoes what Socrates had already suggested to Meno about elenchus serving not only a negative but also a positive purpose (cf. the discussion in the Introduction). But when we consider the *Meno*, our attention is arrested by something even more striking. For, coming fresh from our initiation into the hidden truth of argument beneath the surface of the uninitiates' *reductio*, we now have to ask ourselves: Was not this in fact what Socrates was preparing us for in the *Meno*? Had we (with Meno) waited for initiation into "the mysteries" (cf. *Meno* 76e8-9),[4] might we not have understood Socrates' warning about just this kind of *reductio*? After all, he did draw explicit attention to two distinct readings of Meno's (reconstructed) argument which, it turns out, exactly parallel the two readings I have distinguished here; he did, moreover, even identify the version I am attributing to the uninitiated as "an eristic argument" (*Meno* 80e2; 81d6), whereas the version I am attributing to the *kompsoteroi* is clearly more characteristic of the kind of "dialectical" approach he had just contrasted with eristic (*Meno* 75c8-d7). The argument in question is, of course, the well-known *reductio* from the *Meno*.

ERISTIC ARGUMENT	DIALECTICAL ARGUMENT
Meno's interpretation: a negative reading which Socrates finds an "eristic argument"	Socrates' interpretation: a positive reading which Socrates proposes as more "dialectical"
(*Meno* 80d5-e5)	(*Meno* 81a4-86c2)

ERISTIC ARGUMENT	DIALECTICAL ARGUMENT
	1. *c*: inquiry is possible
1. *Either a*: we do know the object sought in inquiry *or b*: we do not know the object sought	2. *Either a*: we do know the object sought in inquiry *or b*: we do not know the object sought
2. *If a*: we know the object *then not-c*: inquiry is not possible	3. *If a*: we know the object *then not-c*: inquiry is not possible
	4. *Therefore not-a*: it is not the case that we know the object sought
3. *If b*: we do not know the object sought *then not-c*: inquiry is not possible	5. *If b*: we do not know the object sought *then not-c*: inquiry is not possible
	6. *Therefore not-b*: it is not the case that we do not know the object sought in inquiry
4. *Therefore not-c*: inquiry is not possible	7. *Therefore not-(either a or b)*: it is not the case that either we do know or we do not know the object sought.

Interpreting the argument along the same reductive lines as the uninitiates' version of the dice argument which caused Theaetetus such puzzlement, Meno finds it "a good argument", and concludes that inquiry is not possible. Socrates, by contrast, discounts Meno's version, and proceeds instead to interpret it along precisely the lines this paper has proposed here in the *Theaetetus*: rejecting Meno's original disjunction, he leads him toward a solution which, denying the simple either-or, will integrate *both* disjuncts. For that is what the theory of Recollection does: by arguing that the object sought in inquiry is in one sense already known (at least enough to be recognized), but in another sense not known ("forgotten"), he has made room for his positive affirmation that inquiry is indeed possible.

The importance of this move to uncover an argument's hidden truth beneath an apparent *reductio* will prove to be far-reaching, for it provides the framework for eventually coming to understand both the final discussion and the enigmatic conclusion of the dialogue. For the moment, however, here in the immediate context of understanding the significance of Theaetetus' first definition and its relation to the various interpretations of the Heracleitean formula, we will find Socrates again resorting to this kind of argument, this time in order to elucidate the doctrine of motion in relation to language. The argument about the role, and even the possibility, of language will thus follow the same pattern as those about the possibility of emergent generation (in the dice illustration) and the possibility of inquiry (in the *Meno*).

Motion and Language

Focusing on what the Heracleiteans mean when they say that "all is motion," the argument will examine the possibility of language *within the context of that very claim itself.* This examination will provide the occasion to point up difficulties in certain interpretations of the Heracleitean formula; at the same time it will direct us back to the *kompsoteros* interpretation of the same formula, and thereby to a fruitful interpretation of Theaetetus' first definition.

As has just been suggested, what is interesting in this cross-examination of the Heracleitean formula is the way in which we find Socrates resorting to this same form of *kompsoteros* argument embedded in an apparent *reductio*. Noting once again the ambiguity in the claim that all is motion, Socrates opens the examination by drawing attention to two rather different interpretations of "motion" or change: *motion in space* (*phora*: 181d6), i.e., "when a thing changes its place or turns around in the same place" (181c6-7), and *motion as alteration* (*alloiōsis* 181c9-d3). He then proposes that "motion" as it occurs in the Heracleitean formula "all things are in motion" must be understood in one or other of these senses. As the discussion continues, *phora* comes to represent the specific motion of relatively determinate entities, and *alloiosis* that of flux in total indeterminacy. The argument proceeds in the characteristic form of dilemma:[5]

1. *Either a*:   all things move with both kinds of motion

   or b: some things move in both ways, others with only one of these kinds of motion (181d9-e2)

In the now familiar sequence, both disjuncts lead to a denial of the possibility of language—and specifically of the language needed to make the Heracleitean claim in the first place:

2. *If a*:   if all things move with both kinds of motion, (i.e., there is nothing but indeterminate flux)

then the clarity and consistency of language is denied, and with it the possibility, not only of talking about perception rather than non-perception (182e3-5) or knowledge rather than non-knowledge (182e10-11), but

then not-c: language (even language in which to assert the doctrine itself) is impossible:

"Is it possible to give any name to a color, and yet to speak accurately . . . if while we are speaking it always evades us, being as it is, in flux? . . . [In that case] we must not speak of seeing more than not-seeing if all things are in all kinds of motion . . .

"If all things are in motion, every answer to any question whatsoever is equally correct, and we may say it is thus or not thus . . . but we ought not even to say "thus," nor again "not thus" . . . but some other expression must be supplied for those who maintain this doctrine, since now they have, according to their own hypothesis, no words, unless it be perhaps the word "nohow" [*oud'houtōs*].* That might be most fitting for them, since it is [similarly] indeterminate. (182d4-e5; 183a4-b5).

3. *If b*:   some things move with only one of these
                       kinds of motion, then
                       "they will find that things in motion are also things at rest [because unchanging in the other respect],"
                       and therefore "it will be not more correct to say that
                       all things are in motion than that
                       all things are at rest" (181e5-7)

then not-c: language (even language in which to assert the doctrine itself) is impossible.

4. *therefore not-c*: language is impossible.

---

*The text is corrupt at this point. Both the ninth-century Codex Bodleianus and the twelfth-century Codex Venetus read *oud'hopos,* and this is the variant Fowler opts for in the Loeb edition. but Codex Vindobonensis 54, Suppl. graec. 7, reads it as *oud'houtos,* and although Conford argues that the latter cannot be right (*Plato's Theory of Knowledge*, 1935, p. 100),l Burnet apparently accepts it. See also McDowell's comments (*Plato: Theaetetus.* 1973, p. 182). Translations correspondingly vary from Fowler's "nohow," to Conford's "not even no-how," to McDowell's "not even so."

As in the various cases already considered above, the hidden *kompsoteros* argument beneath the apparent *reductio*[6] should, by contrast, be understood as denying the disjunction, thereby making room for a sense in which *both a and b* can be true. This of course brings us back again to the *kompsoteros* doctrine which claims just that (i.e., *both a:* everything is motion [156a3-5], *and b:* some things move with only one of these kinds of motion [i.e., with *phora*: 156d2-3]). This is presumably why, right here in the middle of the argument, we are explicitly reminded of the *kompsoteros* interpretation of the formula; a thumbnail reiteration of the doctrine recalls that, although, on the one hand, "nothing is of itself any one thing" (182b3-4), nevertheless, on the other, determinate subjects do perceive determinate properties (182b4-7). Thus, in the first place, according to the earlier detailed account of the *kompsoteros* mysteries, in affirming disjunct *a* as the original stage of indeterminate flux, the theory recognizes that (as was actually argued under disjunct *a*) language is at this stage, strictly speaking, inapplicable (157a7-b7). In the second place, *kompsoteros* theory also affirms disjunct *b*, since it asserts determinate generation; as a result (just as argued under disjunct *b*,) "things in motion will also be things at rest" (181e5-6) (but in a different sense of rest, i.e., that of stability imposed by language). In short, *kompsoteros* theory maintains *both* the original claim that all is motion (*alloiōsis*) and therefore indeterminate, *and* some things are relatively determinate and so located in space (and move with *phora*). This will make room for the possibility of language (even language in which to make the *kompsoteros* claim about motion)—but the role of language will be conceived of in a significantly different way.

If the function of language were simply passively to mirror reality as "given" according to nature, then our position would indeed be incoherent and absurd, for, as the argument shows, language would in that case be impossible. But the hidden truth beneath the *reductio* makes room for the positive assertion that language is not a mirror, but rather a tool to cut the flow of indeterminacy (see above, chapter 3), so that out of the irrational and incoherent (*alogon*) we separate out those elements that will eventually become the rational structure that we know as reality. Although language is naturally learned in ignorance of its real function, it is clear that, if we are to pursue rational human lives, and ever to seek knowledge, then we "must" (*ēnagkasmetha*: 157b2-3) introduce distinctions and apply to our experience linguistic terms which, introducing "fixity" into the flux (183a7), "make things stand still" (157b5). Hence we discriminate and have "names," not only for the senses (names like *sight* and *hearing* etc.: 156b3-5, d3-e2—contra the claim in the *reductio* that this is not possible: 182d8-e6) and the corresponding sensibles (names like *sound, heat, whiteness,* etc.: 156b7-c3, d3-e2; cf. 182a3-4, b1-2—contra the claim in the *reductio*: 182d1-7), but also for the actual perceivings and perceived (names such as *white-seeing* or *seen-white*: 156e2-8; 182a6-b2—contra the assertion in the *reductio*: 182d4-5).

The mistake of the "drifters," as Theodorus calls them,[7] lies not, as we should now recognize, in their affirmation of radical flux, but in their uninitiated supposition that, just because reality, or being, is in this original sense "nothing other than motion," it therefore follows that such a statement offers an adequate account. That is to say, their error lies in the failure to recognize that the formula "Everything is really motion and nothing else besides" (156a5) is but a first stage in the process of providing an account (*logos*) of being, for it focuses simply on the first requirement of logos, i.e., the sense in which being is to be understood as an "infinite" (see above, chapter 4). By analogy, this study is arguing, Theaetetus' mistake likewise consists, not in his recognition of perception as starting point of knowledge, but in his uninitiated supposition that just because it is true that, in this original sense of basic stuff prior to determination, knowledge is indeed "nothing other than perception," it therefore follows that such a statement offers an adequate account. That is to say, his error likewise lies in his failure to recognize his first definition as but a first stage in the process of providing a logos of knowledge, for it focuses only on the sense in which knowledge is indeterminate, or an "infinite." The challenge is now to move from the "infinite" to the "one" (i.e., to knowledge as the "one" whose logos is being sought), seeking to discover "just how many it is" in terms of its constituent elements so that they might "end by passing from all to one" (*Phil.* 18b2-3). This, as I understand it, is the task undertaken in the remainder of the dialogue. Before moving into the second and third definitions, however, Socrates pauses to take stock of where they stand.

Perception has been represented as an activity in which, first, senses and sensibles have, as "fitting" elements, been discriminated out from an original flow; second, brought together in generative combination, the interacting elements have in each case brought into existence an emergent product (e.g., the white-seeing of seen-white, the sweet-tasting of tasted-sweet, etc.), which infallible occurrences may be "named," but of which, *in the act of perception as such*, no judgment may be made (152d3-e1; 153d8-154b6; 156a3-157b8; 159c14-160c2; 182a3-b7).[8] Thus, couched in terms of a twofold operation—the separating out of "fitting" elements, and the generative combination in which is "born" an emergent product—the activity of perception already embodies (even though at a primitive level) the character-istically rational activity that Socrates associates with "dialectic" (see above, chapter 4). As we have already seen, these two operations of (1) discriminating "many" elements, and (2) collecting the (fitting) many into a "one" that will be fruitful in the sense that it constitutes an emergent product, presuppose certain criteriological conditions. It will therefore be important to make these conditions explicit, for they will be the basis of any further generative activity and, correspondingly, the basis of any further realms of structure or order (logos). This is what Socrates now leads Theaetetus to recognize.

Since each organ of sense has its own proper and exclusive object (a proposition defended inductively: 184e8-185a2), it follows that it must be something other than an organ of sense that is able to reach across objects of sense, or across acts of sense, in order to discriminate between and then fruitfully combine them. They conclude that it cannot be, therefore, any of the senses, but only soul itself[9] that performs these operations of dividing into, and collecting under, appropriate kinds, for "their essential nature and the fact that they exist, and their opposition to one another, and in turn, the essential nature of this opposition, the soul itself tries to determine for us by reverting to them and comparing them with one another" (186b6-9). Thus, operating in light of the *kompsoteros* criteria required for separation and combination, it is soul alone which sees (1) that there *exist* these various kinds in the first place; (2) that each is a distinct and identifiable kind (*different* from others and the *same* as its own kind); (3) that although each is separately one distinct kind, together they are *two* of a comparable kind, depending on (4) whether they are being collected together because of *likeness* into one kind, or separated because of *unlikeness* into two kinds. To determine the elements as "fitting" and the product as "genuine" requires a separating and combining of elements that are both *like* and *unlike* in such a way that, although separately *two*, they are in combination *one*, the product being in one sense composed of, and to that extent the *same* as, its elements—in another sense, not reducible to, and therefore *different* from, those elements. Accordingly, it is these "common" criteria or characteristics (*ta koina*) which underlie the organization, not only of perception, but of any or all experience. And so, step by step, Socrates has led us to the heart of the problem: By what are these criteriological conditions themselves perceived—"that which is common to all things as well as to those of which we have been speaking: existence and nonexistence, and likeness and unlikeness, and identity and difference, and also unity and plurality as applied to them" (185c4-d1). His answer is that these common factors (*ta koina*) that both make possible and at the same time define, the organizing activity of reason, are recognized "by soul itself, through itself" (185e6-7).

This initial naming-and-perceiving process is, then, the first step in a cognitive process that now anticipates the next stage—one which will presumably, in light of these criteria, pursue that same twofold

operation that constitutes the work of reason. This continuing production of a whole, or one, that is coherent and rational (*logon*) out of a
many that is incoherent and irrational (*alogon*) is what constitutes the
operation par excellence of soul—whether in the realm of cognition, of
mathematics, or indeed, of any other field of endeavor, for, as Socrates
(elsewhere) maintains, "one and many are identified by reason. This is
no new thing and will never cease; it is, in my opinion, a quality within
us which will never die or grow old, and which belongs to reason [*logos*]
itself as such" (*Phil.* 15d4-8).

The next chapter will try to follow Plato as, again applying these
same principles, he leads us to the next stage of the cognitive process,
thereby effecting a natural transition from (nonjudgmental but infallible) perception to (judgmental and fallible) opinion.

RETROSPECTIVE

Discussion of Theaetetus' first definition has now taken up roughly
half the dialogue. It should, however, begin to be clear why Plato has
spent what originally looked like an inordinate amount of time on a
definition apparently so unpromising. For what this section has
established are certain pivotal principles which (according to the
overall thesis of this work) provide an essential key to understanding
the *Theaetetus*—and, I do believe, Plato's philosophy as a whole.[10] These
principles include the following:

1. Language (at least language about what is important in a
   culture) is riddled with ambiguity,[11]
   (a) in formulation of doctrine, and
   (b) in elaboration of argument.
2. Confrontation with conflict due to ambiguity leads to *aporia*
   and wonder.
3. *Aporia* should not be merely negative, but, with wonder, should
   rather be the beginning of philosophy (cf. *Theaet.* 155d2-5).
4. At the beginning of philosophy, one often needs a guide to help
   uncover hidden truth embedded in the ambiguities of language.
5. The most effective tool for this educational guidance is the
   purification (elenchus) which sorts out conflicting claims in
   order to discard the worse and retain the better, thereby making
   room for positive teaching.
6. As guide and teacher, Socrates uncovers/reveals/initiates Theaetetus into hidden truth embedded in
   (a) formulations of philosophical claims ("all is motion," held by
   the tradition from Homer to Heracleitus; "man is the measure,"

taught by Protagoras; and "knowledge is perception," proposed by Theaetetus); and

(b) formulations of philosophical argument (the dice argument apparently denying the possibility of generation; the motion argument apparently denying the possibility of language).

7. As guide and teacher, Socrates leads Theaetetus (while Plato leads the reader) out of *aporia*. This is achieved

(a) through elaboration of a form of argument which defends the possibility of positive doctrine beneath the appearance of negative *reductio*; and

(b) through the elaboration of a theory which embodies hidden truth within Protagoras', Heracleitus' and Theaetetus' formulations; this is "the secret doctrine" of emergent generation which he attributes to the "subtle thinkers" (*kompsoteroi*).

8. The dialogue prepares for, and constantly reinforces, this secret doctrine of the *kompsoteroi* by referring back to Theaetetus' work in geometry and to Socrates' work as midwife and matchmaker.

Plato has taken pains (and space) to establish these principles; in the sequel we will come increasingly to understand their significance.

SIX

"KNOWLEDGE IS TRUE OPINION (*doxa alēthēs*)":
187b5-6; 200e4

Having brought Theaetetus to the point of focusing on soul and on the principles that define its activity as rational, the ground is now prepared for a swift move through the next phase of cognition, since the pattern has now been established at some length and the application should be relatively straightforward. But of course it is not; for the next phase, opinion (*doxa*), turns out to be one of the more elusive concepts in Plato's epistemology.

In this chapter I should like to consider, first, what the *kompsoteros* pattern of the dialogue so far has led us to expect of *doxa*; second, what actually happens in the exchange with Theaetetus as they tackle the problem of *doxa*; and third, what our interpretation of *doxa* should perhaps be.

THE *KOMPSOTEROS* PATTERN FOR *DOXA*

Through its careful presentation of *kompsoteros* method, the dialogue seems now to have led us to a twofold expectation. First, we might anticipate further application of the same rational principles of separation and combination. This would mean that from the flow of perception soul can be expected to generate a further emergent cognitive state which will be in one sense "nothing other than" (and to that extent "the same as") its perceptual elements; in another sense it will be "quite other than" (and to that extent different from its) perceptual elements. In other words, we have been led to anticipate discussion of opinion as a rational activity beyond sheer perception.

Second, insofar as we find Socrates' distinction between uninitiated and the *kompsoteroi* paralleled by his distinction between eristic and dialectic, then we might perhaps expect a problem, should Theaetetus fall into the eristic trap of "moving too quickly or too slowly between the one and the infinite, thus ignoring all that lies between them" (*Phil.* 17a1-3). From a *kompsoteros* point of view, such a move would be failing to take account of the successive emergence that must take place *between* perception (as indeterminate or "infinite") and knowledge (as the "one" whose logos they seek), thus collapsing the distinction between opinion and knowledge. In other words, we have been led to expect a consideration of opinion as a rational activity in which soul's creative response to perception will generate a state beyond perception, but one nevertheless to be radically distinguished from knowledge.

Both aspects of our expectation will, I believe, be borne out—but along with such virtuosity that it is easy to be distracted by the pyrotechnical display.

THE PROBLEM OF *DOXA*

There are obviously different ways in which to break down the discussion that follows. It will be convenient here to distinguish a first phase (roughly 184b-187c) in which Theaetetus is initially led beyond perception to the clear notion of opinion as such; a long second phase (roughly 187d-200c) in which he tries, unsuccessfully, to given an account of false opinion; and a brief third phase (200e-201c) in which he is forced to recognize a real difference between true opinion and knowledge.

Phase 1: The Move From Perception to Opinion

To effect this move, Socrates will present it in two steps: first he argues for a subject's being a single agency; second, he argues that such an agency operates not only through, but also to some extent independently of, the senses. The first step gives us soul or mind over and above the senses; the second gives us opinion over and above perception.

Socrates' first step (from the bodily senses to soul, or mind, as agent and cause operating as it were behind or through those senses) recalls the similar move in his own autobiographical sketch in the *Phaedo*. For, apparently, Anaxagoras' claim that it is mind that orders and causes all things (despite Anaxagoras' own inadequate interpretation of the claim) did present itself to Socrates as the answer to his own epistemological questions:

> I was always unsettling myself with such questions as these...Is it the blood, or air, or fire, by which we think? Or is it none of these, and does the brain furnish the sensations of hearing and sight and smell, and do memory and opinion arise from these, and does knowledge come from memory and opinion (*Phaedo* 96a8-b8)

Gradually he came to differentiate mind-as-cause from those bodily instruments "without which a cause could never be a cause" (*Phaedo* 99b2-4). So too now in the *Theaetetus* he will draw a parallel distinction between the senses and that "one thing, whether we call it soul or something else, by which we perceive, through these as instruments, the objects of perception" (184d3-5).[1] This first step, giving us soul or mind over and above the senses, is here actually countering both the stronger proposal behind Protagoras' version of the subject as a bundle of changing impressions—"would [a Protagorean] ever admit that a person who has become unlike is the same as before he became unlike?... would he admit that a person is one at all, and not many?" (166b6-8)—and also the weaker proposal that the subject might be not a single entity but rather a "strange" collection of separate senses (184d2). Instead, we now have Socrates' proposal that a person is actually a single agent, whether we call it "soul" or something else (184d3), that operates *through* the various senses (see chapter 5).

With the second step, Socrates marks a further distinction, this time between two relevant kinds of operation: that achieved through the physical instrumentality of the senses as bodily powers on the one hand (185e7), and on the other a different kind of operation in which the soul "views some things by itself directly" (185e1-2, e6-7). It is, of course, this latter operation which, going beyond sheer perception, precipitates us into opinion. The argument for opinion as a distinct operation makes two separate points: first, that there is a different kind of object involved, and second, that there is a different mode of acquisition. These points are worth taking one by one.

First, a different kind of object is involved. The argument runs as follows: since in general a different kind of object indicates a different power of apprehension, and since a different kind of object is in question here, it follows that a different power of apprehension is indicated. The general principle appealed to here was already similarly asserted (and similarly applied) in the *Republic*:

> Shall we say that powers [*dynameis*] are a class of entities by virtue of which we and all other things are able to do what we or they are able to do?... In the case of a power I look to one thing only—that to which it is related and what it effects. It is in this way that I come to call each one of them a power, and that which is related to the same thing and accomplishes the same thing I call the same power, and that to another I call other. (*Rep.* V, 477c1-2, c9-d5)[2]

In the context of the *Republic* this principle of differentiation according to object was illustrated and supported from the area of sensation (477c3-4)—just as Socrates now proceeds to do here with Theaetetus.

Recalling their earlier recognition of the essential relativity of sensory power to its object (157a4-6; 160a8-b1), Socrates now reminds Theaetetus of the unique differentiation of each of these sensory powers with reference to its own proper object: "It is impossible to perceive through one sense what you perceive through another; for instance to perceive through sight what you perceive through hearing, or through hearing what you perceive through sight" (184e8-185a2). Thus it seems that any power is differentiated according to its object—and, by inductive inference, we have the principle that functions now as first premiss in the argument for opinion. In order to furnish the second premiss, however, Socrates must establish an object for opinion that will be different from that of any (or all) of the senses. He will therefore look for an operation that focuses on something other than the simple objects of the individual senses, because (as he now puts it to Theaetetus) "if you have any thought about both of these together [i.e., object of sight and object of hearing] then you would not have *perception* about both together, either through one organ or through the other" (*Theaet.* 185a4-6; cf. *Charm.* 168d3-e1; 167d1-9). Theaetetus acknowledges at once that there is in fact apprehension across the various senses, for example, the recognition that both sound and color actually exist in terms of phenomenal content, each like the other in being a sensory experience, but unlike in each being unique itself and different from the other. Apprehension of these features (which span objects peculiar to the separate senses of sight and hearing) evidently involves apprehension of something which is different from either color or sound as such, but rather is by contrast common to both. Since therefore "it is impossible to grasp that which is common to them both either through hearing or through sight" (185b7-9), these common features (*ta koina*)—being and nonbeing, likeness and unlikeness, identity and difference, unity and plurality (185c9-d1; cf. 185a9-b5 and 186a2-b1 which add beautiful and ugly, good and evil to the list)—together constitute an object other than that of perception, and so furnish us with the second premiss needed for Socrates' argument. It is therefore concluded that although some things are viewed through the instrumentality of the bodily senses and constitute the proper objects of the various powers of perception, there are at the same time other, radically different, objects which compel us to recognize another, radically different, power—one in which the soul views some things not now through the instrumentality of the senses, but "by itself directly" (186e1-2; 187a3-6).

The second point of Socrates' argument to shift our attention from perception to opinion reinforces this important distinction. Since different modes of acquisition mark a difference in that which is acquired (cf. Gorg. 454c7-455a6; *Tim.* 51d3-e3), and since perception comes through the spontaneous exercise of natural ability whereas opinion is developed only through educated reflection, it follows that perception and opinion must be different:

> All sensations which reach soul through the body can be perceived by human beings and also by animals from the moment of birth [i.e., by nature] whereas reflection about these with reference to their being and usefulness are acquired...with difficulty and slowly...through education. (*Theaet.* 186b11-c5)[3]

This difference in the mode of acquisition clinches the differentiation of opinion from perception.

Phase 2: Opinion—False as well as True

Having now recognized the existence of opinion as distinct as from perception (in terms of both object and acquisition), the task forthwith becomes that of giving a fuller account of opinion itself. For even it it were the case, as Theaetetus goes on to propose, that "true opinion is probably knowledge" (187b5-6), we still need to know just what opinion itself, whether true *or* false, actually is. It will be this tricky question of truth and falsity that will now prove their undoing.

Clearly, if our quarry is knowledge, then the move from the "becoming" of perception to the "being" of opinion is the right one, since the notion of knowledge is inseparable from the notion of truth, and the notion of truth in turn inseparable from the notion of being. Thus it is not possible "for one to attain truth who cannot even get as far as being" nor "will a man ever have knowledge of anything the truth of which he fails to attain" (186c7-d1). This is why Socrates can acknowledge that "we have progressed so far at least as not to seek for knowledge in perception at all, but in that function of soul, whatever name is given to it, when it alone and by itself is engaged directly with realities [*ta onta*]" (187a3-6). But there's the rub. For it is this very approach, sound though it is, that will account for Theaetetus' confusion between true opinion and knowledge. For, although truth-in-its-full-sense about being-in-its-full-sense will take us all the way to knowledge, it is nevertheless the case that the ordinary experience of making false judgments points to a critical difference between opinion and knowledge (187d1-e1, b5). As the *Gorgias* will point out, a decisive distinction between the two consists in the contrast between knowledge as infallibly true, on the one hand, and opinion as able to be either true *or* false, on the other, "so it is evident that they are not the same" (*Gorg.* 454d8). Moreover, it is in the long run because of the *possibility* of being false that opinion as such, even true opinion, can never be the same as knowledge. After all, it is precisely on this point that we have one of Socrates' rare emphatic claims:

> Indeed I speak as one who does not know but only conjectures; yet that there is a difference between right opinion and knowledge is not at all a conjecture with me, but something I would particularly assert that I knew; there are not many things of which I would say that, but this one, at any rate, I will include among those that I know. (*Meno* 98b1-5)

It is of course at this point that Theaetetus has missed the mark by equating knowledge and true opinion. Whereas our task ought to be to discover what it is about opinion that is common both to true and to false opinion (and thereby different from knowledge), what has happened is that by assimilating true opinion to knowledge, Theaetetus has in fact eliminated the realm of opinion proper—most obviously the realm of opinion that is false, but actually in the same stroke the realm of opinion that is true. In other words, he has opted for an exhaustive "knowledge versus no-knowledge" dichotomy—which will turn out to land him in precisely the same difficulties that bedevil that same paradox when it is proposed in the *Meno* (80e2-5). For if there is nothing "between" (*metaxu*) ignorance and knowledge, then the very notion of learning and inquiry is self-contradictory, just because (as the *Meno* will go on to explain, and as both the *Symposium* and the *Republic* also note) the possibility of opinion as such is being denied (*Symp.* 202a2-9; *Rep. V,* 478c8-d4). It is therefore incumbent on Socrates to convince Theaetetus, just as he finally managed to convince Meno, that this is a false dichotomy. According to this reading, therefore, it is this necessity that directs the discussion that follows. The form of argument will once again be that of a *reductio* which, to all appearances (on the model of those earlier eristic arguments which purported to establish, first, the impossibility of generation, and later the impossibility of ordinary language: see above, chapter 5) will now establish the impossibility of false opinion. As with those other arguments, there will be a hidden truth which offers escape from the impasse, but Theaetetus does not find it.

Introductory Skirmish. The false dichotomy is initially run through quickly—first, in the epistemological mode, focusing on the mental state of the cognizing subject, and second, in the ontological mode, focusing on the status of the apprehended object. This whole inquiry into false opinion, which founders on just this dichotomy, argues implicitly against both versions—as the *Meno* (in many ways a companion piece to the *Theaetetus*)[4] will argue explicitly against the epistemological version ("either knowledge or no-knowledge") and the *Sophist* (the obvious continuation and companion piece of the *Theaetetus*) will argue explicitly against the ontological version ("either being or nonbeing").

(1) The epistemological version of the disjunction is introduced:

> *Socrates:* It is possible for us is it not, regarding all things collectively and each thing separately, *either* to know *or* not to know them. (For learning and forgetting as intermediate steps I leave out of account for the present). (188a1-4)

This disjunction is then taken to be exhaustive:

> *Theaetetus:* Certainly Socrates, nothing is left in any particular case except knowing or not knowing it, (188a5-6)

with the alternatives understood as mutually exclusive:

> *Socrates:* And it is surely impossible that one who knows a thing does not know it, or that one who does not know it knows it. (188a10-b1)

On this disjunctive premiss their conclusion proves to be unsatisfactory because it fails to account for the possibility of false opinion: "Inasmuch as all things are either known or unknown to us, it is impossible, I imagine, to form opinions outside of these alternatives, and within them it is clear there is no place for false opinion" (188c5-7). This exchange then leads them, in this initial skirmish, to consider the ontological status of the opined fact—but in correspondingly disjunctive terms.

(2) The ontological version of the disjunction is then developed, to similar effect: "Had we not, then, better look for what we are seeking, not by this method of knowing and not knowing, but by that of being and not-being?" (188c9-d1). The conclusion here is equally unsatisfactory, for on this premiss (that to hold a false opinion is to hold an opinion of nonbeing: 188d3-e1), we now have the following sequence:

> "he who holds an opinion of what is not holds an opinion of nothing," [and]
> "he who holds an opinion of nothing holds no opinion at all," [therefore]
> "it is impossible to hold an opinion of that which is not" [therefore]
> "false opinion must be something different from an opinion of non-being" (189a10-b4).

Finally, in a third attempt that will concentrate only on the positive term of each disjunction (i.e., *knowledge* and *being*), their introductory conversation will explore yet one more possibility.

(3) The interchange of opinion—but still within the framework of the disjunction—first raises, then dashes, their hopes. For once they register that "it is possible for the mind to regard one thing as another

and not as what it is" (189d7-8), it looks as though this fact will perhaps account for false opinion, through a simple exchange of one (i.e., false) opinion for another (i.e., true) opinion. Although this recognition—that to be an object of false opinion is not to be nothing at all but rather to be an object "other" than the true one—will in fact turn out to lead to a solution of the problem, the effort cannot yet at this point succeed because it it still framed by the original disjunction between knowledge and ignorance. Since on this assumption both exchanged opinions must truly be known, they are therefore forced to conclude that

> no one who talks and forms opinions of two objects *and* apprehends them both with his soul could say and have the opinion that one is the other (190c6-8)

> —and so anyone who sets out to define false opinion as interchanged opinion would be talking nonsense. (190e1-2)

This completes what I have been calling the "introductory skirmish." And the puzzle is now complete, for

> neither by this method [i.e., (3)] nor by our previous methods [i.e., (1) and (2)] is false opinion found to exist in us...

> But yet if this is found not to exist, we shall be forced to admit many absurdities. (190e2-3, 5-6)

The all-or-nothing dichotomy seems to have ruled out the possibility of what is a general, familiar, and commonsense experience—whereas, as the reader recognizes, it is of course just the affirmation of that possibility that the *kompsoteros* "hidden" version of the argument makes room for, as it did for the possibility of inquiry with Meno, and the possibility both of generation and of language earlier with Theaetetus (see above, chapter 5). Let us not, however, underestimate the persistence and ingenuity of that "garrulous" gadfly (*adoleschēs: Theaet.* 195b10), for now, still without a solution, we are about to be presented with his two famous models: the wax block and the aviary.

Models of mind. 1) *The wax block.* What motivates this second phase of the inquiry into opinion is the hope that clarification of the notion of knowledge might enable us to escape the current impasse of selfcontradiction. What actually initiates this new direction is the reintroduction of the notion of learning which had been set aside at the outset of the introductory skirmish (188a2-4). Now, however, it warrants a second look, for the time factor involved in learning will permit an important distinction. Although it starts out simply as a distinction between a current perception (as actual impression) and a remembered interpretation (as "known" imprint), this contrast develops in the course of the conversation into a more general distinction between immediate and interpreted. The proposed model is that of a wax block: as with actual impressions leaving the more lasting imprint of a seal ring, perceptual impressions are similarly seen to leave their more lasting imprint. Opinion occurs as judgment based on comparison between imprints and impressions; false opinion occurs as mismatched comparison (193c2-d2; 194b2-6). The fourteen cases in which false opinion cannot occur (listed at 192a1-c5, and systematically tabulated by McDowell) are then clearly contrasted with the three cases of possible mismatching (192c9-d1). As Socrates sums up the position (still within the framework of the disjunction "either knowledge or no--knowledge"):

> In a word, if our present view is sound, false opinion or deception seems to be impossible in relation to things which one does not know and has never perceived; but it is precisely in relation to things which we know and perceive that opinion turns and twists, becoming false and true—true when it puts the proper imprints and seals fairly and squarely upon one another, and false when it applies them sideways and aslant. (194a8-b6)

Theaetetus' satisfaction is, however, unfortunately short-lived, for the model will fail to account for the kind of error in judgment illustrated in supposing 5 + 7 to yield 11 instead of 12—since, in terms of the theory, this is to confuse (not a perception and an imprint, but) two imprints, both of which are supposedly "known." But, since confusion implies *lack* of knowledge, this problem has now brought us, in circular fashion, back to the original problem of how error is possible when it apparently involves simultaneously knowing and not knowing the same thing. In short, as Socrates puts it to Theaetetus:

> Have we not then come back again to the beginning of our talk? For the man who is affected in this way imagines that one thing which he knows is another thing which he knows. This we said was impossible, and by this very argument we were forcing false opinion out of existence, that the same man might not be forced to know and not to know the same things at the same time. (196b8-c2)

Their efforts prove, however, to involve another kind of circularity, equally damaging; for how can we define knowledge in terms of opinion—and then turn around to use the term *knowledge* in our account of opinion (cf. 196d7-e7)? At this point it looks as though they must take the bull by the horns and clarify at least some of the ambiguity behind the notion of knowledge. This effort now prompts the model of the aviary.

(2) *The aviary.* One way of relating the models of wax block and aviary might be to see them as succinctly picking up those two issues set aside at the beginning: "Learning and forgetting, as intermediate stages, I leave out of account for the present" (188a2-4). The preceding clarification of knowledge (distinguishing interpretation from perception) became possible only by taking account of that first intermediate, learning. Accordingly, the wax model, introduced by Socrates' question, "Can a man who did not know a thing at one time learn it later?" (191c3-4), went on to develop the contrast between impression as current perception and imprint as remembered interpretation. It seems to be the second intermediate, that is, forgetting (as having originally in mind but not now in hand), that will permit a further clarification of the notion of knowledge, and accordingly now prompts the development of the aviary model.

The aviary is introduced in order to represent the difference between knowing in the sense of possessing knowledge (but not now having it actually in hand) over and against the sense of actually having it in hand for effective use. This difference permits the quite literal model of an aviary, in which enclosed birds represent, not objects of knowledge, but rather conceptions latently "possessed" as various kinds of knowledge, although only those at any moment actually caught and held are said to be knowledge actually "had" in hand for effective use. This image now allows them to model the $5 + 7 = 11$ error while apparently avoiding the previous self-contradiction that required the subject both to know and not to know the same thing. Thus, in the aviary

> it never happens that a man does not know that which he knows, but that it is possible to conceive a false opinion about it. For it is possible to have not the knowledge of this thing, but some other knowledge instead, when in hunting for some one kind of knowledge, as the various kinds fly about, he makes a mistake and catches one instead of another; so in one example he thought eleven was twelve, because he caught the knowledge of eleven, which was within him, instead of that of twelve—caught a ringdove, as it were, instead of a pigeon. (199a8-b5)

The objection to this ingenious proposal—underscoring its reliance on the same disjunctive premise—returns to the problem of trying to explain ignorance of something known. How could knowledge of something be the reason for ignorance of that very thing (199d1-8)? Nor will Theaetetus' last-ditch effort save the situation; for even if the flying birds were reinterpreted to include pieces both of knowledge and of ignorance[!], we still run the danger of falling backward into the same old problem that has dogged us from the beginning; for, at one step removed, we now have to explain the analogous mistaking of the piece of ignorance for a piece of knowledge. It has become abundantly clear that if one starts out from Theaetetus' disjunctive premiss, according to which the only alternatives are knowledge and ignorance, we really are caught in Meno's dilemma, for there is by definition now no place at all for opinion: with true opinion assimilated to knowledge, false opinion has become as impossible as false knowledge would be. And so, as Socrates exclaims to Theaetetus,

> after our long wanderings, we have come round again to our first difficulty...And in this fashion are you going to be compelled to trot about endlessly in the same circle, without making any progress? (200a11-12, c3-4)

Phase 3: True Opinion Is Not Knowledge

When Meno originally posed his dilemma (with the denial of the possibility of learning carrying the implicit denial of the possibility of opinion, either true or false), it finally turned out to be not through conceptual argument that Socrates was able to convince him, but rather on empirical grounds. Through the practical demonstration with the slave boy, Socrates confronted him with an actual case of learning, that is to say, with the boy's transition in actual practice from holding a false opinion to hold a true one. Whatever the initial plausibility of the theoretic dilemma, Meno found himself *persuaded* by confrontation with the facts. (In making his own transition from a false to a true opinion, Meno admits the persuasion: "What you say commends itself to me, Socrates, I do not know how": *Meno* 86b5). So too now with Theaetetus, Socrates will give us the same routine. Where theory has failed to extricate them from the dilemma (and so Theaetetus has, like Meno, failed to attain true opinion), Socrates will similarly confront him with the actual fact of judgment in the law courts, where the main business proves to be the acquisition of true opinion without knowledge. Stressing the now familiar contrast between persuasion and teaching, Socrates concludes: "If true opinion and knowledge were the same thing in law courts, the best of judges could never have true opinion without knowledge; in fact, however, it appears that the two are different" (201c4-7). Theaetetus, like Meno before him, is now himself also *persuaded* from a false opinion (that knowledge is true opinion) to a true opinion (that the two are different).

In the long run, however, it may be that it is impossible to understand false opinion until (as the *Sophist* will also demonstrate with falsity and truth on the one hand, and with nonbeing and being on the other) we are able to contrast it with true opinion; and to do that we must first try to understand opinion itself as such. To that problem we now turn.

THE INTERPRETATION OF *DOXA*

My argument in this section will propose that the clue to an understanding of opinion—hence to understanding both true *and* false opinion—is to be sought in *kompsoteros* theory. The challenge will therefore be to elaborate an account of opinion which, (1) insofar as both true and false opinion are each nevertheless opinion, will describe a single operation which will in one sense be the same for both true and false opinion, but (2) insofar as true and false opinion are radically opposed, will describe contrasting operations to account for the difference between true and false opinion.

Pursuing the basic *kompsoteros* insight that mind is generative, and its cognitive products emergent wholes, my thesis here—echoing the *kompsoteros* account of sensation provided earlier in the dialogue—will interpret opinion as involving an analogous operation of soul in which "one" will be generated from an interactive combination of "many" elements that have been discriminated out from an original "infinite" (see chapter 4 above). To understand the details of this operation we must return to the original source of all cognition—those "swifter motions" (156d1-3) whose mutual interaction constitutes sensation. As already noted, however, cognition must take as starting point, not brute sensation, but rather conscious perception. The "infinite" which in this case soul confronts is thus the stream of conscious perception, the multidimensional perceptual flow—visual, auditory, tactile, etc. The first task of the opining soul will therefore be to separate out the many elements that will come to function as parts of a higher-order whole. To do this, soul must discriminate distinct perceptions, evaluating some as "fitting" elements in terms of the criteria already elaborated in the discussion of *kompsoteros* method above.[5] The second phase of the opining operation will then consist in productively combining those fitting elements so as to generate new offspring as an emergent whole. As in the earlier accounts of *kompsoteros* theory, emergence here too will be marked by radical novelty. Thus, over and against the subjectivity of perception we will now have the objectivity of opinion; over and against the relativistic privacy of perception we will now have the public testability of opinion; and finally, over and against the "infallibility" of perception, we will have the possible falsity of opinion. According to the *kompsoteros* approach, therefore, the response to the first part of the above challenge proposes that opinion (as common now to both true and false opinion) involves a generative move from many subjective elements in phenomenal experience to an objective judgment within the public realm of spatiotemporal reality.[6] But what about the second part of the challenge, the demand for an account of the difference between true and false opinion?

As already suggested above in the discussion of *kompsoteros* method in general, the overall test of emergent wholeness must ultimately be power of coherence—coherence expressed, first, as the *dynamis,* or power, of the newly emergent entity itself to act coherently, that is, to do (and thus be), more than its elements either singly or together (this is demonstrated in the radical novelty that has just been noted); and second, as a *dynamis* to participate with, that is, cohere with, other comparable entities as elements to form ever more complex wholes. Here we might follow Socrates in his characteristic invocation of language to illustrate the point. Thus, as language involves successive moves—from the infinite flow of sound, through the discrimination of many letters, to their combination in words, and the combining in turn of words in the various concatenations that go to make up sentences, etc.—so too opinion will involve successive moves from the infinite flow of perception, through the discrimination of many impressions, to their combination in judgment or opinion about objects, and the combining in turn of these in the various concatenations that go to make up opinion about facts and events.

Moreover (as we have seen above, in chapter 4), the twofold test for whether a given combination of letters has been effective in producing a genuine whole (i.e., a real word) will involve, first, testing to see whether the particular combination of letters has produced a new entity with not only sound but also meaning—or whether it is simply "sound without meaning" (cf. *Crat.* 429e8-9; 430a4-5); and second, testing to see whether the new entity is able to enter into combination as one element with other comparable elements to form a more complex whole like a sentence. In light of these criteria, we can now distinguish between true and false opinion. For true opinion consists in soul's successful exercise of this generative operation, as judged by these criteria; false opinion consists in its unsuccessful exercise, as judged by those same criteria. That is to say, if soul combines the given perceptual elements in such a way that what is produced is not a genuine emergent whole according to these criteria, first, vis-à-vis the level of elements (that is to say, if all the perceptions do not mutually "fit" so as to yield a coherent situation), or second, vis-à-vis the level of its own further participation in more complex structures (that is to say, if the opinion or belief produced is unable to enter coherently into combination with other opinions and beliefs), then it has failed to meet the criteria of emergent wholeness, and therefore under cross-examination may be expected to disintegrate into what the *Philebus* calls an "uncompounded jumble" (64e1) and the *Theaetetus* calls a "windegg" (161a1; 210b9; cf. 150a9-b1).

If, however, this *kompsoteros* account of opinion as the successful or unsuccessful generation of emergent wholes is really what Socrates has in mind, then how are we to interpret this long discussion with Theaetetus? Let us return to review that discussion, but now within a *kompsoteros* perspective.

A *kompsoteros* Interpretation of Phase 1: The Move from Perception to Opinion

Coming to the text from the earlier initiation into the mysteries of the *kompsoteroi*, certain otherwise inconspicuous, or hidden, aspects of the conversation spring into relief. Thus one hears Socrates explaining to Theaetetus that soul must move beyond perception through an entirely different activity that seems to involve two now-familiar steps. First, in an operation that is to be sharply differentiated from that of any of the senses, it will reckon up the various sensations which reach the soul through the body,[7] discriminating a "plurality" of different perceptions in terms of actual occurrence, similarity, and dissimilarity, etc.— as, for example, the "hot" of temperature, the "hard" of texture, the "light" of weight, and the "sweet" of taste (184e4-5). Thus:

> In regard to sound and color, you have in the first place this thought about both of them, that they both exist?
> Certainly.
> And that each is different from the other and the same as itself?
> Of course.
> And that both together are two and each separately is one?
> Yes, and that also.
> And are you able also to observe whether they are like or unlike each other? (185a8-b4)

Second, after "viewing these in relation to one another," "seeing their opposition to one another," and "comparing them with one another" (186a9-b9), soul will bring them together in a kind of collected unity (*syllogismō*) (186d3).[8] The result, moreover, will differ radically from perception, which, as subjective experience, simply occurs and to that extent is, for the subject, infallibly so (160c7-9); for the first time we are enabled to move beyond the perceptual world of subjective becoming to a world of objective "being," beyond an experience of privately infallible occurrence to judgment which may be "true" (or, indeed, "false"). As Socrates puts it here to Theaetetus:

Is it possible for one to attain "truth" who can never even get as far as "being"?...
Then knowledge is not in the sensations, but in the process of collecting them [*en de tō peri ekeinōn syllogismō*] for through that it is possible, apparently, to apprehend being and truth, but not by sensation. (186c7-d5)[9]

In terms, then, both of operation (the judgment of opinion) and of product (objectively existent "being"), we have now found a cognitive state and activity quite distinct from that of perception. How should it be identified?

Socrates: Will you call the two by the same name when there are so great differences between them?...Perception includes seeing, hearing, smelling, being cold, and being hot, but by it we are quite unable to apprehend truth, since we cannot apprehend being either...[Rather, we must look to] some function of the soul, whatever name is given to it when it alone and by itself is engaged directly with realities [*ta onta*].

Theaetetus: That, Socrates, is, I suppose, called having opinion.

Socrates: You suppose rightly, my friend. (186d7-187a9)...
when soul has arrived at a decision, whether slowly or with a sudden bound, and is at last agreed, and is not in doubt, we call that its opinion. (190a2-4)[10]

The problem Theaetetus now must face is, of course, that in going on to assimilate true opinion to knowledge (187b5-6) (in line still with his original dichotomy), he has left no room for *false* opinion (187d1-6). So how (from a *kompsoteros* point of view) does the dialogue deal with that problem?

A *kompsoteros* Interpretation of Phase 2: False Opinion

According to the proposed interpretation (as just indicated above), the *kompsoteros* clue to the inconclusive discussion of false opinion lies precisely in this conception of emergence—and more specifically in the denial of that conception in the disjunctive dichotomy that frames the discussion from start to finish.[11] Not only is it actually possible both to know and not to know (to know the elements, for example, but not to know how they fit together as a genuine whole), but it is also in fact this very recognition that is needed in order to understand and account for false opinion.[12] In other words, to settle for the disjunction "either one knows or one does not know" (which from its first adoption at 188a1-b1 functions as the premiss on which the entire discussion is based) is, quite simply, to lack subtlety.[13] It is not just that this uncritical assumption of disjunctive dichotomy so readily lends itself in each case to a *reductio* which renders impossible what we all in fact accept (such as the reality of inquiry, of language, and now of false opinion—although the very act of denying each actually provides a case in point that illustrates, and thereby affirms, exactly what has been denied). As I read the dialogues, the question to which Socrates returns again and again is: What has gone wrong? How account, not just for false opinion in general, but for those original misguided divisions that yield the false dichotomies in the first place? Plato's effort to grapple with this question (largely through the person of Socrates) leads to the very heart of Plato's philosophy and to what he conceives of as the role of the Good. For Socrates does believe that there are better and worse ways to cut the continuum and make our divisions; there are better and worse ways to combine elements.[14] These disjunctive dichotomies with their eristic *reductio* he finds to be sterile, and against such negativity he will "fight in word and deed" (*Meno* 86c1-2).

Introductory Skirmish: A *kompsoteros* Interpretation. What I have been calling the "introductory skirmish" (see above) may now be seen as succinctly laying out three variations on the general theme of the uninitiated stance: (1) the epistemological disjunction of "either knowledge or no-knowledge" (*Theaet.* 188a1-b1); (2) the ontological disjunction of "either being or nonbeing" (*Theaet.* 188c9-189b1); and (3) the simple interchange between "beings" that are "known"—all of which, as we now understand, must and do fail. As we have just seen, eristic fails to make appropriate distinctions: where the distinctions of dialectic are subtle and fruitful, those of eristic are gross and sterile. This is why Meno's adoption of the epistemological version of the uninitiates' dilemma, which is set by Plato right after Socrates' contrast between dialectic and eristic (*Meno* 75c8-d4), is in that dialogue criticized as "an eristic argument" (80e2; 81d6). Similarly, the ontological version of the dilemma, will shortly be criticized in the *Sophist*, where it likewise leads to denial of the possibility of false opinion (*Soph.* 239d2-241b3). What the Eleatic Stranger there attributes to the Sophist's "twisting of our words" (239d2) is made even more explicit in the *Republic*:

> Many suppose they are practicing not eristic but dialectic, owing to their inability to apply the proper divisions and distinctions to the subject under consideration. They *pursue purely verbal oppositions*, practicing eristic, not dialectic, on one another (*Rep.* V, 454a4-9)

Here in the *Republic*, Socrates goes on to make one other point which is of special interest for this study, in light of its contrast between literal and subtle interpretations corresponding to uninitiated and initiated understandings. For this passage in the *Republic* follows up the distinction between eristic and dialectic by associating eristic with literal interpretation—Socrates going on to upbraid himself and Glaucon for failing to make proper distinctions, and instead interpreting their conclusions "most manfully and eristically, in the literal and verbal sense" (*Rep.* V, 454b5-6). This now familiar Platonic sensitivity to levels of interpretation[15]—along with the need to cross-examine and purify ambiguous logoi in order to retain the better and discard the worse interpretation—brings us back to the task of interpreting the graphic models of mind that Socrates now lays out for us.

Models of Mind: Wax Block and Aviary: A *kompsoteros* Interpretation

Just as earlier, in the context of perception, the dialogue sought to cross-examine and so purify the formulations of both Protagoras and Heracleitus in order to retain their genuine insights while discarding their misleading aspects, so too now, in the context of opinion, the dialogue will likewise cross-examine and so purify the theories of two other groups in order to retain their insights while discarding their errors.

Given the *kompsoteros* theory of opinion, it is relatively easy now to see what is sound and unsound about the view of knowledge embodied in the wax block model. The characteristic feature of this model is its twofold insistence, first, on perception as providing the content of knowledge, and second, on a central distinction between perceptual impressions and interpreted imprints. Both claims have turned out to be in one sense right, in another wrong. For we now understand that the insistence on perceptual input is right, insofar as perception does indeed provide the multiplicity of elements for emergent wholeness. Moreover, it is truly the case that there is a radical distinction between the immediate impressions of perception and the mediated interpretations of opinion. It is these important insights that give the model its initial plausibility; at the same time, however, they lead directly to its downfall. For we now understand that it is not through any simple accumulation of perceptions that the judgment of opinion arises. On the contrary, the position of the *kompsoteroi* has been set over and against that of the uninitiated, for whom the only modes of change are addition and subtraction (see discussion of the dice illustration). What the model assumes, however, is that the mere occurrence or repetition of impressions is sufficient to produce the judgment of an interpreted imprint. Thus, although the *kompsoteros* account also holds that perception provides the material for opinion (both true and false), it nevertheless at the same time insists that what is required is a generative act of rational soul to transform these impressions into the interpretation characteristic of opinion. In short, what is wrong with the wax-block model is that, whereas it gives us the parts, it gives no consideration to how those parts might be combined— whether truly, so as to constitute a genuine whole (like 5 + 7 = 12), or falsely, so as to constitute a windegg (like 5 + 7 = 11) (195e1-196b6).

By contrast, the aviary model seems in many ways to stand at the opposite extreme. What is right about this model is, first of all, its emphasis on the presence of the conceptual, and second, its distinction between latent and exercised knowledge, between "possessing" and "having" knowledge. But what is wrong is really very wrong—and on just these two same scores. For, first of all, there is here no evidence of perceptual input at all, but rather what appear to be simply ready-made opinions. In fact, what we now seem to have are conceptual units that have no parts[16] (like the ringdove that is 11, and the pigeon that is 12: 199b3-5). (It is as though the birds were deliberately designed to pick up the earlier interpretation of "being" as a single unit or *hen* [188e7, 8, 10; 189a1, 6, 8], and to anticipate its recurrence as a problem in the discussion of Socrates dream.)[17] By talking, moreover, of pieces of conceptual knowledge as transmitted and received (*paradidonta...paralambanonta*: 198b4-5) for latent possession, impoundment, or enclosure (*katheirxē eis ton peribolon*: 197e4) in the mind, it has offered, instead of a genuine account of recollection as a condition of productive combination, only a windegg that is a travesty of recollection.[18] In other words, the conceptual birds in the aviary seem to raise as many problems as did the perceptual seal ring impressions in the wax.

Let us now for a moment step back to look at the two models side by side in somewhat larger compass. The contrast seems to be as ingenious as it is complete. Over by the block of wax we now recognize the "giants" of the *Sophist*, those men of solid earthiness who "define existence, and body or matter, as identical, and if anyone [such as those over by the aviary] says that anything else which has no body exists, they despise him utterly" (*Soph.* 246b1-3). Since, moreover, "they maintain that that alone exists which can be touched and handled" (246a9-b1), it naturally follows that the only epistemological source, as well as touchstone of verification, will be for them perception. From the *kompsoteros* point of view, then, these "earthborn" giants (*Soph.* 247c5)—ontologically materialists, epistemologically empiricists[19]— are to be understood as in one sense right, in another sense wrong. Thus, their insistence on the role of perception is right insofar as perception provides the elements (as necessary but not sufficient condition) for the emergent wholeness of opinion. By concentrating exclusively, however, on the fleeting impressions of perception, they have imprisoned themselves in an earthbound blindness as surely as if they were in the dark of a cave. For perception alone leaves us with a kind of cognitive blindness.

Meanwhile, over by the aviary we recognize the airy spirits or "gods" of the *Sophist* who, by contrast, "with weapons from the invisible world above, maintain that real existence consists of certain ideas which are only conceived by the mind and have no body" (*Soph.* 246b7-8)—conceptions, as it were, flying around in the "invisible world above" without even so much as a foot on the ground. These ideas are, moreover, to be understood as unitary, for "surely that which is really one must according to right reason be affirmed to be absolutely without parts" (*Soph.* 245a8-9). From the *kompsoteros* point of view, then, these ethereal spirits—ontologically idealists identified as "Friends of the Forms" (*Soph.* 248a4), epistemologically espousing a kind of direct conceptual input that makes them appear to be "Friends of Recollection"—are also to be understood as in one sense right, in another sense wrong. Thus their emphasis on the role of the conceptual is right insofar as form provides a unitary "shape" (a necessary but not sufficient condition) for the emergent wholeness of opinion. By concentrating exclusively, however, on bare conceptual unities, they have severed their connection to the perceptual ground of knowledge, casting themselves aloft as it were in a rarefied atmosphere of invisible emptiness.

As we finally leave both wax block and aviary behind, to head off towards the law courts of Athens (200e7-201c7), we can see that the purification through elenchus is now complete. On the one side are the earthborn wax block giants whose materialist empiricism, while offering genuine insights, at the same time distorts that glimpse of the truth; on the other side are the ethereal spirits whose idealist "recollection-ism" likewise offers genuine insights, but at the same time distorts their glimpse of the truth. With that phase of elenchus complete, the purified interpretations can now highlight a further difference that sets in stark opposition the proposed approach of the *kompsoteroi* and that of *both* these models. For we can now see the clear contrast between the generative operation being proposed by Socrates and the sheer receptivity of "givenness" proposed by *both* the models—where in the case of the wax we have the image of a tabula rasa that is simply receiving the stamp of impressions, in the case of the aviary we have the image of "empty" space (197e2-3) which is simply receiving, by impoundment and transfer, the piece-meal input of conceptual units. Once again the wax block and aviary models serve to illumine by contrast the *kompsoteros* conception of a "taking" and structuring that characterizes rational soul's generative, and truly productive, activity.

When, at last, we broaden out our lens to take in the wide-angle view, we recognize another feature, present throughout, that enables us better to focus the whole discussion. For the picture reveals Socrates' continuous play on the comprehensive contrast between sophistry and true philosophy. Although eristic is superficially very like dialectic—as a wolf is very like a dog (*Soph.* 231a6)—one way to interpret the whole discussion is to realize that, underneath all the ballyhoo, the dichotomizing cleaver of eristic has been replaced by the healing scalpel of dialectic (cf. *Phaedr.* 265e1-3; *Stat.* 287c3-5).[20]

RETROSPECTIVE

By this stage of the *Theaetetus*, Plato has carefully established his pattern and method. What he is proposing is a theory of complex emergence— the successive generation of radically new entities. At each level, an entity is to be understood as a unified whole (a "one") generated out of diverse elements (a "many"), these in turn having been separated out from a prior continuum (an "infinite"). In each case, moreover, the elements must be first discriminated out as "fitting" (according to quite specific criteria, which might be regarded as necessary but not sufficient conditions), and then combined in a peculiarly generative interaction so as to yield a genuinely emergent product (again meeting the specific conditions for genuine emergence).

First elaborated in the context of perception, or *aisthēsis*, this theory of emergent generation has now been reiterated in the context of *doxa*. Confronted at each level with some sort of indeterminate range, mind proceeds to do what defines it as mind—introducing measure into what has hitherto been unmeasured, ratio or rationality into what has been irrational. Ordering and organizing, it is the activity of mind or soul which generates the organic wholes that define our universe. Mind's activity does not, however, cease with the generation of opinion. Hence the move to logos, and finally to knowledge as *epistēmē*. These moves the dialogue will now take up, following this same clearly established pattern.

SEVEN

"...AND LOGOS (*meta logou*)":
201c9; 206c3-5

With Theaetetus' final effort at definition ("knowledge is true opinion with logos"), we are confronted with yet another puzzle and challenge. One of the most pervasive terms in Plato's dialogues, *logos* is perhaps at the same time one of the most ambiguous—its meaning ranging all the way from speech, statement, and definition to argument, account, discourse, structure, rationality, and even rationally structuring mind itself.

Perhaps a good way to pursue the inquiry of the present chapter is to break it down into four sections. The first will consider what the pattern of *kompsoteros* theory, as thus far developed, has led us to expect of logos. A second section will then examine logos as we meet it in the *Theaetetus* itself—from the original paradigms of logos as definition in the beginning to the rejected accounts at the end. This examination will then provide background for a third section which will look to the dialogues in general to see how far Plato's overall presentation of logos conforms or fails to conform to the predictions of *kompsoteros* theory. Finally, a fourth section will raise the question of how any of this relates to the puzzling introduction of Socrates' "dream."

THE *KOMPSOTEROS* PATTERN FOR LOGOS

From the point of view of *kompsoteros* method, as this study has been exploring it, it is not surprising that the term *logos* should thus span linguistic and cognitive meanings. After all, language, it has been suggested (see above, chapters 3 and 4), is the primary tool of cognitive activity, the device through which we first structure our experience, and thereby reality as we know it. Approaching the question of logos, therefore, from within the perspective of *kompsoteros* theory, we must go back to the starting point of "the mysteries" and to the claim that everything is motion. For viewed from this angle, the generative activity of logos in its linguistic mode (i.e., in the increasingly complex structuring of speech) will parallel the generative activity of logos in its cognitive mode (i.e., in the structuring activity that marks increasingly complex stages of cognition).

Thus, brought to the awareness of human consciousness, it will be the originally indeterminate motion of sound that becomes the flow of human speech, the continuum or "infinite" from which (as Socrates repeatedly observes) the rational activity of soul will generate language. Thus, from soul's successive separations and combinations, there will come about a cumulative emergence of linguistic entities: first, syllables or words which, as a combining or weaving together of sounds or letters, may (unlike mere letters) be meaningful;[1] second, statements which, as a weaving together of words, may (unlike mere words) be either true or false;[2] and third, we can anticipate a weaving together of statements to yield arguments which may (unlike mere statements) be either sound or unsound.[3] Socrates' fascination with this process in the *Theaetetus* is echoed in dialogues like the *Cratylus* (424c5-425a3), *Sophist* (253a1-6; 261d1-263d4), *Statesman* (277e3-278d6), and *Philebus* (17a8-b9; 18b3-d2).

It is easy enough to see how this *linguistic* structuring corresponds to the *kompsoteros* view of *cognitive* structuring as thus far developed. For, at the lowest level of cognitive awareness, we have the swifter motion of sensation, which, once similarly brought to the awareness of human consciousness, becomes the perceptual flow, the continuum that constitutes the cognitive unlimited or "infinite" from which rational soul will ultimately generate knowledge. Thus, from soul's successive separations and combinations there similarly comes about the cumulative emergence of cognitive operations: first, perceptual impressions which, as subjective occurrences, can attain neither to being nor to truth (*Theaet.* 186c7-d5), but simply occur and are given names (156b2-7). At a second level, we have just seen (see above, chapter 6) how perceptual impressions may be combined to generate opinion as an emergent whole, how in that emergence opinion can reach beyond the subjectivity of perception to objective being, and beyond the private relativism of perception to public truth; in other words, opinion may be either true or false. What *kompsoteros* theory has therefore prepared us for is a third cognitive phase which, at the next level, may now be expected to apply the same *kompsoteros* principles of separation and combination, only this time to the material of opinion, in order thereby to generate a further emergent whole. In one sense, as always, this emergent will be the same as, in another sense quite different from, the elements from which it is generated. It is to be expected, moreover, that following *kompsoteros* theory, the elements will meet the criteria for "fitness," and that the generated whole will meet the criteria for genuine emergence (see above, chapter 4). A diagram might at this point illustrate the picture of *kompsoteros* expectation (fig. 4).

Figure 4.
kompsoteros **Perspective:**
Linguistic and Cognitive Patterns of Successive Emergence

	SUCCESSIVE COGNITIVE OPERATIONS		SUCCESSIVE LINGUISTIC ENTITIES
Starting point	*Flow of perception* — with original discrimination of senses and sensibles which in interaction will generate the first truly cognitive, operation, i.e.:		*Flow of speech* — with original discrimination of letters which in combination will generate the first truly linguistic entity, i.e.:
First level of emergence:	*Perceptions*	CAN BE NAMED ONLY	*Words*
Second level of emergence:	*Opinion*	CAN BE TRUE OR FALSE	*Statements*
Third level of emergence:	*Logos* as reasoning	CAN BE SOUND OR UNSOUND	*Logos* as definition and argument

According to my reading of the *kompsoteros* approach, it is because this multi-dimensional operation of language corresponds so perfectly with the multidimensional operation of knowledge, that Plato has Socrates so readily resort to it as a paradigm for rationality. The question that now confronts us, however, is whether this *kompsoteros* expectation will be borne out in Plato's presentation of logos, first within the *Theaetetus* itself, then within the dialogues in general.

LOGOS IN THE *THEAETETUS*

The Problem of Logos

Whatever its exact role in the evolution of knowledge, it is persistently and abundantly clear throughout the dialogues that logos is cognitively crucial (see discussion in Introduction, "Apparent Failure"). Much would therefore seem to ride on the *Theaetetus'* examination of logos. Fortunately for our inquiry, Plato makes a point of providing not only a detailed analysis (at the end of the dialogue), but also (from the beginning) specific examples to illustrate what he means by logos as definition.[4] Thus, not only does he have Socrates very early offer a definition of clay, but it is especially Theaetetus' account of surds that is hailed and endorsed as a model for a definition of knowledge (*Theaet.* 148d4-7). The trouble is that, on closer examination, this model of definition will reduce both Theaetetus and the reader to *aporia*; for in the end, it is of course on just this point that the dialogue apparently founders—bringing us full circle from the original *model* of logos round to the final failure to reach a *definition* of logos. The real crux of the problem, is, however, that the triple account of logos that is rejected at the end does actually seem to be modeled on the exemplar of definition that was lauded at the beginning.[5] How is it that the analogous operation, when presented by Theaetetus at the beginning, is accepted as an admirable model of logos, but when described at the end, is apparently rejected as an unacceptable account of that same logos? The question warrants a closer look, first at the models proposed, and then at the logos of "logos" that is apparently rejected at the end.

The Models of Logos

In light of the importance Socrates has attached to Theaetetus' model of logos, it becomes all the more interesting to recognize that that master juggler, Plato, now has four balls in the air: for not only is our attention being directed to the explicit examples provided in the logos of clay and of surd—as well as in Theaetetus' later attempt at a logos of logos—but for the reader there is the further encompassing example being provided in their joint effort to arrive at a logos of knowledge. If we can clarify our own understanding of logos, it will be desirable then to return and evaluate the success or failure of their logos of knowledge. (This will be the goal of the next chapter.) Our task, meanwhile, is to examine more closely these models provided within the dialogue, in order to see how far they conform (or fail to conform) to *kompsoteros* expectations with respect to emergent generation.

As we draw nearer to look more closely at these various models of logos, we realize that Plato's moves in each become successively more subtle. Thus, in light of *kompsoteros* theory, we realize first of all that even Socrates' first example (147a1-c6)—so disarmingly innocent in its apparently simple spontaneity—contrives to set the tone for the rest of the inquiry. For beneath the casual illustration, our attention is directed to the fact that clay is actually a whole, composed of earth and water. In terms of *kompsoteros* theory, earth and water meet all the criteria for fitness of elements (similarity, dissimilarity, relativity, mutuality), while clay itself meets the criteria for genuineness of product since the defining characteristic of plasticity, shared by neither earth nor water, is generated in their interaction. What we are being thus casually offered at a practical level in the beginning of the dialogue will, on the *kompsoteros* reading I am proposing, turn out to be echoed at the theoretic level at the end. For, expressed as "earth together with moisture" (147c5-6), Socrates' definition of clay in fact foreshadows the final definition of knowledge as "true opinion together with logos." On my reading, the point of the clay analogy is to prepare us to recognize that just as the interaction of earth and water (as fitting elements) will yield a genuinely new entity characterized by a *dynamis* beyond that of either of the elements that constitute it (i.e., plasticity), so too the interaction of true opinion and logos (as fitting elements) will also yield a genuinely new entity characterized by a *dynamis* beyond that of either of its elements. In other words, just as clay may be defined in terms of those elements that constitute its material components, so too, analogously, knowledge may be defined in terms of those elements that constitute its cognitive components; moreover, just as in the long run what we also need to understand about clay is that, generated in the mixture of those elements is a new *dynamis*, hence a new entity, so also in the long run what we need to understand about knowledge is that, generated in the mixture of those elements is also a new *dynamis*, hence a new entity. Thus, framing the whole inquiry, this initial *demonstration* of logos and the final *account* of logos will together hold the clue to the sought-for logos of knowledge. Let us, however, now look at the models to see how far the kind of operation they represent might accord with *kompsoteros* expectations with respect to separating and combining activity.

If the dialogue were indeed pursuing a *kompsoteros* approach, then these models of logos would take as starting point the "flow" or "course" of experience, out of which certain items would then be separated in order to give us a multiplicity of particulars, identified through opinion, and ready to be tested according to the *kompsoteros* criteria for fitness of elements. Interestingly enough, reference to elements drawn in this sense from the course of our experience is in fact meticulously adherred to in the fashioning of the dialogue's various models of logos—whether it is the listing of an actual variety of clays with a view to a definition of clay—"the potters' clay, and the oven-makers' clay, and the brickmakers' clay" (147a3-4)—or the listing of Theodorus' variety of surds in preparation for the definition of surd—"the squares containing three square feet and five square feet...and so up to seventeen square feet" (147d3-6)[6]—or the listing of a variety of actual kinds of knowledge as a first step towards defining knowledge—"geometry and all the things you spoke of just now [i.e., astronomy, arithmetic, music: 145a5-8]—and also cobblery, and the other craftsmen's arts" (146c8-d1)—or, finally, for the reader, the actual succession of logoi themselves, preparing us for a definition of logos—that is, Socrates' logos of clay, Theaetetus' logos of surd, and their joint effort at a logos of knowledge.

What *kompsoteros* theory might now expect by way of cognitive operation would be something analogous to that generative combination in which opinion combines (*syllogismō*) perceptions to give us the empirical dimension of experience in the first place (186d3)—that is to say, we might expect a move from the sheer listing of a multiplicity of concrete instances, to their collection, or generative combination, into a single and emergent whole. This too we seem to find in Theaetetus' determination "to try to collect them into one [*syllabein eis hen*] according to which we could call all the roots" (147d8-e1).[7]

The term Theaetetus uses for this particular bringing together of many instances in order to combine them in one is *syllabein*. This is, of course, the same term that is used of that combination of letters which generates a "syllable" as the first unit of meaning—and it is in this literal sense that Plato often uses the word (e.g., *Theaet.* 202e6ff.; cf. *Stat.* 278b6; *Crat.* 423e8, 431d2). But from the point of view of the *kompsoteros* thesis, it is of considerable interest to discover that *syllabein* is also used (as by Aristotle)[8] for a female's "conceiving." It would seem that, for Plato, to say that both a child and a logos are "conceived" (as is also possible in English through the ambiguity of *conception*, from the Latin *conceptus*) is not so much a pun, but an illuminating analogy.[9] Hence it is the term that Plato uses, as here in the "surd" model, for that combining act in which mind literally and constructively brings together a many in a single hold, combining a number of instances under a single concept (*syl-labein*: grasp or hold together; cf. *Soph.* 218c5-6; 235b10; *Stat.* 263d8). His choice of this term, moreover, with its double entendre that links concrete and abstract generation, seems clearly to echo the original language of sexual intercourse in the *kompsoteros* mysteries of generation and perception. It is thus demanded, by the models as well as by the *kompsoteros* theory of emergence in general, that in logos a multitude of concrete cases be collectively "taken hold of" and constructively "held together" by mind, so as to generate a single "con-cept" as the subject of definition. This, now at the end of the dialogue, both Theaetetus and the reader are finally called upon to do: first for logos, then for knowledge itself—the ultimate quarry of the whole dialogue.

Integrating this interpretation of the models of logos into the broader *kompsoteros* theory of emergence, we are now led to recognize the epistemological implications for a theory of meaning and a method of explanation. To explain anything (*logon didonai*) will therefore, according to *kompsoteros* theory, involve focusing on three distinct dimensions of the explicandum. First, we must recognize a continuum, or "infinite," whose more-or-less-ness provides not only a starting point but actually the stuff out of which the explicandum will arise. Thus, sound is the stuff both of music and of speech (*Phil.* 17b3-c2; cf. *Soph.* 263e7-8; *Theaet.* 206d2-4); power, the stuff of being (*Soph.* 247d8-e4; cf. *Theaet.* 156a5-7); magnitude, the stuff of mathematics (my reading of *Theaet.* 147e5-148b1); human temperament, the stuff of virtue (*Stat.* 306a1-3; 308c1-309a3); motion, the stuff of things (*Theaet.* 156a5); and perception, the stuff of knowledge (*Theaet.* 151e2-3)—and in each case it is quite literally true to say that the explicandum is "nothing other than this" (e.g., *Soph.* 247e4). But simply to have recognized this is—as in the case of Theaetetus' first definition of knowledge as "nothing other than perception"—only a first step. Thus in the case of language,

> sound, which passes out through the mouth of each and all of us, is one, and yet again it is infinite in number. And no one of us is wiser than the other merely for knowing that it is infinite or that it is one; but what makes each of us a grammarian is the knowledge of the number and nature of the sounds. (*Phil.* 17b3-9)

In a second phase, therefore, logos (as account or explanation) will focus on a number of discrete particulars as a "many" separated out from the original indeterminate range as distinct, and often opposed, elements. But here again, this operation is a necessary, but not a sufficient, condition for understanding or explaining in the sense of "giving an account." Plato insists on this point in a number of contexts:

> But knowledge of the various high and low and intermediate sounds would not suffice to make you a musician, although ignorance of them would make us, if I might say so, quite worthless with respect to music. (*Phil.* 17c4-9)

> If a musician met a man who thought he understood harmony because he could strike the highest and lowest notes . . . he would say: "My friend, he who is to be a harmonist must know these things you mention, but nothing prevents one who is at your stage of knowledge from being quite ignorant of harmony. You know the necessary preliminaries of harmony, but not harmony itself." (*Phaedr.* 268d7-e6)

Again, with regard to medicine:

> If anyone should go to Eryximachus or to his father Acumeneus and should say, "I know how to apply various drugs to people so as to make them warm or, if I wish, cold, and I can make them vomit if I like, or can make their bowels move, and all that sort of thing; and because of this knowledge I claim that I am a physician and can make any other man a physician to whom I impart the knowledge of these things," . . . they

would say the man was crazy...for he knew the preliminaries of medicine, but not medicine itself. (*Phaedr.* 268a8-269a3)

And so with Sophocles or Euripides with the writing of tragedy (*Phaedr.* 268c5-269a2), or the necessary but not sufficient niceties of speech and rhetoric (*Phaedr.* 266d5-269b8). So too, of course, while recognizing that, as a necessary condition of explaining knowledge, Theaetetus should separate out true opinion and logos as the "many" elements, we must not mistake this for an adequate account or explanation exhibiting true understanding of "what knowledge really is" (*Theaet.* 145e9; 146e9-10; 151d4).

A third phase will therefore be required in this process of explaining and understanding—a phase which will reveal how the combination of these elements may generate, not a "jumble" (*Phil.* 64e1), nor a "windegg" (*Theaet.* 151e6; 157d3; 210b9), but rather a "one" that will be a genuine and radically emergent whole, since (for the *kompsoteroi*) "what is brought into existence always comes into existence as a whole" (*Soph.* 245d4). Thus, picking up the earlier question, Phaedrus recognizes that Sophocles and Euripides "would laugh at one who imagined that tragedy was anything else than *the proper combination of these elements* in such a way that they harmonize with each other and with the whole composition" (*Phaedr.* 268d3-5) and in the case of music, Socrates explains that

> when you have grasped the number and quality of the intervals of the voice in respect to high and low pitch, and the limits of the intervals, and *all the combinations generated from them* [*systemata*], when you have grasped them in this way, then you have become a musician. (*Phil.* 17c11-e1)

The logos of Logos

Throughout our discussions of the ambiguity that pervades the *Theaetetus*, we have recognized Socrates to be not so much rejecting as actually purifying interpretations, thereby opening up cumulative, and to that extent, richer, understanding. When, therefore, here at the end of the dialogue, he asks: What is the meaning of *logos*? (*Theaet.* 206c7-8), we are by now prepared for a cumulative response that will encompass identification of an infinite or indeterminate as starting point, discrimination into many elements, and combination into a single whole. And, sure enough, this does seem to be how the final section of the dialogue now unfolds. What makes the ensuing discussion somewhat tricky to follow is that Socrates is making his point simultaneously at two distinct (though inseparable) levels—the one more obviously focusing on logos as *product* of definition (e.g., the definition of *wagon*), the other more significantly reflecting on logos as defining *activity* (in which the defining of *wagon* functions as example). We will return to disentangle these in a moment. For now, however, let us follow Socrates as he moves between the two.

Turning Theaetetus round to focus now on logos, Socrates takes him, as it were, by the hand:

> I think, says Socrates, logos means one of three things. The first would be making one's own thought clear through speech by means of verbs and nouns, imaging the opinion in the stream that flows through the lips as in a mirror or in water. (206c8-d4)

Like Heracleitus' river itself, this streamlike flow of speech constitutes the starting point and stuff, the "infinite," of logos. To stop there would, however, reduce the proposed definition of knowledge to nonsense, for, although it is of course literally true that logos is "nothing other than" a flow of words, this interpretation, as Socrates goes on to point out, would mean that any expression of opinion would automatically be knowledge (206d9-e2). He concludes: "Let us not, therefore, carelessly accuse him of talking nonsense who gave the definition of knowledge we are now considering; for perhaps that is not what he meant" (206e4-6).

Thus, while recognizing the basic stuff of logos to be indeed the flow of language or speech, we will now be led into an account of logos as involving "many." This, not surprisingly, points to logos as description in terms of constituents, an enumeration of those fitting elements which, in right relation, will constitute the parts:

> He may have meant that each person, if asked about anything, must be able to give his questioner an account of it in terms of its elements; as for example. . . if we were asked what a wagon is, we should be satisfied if we could say, "wheels, axle, body, rims, yoke". . . It is impossible for anyone to give a rational explanation of anything with knowledge until he gives a complete enumeration of the elements, combined with true opinion. . . an orderly description in terms of its elements. . . describing the whole in terms of its elements. (206e6-207c4)

On examination, however, they realize that (as *kompsoteros* theory has already explained), for the correct enumeration of elements, right opinion is sufficient (207b5; 208a10)—just as it proved to be sufficient to direct people on the right road to Larissa (*Meno* 97a9-11). Since, moreover—recalling the earlier excursion into the Athenian law courts (201a4-c7)—they realize that it is possible to have right opinion *without* knowledge (208b1-2; cf. 210b4-7), it follows that on this interpretation (i.e., on the reduction of logos to true opinion's enumeration of

elements), the would-be definition of knowledge is again unacceptable
(208b1-9). Meanwhile, of course, the reader recognizes that, according
to *kompsoteros* theory, logos as emergent (that is to say, as conceptual
account or definition) represents apprehension in a different dimension
of reality from that of right opinion. For it is one thing to know in
practice (i.e., to judge or opine) *that* in fact these are the elements of a
thing; it is another to know in theory (i.e., to understand in light of a
theoretical concept) *why* these—all these, and only these—are the
elements. This is why "true opinions. . . are of no great value until one
makes them fast with casual reasoning [*aitias logismō*]" (*Meno* 98a3-4).[10]
Recognition of the conceptual unity that both defines as fitting, and
holds together as one, these—and just these—elements is what logos
must now achieve.[11] It leads therefore into the third and last interpretation of logos—which, from the *kompsoteros* point of view, points to
another, necessary and complementary, element of the defining
operation. This will involve identification in terms, not now of
constitutive components, but rather of unique differentia. In other
words, definition needs to zero in on the emergent *dynamis* which
characterizes the thing as a single whole, and in terms of which the
elements were originally determined. (It is, for example, the peculiar
power of vehicular transportation that characterizes the wagon, and
accounts for the selection of these particular elements—wheels, axle,
rims, etc..) This task calls for the "identification of some characteristic
by which the object in question differs from all the others" (208c7-8), "a
comprehension of the difference which distinguishes it from other
things" (208e3-4).

According to the *kompsoteros* approach as developed throughout
the dialogue, we are now speaking simultaneously on two levels at
which "many" are made "one"—first, with respect to the concept as
object of definition, and second, with respect to the process of
definition itself. For while logos presents the definiendum as a
conceptual "one" in which the enumerated elements are collected into
a single abstract entity, the defining operation itself also thereby
becomes a "one," as it combines into a single activity both the
enumerating of elements and the identifying of unique differentia. But,
reflecting Theaetetus' failure to recognize the operation of logos as
requiring this generative move to the abstract realm of the conceptual,
they proceed instead to take as their example, not an abstract concept
from the realm of being (*ousia*), but rather a concrete particular from the
three-dimensional realm of becoming (*genesis*)—where the mode of
apprehension is not through logos as definition at all, but rather (as we
have just seen) through right opinion (208d1-3; 209a1-d2). In other
words, given *kompsoteros* theory—according to which the sense of logos
they seek is necessarily restricted to the dimension of *ousia* in contrast

to that of *genesis*—this interpretation, which attempts to define a concrete particular, once again reduces the proposed definition of knowledge to absurdity (209d6).

At this point, all three proposed interpretations of logos are found to be, on the face of it, inadequate. Consistently with the approach of this study, however, it would rather seem that here again Plato is insisting on the radical ambiguity of verbal formulations. For like the doctrines of both Protagoras and Heracleitus, and like the earlier definitions of Theaetetus, this logos too will prove to be equally susceptible of a true interpretation. In other words, it is not the logos itself which is to be rejected, but only certain interpretations that have been put upon it. For this reason, Theaetetus' understanding of the logos of logos—and ultimately of the equally ambiguous logos of knowledge as "true opinion with logos"—remains only a dreamlike recollection of the truth (cf. *Meno* 85c9-10). In the words of the *Statesman*, Theaetetus' dreaming opinion has not yet been transformed into waking knowledge (*Stat.* 278e10; cf. *Meno* 86a7-8), for, as they had recognized earlier in this dialogue, it is the difficulty of distinguishing between resemblance and reality that characterizes the dreaming state (*Theaet.* 158b9-c8; cf. *Rep.* V, 476c5-7). It is in this sense, I believe, that we must read Socrates' exclamation that "the perfectly true definition of knowledge, which we thought we had, was but a golden dream" (208b11-12).

By the way of concluding this section, therefore, we can see that, approached from within the perspective of *kompsoteros* theory, we find in the *Theaetetus*—both in the models of logos and in the logos of logos—a structure which might be paralleled for the various cases as in figure 5.

Figure 5.
Parallelism between Models of Definition

	Clay	*Surd*	*Logos*	*Knowledge*
Basic stuff as starting point i.e., AN "INFINITE"	Continuum of matter	Continuum of space	Continuum of sound (in speech)	Continuum of perception
Elements "fit" for mutual interaction i.e., A "MANY"	Earth AND water	Size AND shape	Enumeration of material elements AND identification of formal differentia	True opinion AND logos
Generated whole with unique *dynamis* i.e., A "ONE"	Plastic substance taking permanent shape	Side of square shape with oblong size	Identification of formal unity to determine material multiplicity	Infallible reasoned rightness

It is instructive now to compare this diagram that relates the various *models* of definition with one that highlights the parallelism between the *logoi* of definition (fig. 6).

Figure 6.
Parallelism between the Logos of *knowledge* and the Logos of *Logos*

Logos of knowledge	*Logos of logos*
(1) As *infinite:* a stream of sensation where particular appearings, as phenomenal "images," are apprehended in perception and can only be named: i.e., *Definition #1:* 151e2-3 *"Knowledge is perception"*	(1) As *infinite:* a stream of speech where particular words, as "images," are simply heard as names *(onomata):* i.e., *Definition #1:* 206d2-4 *"Logos is a stream of speech"*
(2) As *many:* apprehension of particulars in opinion which may be true or false: i.e., *Definition #2:* 187b5-6, 200e4 *"Knowledge is true opinion"*	(2) As *many:* enumeration of particulars in statements of opinion which may be true or false: i.e., *Definition #2:* 206e5-208a10 *"Logos is enumeration of elements"*
(3) As *one:* apprehension in logos of many as one [may be tested in logos as argument]: i.e., *Definition #3:* 201c9-d1 *"Knowledge is true opinion and logos"*	(3) As *one:* formal differentiation of definable concepts [may be tested in logos as argument]: i.e., *Definition #3:* 208c7-8 *"Logos is indentification of unique differentia"*
kompsoteros implication: Knowledge will be that which (while "nothing other than perception") will combine true opinion AND logos in that emergent wholeness which will constitute, and be properly called, genuine "knowledge."	*kompsoteros implication:* Logos will be that which (while "nothing other than speech") will combine enumeration of elements AND unique differentiation in that emergent wholeness which will constitute, and be properly called, genuine "logos."

If, in line with the diagram, we take as a paradigm of logos, not the dreaming frustration of Theaetetus' effort, but rather Plato's own dialogues, then this threefold logos of logos becomes susceptible of an interpretation fully consonant with *kompsoteros* expectation. According to this reading, the *Theaetetus'* cumulative account of logos is not only an account consistent with all that is said about definition in this and other dialogues, but the dialogues themselves, when measured against this account, stand revealed as logoi par excellence.

THE DIALOGUES AS LOGOI

Approached in this way, from the angle of *kompsoteros* theory, it is not difficult to recognize in Plato's own dialogues the consistent pursuit of a method which successively develops these three phases of logos. Whether the subject of inquiry is the nature of virtue (as in the *Meno*), or discourse (as in the *Phaedrus*), or justice (as in the *Republic*), or the sophist (as in the *Sophist*), or pleasure (as in the *Philebus*), the moves are analogous, and the overall method basically the same. As the roadway Socrates has "always loved" and tried to follow, Plato calls it the *hodos* (road or way) of dialectic (*Phil.* 16b5-17a5). (See above, chapter 4.)

One of the first things to strike a reader of the dialogues is that so many of them set out from an apparently casual introductory conversation, during the course of which some significant term is found spontaneously and naturally to occur. In the language of this section of the *Theaetetus*, we are being presented with the first level of logos, that is to say, with a term (*onoma*) which fleetingly appears in the stream of ordinary speech—the different character of each particular dialogue being established through the various ingenious ways in which Plato casts this "vocal image of thought" on the natural flow of conversation (208c5). Thus, against various real-life settings, terms such as "temperance" in the *Charmides*, "courage" in the *Laches*, "virtue" in the *Meno*, "justice" in the *Republic*, both "discourse" and "love" in the *Phaedrus*, "being" in the *Sophist*, and here in the *Theaetetus* "logos" and "knowledge" itself—are all introduced with studied casualness as "imaging opinion on the stream that flows through the lips, as in a mirror or water" (206d3-4). But, as with images in flowing water, the edges are often fuzzy, and although Plato would agree with Wittgenstein that such fuzziness is often inconsequential, he does believe that in certain cases the way we understand key concepts (like piety, love, or justice, for example) will make a difference to the way we act. In such cases, accordingly, the question is posed: What exactly is it that is being thus imaged in the sound-flow of speech? Taking as starting point the relative indeterminacy of ordinary usage, the dialogue will therefore go on to determine first the extension of the term through the enumeration of characteristic instances, and then its intension through the identification of unique differentia.

In line, therefore, with Theaetetus' second account of logos as enumeration of elements, the second phase of Platonic inquiry normally moves to some form of description via ostension—that is to say, to some listing of instances drawn from the participants' stream of conscious experience to which, through true opinion, the term is judged to apply. Moreover, this instantiation will very often take place on two different, but synchronized, levels. For, in addition to the obvious level addressed to characters as participants in the inquiry, there is a further level in which, addressing the reader, Plato at the same time takes us, the readers, through a parallel inquiry. As a result, the dialogue as a whole moves simultaneously on both a surface and a deeper-level pursuit—the interplay between the two often resulting in drama of quite extraordinary subtlety. Thus, for example, in the *Republic*, not only are we (along with Glaucon and the rest of the group) reflecting on justice writ large in the state and small in the individual, but at the same time we are reflecting on the actual presentation of justice and injustice in the persons of the participants and in their interrelations; in the *Phaedrus*, not only do we look (with Phaedrus and Socrates) at Lysias' and Socrates' discourses about love, but we also respond to the quality of love actually demonstrated by Lysias and Socrates for Phaedrus. In light of *kompsoteros* theory, supported by Theaetetus' second interpretation of logos, we recognize this move in the dialogue as a necessary phase of the inquiry, both for the participants and for the reader;[12] for this reference to instances apprehended in opinion is, in terms of the theory of emergence, actually the enumeration of "many" elements which, in proper combination, must fit together as parts to generate "one" as-yet-but-glimpsed whole. As I read it, this is why the second interpretation of logos is described as "an orderly approach *to the whole* through the elements" (*Theaet.* 208c6; cf. 107c3-4).

It is finally, therefore, to this whole as an emergent concept that the third phase of a dialogue will direct itself; for, as the Stranger explains in the context of the inquiry into the term *sophist:* From a starting point of common usage (i.e., shared acceptance of the term, or name, as it occurs in the ordinary course of conversation), we must move next to agreement about the actual things referred to by that term (i.e., to consensus about the extension of the term), and finally to agreement about the conceptual definition (i.e., to consensus about the intension of the term). Thus

> we must inquire together . . . to search out the sophist and make manifest in logos what he is. For as yet you and I have nothing in common about him but the name; but as to the thing to which we give the name, we may perhaps each have a notion of it in our own minds; however, we ought

always in every instance to come to an agreement about the thing itself
through logos, rather than about the mere name without logos. (*Soph.*
218b6-c5)

This third phase of Plato's method of inquiry as he pursues it in the
dialogues seeks, therefore, to elaborate a definition of the abstract
entity as "one," for "one and many are identified by logos" (*Phil.* 15d4).
As the *Laws* puts it,

[One who would excel] must not only be able to pay regard to the many,
but must be able to press towards the one, so as to discern it, and on
discerning it, to survey and organize all the rest with a single eye to
it...Can any man get an accurate vision and view of anything better than
by being able to look from the many and dissimilar to the one unifying
form? It is certain that no man can possibly have a clearer method than
this. (*Laws* 965b8-c6; cf. *Rep.* VI, 507b5-7)

The problem is, however, that in this third phase, all is not plain sailing
(as Plato would say)—either for the participants or, often enough, for
the reader, for in many of the dialogues this third phase seems to be
frustrated and left hanging. Sometimes, of course, this is not the case,
as, for example, with Socrates' definition of love (*Phaedr.* 265a6-b5; cf.
244a6ff.; 249d4-e4) or justice (*Rep.* IV, 443c9-e2), with Theaetetus'
definition of surd, or the Stranger's definition of sophist (*Soph.* 268c8-
d4). In these cases the definition is achieved through systematic
identification of that *dynamis* which differentiates the object of inquiry
from all else in terms of unique and essential properties. On other
occasions, however—as, for example, at the end of both the *Euthyphro*
and the *Meno*, and now again here in the *Theaetetus*—the effort at logos is
to all intents and purposes fruitless, and the dialogues themselves
apparent failures. According to the *kompsoteros* interpretation of a
dialogue as a complex inquiry simultaneously addressing both participants and readers, what we are really witnessing in these cases is rather
a question of contrast and interplay between the two levels, with the
participants taking what is said in one way, and the reader taking it (or
intended to take it) in another. And this is why the present study is
cautious about taking the apparently aporetic dialogues at face value.
On the contrary, these dialogues seem deliberately designed to
highlight for the reader the ambiguity of logos, challenging us to
discover for ourselves the deeper-level interpretation that is provided
in a dialogue's "hidden truth" (cf. *Theaet.* 155d10).[13] The problem is that
the effort to move from "many" to "one" will normally lead to
perplexity, because the *kompsoteros* criterion of dissimilarity among the
elements is deliberately exploited in such a way as to thwart any

temptation to mere addition, thereby encouraging us to search instead for an effectively generative combination that will result in a new and genuine whole. It will be instructive to look at some details here.

When pressed in the *Meno* for an account of "what virtue is," Meno happily launches into the familiar list of what, in his (unsupported) opinion, he judges to be examples of virtue:

> Why, there is no difficulty, Socrates, in telling. First of all, if you take the virtue of a man, it is easily stated that a man's virtue is this: that he be competent to manage the affairs of his city...Or take a woman's virtue...And the child has another virtue, one for the female, and one for the male; and there is another for elderly men, one if you like for freemen, and yet another for slaves. And there are very many other virtues besides, so that one cannot be at a loss to explain what virtue is. (*Meno* 71e1-72a2)

Socrates' reaction to being provided with "many" when they are seeking "one" precipitates, of course, the second step and the well-known illustrations in which he defines figure and color in such a way as to encompass the variety of particulars in a single formula. Similarly in the *Sophist*, when asked by the Athenian Stranger, "What exactly do we mean by 'image'?" Theaetetus replies: "Obviously we mean the images in water and in mirrors, and those in paintings too, and sculptures and all the other things of the same sort" (*Soph.* 239d6-8). Again, what are offered here are judgments of opinion about actual physical cases. These are the empirical "many"—the elements selected out from Theaetetus' own experience; the next step opens up the challenge to move beyond these many elements to that which binds them together. Thus, Socrates goes on to make clear that what they seek is "that which exists throughout all these things which you say are many but which you saw fit to call by a single name when you said 'image' of them all, as if they were one thing" (*Soph.* 240a4-6). The principle throughout is the same, for, as Socrates explains to Euthyphro, what is being sought in definition is "not one or two out of all the numerous actions that are holy, but something that is essentially one" (*Euth.* 6d9-11). In other words, it is through "seeing and bringing together in one idea the scattered particulars, that one may make clear by definition the particular thing he wishes to explain" (*Phaedr.* 249b7-c1). So too now, it is the same process that is illustrated for us here in the *Theaetetus*. Asked "what knowledge is," Theaetetus selects out from his experience a number of concrete instances, identified on the basis of his (as yet unsupported) opinion as examples of knowledge: "Geometry, and all those things you spoke of just now [astronomy, and harmony, and arithmetic (145d1-2)] and also cobblery and the other craftsmen's arts, each and all of these are nothing else but knowledge" (146c8-d2).

As usual, in a second step, Socrates responds to this move by pointing out that

> you are noble and generous, my friend, for when you are asked for one thing you give many, and a variety of things instead of a simple answer... the question we are asking is not how many objects or sorts of knowledge there are; we did not want to count them, but to find out what the thing itself is. (*Theaet.* 146d3-4, e7-10)

Sometimes Socrates is even more explicit in his hints that what we are really seeking is not just an aggregate, but rather a special kind of whole. Thus in the *Philebus* we are urged to collect together the multiplicity of instances as though they have been "torn and split apart" (*Phil.* 25a1-3). In the *Meno,* this image of a conceptual unity broken into instantiated concrete parts is further developed when Socrates jokingly draws an analogy with the parts of a broken plate, and goes on to urge Meno to stop "making many out of one" (by listing particular instantiations), but rather to "leave virtue whole and sound" (*Meno* 77a7-9). In order for elements to constitute a whole, however, they must according to *kompsoteros* theory meet certain conditions of "fitness" (see above, chapter 4). It will be important, therefore, to look more closely at the way in which the dialogues introduce these elements (i.e., the concrete instantiations that are to function as parts within the conceptual whole required by logos).

Testing the Dialogues:
Criteria for "fitness" of elements of logos

The first criterion for fitness required by *kompsoteros* theory (see above, chapter 4) was that the elements be *similar*. Confirmation of this requirement is not difficult to find; indeed, again and again Socrates will ask: What is the similarity in all these particular cases that justifies our calling them by the same name—whether the particulars in question are virtues (*Meno* 72c1-3), clays (*Theaet.* 147a1-c6), figures (*Meno* 73e3-75a8; *Phil.* 12e6-13a2), colors (*Meno* 74c5-d1; *Phil.* 12e3-6), images (*Soph.* 240a4-6), sophists (*Soph.* 232a1-6), or whatever?

The second *kompsoteros* criterion for fitness was, by contrast, *dissimilarity*. Thus in the *Meno*, the problem with moving from particular instances of figure as round, square, etc., to 'figure' as definable concept, is that round and square are antithetical to each other in just this sense: they do not lend themselves to being simply put together to yield a concept of 'round-square' or 'square-circle'. Hence Meno's difficulty when Socrates asks him, "Even though they are the contrary of each other, tell me what this is which embraces round as well as rectangular" (*Meno* 74d6-8)—which response is then of course intended as the model for Meno's definition of virtue, because that too must embrace opposite instantiations (such as the governing of others on the one hand, and the obeying of others on the other: 73c9-d4). This pattern, in which it is recognized that, although no more round than square, figure itself must embrace both, is in fact a familiar one. It is often enough, after all, the point of departure for inquiry, as in the *Charmides*, when *sōphrosynē* is recognized to be no more slowness than quickness (*Charm.* 160b9-d3), or in the *Republic*, when justice is seen to be no more the returning, than the refusal to return, what has been received (*Rep.* I, 331c1-8). The issue of color, which Socrates had noted in the *Meno*, is picked up again later in the *Philebus:*

> Insofar as every particular color is a color they will be all the same, yet we all recognize that black is not only different from white, but is its exact opposite. And so too, figure is like figure; they are all one in kind; but the parts of the kind are in some instances absolutely opposed to each other, and in other cases there is endless variety of difference; and we can find many other examples of such relations. (*Phil.* 12e3-13a3)

The *Philebus* goes on to develop this point in the context of finding a single definition of pleasure, pointing out that "pleasure has various aspects...she takes on all sorts of shapes which are even, in a way, unlike each other. And would not any person who said these two kinds of pleasure were like each other be rightly regarded as a fool?" (*Phil.* 12c4-d6). Already here in the *Theaetetus* we have been prepared for this sort of opposition among particular instances when, in first looking to identify knowledge, Theaetetus points, on the one hand (as we have just noted), to cases of the most abstract and theoretic kinds of knowledge (mathematics, etc.) and on the other, to the most concrete and practical kinds (cobblery, etc.) (146c7-d2)—an opposition which we now recognize to be ingredient in the *kompsoteros* pattern.

The third condition which, according to the *kompsoteros* view, seemed to be necessary for the "fitness" of elements was a kind of mutual *relativity*. This condition has already been met in our various illustrations from the dialogues: for example, black and white in the context of color, governing and obeying in the context of virtue, practical and theoretic in the context of knowledge—all are mutually relative in a way that is comparable to that of the active and passive motions that constitute the original elements of the physical world (*Theaet.* 156a5-7).

All the examples seem, moreover, to meet the fourth *kompsoteros* criterion. No element—whether a particular action, object, or event—is, in isolation, of any use to mind in its effort to generate logos. For it is only in the comparison and combination of different elements that that which is one and definable emerges as an abstract complex embracing a variety of concrete instances. By contrast (meeting the fifth criterion) there is a sense in which, if properly matched with other fitting elements, each, while remaining the same, nevertheless exhibits a kind of power or *dynamis* to become something more than it is in isolation— just as the twisted threads become warp and woof, the sounds or squiggles become letters, the lines become the sides of a square, and so on.

This brings us to the sixth—and probably the most puzzling—of the criteria. For, as suggested earlier in the case of the linguist separating out letters as vowels and consonants, or the weaver separating out hard and soft threads as warp and woof, there seems to be a strange condition required. In order in the first place to recognize squiggles or sounds as having the power to become letters and so to generate a word, or in order to recognize twisted thread as having the power to become warp and woof and so to produce woven fabric, it would seem that—although neither word nor web has as yet been generated—some idea or vision of what a word or web might be must nevertheless, in some degree, be already present to the mind. So too it would likewise seem that, in order to discriminate particular instances of color or figure or virtue or knowledge or whatever, we must in the first place have some idea or vision of what color, figure, virtue, or knowledge might be. This, of course, was the point of Meno's dilemma. Since the whole is not given (that is, after all, why it is the object of search), it seems clear that one does not initially know the whole, but must on the contrary first know the parts (the *many*) as the condition of ever coming to a knowledge of the whole. (This is the empiricist alternative, and is represented by the wax block model.) On the other hand, however, since the particular elements can be picked out and identified *as* elements or parts of the thing in question only in light of some prior knowledge of that thing as whole, it seems that one cannot initially know the parts, but on the contrary must already first have knowledge of the thing (the *one*), as condition of ever coming to know the parts. (This opposite alternative seems to be represented by the aviary model's knowledge of unitary entities.) If this dilemma were indeed to hold, then, as Meno points out, learning, and with it all inquiry, would be impossible. It is to break this bind that Plato proposes an epistemologically prior condition which permits us, while not *fully* to know the whole which we seek, yet to have sufficient awareness that we are nevertheless able to pick out the relevant parts. To acknowledge such a power of recognition (re-cognition) successfully resolves the dilemma of "complete knowledge or complete ignorance," thereby making room for opinion as a state "between," and thereby in turn reinstating the possibility of learning and philosophical inquiry (*Meno* 81d4-5; 86b7-c2). (For a discussion of the argument, see above, chapter 5.)

Testing the Dialogues:
Criteria for genuineness of emergent logos

The criteria found by *kompsoteros* theory to be necessary for the genuineness, or real existence, of the emergent product seem also to be met in Socrates' search for logos as this is depicted in the dialogues. First, since genuine existence or being (*ta onta*) is assimilated to power (*Soph.* 247d8-e4; cf. *Phaedr.* 270d4-7), a genuinely emergent entity must itself exhibit a power (a character or property) not evidenced by its elements. Clearly, this criterion is met in the case of logos, where the abstract or formal quality of the definable concept constitutes it a radically different kind in a radically different dimension of reality from that of the objects and events of the concrete, three-dimensional world. Plato frequently talks of this kind of formal reality as "being" (*ousia*), in contrast to the "becoming" (*genesis*) of the physical world, and its genuineness in terms of emergent properties is a theme familiar to any reader of the dialogues. Thus, formal essence as apprehended by mind—in logos and as logos—is "one" in contrast to the elements which are "many"; it is the abstract object of thought, in contrast to the elements as concrete objects of the senses; it is unmixed and unchanging, in contrast to the elements as impure and changing reflections or manifestations of the formal reality. What the *kompsoteros* theory of emergence does is simply to cast in a slightly different light those familiar assertions from dialogues like the *Phaedo* and the *Republic*—for example, Socrates' insistence that

> the absolute essence of which we give an account is uniform and exists by itself, remaining the same and never in any way admitting of any change [in contrast to] the many things . . . which bear the same names but which are, in direct opposition to these, constantly changing in themselves, unlike each other, and never the same . . . And you can see and touch them, and perceive them by the other senses, whereas the things which are always the same can be grasped only by reason. (*Phaedo* 78d1-79a4; cf. *Rep.* VI, 479a1-b2; 507b5-10)

This contrast is echoed in the distinction between becoming (*genesis*) and being (*ousia*) that is marked in the *Timaeus* (27d6-28a4), and in later dialogues like the *Sophist* (e.g., 248a7) and *Philebus* (e.g., 54a5-6)—a distinction on the one hand paralleled in the kind of knowledge appropriate for the apprehension of each (e.g., *Phil.* 58a2-59c6; cf. *Stat.*

258d4-e5; Tim. 51d3-52a7), and on the other, embodied in the kinds of linguistic expressions that can embody each.

According to this approach, then, the move from opinion to logos is seen as a productive act strictly analogous to the move from perception to opinion. In opinion, the opinable object emerges as genuinely novel product—one, three-dimensional, enduring—through a generative combination of perceptual elements that are, by contrast, many, phenomenal, ephemeral. Here now, analogously, as the product of reasoning or *dianoia*,[14] logos emerges as a radically novel whole—one, abstract, and unchanging—through a generative combination of elements that are, by contrast, many, concrete, and changing.

The second condition specified for genuine emergence requires that the new product have the power to become now itself in turn an element or "power" to interact with other elements so as together to generate an even more comprehensive whole in a yet richer dimension of reality. The fulfillment of this requirement will (very shortly) lead us into the analysis of knowledge itself.

Summary

According to *kompsoteros* theory, then, we can summarize the meaning of logos—both as it is pursued by Socrates within the dialogues, and as it is presented by Plato in the form of dialogue. To give, or receive, an account[15] requires that we take cumulatively all three interpretations of logos proposed by Theaetetus, so that explanation or logos in the enriched sense that Plato envisages consists of that now familiar threefold method of inquiry, "a gift of gods to men, tossed down from some divine source" (*Phil.* 16c5-6). In a first phase we confront ordinary loose usage in which terms (*onomata*) occur as fuzzy images in the flow or "course" of speech (an "infinite" which corresponds to the first interpretation of logos); a second phase will then involve an enumeration of instances as elements (the enumeration of a "many" which corresponds to the second interpretation of logos); and a third phase will finally seek to define the abstract entity in terms of its emergent (unique and essential) properties (a "one" which corresponds to the third interpretation of logos). Such a method of inquiry describes a cognitive sequence in which we are led from an initial phase concerned with images, linguistic images in the flow of speech and phenomenal images in the flow of perception (compare Theaetetus' first definition of knowledge as perception), to a second phase in which true opinion judges concrete entities and events (compare Theaetetus' second definition of knowledge as true opinion), to a phase in which reason, through logos, argues for definitions of abstract entities (compare

Theaetetus' third definition of knowledge as true opinion and logos).
As I understand him, these three phases correspond to those that Plato
diagrams as the first three sections of his divided line in the *Republic:* a
first phase in which a kind of conjectural picturing (*eikasia: Rep.* VI,
511e2; VII, 534a1) apprehends images of the physical world which
appear as "shadows and reflections in water" (*Rep.* VI, 509e1-510a1) and
which can apparently be "named" (515b5; cf. 516c9-d2, e8-9); a second
phase which, as opinion (508d8; 510a9; 534a1-4), apprehends with belief
(*pistis*) the three-dimensional things of the physical world (510a5-6);
and a third phase concerned with abstract intelligibles apprehended
conceptually and tested for coherence through *dianoia* (510d5-511a1).

According to the *kompsoteros* theory of emergence, these phases are
to be understood as successive combinations of elements that "fit
together" so as to generate increasingly ordered or "rational" complexes. Moreover, this successive ordering by mind or soul is achieved
through and expressed in successively complex logoi—from logos as
the flow of words through which the first cognitive elements, apprehended in perception, can simply be named; to logos as statement
through which, at the next cognitive level, concrete objects and events
can be objectively determined through opinion and tested for coherence in experience; to logos as definition through which abstract
concepts can be hypothetically determined and tested for theoretic
coherence in dianoetic argument.

Standing back finally to evaluate the *kompsoteros* expectations, it
would seem that not only do the dialogues present themselves as
consistent with the *kompsoteros* approach, but they may in fact be seen
as offering a relatively detailed elaboration of *kompsoteros* theory. A
slightly expanded version of the earlier diagram might be helpful at
this point (fig. 7).

LOGOS IN SOCRATES "DREAM"

What at this point in the dialogue is first arresting and exciting, then
puzzling and challenging, is that, enigmatically, it seems to be just this
same *kompsoteros* vision which Plato now has Socrates first express,
then apparently refute, in his notorious "dream" (*onar*):

> The primary elements...each alone by itself can only be named...but
> none of the primal elements can be expressed in a statement; they can only
> be named, for they have only a name;...and thus the elements are the
> objects of perception only.

By contrast, however,

Figure 7.
Patterns of Successive Emergence: Ontological Epistemological,
and Linguistic

	Successive ontological entities, APPREHENDED THROUGH ⟶	Successive epistemological operations, AND EXPRESSED IN ⟶	Successive linguistic expression:
Starting point: discriminated into: Original elements, i.e.:	Continuum of motion Swift motions of sensibles	Continuum of motion Swift motions of sensings	Continuum of sound Letters or sounds
	[Strictly speaking, these simply occur as mere motions or noises.]		
First level of emergence	Phenomenal images ("private" and "two-dimensional")	Perceptual impressions ("infallible" occurrences)	Words (for a given society "meaningful")
	[As the first level actually employing language, these can be linguistically identified, or "named."]		
Second level of emergence	Objects and events (in the "public" and "3-D" world)	Opinion or belief (that can be true or false)	Statements (that can be true or false)
Third level of emergence	Abstract entities in the intelligible world	Logos/*dianoia* i.e., reasoning (that can be sound or unsound)	Theoretic arguments (that can be sound or unsound)

the things composed of these elements are themselves interwoven complexes, so their names are combined to generate a logos—for the interweaving of names is the essence of logos...As the products of combination, these then become the objects of knowledge and rational speech and true opinion. (201e1-202b7)

In light of *kompsoteros* theory as it has gradually been unfolded for us through the dialogue, this statement of doctrine in Socrates' dream comes (with a shock of recognition) as a succinct summary of the theory of emergent logos[16]—but then seems to be immediately, and disconcertingly, snatched away again. Whatever are we to make of this? It is certainly understandable that, in general, scholarly commentary represents bewilderment as to why the dream should be introduced at all, sometimes a passing wonder as to why it should be introduced at just this point, a conviction that it bears little or no relation to anything that has gone before or follows after, and an almost universal assumption that, whatever the purpose of its introduction, it is at any rate decisively refuted.[17] Floundering in confusion as to what is going on, we might for a start grasp at two straws. First, we ought perhaps to recall an important insight from the beginning of the dialogue. For what we were there led to understand was that meaning is elusive, language fragile, and accounts of doctrine clothed with ambiguity. As itself a verbal formulation, therefore, this "dream" account can also be expected to prove ambiguous, with surface and deeper-level interpretations to be disentangled. Second, there is the metaphor of "dreaming" itself. It will be appropriate, for a moment, to consider possible reasons for Plato's introducing this final statement of *kompsoteros* doctrine in the form of a "dream" before turning (in the next chapter) to cross-examine it.

Socrates' dream here in the *Theaetetus* is, of course, not the only occasion on which a dream is introduced into the conversation of a dialogue.[18] The first point, therefore, reiterating the fact that talk of a "dream" should evoke echoes of similar Socratic "dreams" in other dialogues, suggests that the reader should be thereby alerted to caution in what follows.

References to dreams and dreaming occur throughout the dialogues. Sometimes these references involve a derogatory contrast with the waking state (e.g., *Lysis* 218c8; *Rep.* V, 476c4-8; VII, 520c6-7; IX, 576b4-5; *Tim.* 52b3-c2; *Laws* 969b5-6; even here at *Theaet.* 158b1-4); but as far as I can discover, the deliberate introduction of material as being the *content* of a "dream" is invariably significant. In this context a "dream" represents a kind of divine or oracular statement which (like the Delphic oracle itself: *Apol.* 21bff.) is the vehicle of important, if "riddling," truth; at the same time, being susceptible of misinterpretation, it requires cross-examination if it is to yield up its true content and relevance.[19] That this is what Plato intends by the deliberate introduction of "dream" material seems to be confirmed by his discussion of divine inspiration in the *Timaeus*. Talking of the gift of divination, which "in some degree may lay hold on truth," he continues

No man achieves true and inspired divination except when the power of his intelligence is fettered in sleep . . . But it belongs to a man when in his

right mind to recollect and ponder the things spoken in dreams [*onar*]...
and by means of reasoning to discern about them wherein they are
significant. (*Tim.* 71e2-72a1; cf. *Symp.* 203a3-4; *Soph.* 266b9-c6; *Laws* 800a2-3)

Such an interpretation accords, moreover with Plato's representation
of Socrates' own response to dreams as being of divine origin—hence
to be taken seriously and pressed for their hidden meaning (e.g., *Crito*
44a5-b4; *Phaedo* 60d8-e7). What should be even more sobering, however,
is the fact that in two other dialogues, at just such comparable points of
climax as we find here in the *Theaetetus*, it is the introduction of a
"dream" (*onar*) which provides the crucial clue and turns the dialogue
in the direction of Plato's desired conclusion. Thus in the *Charmides*,
after the long and tortuous examination of *epistēmē epistēmēs* shows it
to be—on Critias' interpretation—empty and worthless, Socrates
moves in to point the direction in which one might properly seek that
knowledge which will constitute virtue:

> I expect I am talking nonsense; but still one is bound to consider what
> occurs to one and not idly ignore it...Hear, then, my dream [*onar*]...
> [He proceeds to show the inadequacy of mere knowledge, as such, as far as
> happiness or virtue is concerned, and concludes] you have all this time
> been dragging me round and round, while concealing the fact that the life
> according to knowledge does not make us do well and be happy, not even
> if it be of all the other knowledges together, but only if it is of this single one
> concerning good and evil. (*Charm.* 173a3-174c3)

And so we are directed to the final (and ultimately illuminating)
account of *sōphrosyne*. So too in the *Philebus*, when the inquiry seems to
have become bogged down in a kind of either-or impasse, Socrates
breaks in:

> I think some god has given me a vague recollection...I remember now
> having heard long ago in a dream [*onar*], or perhaps when I was awake,
> some talk about pleasure and wisdom to the effect that neither of the two
> is good, but some third thing, different from them and better than both
> (*Phil.* 20b3-9)

—which inspiration then defines the direction of the remainder of the
dialogue. So too, finally, here in the *Theaetetus* we seem to have a
repetition of the same pattern. At just that crucial moment when the
inquiry seems to be drawing to its close after a long and frustratingly
futile exercise, Plato makes exactly the same move and introduces "the
dream of Socrates." Let us look more closely for a moment at this latter
comparison.

At this point in the *Theaetetus* it has just been suggested that some combination of true opinion and logos is necessary in order to yield *epistēmē*; in the *Philebus* the dream suggests that some combination of pleasure and *phronesis* is necessary in order to produce the best and happiest life. The *Philebus* then goes on to develop at great length a theory of combination which contrasts the mere addition of components (yielding only an aggregate, or sum of would-be parts) with an effective mixture in which the parts, "made commensurable and harmonious" (*Phil.* 25e1), actually achieve the kind of coherence that transforms them from a mere sum of parts into a new and genuine whole. For "everybody knows that . . . any compound, however made, which lacks measure and proportion, must necessarily destroy its components and first of all itself; for it is in truth no compound, but an uncompounded jumble, and is always a misfortune to those who possess it" (*Phil.* 64d7-e3). Echoing the concern of the *Theaetetus*, it is claimed that out of such an act of "proper combination" (*orthē koinōnia: Phil.* 25e7) are generated *both* the objects of knowledge in the world ("all the beautiful things in our world") *and* the knowledge in the soul by which they may be known ("the many glorious and beautiful things in the soul") (*Phil.* 26b1-7).

The original introduction of this discussion of components and compounds in the *Philebus* seems to leave both Protarchus and Philebus as bewildered as the introduction of Socrates' "dream" about elements and complexes leaves most of its readers:[20]

> *Protarchus:* I think, Philebus, that what Socrates has said is excellent.
> *Philebus:* So do I; it is excellent in itself, but why has he said it now, to us, and what purpose is there in it? (*Phil.* 17e7-18a2)

Perhaps Socrates' response (which, as in the *Theaetetus*, depends on illustration from the letters of the alphabet: *Phil.* 18b3-d2) would stand equally well for the *Theaetetus*:

> *Socrates:* Do you mean, Philebus, that you do not see what this has to do with the question?
> *Philebus:* Yes; that is what Protarchus and I have been trying to discover for a long time.
> *Socrates:* Really, have you been trying, as you say, for a long time to discover it, when it was close to you all the while? (*Phil.* 18d6-e1)

The next chapter will explore the possibility that the point of Socrates' dream, "so close to us all the while," is meant to provide an important clue for our coming to understand the nature of knowledge—both the objects of knowledge and the knowing itself.[21] This challenge now precipitates us into the final consideration of knowledge as such.

EIGHT

"...WHAT KNOWLEDGE (*EPISTĒMĒ*) REALLY IS"
145e9, 146e9-10, 151d4

With our initiation into the *kompsoteros* mysteries of perception, true opinion, and logos, the ground has now been carefully prepared for the denouement of the dialogue. For in the generation first, of perception, then of opinion, and now of logos, mind or soul has in each case first discriminated out, then combined, elements whose mutual fitness is proved in the emergence of a new product in a radically different dimension—thus, on direct analogy with geometry, rendering increasingly commensurable and rational what was originally incommensurable and irrational (e.g., 148b1-2; 202b5-7; see also appendix A). Following with Socrates along this, his "beloved roadway" (*Phil.* 16b5-6), we have been led to expect that it will likewise be in a proper combination of fitting elements that knowledge itself will be generated as a genuinely emergent whole.

Like so much else in the *Theaetetus*, this last section seems, however, to be anything but straightforward. It is introduced by Socrates' notoriously puzzling "dream" theory, proceeds through a careful and seemingly definitive refutation of that theory, and concludes with an acknowledgment of apparent failure in the joint quest for an account of knowledge. As already anticipated, this chapter will propose a rather different interpretation, arguing first, that what Socrates' dream offers is in fact a rēsumē of *kompsoteros* theory; second, that the apparent refutation is not in reality refutation at all but rather clarification of, and support for, the dream theory; and third, that the dialogue does not fail, but is instead a dazzling, though subtle, success.

SOCRATES' "DREAM" AS RÉSUMÉ OF *KOMPSOTEROS* THEORY

The "dream," it will be recalled, is introduced in order to expand on Theaetetus' memory, according to which he had heard it said that knowledge is true opinion with logos, and that things of which there is logos are knowable, whereas those of which there is no logos are unknowable (201c8-d3).[1] The reader gradually becomes aware, however, that, according to Socrates' version of the "dream," the substance of the assertion has actually become a generalized statement of the *kompsoteros* doctrine of emergence—and lest we fail to recognize it as an echo of that theory, Socrates makes a point of using exactly the same rare term to focus our attention on its central claim: "that point which seems to be the subtlest [*kompsotata*]: the assertion that the elements are unknowable but the complex knowable" (202d10-e1).

According to the *kompsoteros* account, it will be recalled, the starting point of knowledge is simply motion: swift streamings of subjective and objective sensibility, in whose productive interaction sensation is generated (156d6-157a3). In perception, soul discriminates out for conscious focus certain appearings from the flow of sensation—visual, audible, tactile, etc. These, as part of our very being (160c7-8) and given by nature (157b6), constitute the primary elements of our knowing—and therefore of the world as we know it. In the act of perception, soul consciously and "infallibly" (160c7-9; 171d9-e3) experiences these sense-occurrences, and using language to mark the experience, compels the fleeting occurrence as it were to stand still (157b5, b7; 183a7) in order that each be distinguished and identified by a name (cf. 156b2-7). Beyond the unadorned naming, however, nothing can be asserted: in the simple act of perceptual awareness, no reference beyond the instantaneous occurrence can be made—neither to situate it with respect to other such occurrences, as *"this* soft," "red *alone,"* or whatever (for that would require reflection and comparison beyond perception as such: 185a4-6), nor to assert for it any kind of corresponding objective "being" (for judgment involving existential reference requires a level of reflection that will project us beyond perception: 186a2-e5). These, then, are for the *kompsoteroi* the primary elements of knowledge: nameable occurrences which are the object of perception only.

On examination, however, we come to realize that it is this same account of perception that is being echoed in Socrates' parallel account (originally introduced as secret truth requiring initiation, here reintroduced in equally cryptic terms as a "dream" requiring interpretation). Socrates recalls "having heard certain people say" that

> the primary elements, as it were, of which we and all else are composed admit of no logos; for each alone by itself can only be named, and no qualification can be added, neither that it is nor that is is not, for that would at once be attributing to it existence or nonexistence, whereas we must attribute nothing to it if we are to speak of that itself alone. Indeed, not even "itself," or "that," or "each," or "alone," or "this,"...must be added...

> But none of the primary elements can be expressed in a logos; they can only be named, for they have only a name...Thus the elements are objects...only of perception. (201e1-202b6)

Back in the earlier version of the *kompsoteros* account, we were eventually led beyond perception to a different dimension of the cognitive process. For that activity of soul in which the perceptual elements are reflectively compared (*pros allēla krinein:* 186b8), reckoned in judgment (*analogismata:* 186c2-3), and effectively related (*syllogismō:* 186d3) was presented as an operation which Socrates distinguished radically from that of perception (186d7-e10). Judgments about those "objects" which, combining many perceptual elements in a single complex, are now said to *exist* (186b6, c3; 187a6), are given the name of "opinion" (187a7-8); and, since in opinion the objects themselves are both generated and apprehended as complexes made up of perceptual elements, so the expression of that opinion will take the form of linguistic complexes made up of such linguistic entities as those that originally named the elements.

When, now, this earlier *kompsoteros* account comes to be reiterated in Socrates' dream version of the theory, we will find that the counterpart to this second phase of cognitive development similarly involves combination and the generation of complexes:

> ...the things composed from the combination of these primary elements being themselves complexes, the names are likewise woven together to generate a logos. Thus...the combinations of the elements are objects of cognition and expression and true opinion. (202b2-7)

This telescoped account has thus brought us to logos, and to the threshold where cognition will at last be brought to completion in knowledge. For, just as the complex that is generated from a proper combination of perceptual elements is grasped in opinion, is referred to physical reality, and is expressed in (true or false) statements, so too analogously (see above, chapter 7) the complex that is generated from a proper combination of judgments as elements is grasped in *dianoia*, is referred to concepts as definable abstract entities, and is expressed in logos as theoretic and reasoned account. When finally right opinion, operating in the realm of the practical, is combined with true logos in the realm of theoretical structuring, then perhaps—that is to say, if the combination is genuinely generative—knowledge as emergent product may be brought to birth in the soul. All this is now summarized in Socrates' "dream":

When, therefore, a man acquires without logos a true opinion about something, then his mind has the truth about it, but he still has no knowledge; for he who cannot give and receive an account is without knowledge of that thing. When, however, he grasps the logos as well, then he may possibly become all that I have said, and may be perfect in knowledge (*epistēmē*). (202b8-c5)

What poses a difficulty for this proposed interpretation of Socrates' "dream," and indeed lays down a challenge to the whole thesis of this study, is of course the fact that the "dream" (and therefore *kompsoteros* theory with it) is in the ensuing exchange apparently attacked and definitely refuted. Where then does this leave my thesis?

REFUTATION OF SOCRATES' "DREAM"

If there is one thread of warning that runs through this dialogue, from beginning to end, it is that verbal formulations as such are shot through with ambiguity. Since every major statement in the dialogue has proved to be susceptible of both true and false interpretations, we must surely not be surprised now to find this third definition to be vulnerable in the same way. A final task of the dialogue will therefore presumably involve the kind of purification which, through cross-examination, will discard the false, in order to retain the true meaning of this last definition.[2] Our awareness of this dual stance—involving, on the one hand, the *kompsoteros* affirmation that knowledge is to be understood as an emergent state generated in interactive combination of true opinion and logos as its constitutive and fitting elements, and, on the other, the recognition that simply to state that claim inevitably leaves it vulnerable to the ambiguities of interpretation and misinterpretation—finds echo in the nuances of Socrates' remarks immediately following the elaboration of the "dream": Why yes, of course true opinion and logos will now constitute the elements of knowledge—but can the meaning, even of such a simple formulation, be unambiguously clear?

Socrates: Are you satisfied then, and do you state it in this way, that true opinion together with logos is knowledge?
Theaetetus: Precisely.
Socrates: Can it be, Theaetetus, that we now, in this casual manner, have found out on this day what many wise men have long been seeking, and have grown grey in the search?
Theaetetus: I, at any rate, Socrates, think our present statement is good.
Socrates: Probably this particular statement is so; for what knowledge could there still be apart from logos and right opinion? (202c7-d7)

As I understand Socrates, it is this double anticipation that provides the clue to the remainder of the conversation—and to the otherwise enigmatic conclusion of the dialogue. For the entire thrust of the inquiry has led us to the irony of a position in which we recognize, on the one hand, the truth of the claim that the proper combination of true opinion and logos will indeed generate knowledge, and, on the other, the deceptive ambiguity of any linguistic formulation—and specifically, of this statement itself, that *knowledge is true opinion together with logos*. The cross-examination that ensues will therefore proceed to purify of false or inadequate interpretations not only the conception of logos as fitting element (206c7-210a9: this we have already explored in chapter 7), but especially the notion of combination, or "coming together," as it applies to elements which combine to form a complex (202d10-206b12). In short, the challenge that confronts us is to discover "what is *meant* by the doctrine that the most perfect knowledge arises from the coming together of logos and true opinion [*to meta doxēs alēthous logon pros-genomenon*]?" (206c3-5).

The first phase of Socrates' cross-examination of this final definition will therefore focus on the now familiar notion of generative combination—the generation of a complex, or whole, as genuinely emergent from its elements (which thereby have become no longer simply elements, but now parts of the generated whole). Thus, although Socrates is satisfied that this final definition itself is fine (*kalos:* 202d4-6), the trickier problem is its commitment to emergent properties (202d8-e1)—although this *kompsotata* assertion is one which Socrates himself "decidedly" shares (203a3-6). It is, of course, an affirmation that is supported by the specific example chosen to illustrate and reinforce the "dream" theory: the emergence of meaning in a syllable that is composed only of meaningless letters.[3] For although a syllable is analyzable in terms of its component letters, it is nevertheless not reducible to those mere sounds. In other words, the syllable is, and yet is not, just its letters.

This simultaneous insistence *both* that there is nothing else besides the elements, *and* that there is much else besides, has stood throughout as a paradox—resolved, however (for those initiated) in the *kompsoteros* theory of emergent generation. For those uninitiated into the mysteries, by contrast,[4] there are (as we already saw in the case of the dice illustration) two distinct ways of denying the theory of emergence. For whereas the *kompsoteroi* seek, on the one hand, to avoid such sheer sameness that the generated product would be seen as *simply the same* *as*, and therefore reducible to, its elements, and, on the other, to avoid such sheer difference that the generated product would be seen as *radically different from*, and therefore not even analyzable into, its elements, by contrast, one might expect those who have not been initiated into the mysteries of *kompsoteros* doctrine to fall into one or other of these rejected positions—maintaining *either* reducibility to a plurality of elements (because the generated whole has been taken as simply the same as its elements), *or* the irreducibility of simple unity (because the generated whole has been taken as radically different from its elements). Failure to understand the "mysteries" of emergent generation, and the consequent blindness to the necessity of both-and, can therefore only leave the uninitiated stranded on the horns of just such a dilemma, so that for them, either

a) the generated product is nothing other than, in the sense of being wholly reducible to, its constitutive elements—so that, if the elements are not f, then the generated product cannot be f; or

b) the generated product is radically other than its elements, in the sense that it is an irreducible, indivisible, and unanalyzable unity.

This is the argument that becomes, of course, the dilemma of Socrates' "dream."

As should come as no surprise, the section that follows develops this dilemma along the now familiar eristic lines:

PURPORTED ARGUMENT: "Refutation" of Socrates' Dream

1. *Either a:*   "Shall we say that the complex is its elements—two elements, or if there be more than two, then all of them?" (203c4-5)

   or b: "or is it a single idea that has arisen from their combination" (203c5-6)

2. *If a:*   "if the complex is nothing other than, and therefore simply the sum of, its parts, so that everything that has parts consists of parts," then:
   "There is no difference between the sum and the whole; if there are parts of anything, the whole and the sum will be all the parts...if the complex is the same as its elements" (204a7-8, e3; 205a7-9, b2)

   then: if the elements are not f, then the complex cannot be f, for:
   "being the same as the elements, it is equally knowable with them.
   How could it be that knowing neither of the elements, he knows them both together?...yet, if knowledge of each element is necessary before one can know both,

then he who is ever to know a complex must certainly know the elements first" (205b2-3; 203d4-5, d7-9)

therefore not-c: i.e., on assumption *a,* the complex, along with its elements, is unknowable, and the dream theory of *kompsoteros* emergence is false:
"it will have run away and vanished, monstrous and absurd" (203d10, d6)

3. *If b:*   if the complex is radically other than, and therefore not even analyzable into, its parts, so that:
"the complex is not its elements but a single idea that has arisen from them, having a single form of its own, different from its elements" (203e3-5)
"and it is the same with words and all other things" (204a2-3)
"so there must be no parts of it" (204a5)
"and the complex would be an indivisible idea" (205c2)

then: analytic explanation is ruled out, and any complex therefore becomes, by definition, rationally unknowable, for:
"[just as] there can be no logos of the primary elements because each is not composite [*asyntheton*]...and for this reason it is irrational [*alogon*] and unknowable" (205c5-10)
"[so now] the complex falls into the same class with the elements, if it has no parts and is a single form" (205d4-5)

therefore not-c: i.e., on assumption *b,* the complex proves to be as unknowable as any element and the dream theory of *kompsoteros* emergence is likewise false

4. *Therefore not-c:*   The dream theory of emergence is false

By way of conclusion, the argument is finally summarized:

If a: "if the complex is a plurality of elements and is a whole of which the elements are parts, then the complex and the elements are equally knowable and expressible, if all the parts were found to be the same as the whole. But:

if b: if the complex is one and indivisible, then complex and likewise the element are equally irrational and unknowable

Therefore   we must not accept the statement of anyone [such as the *kompsoteroi*] who says that the complex is knowable and expressible, but the element is not" (205d7-e3)

Thus to accept what we now recognize as an eristic version of the argument (see above, chapter 5) is to rule out both elements and complexes as possible objects of knowledge. But, insofar as everything is either simple or complex, this in turn rules out everything whatever as object of knowledge—and, to that extent, knowledge itself has been rendered impossible. In other words, just as the eristic version of the earlier arguments purported to prove the impossibility of generation and the impossibility of language, so now this eristic argument purports to prove the impossibility of knowledge. Strangely enough, in spite of his earlier initiation into the theory of emergence, Theaetetus— despite one brave but unsustained effort[5]—seems prepared to accept this argument at face value, i.e.:

1. *Either a or b*
2. *If a then not-c*
3. *If b then not-c*
4. *Therefore not-c*

It is true that Plato does represent Theaetetus as somewhat uneasy at this conclusion (maybe as a warning to the reader?), for in acquiescing in this conclusion, he has him add, "—if we are convinced by this argument" (205e8). Nevertheless, what Theaetetus does not seem to recognize (in terms either of logic or of earlier *kompsoteros* criticism of the uninitiated) is that the hidden significance of this argument (as we have seen) lies not in the fact that it disproves *c*, for of course it does not, but rather in the fact that it allows us to deny the original disjunction (see chapter 5). In other words, all that is needed to escape the horns of the dilemma is a rejection of the uninitiates' assumption that the disjunction "either *a* or *b*" is exhaustive. Taken in this light, the hidden *kompsoteros* argument stands:

1. *c:*   *kompsoteros* theory of emergent generation (introduced on the authority first, of *kompsoteros* initiation, and second, of Socrates' "dream")
2. *Either a or b*
3. *if a, then not-c*
4. *therefore not-a*

5. *if b, then not-c*
6. *therefore not-b*

7. *Therefore not (either a or b)*

As I am reading it, therefore, the so-called refutation of Socrates' dream should be understood as a *reductio, not* of the dream theory, but only of the eristic disjunction—which I understand the dream theory (echoing *kompsoteros* insistence throughout) to be also denying. According to this approach, then, the hidden *kompsoteros* argument of the so-called refutation should be read in the following way:

REAL ARGUMENT OF "REFUTATION": *reductio of the one-many disjunction*

1. *c:*	knowledge is possible—in the sense that there are objects of knowledge (i.e. knowable complexes)	

2. *either a:*   a complex is ultimately many,
i.e., it is merely the sum of, and therefore the same as, its elements (203c4-5)

or b: a complex is a simple unity,
i.e., different from its elements (203c5-6)

3. *if a:*   if a complex is merely the sum of, and therefore the same as, its elements, it will be equally irrational and unknowable, (203d4-9; 205b2-3)

then not-c: then there will be no knowable complexes (i.e. no objects of knowledge)—so that in this sense knowledge is not possible (203d7-10; 205d5-10)

4. *therefore not-a*   [by implication, if not for Theaetetus, then at least for the reader]

5. *if b:*   if a complex is simply one, being a single form different from the elements (203e3-5; 204a5)
it will be an unanalyzable unity, and so irrational and unknowable (205c2-10; d4-5; e1-3)

then not-c: (205e6-7)

6. *Therefore not-b* [again, by implication]

7. *Therefore not-(either a or b)*

Recognizing the characteristic pattern, we should realize that the hidden argument opens up to the simultaneous *both-and* and *neither-nor* of emergent generation. Far from being impaled on the horns of a dilemma, the dream theory (to use Plato's colorful imagery) allows us to slip through between both at once (*Soph.* 251a1-3). Like the Minoan bull dancers who, grasping both horns at once, soar exquisitely into escape beyond them, so in the dream theory, grasping both disjuncts at once, we similarly soar to escape beyond reach of the *reductio*. In other words, we recognize that the complex will on the one hand be

neither   simply the same as its elements, in the sense of nothing other than the mere sum of those elements (for then the complex could be *f* only if the elements were *f*),

| *nor* | simply different from its elements, in the sense of a single absolute unity unanalyzable into those elements (for then it would not be susceptible of rational analysis). |

On the other hand, it will nevertheless be

| *both* | "the same as" its elements, in the sense of being analyzable into those elements |
| *and* | "different from" its elements, in the sense of not being reducible to those elements. |

Against the background of the *kompsoteros* doctrine of emergence, the real argument is thus seen to be defending the possibility of generation—including the generation of knowledge. Thus we have come full circle back to the parallel argument implied in Socrates' dice illustration (see chapter 5), and to Theaetetus' wonder which precipitated the sophisticated version of "the mysteries" of generation in the first place. In fact, we now see that the whole thrust of the dialogue, from the introductory discussion about surds and matchmaking midwives, has prepared us for just this interpretation of Socrates' "dream."[6]

THE ACCOUNT OF KNOWLEDGE

Approached from the viewpoint proposed in this paper, Socrates' "dream"—together with its apparent refutation—can now be seen as providing the clue for finally understanding the nature of knowledge, the quest of the whole dialogue. Not only has the dream provided a final résumé of *kompsoteros* theory, but the apparent refutation has offered the clarification needed to understand its power as well as its pitfalls. In short, the argument has enabled us to assert the possibility of knowledge and objects of knowledge; moreover, it has explained what must be the case for there to be either. For on analogy with the syllable-complex, each must now be understood as a whole that is analyzable in terms of, but not reducible to, its formal unity and material plurality.[7] In thus playing off the either-or of sameness and difference, Plato is (on this reading) deliberately directing us towards the conception of an emergent whole-of-parts. For it seems that here too, "everything stands to everything else in one of the following relations: it is either the same or different; or if neither the same nor different, its relation is that of part to a whole or of a whole to a part" (*Parm.* 146b2-5).[8] With this understanding of knowledge and the object of knowledge, we can now return to the interpretation of Theaetetus' final definition.

What we are seeking in the *Theaetetus* is a *logos* of *knowledge;* and unless we come to understand these two pivotal terms, our search will be to no avail. According to this reading, therefore, the function of the "dream" passage at just this point is to prepare Theaetetus—and with him the reader—for the final phase of the dialogue, by providing the key to both concepts. But for it to be such a preparation, we have to read the argument the way this study is suggesting—and then apply it first to the concept of logos, then to the concept of knowledge itself.

ARGUMENT FOR LOGOS: *reduction of the logos disjunction*

The argument will undercut the uninitiated claim that logos is an account of a complex as:

either	the same as its elements i.e., as ultimately many (thus an account simply in terms of its constituent matter)
or	different from its elements i.e., as ultimately one (thus an account simply in terms of differentiating form) (see 203c5-6; 204a1; 205c2, d1, d5)

Theaetetus' understanding of this discussion of logos falls into the familiar pattern of Meno's "eristic" dilemma:

1.	*Either a:*	logos is an account in terms of constitutive matter, i.e., an enumeration of elements,
	or b:	logos is an account in terms of differentiating form, i.e., an identification of unique properties
2.	*If a:*	logos is an account in terms of an enumeration of elements (206e6-c4; 208c5-6)
	then not-c:	it is not the case that a combination of true opinion with logos will constitute knowledge (207c6-208b9)
3.	*If b:*	logos is an account in terms of unique differentia (208c7-e5)
	then not-c:	it is not the case that a combination of true opinion with logos will constitute knowledge (209d5-210a5)
4.	*Therefore not-c:*	[The dialogue's apparent conclusion.]

By contrast, of course, what I am urging is the now familiar *kompsoteros* twist:

1.	*c:*	knowledge consists of a combination of true opinion and logos.

2. *Either a:*   logos is an account in terms of an enumeration of elements

   or b: logos is an account in terms of unique differentia

3. *If a:*   if logos is an account in terms of an enumeration of elements—thus taking the definiendum as ultimately many (206e6-207c4)

   then not-c: it is not the case that knowledge consists of a combination of true opinion and logos (207c6-208b9)

4. *Therefore not-a:* (208b8-12)

5. *If b:*   if logos is an account in terms of unique differentia—thus taking the definiendum as simply one (208c7-e5)

   then not-c: it is not the case that knowledge consists in a combination of true opinion and logos (209d5-210a5)

6. *Therefore not-b:* (208e7-209e4)

7. *Therefore not-(either a or b)*

Once again, the implied conclusion will be that logos provides an account of a thing *neither* simply in terms of an enumeration of its elements *nor* simply in terms of unique differentia, but in a significant sense in terms *both* of an enumeration of elements *and* of unique differentia. Such an interpretation of logos accords, I believe, with what, for example, the *Phaedrus* also seems to be telling us: true logos must both enumerate the elements of the things to be defined ("determine whether it is simple or multiform...and if multiform, number them") and identify the unique function or power in terms of which it is what it is ("inquire what power it possesses of action or being acted upon, and by what") (*Phaedr.* 270c10-d7). The *Phaedrus* goes on to suggest that "any other mode of procedure would be like the progress of a blind man" (270d9-e1)—which recalls, of course, that Theaetetus' present failure to recognize this conclusion is also represented as a kind of blindness "very like a man whose sight is mightily darkened" (*Theaet.* 209e4).

And now we come to the last lap, for the real thrust of this interpretation is to argue that the reader is called upon to make one more, and final, application of the *kompsoteros* argument. So far the pattern of argument has denied the would-be disjunction of one versus many, thereby making room for the *kompsoteros* demand that an object of knowledge be viewed as both; it has similarly denied the would-be disjunction of an enumeration-of-many-elements versus singularity-of-unique-identification, thereby making room for the *kompsoteros* demand that logos provide both. Now, I believe, this same form of argument must be once more applied, in order to throw light on the nature of knowledge itself; in other words, it must likewise deny the would-be disjunction of knowledge defined as the-same-as-its-elements versus knowledge defined as uniquely-different-from-its-elements. In order to see how the dialogue makes room for what I believe is the *kompsoteros* demand that knowledge must be both, let us look for the last time at the form of the argument:

ARGUMENT FOR KNOWLEDGE: *reduction of the knowledge disjunction*

The argument will undercut the uninitiated claim that knowledge is

either	the same as its elements i.e., ultimately many (thus defined simply as the sum of its elements)
or	different from its elements i.e., ultimately one (thus defined simply in terms of differentiating form)

For the last time, we must make the *kompsoteros* turn:

1. *c:* a logos of knowledge is possible (original hypothesis of the dialogue)

2. *Either a:* knowledge is the same as its elements

   or b: knowledge is different from its elements

3. *If a:* knowledge is the same as its elements and therefore to be defined as the sum or addition of its elements (i.e., of true opinion and logos)

   then not-c: there is no logos of knowledge

4. *Therefore not-a*

5. *If b:* knowledge is different from its elements, and therefore to be defined independently of its elements (i.e., of true opinion and logos)

   then not-c: there is no logos of knowledge

6. *Therefore not-b*

7. *Therefore not-(either a or b)*

Once again, I believe, the implied conclusion must be that knowledge is *neither* simply the same as *nor* simply different from its elements, but in a significant sense *both* the same as *and* different from, those elements.

In contrast, however, to the kind of *generative* combination of true opinion and logos which would be thus productive of knowledge as genuinely emergent, Theaetetus is "satisfied" (*areskei:* 202c7-9) with an interpretation which takes the relation between the elements as simply one of juxtaposition or *addition.* This is, of course, to ignore or deny entirely the role of emergence—and there, in a nutshell, lies Theaetetus' problem. Throughout the remainder of the dialogue, therefore, the combination of true opinion and logos that is found wanting as an account of knowledge turns out to be expressed either by the preposition *meta,* meaning simply "with," "along with," "in addition to," (e.g., 202c8; 206e1; 208b8, c3; 210a4), or by the verbs *proslambanō,* "to take in addition" (e.g., 208e4; 209a2, d4, e6), or *prosgignomai,* to "come together" or to be "added" (e.g., 206c4; 210b1)—thereby failing to heed Socrates' original warning in the dice illustration (see argument in chapter 5, and appendix A). As readers, we recognize the explicit echo of the dice argument's original focus on mere addition (*prostithēmi:* 155a7)—the rejection of which originally precipitated the whole initiation into the mysteries of emergence. It is this persistently non-emergent interpretation of the third definition that now accounts for Socrates' final pessimistic summary of their efforts (210a9-b2).

If, by contrast, the *kompsoteros* interpretation is correct, then this would mean that any adequate account of knowledge must do two things. First, it must recognize that knowledge is in one sense the same as its elements: a logos of knowledge must therefore enumerate the constituent elements of knowledge (that is, it must analyze knowledge in terms of its components); second, it must recognize that knowledge is in another sense different from its elements: a logos of knowledge must therefore show that a mere addition of the elements can never amount to knowledge (that is, it must show that knowledge is not reducible to its elements). On this reading, therefore, it is only to be expected that the dialogue will, on the one hand, enumerate true opinion and logos as the constituent elements of knowledge—and will moreover have Socrates explicitly endorse this enumeration as an account of knowledge: "This account ['knowledge is true opinion and logos'] is probably fine, for what knowledge could there still be apart from logos and true opinion?" (202d6-7; cf. *Meno*98a1-8; *Symp.* 202a5-7). On the other hand, however, the dialogue must demonstrate that, although a necessary condition, the mere presence or even addition of these elements is not sufficient for a logos of knowledge; it will therefore have Socrates emphasize that, understood as the mere sum of those elements, it equally clearly will not do: "Neither perception, nor true opinion, nor the addition [*prosgignomenos*] of logos and true opinion could be knowledge [*prosgignomenos* = juxtaposed, added as in a sum, brought side by side] (210a9-b2).

For anyone who has taken seriously Theaetetus' initiation into the mysteries of the *kompsoteroi,* the impact of this conclusion, far from being merely negative, is integral to the thesis of the whole dialogue. Anticipated from the very beginning, in both Theaetetus' account of his work with surds, and in Socrates' talk of midwifery and match-making, it climaxes the entire discussion with a forceful highlighting of the *kompsoteros* rejection of mere addition in favor of a truly generative combination that will be productive of genuine emergence—an act analogous, in the words of "the mysteries," to the bringing to birth of living offspring (e.g., 156a7-8, b2, c3, d1, d4, e2, e4; 157a1-2) or the kindling of flame (156a8). By setting the discussion of this last definition within the framework of Socrates' "dream," Plato has provided us with a subtle (*"kompsoteros"*) interpretation of just how this logos of knowledge is, and is not, to be understood if the inquiry is to be fruitful—if not for Theaetetus, then at least for the reader.[9]

Read in this way, with Socrates' dream version of emergence recapitulating the *kompsoteros* mysteries, the *Theaetetus* is seen to be a beautifully articulated whole. In a comprehensive inquiry which follows the same procedure which the *Philebus* identifies as "the dialectical method" (*Phil.* 17a3-5), it "gives an account" of knowledge, by offering us a cumulative logos that successively embodies each of the senses of logos explored at the end of the dialogue. In other words, the dialogue self-referentially presents knowledge first of all as "infinite": a flow of images (perceptual appearances on the stream of consciousness, and linguistic images on the stream of speech) which constitutes the raw material with which soul starts its cognitive structuring; accordingly, it is important to understand that, in this sense, "knowledge is nothing other than perception" (Theaetetus' first definition: 151e2-3). Second (still doing what it is describing), the dialogue presents knowledge as "many," through analysis into its elements; diverse but fitting, these will have the "power" to generate radical novelty; accordingly, it is important to understand that, in this sense, "knowledge is true opinion" (Theaetetus' second definition: 187b5-6) and "knowledge is true opinion with logos" (Theaetetus' third definition: 201c8-d1). In the course of purifying this third definition of misinterpretation, the cross-examination of Socrates' dream points to the sense in which knowledge must be recognized, and actually achieved, as not only many but also "one": an emergent whole born in generative interaction between its constituent elements.

When anything is grasped in this way as infinite, many, and one, then, the *Philebus* tells us, we shall be become wise with respect to that thing (*Phil.* 17e1-3). The inquiry here in the *Theaetetus* should thus help us become wise with respect to "what knowledge really is" (*Theaet.* 145e9).

OVERVIEW

Standing back now from the dialogue in order to view its conclusion in perspective, one cannot help but be awed by the scope of Plato's vision—linguistic, epistemological, and ontological. It is a vision of soul as creative intelligence,[10] operating according to principles which, as we have seen, apply to the expression of rational activity—whether in language, mathematics, the arts, literature, physical science, music, or the political order. Confronted with a flow of sensory experience on the one hand, and the ability to produce a flow of sound on the other, soul generates language itself as a fitting instrument to its purpose (cf. *Crat.* 387a2-8; 388b7-c1). Using language—names, statements, and accounts (through reasoned definitions and arguments)—mind, as *nous* or logos, generates an emergent and multidimensional "reality" that is apprehended in correspondingly emergent phases of multidimensional "knowing." If, by way of summary—heavyhanded, alas, in comparison with Socrates' dream (or with Plato's compact diagram in the *Republic*)—we now seek to "give an account" of that activity, it would have to go something like this:

A. KNOWLEDGE: *The subjective dimension of soul's rational activity*

1. *Perception,* as a complex operation, the elements of which are swift motions of objective and subjective sensibility, may on the one hand be analyzed into those elements; on the other, as radically emergent, it is characterized by our power to experience phenomenally these various appearings, bringing them to consciousness through the assigning of names; in this respect, it is an operation which no mere adding up of motions could ever amount to, and as such is not reducible to those motion-elements.

2. *Opinion,* as a complex operation, the elements of which are perceivings (provided in the phase of perception above), may on the one hand be analyzed into those primary perceptual elements; on the other, as radically emergent, it is characterized by the power to make judgments which may be true or false; in this respect it is an operation which no mere adding up of perceivings could ever amount to, and as such is not reducible to those perceptual elements.

3. *Dianoia* or *logos,* as a complex operation, the elements of which (provided in the phase of opinion above) are individual judgments in the spatiotemporal world, may on the one hand be analyzed into those elements; on the other, as radically emergent, it is characterized by the power to formulate definitions which (defended or justified in arguments that may be sound or unsound) seek to structure a theoretical realm of abstract entities; in this respect, it is an operation which no mere adding up of judgments of opinion could ever amount to, and as such is not reducible to those opining elements.

4. *Knowledge (epistēmē)*, as a complex operation, the elements of which (provided in the two phases of opinion and logos above) consist of *both* judgments in the realm of practical structuring *and* logoi in the realm of theoretical structuring, may on the one hand be analyzed into those practical and theoretical elements; on the other, as radically emergent, it is characterized by the power to provide infallible or nonhypothetical guidance to right judgment and action in the realm of practice, and infallible or nonhypothetical principles for true *dianoia* and logos in the realm of theory; in this respect, it is an operation which no mere adding up of right opinions and true logoi could ever amount to, and as such is not reducible to those fallible and hypothetical elements.

B. BEING OR REALITY: *The objective dimension of soul's rational activity*

1. *Appearances,* as the objects of perception, are also to be understood as complexes, the elements of which in this case are subconscious "motions." This means, again, that on the one hand appearances may be analyzed into those motion-elements; on the other, as radically emergent, appearances have the power to impinge with phenomenal qualities on consciousness; in this respect the object of perception exhibits properties that no mere adding up of motion-elements could ever amount to, and as such is not reducible to those elements.

2. *Concrete particulars* (things and events) in the realm of practical experience, which are the objects of opinion, are also to be understood as complexes, the elements of which in this case are phenomenal and nameable appearances. This means, again, that on the one hand concrete particulars may be analyzed into those phenomenal elements; on the other, as radically emergent, objects of opinion exist in a three-dimensional realm of space and time, exhibiting a power of enduring existence that interactively combines, or "holds together," all possible perceptual appearances; in this respect, the object of opinion exhibits properties that no mere adding up of appearance-elements could ever amount to, and as such is not reducible to those elements.

3. *Abstract definable entities* in the realm of theoretical structure, which are the objects of *dianoia* and logos, are also to be understood as complexes, the elements of which in this case are the spatiotemporal objects and events provided by opinion. This means again that, on the one hand, these abstract entities may be analyzed in terms of those three-dimensional elements; on the other, as radically emergent, the objects of *dianoia* and logos have their being in a formal realm that transcends both space and time so that—as abstract (in contrast to the elements which are concrete), unmixed and unchanging (in contrast to the elements which are impure and changing), and apprehended through thought alone (in contrast to the elements which are apprehended through the senses and opinion)—they exhibit a power to "hold together" all possible instantiations; in this respect, the object of *dianoia*

and logos exhibits properties that no mere adding up of material elements could ever amount to, and as such is not reducible to those elements.

4. *Being or reality in its most complete sense,* as the object of knowledge in its most complete sense (202c4; 206c4), is also, finally, to be understood as a complex, the elements of which in this case are *both* the objects of opinion in the world of material becoming *and* the objects of *dianoia* and logos in the world of formal being. This means yet again that, on the one hand, reality in this comprehensive sense may be analyzed into "all that is in motion" in the world of becoming and "all that is at rest" in the world of being (cf. *Soph.* 249c10-d4). On the other hand, as radically emergent, reality in this ultimate sense (as the *Sophist* is shortly to make explicit) "is not simply motion and rest both together but something else different from both...outside both these dimensions" (*Soph.* 250c3-d3). Accordingly, we attribute to the objects of knowledge properties which no mere adding up of concrete and/or abstract elements could ever claim, and therefore reality in this ultimate sense is not reducible to those elements.

   As the ultimately real (e.g., *Rep.* VI, 511b3-7; VII, 516b4-6; cf. *Phaedr.* 247c6-e2), it is to be identified neither simply with the many concrete and changing manifestations (as the materialists and uninitiates of the *Theaetetus* would have it), nor simply with abstract form, always one and the same (as the proponents of the aviary model would have it). The rejection of precisely this disjunction—either one form or a material many—is what the discussion of Socrates' "dream" has undertaken to argue.

Carefully situated between the dream account that leads up to that "complete" kind of knowledge at 202c4, and the reference back to that same "most complete knowledge" at 206c4, the cross-examination of Socrates' "dream" explores the nature of that which is rational and knowable (*logon* and *gnoston*). In light of this final search for the object of complete knowledge, we recognize that the uninitiates' disjunction which is now rejected is the same disjunction, with a parallel rejection, that the *Sophist* describes as "a battle like that of gods and giants due to their disagreement about being" (*Soph.* 246a4-5). In the *Sophist,* the dilemma is pursued in terms of "being" viewed as either one or many (*Soph.* 244b9-245e2), either at rest or in motion (248d10-249d4). Here in the *Theaetetus,* the dilemma is elaborated in terms of "being" viewed as either the multiplicity of elements that provide the matter of a thing (for example, the letters that make up the syllable: 203c4-d3; 205b8-13; the physical parts that make up the wagon: 207a3-7, etc.) or the unity that constitutes the *form* of the complex: *mian tina idean* (203c5-6), *en ti...eidos* (203e3-4), *mia idea* (204a1), *en ti eidos* (204a8-9), *mia tis idea ameristos...asyntheton...monoeides* (205c2, c7, d1), *mia estin idea* (205d5).

To seek to attain knowledge of anything—from the most primitive compounds all the way up to the most complex reality—simply in terms of either material multiplicity or formal unity turns out, on examination, to be selfcontradictory, undercutting the very possibility both of logos and of knowledge itself (203c4-205e8). By contrast, complete *epistēmē* requires apprehension *both* of material multiplicity in the realm of the concrete and practical (via true opinion in the world of becoming and motion), *and* of formal unity in the realm of the abstract and theoretical (via *dianoia* or logos in the world of being and rest). These elements are, in the language of this dialogue, the ultimate epistemological incommensurables that we are finally called upon to render commensurable (see discussion in Mathematical Interlude and Epilogue).

In order, therefore, to attain that knowledge which is the quest of the *Theaetetus,* we must ourselves come to apprehend knowledge through *both* the concrete and practical dimension of experience (which Plato points to in the dramatic action of the dialogue), *and* the abstract and logical dimension of thinking (which Plato provides in the discursive argument of the dialogue). But we must not, like Theaetetus, stop short with a simple addition or juxtaposition of these two modes of apprehension. On the contrary, these must in turn be generatively combined if the dialogue is to prove effective in delivering us—not of a windegg—but of genuine knowledge of knowledge. This is what I have tried to do.

CONCLUSION

> Any discourse ought to be constructed like a living creature, with its own body, as it were; it must not lack either head or feet; it must have a middle and extremities so composed as to fit each other and the whole work.
>
> (*Phaedr.* 264c2-5)

It was with this counsel in mind that this study first set out to read the *Theaetetus* as an organically structured whole. What has now been proposed as an account of the *Theaetetus* turns out to be itself a "logos" according to the criteria that have been developed within the context of *kompsoteros* theory (chapter 7). Thus, it has tried, on the one hand, to enumerate and take seriously the various elements of the dialogue— the cast of characters, dramatic images, mathematical analogies, successive definitions of knowledge, and the arguments in which their meanings have been clarified and purified of ambiguity. On the other hand, since it is a major thesis of this study that Plato not only discusses, but also demonstrates, his philosophical commitments, it has tried to show how, holding all these elements together (literally, *syl-labein*), Plato has interwoven (*symplokein*) dramatic and poetic with logical and mathematical elements in such a way as to produce, bring forth, or create one, whole, and beautiful web of philosophical literature (cf. *Crat.* 425a2-3).

The core of the dialogue's account of knowledge is provided in the *kompsoteros* mysteries of generation and emergence, as these are first revealed in the so-called initiation of Theaetetus (chapters 2 and 3) and later recollected and recapitulated in Socrates' "dream" (chapter 8). The role of mind or soul, both in matching elements which will be fitting, and in judging the genuineness of the emergent product, is foreshadowed in the image of Socrates as matchmaker and midwife (chapter 4)—which also provides the metaphor for contrasting the

169

apparent inconclusiveness with the real conclusiveness of the dialogue. The real but hidden conclusiveness is found to rest, at a number of crucial points, on the distinction between eristic and dialectical readings of a characteristically Platonic argument (chapter 5 and 6). The dialectical reading rests in turn on the resolution of an eristic dilemma framed by the horns of sheer sameness or sheer difference, sheer unity or sheer plurality (chapter 8). The sophisticated resolution of this eristic disjunction culminates in the *kompsoteros* theory of emergence through the generative activity of creative intelligence (appendix A, and passim).

It is the irony of the dialogue that the role of reporting this rejection of the eristic disjunction and the resolution of the eristic dilemma is put into the mouth of Plato's friend, Eucleides the Eristic.[1] For the solution to the overall problem of the dialogue—"what knowledge really is"—is provided through the mode of problem solving known to the mathematicians as "reduction" or *apagōgē* (see appendix A)—a method used to powerful effect by Hippocrates of Chios and Theaetetus of Athens but, on the basis of the same eristic disjunction, emphatically rejected by Eucleides,[2] who, apparently unaware that the dialogue presents a complex and serious challenge to his own position, is here represented as reporting just such a case of reduction as a discussion "well worth hearing" (*Theaet.* 142d1). Meanwhile, Theaetetus' work with irrationals provides the reductive solution to the problem of knowledge (Mathematical Interlude, appendix A, and Epilogue), for the generation of radically emergent entities in increasingly complex dimensions of reality—rendering ever more rational what was originally irrational— is, both in geometry and in knowledge as a whole, the essence of that creative operation which we know as the rational enterprise.

EPILOGUE
The Mathematical Paradigm
(147d3-148b2)

One of the persistent themes of this paper has focused on the binding together of elements so as to generate an emergent whole in a radically new dimension. In fact, it has been argued, it is Theaetetus' failure to recognize the demand for (let alone himself achieve) just such a combination that allows him to settle for a mere addition of true opinion and logos—thereby encompassing the apparent failure of the dialogue. At one remove, it has further been suggested, the reader too is called upon to achieve a generative combination of elements (in this case the elements of dramatic presentation and discursive argument within the dialogue itself) in order to attain to knowledge of "knowledge" as Plato is presenting it. Partly because of the ambiguity inherent in language, and therefore in all verbal communication, partly because he holds that, in the generation of knowledge, abstract argument is only one element, requiring for completion also concrete experience, Plato chose to present his philosophy, not as a philosophic treatise (*syggramma: Seventh Epistle*, 341c5), but in the form of dramatic dialogues. Here the traditional Greek balance between logos and *ergon* (word and deed), of which Plato is so evidently aware,[1] finds expression *both* in the pursuit of logos as argument and definition *and* in the presentation of *ergon* through examples, myth, and the dramatic action of the dialogues generally. As Theaetetus is (in a confused way) aware that knowledge will involve as its elements both true opinion and logos, so the reader is (often also in a confused way) aware that understanding a dialogue will involve as its elements, participation in both its dramatic and logical dimensions; as with Theaetetus, however, the problem is to achieve not mere juxtaposition but a generative combination wherein the two will reinforce, complement, and eventually transform each other. It has been in thus taking seriously the dramatic dimensions of the *Theaetetus*—for example, Socrates' presentation of himself as midwife and

..atchmaker, Theaetetus' youthful promise in his account of his own work with irrationals, his philosophical wonder before the problem of the dice, Socrates' talk of initiation into the mysteries of generation and emergence, and finally his puzzling report of the "dream"—that this paper has (I believe) found a key to understanding otherwise obscure aspects of the dialogue (such as the meaning of the "dream" theory, the intent of its apparent refutation, and the significance of the dialogue's apparent inconclusiveness). Ideally, moving back and forth between these elements of the dialogue will continue to spark understanding of the vision Plato is trying to communicate. So, although there is yet much to be said about the *Theaetetus* that in this study must remain unsaid, there is nevertheless one further connection I should like to make because of the light it throws on Plato's theory of knowledge.

One of the terms Plato frequently uses in describing that combination of elements in which a whole is generated is *desmon* (bond) and *deō*, or *syndeō* (to bind). Thus, we find the following:

— the binding together of letters to form words through the presence of vowels as a bond (*hoion desmos: Soph.* 253a4-5)
— the binding together of the limbs to form the body as an organic whole (*syndēsas: Tim.* 74b5; *syndoun...desmos: Tim.* 84a1, 3)
— the binding together of soul and body to form one whole (*syndoumenēs: Tim.* 73b4)
— the binding together of the parts of the soul to form one whole person (*syndesanta: Rep.* IV, 443e1)
— the weaving and binding together of temperaments exhibiting opposing kinds of virtue (*syndein kai symplekein; symplokēn kai desmon; syndesmon: Stat.* 309b7; 309e10; 310a4)
— the binding together of citizens to form a polis (*syndē; syndesmon: Rep.* V, 462b2; VII, 520a4)
— the binding together of either instances or species under one name to form a definable class (*syndēsan: Soph.* 227c3; cf. *syndēsomen:* 268c5)
— the binding together of true opinion with casual reasoning to form knowledge (*dēsē aitias logismō: Meno* 98a3-4)
— the binding together of the four elements to form the cosmos (*synedēsen: Tim.* 32b7)
— the binding together of all things whatsoever by the good (*syndein: Phaedo* 99c6)

The concept is pervasive enough, and crucial enough, to tease for further elucidation; and, although the elucidation will lead through a slight detour, it will return us very shortly to the *Theaetetus*, for it turns out that Plato's paradigms of such bonding resort to the same two themes with which we are now so familiar. On the one hand, there is the "concrete" paradigm that draws on the organicity of the living body (e.g., *Phaedr.* 265e1-266a2; *Stat.* 287c3-4)—and which is reminiscent of the imagery of the mysteries of generation, where the bonding is compared with intercourse and the emergent product with living offspring (and of Socrates' role as midwife in judging the genuineness of such offspring). On the other hand, there is the "abstract" paradigm that draws on proportion in mathematics—and it is on this point, reminiscent of Theaetetus' work in geometry, that I should like here to concentrate.

Already in the discussion of justice in Book IV of the *Republic,* Plato has talked of binding the three parts of the soul as a harmony expressible in mathematical terms:

> [The just man will have] harmonized these three principles, the notes or intervals of three terms quite literally the lowest, the highest, and the mean [*mesēs*], and all others there may be between them, and having bound all these together [*panta tauta syndēsanta*], made of himself a unit, one person instead of many (*Rep.* IV, 443d5-e1)

Later, when the *Philebus* asks this very question that lies at the heart of any theory of emergent wholes—"What is it about the mixture that we recognize both as being most to be valued and as being the major cause of its being desired (loved)?" (*Phil.* 64c5-7)—Plato goes on to explain:

> It is quite easy to see the cause which makes any mixture whatsoever either of the highest value or of none at all... Everybody knows that any compound, however made, which lacks measure and proportion [*metrou kai...symmetrou*] must necessarily destroy its components and first of all itself, for it is in truth no compound. (*Phil.* 64d3-e3)

It is therefore "measure, and the mean, and fitness" [*metron kai to metrion kai kairion*] as cause of genuine wholeness that the *Philebus* finally ranks first in value (*Phil.* 66a6-7)—and all these, according to the gloss in the *Statesman,* must be understood with reference to "a mean between extremes" (*eis to meson... ton eschaton: Stat.* 284e7-8). Now from the point of view of emergence, this stress on a mean is particularly significant, because the determination of a mean is, in mathematics, a major mode of generating number—and not only do the different means indicate different modes of generation, but they also imply different assumptions about the nature of number itself.

The Greeks of Plato's time inherited from the Pythagoreans three types of mean—the arithmetic, the harmonic, and the geometric.[2] The arithmetic mean is determined simply by the addition to the first term of the same number as that subtracted from the last term (e.g., *Tim.* 36a4-5; *Epin.* 991a4-5). This of course reflects the arithmetical view of number as essentially discrete, with the consequent mode of generation being through addition and subtraction only (as in the eristic version of the dice argument; see above, chapter 5). The harmonic mean is determined as that number which exceeds the first extreme and is exceeded by the second extreme by the same fraction of each of the extremes respectively (e.g., *Tim.* 36a3-4; *Epin.* 991a6-7). Thus, for example, the harmonic mean between 4 and 12 is 6, for, as Socrates reminds Theaetetus when he prepares to direct his attention towards a mode of generation other than mere addition (see appendix A), "Given six dice, for instance, if you compare four with them, we say that they are more than the four, half as many again; but if you compare twelve with them, we say they are less, half as many" (*Theaet.* 154c2-4). Finally, and in contrast to both the arithmetic and harmonic means, which deal only with number as discrete and rational, there is the geometric mean—so called, one might suppose, because, operating with lines as does geometry, it treats number not as discrete but as a continuous magnitude (see above, Mathematical Interlude). Determined as "that number such that, as the first term is to it, so it is to the last term" (*Tim.* 31c4-32a1), it provides the middle term for a continuous proportion, and was in the subsequent tradition accounted "both proportion par excellence and primary" (*tēn geometrikēn kyrios . . . kai protēn*).[3] One of the reasons for this was presumably that the geometric mean is unlimited in its generative power, since, treating number as continuous magnitude, it can handle irrational as well as rational quantities. Thus, for example, the geometric mean between the two extremes cited above, i.e., 4 and 12, is $\sqrt{48}$.[4] Immediately it becomes evident that the geometric mean permits the generation of either rational or irrational numbers—which is, of course, exactly what Theaetetus is describing to Socrates at the beginning of the dialogue: the generation, not only of the square roots up to $\sqrt{17}$, but the setting up of a schema to generate any root as a geometric mean,[5] covering them all in a single mathematical formula. Given a and c, where a is not equal to c (i.e., the sides of an oblong, not of a square), then one can determine the geometric mean, b (whether rational or not), as $\sqrt{ac}$. But—apart from possible confirmation of the claim that the starting point is to be understood as a continuum rather than as some atomistic discreteness (see appendix A)—what could be the purpose of this reference to a geometric mean in the context of Theaetetus' theory of surds? It seems to me that there are several points here that are intended by Plato to be relevant to the quest of the *Theaetetus*.

First of all, in light of the fact that the challenge of the dialogue finally turns out to be the problem of grasping knowledge as a whole of parts, it comes as something of a shock to realize that this particular proportion that is pointed up at the outset of the dialogue—that is, the continuous proportionality that characterizes the geometric mean, as

in *a:b* = *b:c*—represents for Plato that "bond" which binds together a
whole of parts. In other words, continuous geometric proportion is the
hallmark of wholeness as conceived in the *kompsoteros* mysteries, and as
elaborated in Socrates' "dream" and the subsequent discussion. As the
Timaeus explains:

> The fairest of bonds [*desmon de kallistos*] is that which most perfectly unites
> into one both itself and the things which it binds together; and to effect
> this in the fairest manner is the natural property of proportion [*analogia*].
> For whenever the middle term of any three numbers, cubic or square, is
> such that as the first term is to it, so is it to the last term . . . the necessary
> consequence will be that all the terms are interchangeable, and being
> interchangeable they all form a unity. (*Tim.* 31c2-32a7)

The first point, then, about this mathematical paradigm seems therefore
to be that, in providing this account of Theaetetus' work at the outset of
the inquiry, Plato is setting before us an example of what he believes to
be that most perfect bond to unite elements so as to constitute a
genuine whole.

The second point of interest is that this geometric proportion,
introduced by Theaetetus and regarded by Plato as the fairest of bonds,
is the same proportion as that employed by Plato in the *Republic* when
he diagrams knowledge in terms of a divided line: "Take a line which is
divided into two unequal sections and cut each section again in the
same ratio [*ana ton auton logon*]" (*Rep.* VI, 509d6-8). This might be
diagrammed as follows:

A	B	C		D	

where $A : B = C : D = A + B = C + D$.

As is commonly recognized, it is mathematically impossible to divide a
line according to Plato's stipulations without having the two central
sections, B and C, of equal length—thus giving us, of course, Theaetetus'
geometric proportion, a : b = b : c. For the most part, this fact about the
proportions of the divided line are either ignored or deplored. Maybe
Plato overlooked an unforeseen and unfortunate implication?[6] But
Plato's instructions here are quite clear and can be readily illustrated.
For example:

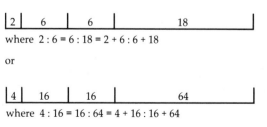

2	6	6		18	

where $2 : 6 = 6 : 18 = 2 + 6 : 6 + 18$

or

4	16	16		64	

where $4 : 16 = 16 : 64 = 4 + 16 : 16 + 64$

—or innumerable other examples. Moreover, contrary to the conviction of many of his commentators, Plato seems perfectly aware of the implications of his diagram, for on the two separate occasions on which he spells out the proportion, he transposes the two central sections—which he could do only if they were equal.

Thus,

$$C + D : A + B = D : C = B : A$$

(Rep. VI, 509d6-510a10; cf. 511d8-e2)

and

$$C + D : A + B = D : B = C : A$$

(Rep. VII, 534a4-5)

But this should not really present such a problem. According to the *Theaetetus* (as interpreted in this study), this is of course just what one ought to expect if the two central sections, *pistis* (as true opinion) and *dianoia* (logos), are the final elements discriminated out for generative combination in *epistēmē*. As "fitting" elements, they meet all the criteria we have already recognized (see above, chapter 4): they are, on the one hand, *dissimilar:* intelligible versus sensible, one versus many, unchanging versus changing, etc.—which dissimilarity is, of course, represented on the diagram by their being respectively "above" and "below" the dividing line; on the other hand, they are *similar:* both are expressible in statements (in contrast to the mere naming of perception), and both can be justified or unjustified (that is to say, right or wrong, true or false, in contrast to the infallibility of perceivings)—as is represented in the diagram by the two sections being of equal length; they are, moreover, *mutually relative:* one-many, form-matter, abstract-concrete, etc., so that, although different in the kind of apprehension they indicate, *as elements* they are on a par and so represented by sections of equal length.

If, however, the two central sections are thus equal, and the line therefore to be diagrammed on the model of Theaetetus' proportion, $a : b = b : c$, then the overtones become even more interesting. For, as a schema of knowledge, the divided line represents not just any old geometric proportion, but one carefully calculated so that not only is there a continuous proportion between the four sections so that $a : b = b : c$, but also $a + b : b + c = a : b = b : c$. Might there not be some formula which would meet those conditions as Plato lays them down? Fascinated by the discovery of this apparent echo between the *Republic* and the *Theaetetus,* where both seem to be presenting knowledge as a complex of the same elements, I began to look more closely at other features of the paradigm—and in particular at the fact (crucial for the *Theaetetus'* approach to knowledge through the mysteries of emergence) that in his account Theaetetus moves from linear to square to cubic measure in the generation of successive, and radically different, dimensions. And suddenly it dawned on me that Theaetetus' illustration of surds gives us the formula for a divided line that meets all of Plato's stipulations in the *Republic*: $a : ab = ab : ab^2$—and hence also $a : a^2 = a^2 : a^3$ (so long as a and $b > 1$).[7] Expressed geometrically, a continuous proportion binding together in perfect unity successively generated dimensions of reality would read as follows: "Take a line which is divided into two unequal sections and cut each section again in the same ratio" (cf. *Rep.* VI, 509d6-8).[8]

This, then, is the second point to be noted about the mathematical paradigm in the *Theaetetus*. For it now seems that at the very outset of the inquiry Plato has provided us with that exact proportion which not only in the *Timaeus* is found to express the unity of a perfect whole, but also in the *Republic* is used to represent the various phases of knowledge in their relations to each other and to the whole according to their various degrees of subjective clarity and objective reality.[9]

The third aspect of the paradigm that strikes one as significant recalls the discussion of the *Philebus*. Much has been said in this study about Plato's conception of explanation, or logos, as "giving an account" of something as at once infinite, many, and one. The argument has even gone on to interpret the various definitions offered as doing just that. Thus:

Theaetetus' *first definition*: "knowledge is nothing other than perception" has been taken as the presentation of knowledge as *infinite*—in the sense that perceptual flux provides the originally indeterminate stuff of knowledge;

Theaetetus' *second definition*: "knowledge is true opinion," and *third definition*: "knowledge is true opinion with logos," have been taken as presenting knowledge as *many*—in the sense that these factors (similar and dissimilar, mutually relative and complementary) constitute those "fitting" elements which must be generatively combined to give birth to knowledge as a radically emergent *one*.

The fact that perception provides the indeterminate stuff of knowledge is commonly recognized—not only by Theaetetus, but also by Protagoras, Heracleitus, and others. So too, the equally conventional recognition that knowledge is one is evidenced in the ordinary use of the single term *epistēmē*. But, as the *Philebus* points out, "no one of us is wiser than the other merely for knowing that a thing is infinite or that it is one" (*Phil.* 17b6-7); the challenge is to pursue the road of inquiry "until we can see not only that the original entity is one and many and infinite, but just how many it is. For we must not apply the idea of infinite to plurality until we have a view of all that lies between infinity and one" (*Phil.* 16d5-e1). The task is therefore to focus on the many "in between"—coming to understand, first, which elements must be discriminated out as many from the infinite, and second, how such fitting elements are to be combined to generate knowledge as one. In other words, given that knowledge is infinite (i.e., perception), and that knowledge is one (*epistēmē*), how does one determine the fitting elements "between" perception and *epistēmē*? Coming fresh from the mathematical paradigm, one readily recognizes the mathematical expression of this challenge as the determination of the appropriate many as a geometric mean between the two extremes of perception and *epistēmē*. That is to say:

a (perception as infinite) : $b = b : c$ (*epistēmē* as one).

This seems to be why the *Philebus* goes on to explain that

> The gods handed down to us this mode of investigating, learning, and teaching one another; but the wise men of the present day...put infinity immediately after unity; they disregard the mean [*ta de mesa*], and this it is that distinguishes dialectic from eristic. (*Phil.* 16e3-17a5)

Seen in this light, then, the third point to note about the mathematical paradigm in the *Theaetetus* is that in mathematical language it poses the epistemological problem—and at the same time points to its solution. For, given perception on the one hand, and *epistēmē* on the other, what is the mean that will bind them in geometric proportion—that fairest of bonds? The answer, of course, again yields the divided line of the *Republic*:

a	:	b	=	b	:	c
aisthēsis		pistis		dianoia		epistēmē
(perception)	:	(true opinion)	=	(logos)	:	(knowledge)

A fourth reason that Theaetetus' description of surds is significant for the quest of the dialogue as a whole was anticipated earlier (see above, Mathematical Interlude). It echoes this issue of multi-dimensionality, but now from a slightly different angle. For Theaetetus' project succinctly illustrates a central feature of the *kompsoteros* theory of emergence. By resorting to the geometric mean, it opens up the possibility of dealing with irrationals; for what in the one-dimensional context of the line is irrational can now in the two-dimensional context of the plane be rendered rational. This feature of geometry struck Plato as important and wonderful—"a miracle of God's contrivance" (*Epin.* 990d5-e1). Its significance for the *Theaetetus* lies in the way in which Theaetetus' generative move toward increasingly rational structure in the context of *geometry* provides a model for the analogously generative move toward increasingly rational structure in the context of *cognition*.

The fifth and final point to note about the mathematical paradigm in the *Theaetetus* is that, in pointing to Theaetetus' own solution to one problem (i.e., finding the mean which, as "root" or *dynamis*, will permit the generation or "growth" of further dimensions), Plato is proposing a transition by analogy to a parallel solution to the problem of knowledge. To the mathematicians of Plato's time this device was known as "reduction" (*apagōgē*). The most famous case of reduction seems to have occurred in connection with the problem of doubling the cube. Hippocrates of Chios apparently effected a reductive solution to this problem by pointing out that if two means could be found in a continuous geometric proportion between the two given volumes as extremes, then the first mean would indicate the length of the side that would generate the desired cubic measure. Thus:

> Reduction is a transition from one problem or theorem to another, where the solution or proof of the second makes manifest also the solution of the original problem—as when those who sought to double the cube transferred the investigation to another problem which it parallels: the discovery of the two means... They say the first to effect the reduction of the difficult construction was Hippocrates of Chios.[10]

Reduction thus corresponds to one of our own problem-solving devices in science, where the solution to a problem is sometimes sought by setting up a model—in the context of which an analogous solution, if not actually provided, is at least indicated. That such a method was thoroughly familiar to Plato seems to be confirmed in the story that, after trying unsuccessfully to solve their problem, the Delians came to Plato for a solution, and Plato, recognizing the need for a geometrical reduction, told them that "the god had given them this oracle, not because he wanted an altar of double this size, but because he wished, in setting this task before them, to reproach the Greeks for their neglect of mathematics and their contempt of geometry."[11]

Although commentators often do not take the mathematical metaphors in the dialogues seriously as models for the solution of nonmathematical problems,[12] it is intriguing that, historically, Theaetetus himself does seem to have recognized the fruitfulness of seeking a solution to an otherwise insoluble problem by modeling it on another that is more readily susceptible of solution.[13] What this means is that, in spite of his failure at the end of the dialogue, Theaetetus does in fact—in his own treatment of irrationals by means of geometric proportion—hold the key to solving the otherwise recalcitrant problem that Socrates posed when he initiated the inquiry: "I am in doubt about one little matter, which should be investigated with your help...it is just this that I am in doubt about and cannot fully grasp by my own efforts: what knowledge really is" (145d6-7, e8-9). By contrast, Eucleides of Megara had the reputation of discounting such a mode of problem solving. As already noted (see conclusion above), a final twist to the dialogue therefore lies in the irony of a situation in which Plato has—of all people—Eucleides present the conversation. For although at face value the inquiry appears to be a failure, nevertheless *the reader* recognizes, not only that the dialogue is on the contrary a spectacular success in giving an account of knowledge, but also that it is the mathematical model at the outset of the inquiry which, by analogy, already indicates the solution to the problem. It is, moreover, in this last ironic fillip that Plato has Eucleides,[14] a distinguished monist who did not admit the existence of even an "illusory" world of becoming,[15] reporting at length (and with obvious admiration) a theory of emergence which actually denies his own position. Finally, in using the form of a reductio ad absurdum, Plato is resorting to the very form of argument for which the Eristic Megarians were famous;[16] but he uses it precisely to deny that eristic approach. This tension between Eucleides' understanding of the dialogue and that of the reader thus adds a final exquisite touch to the overall play on the ambiguity of logoi—in this case, the ambiguity of the logos that is the dialogue itself.

APPENDIX A
SOCRATES' DICE ILLUSTRATION
(154c1-155d5)

Socrates: We find ourselves rather easily forced to make extraordinary and absurd statements...
Theaetetus: What do you mean? What statements?
Socrates: Take a little example, and you will know all I have in mind. Given six dice, for instance...

(Theaet. 154b6-c2)

The argument or illustration that follows is, I have found, one of the most difficult passages of the whole dialogue.

At first I thought Socrates merely meant that we make absurd statements in asserting that things themselves are large, white, hot, etc., whereas, as he had argued earlier, "if you call it large it will also appear to be small" (152d4-5). I was inclined to see the case of the dice introduced simply to illustrate this point: thus, viewed relative to four, six appears as large; relative to twelve, six appears small. But this seems so trivial that I began to be uneasy about attributing such simplicity to Socrates, especially in talking with a major mathematician like Theaetetus. Socrates' next question, and Theaetetus' response, only deepened my suspicion that there must be more to this than was meeting the eye. "Well, then, if Protagoras, or anyone else, ask you, 'Theaetetus, can anything become greater or more in any other way than by being increased?' what reply will you make?" (154c7-9). On the face of it, this seems a harmless enough question—but it reduces Theaetetus to a quandary in which he is torn between answering yes or no. Admitting that the problem is not new to him (155c5-7), Theaetetus goes on to exclaim, "By the gods, Socrates, I am lost in wonder when I think of all these things, and sometimes when I regard them, it really makes my head swim" (155c8-10). Now why? Why should such a simple question precipitate such a reaction in a brilliant young mathematician— especially since, as the critics consistently point out, the supposed puzzle is really no puzzle at all? Most commentators that I have read do not make a point of examining this discussion of the dice; in those that do, what now strikes me as the real significance of this question is never brought to the surface.

Lewis Campbell is prepared to locate the absurdity of which Plato speaks in the fact that "the six dice are more when compared with four. They were fewer when compared with twelve. They cannot be more without having become more, and they cannot have become more without increase" (Campbell, *Plato's Theaetetus*, p. 54). But where is the problem that Theaetetus finds so challenging? The question whether anything can become more unless increased is trivially interpreted as registering some sort of apparent contradiction between saying, on the one hand, that six is more then four, and at the same time, on the other, that six has not been increased. It is difficult to see why a mathematician of Theaetetus' caliber might be fazed by such an elementary non-problem. And indeed Campbell seems to have some difficulty himself in making his theory account for Theaetetus' response. Thus, on the one hand, he maintains that "Theaetetus' answer showed great dialectical aptitude. He perceives the contradiction, and yet will not answer *para to dokoun hauto* [according to what he himself thinks]" (p. 50); on the other, he admits that "the distinction between relative and absolute quantity is so familiar to us, that this is apt to appear a mere verbal quibble." In spite of the triviality, Campbell nevertheless sees Protagoras as coming to the rescue by offering Theaetetus, the subtle mathematician, the trite explanation that "it is true that something cannot be more without addition, but the dice in the two cases are not the same thing, for they are in a different relation" (p. 54).

Cornford's account of what is going on strikes me as hardly more enlightening. To begin with, he sees the introduction of this mathematical illustration as something of a digression:

> If Socrates now proceeded at once to the fuller statement of the theory of sense perception, there would be no difficulty. But here Plato interpolates some alleged puzzles about what we call "relations" of size and number, whose relevance to their context is by no means obvious. (Cornford, *Plato's Theory of Knowledge*, p. 41)

His interpretation of the nature of the absurdity involved resembles that of Campbell, in that he sees simply a contradiction between the assertion that the six are first more (than four) and then less (than twelve), and the commonsense conviction that the only way they could have become first more and then less must be by addition or subtraction. The question thus becomes "How, then, can the dice, which have remained the same in amount, have become less? (p. 43). Like Campbell, Cornford seems apparently satisfied that this trivial

play on words (Campbell's "mere verbal quibble") should have left
Theaetetus dizzy with wonder. His account does not, however, explain
how such banalities might really seem puzzling to an intelligent
adult—"nor is it easy for us to understand why anyone should be
perplexed by them" (p. 41). With his own persistent concern about the
Forms, Cornford proposes the theory that Plato *may* be indicating a
change of position on "Forms of relations" (but then, again, as he adds,
he may not be) (p. 45).

The third interpretation I should like to consider is that of John
McDowell which accompanies his 1973 translation of the *Theaetetus*.
McDowell's account is a joy to read as far as clarity and perception are
concerned; it is also sharper than either of the other two in recognizing
some of the inadequacies of the alternative interpretations he considers.
McDowell attributes the various puzzles of this section (as will Plato
himself shortly, at 155a2-b2) to the attempt to apply jointly three
commonsense principles:

1. As long as something is equal to itself, it does not come to be greater or
   smaller (in size or number).
2. If something has nothing added to it or subtracted from it, it is equal (sc.
   "to itself," as in [1]).
3. Nothing is what it previously was not, without having come to be (sc.
   "that," i.e., "what it previously was not").

McDowell then analyzes the mathematical analogy as being "meant to
yield two puzzles":

A. The six dice were not more numerous (than the four), but now are; so,
   by (3), they have come to be more numerous. On the other hand,
   nothing has been added to them; so, by (1) and (2), they have not come
   to be more numerous.
B. The six dice were not less numerous (than the twelve), but now are; so,
   by (3), they have come to be less numerous. On the other hand, nothing
   has been subtracted from them; so, by (1) and (2), they have not come to
   be less numerous. (McDowell, *Plato: "Theaetetus,"* p. 134)

Although I do think McDowell is right in casting the problem in the
form of apparent self-contradiction, there nevertheless seem to me to
be certain difficulties with McDowell's interpretation of what is going
on at 154c1-5.

First, as he too recognizes, there is something odd about this
interpretation of the intended puzzles, for he warns us to

note the curious assumptions required for these arguments: for (i), that
putting the four dice next to the six makes it newly the case that the six are

more numerous; and for (ii), similarly, that putting the twelve dice next to the six makes it newly the case that the six are less numerous. (p. 134)

Such assumptions apparently seem odd to McDowell. They certainly seem odd to me. And I believe they would seem equally odd to both Theaetetus and Socrates.

Secondly, I do not see how McDowell's remarks account for the second half of Theaetetus' reply at 154d1-2 ("If I consider the earlier question, I should say 'yes' for fear of contradicting myself") when McDowell says that "presumably his inclination to answer the other way is to be explained by an application of principle (3) to what is said at 154c1-5." But neither, apparently, does McDowell himself see how this would explain anything, since he seems to recognize the inadequacy here when he adds, "How this works in detail is not made explicit." Nor does he offer any other explanation of this second half of Theaetetus' answer, except to admit that "some similarly curious assumption [i.e., similar to those in the previous paragraph] would be needed in order to account for the second part of Theaetetus' answer at 154c10-d2" (p. 134).

Third, by his own admission that "in fact these puzzles are not very puzzling" (p. 134), he poses (but does not answer) the question as to why, in that case, Theaetetus, one of the major mathematical minds in an age of mathematical sophistication, should have spent time thinking about such matters, and should find them so challenging as to fill him with wonder (155c5-10).

The only alternative interpretation that McDowell seriously considers relates not to the nature of the mathematical puzzle itself, but to Plato's reasons for introducing the mathematical analogy in the first place. According to this alternative view, the puzzles are meant to illustrate the difficulties one gets into if one uses nonrelational forms of speech when one ought to use relational forms, that is to say, if one uses *larger* and *smaller* unsupplemented by the necessary *than* phrases. But, as McDowell points out, Socrates promises that the theory of perception he is about to expound will contain the solution to the puzzles. This promise entails two decisive objections to McDowell's proposed interpretation: (a) Although it is true that in the theory of perception, nonrelational forms of speech are criticized, the basis of criticism is not that comparative adjectives like *larger* and *smaller* require completion with respect to some object of comparison, but rather that perceptual qualities should be ascribed to things only in relation to perceivers, and vice versa; (b) it is difficult to read the argument immediately preceding (i.e., 154b1-6)—in the context of which the mathematical illustration arises—as a warning against the dangers of nonrelational speech. This point leads me to my final difficulty with McDowell's account of this section.

Fourth, McDowell's own conclusion is that "both the puzzles and the arguments of 154b1-5 are intended by Plato to illustrate the dangers of using 'be,' contrary to the secret doctrine" (p. 135). On this view, however, as McDowell conceives it, we are forced to a position in which we cannot suppose "that Plato sees through the apparent contradictions of the puzzles, [but on the contrary] we have to suppose that he takes the contradiction to be genuine." Although this does seem to make him uneasy, McDowell is prepared to see such gullibility on Plato's part as perhaps due to a "lack of enlightenment about the logic of what may be called 'incomplete predicates'" (p. 136).

By contrast, it seems to me that, although the vocabulary available to Plato proves at times unwieldy for tackling some of the logical and linguistic problems that the logic of our time has made easier to handle, nevertheless he was surely not as logically or linguistically naive as much of the commentary seems to suggest. On the contrary, not only do I not believe that Theaetetus was puzzled by what these commentators seem to think he was puzzled by, but even more strongly do I not believe that Plato himself would have been. Indeed, as I shall argue, I think Plato knows exactly what he is doing at every step of the way— but the steps themselves I see rather differently, for I believe he is operating here on a level quite alien to that of trivial wordplay.

What I should therefore like to propose here is a different reading of (1) what constitutes the puzzle proposed to Theaetetus in the dice illustration; (2) why Theaetetus answers as he does—first no, and then yes; (3) why the sort of wonder generated by these questions is truly philosophic wonder; and (4) why the whole section naturally leads on to the expanded account of perception. (Part of what follows overlaps material discussed in the Epilogue, but this only underscores, I believe, the significance Plato attaches to the use of mathematical paradigms).

II

The primary challenge to any interpretation here will be to show how Socrates' introduction of the dice illustration and Theaetetus' puzzled response rise out of what has gone before, and lead up to what follows after.

Perhaps the first thing to strike a twentieth-century reader is the strange way Socrates introduces the 6 dice in the first place: the 6 are identified as half as many again as 4, half as few as 12. For Socrates, however, this is simply to speak the language of Pythagorean "means."

For—described as simultaneously 4-increased-by-half-its-value, and 12-decreased-by-half-its-value—the quantity 6 measures (in Pythagorean terms) the harmonic mean between 4 and 12.[1] As I read Socrates, it is this introduction of a Pythagorean mean that now gives the necessary nudge to Theaetetus' thinking. For, as the *Epinomis* tells us, and later writers like Nicomachus confirm, there were three means "which came down to Plato and Aristotle from Pythagoras."[2] These were the harmonic, the arithmetic, and the geometric.[3] Each represents different ways of cutting, or measuring off, segments of the more and less—that is to say, the continuum of magnitude. To someone versed in Pythagorean mathematics (as Theaetetus obviously is), it would therefore be naturally and immediately clear that the same quantity "6" could have been equally well measured off, not as a *harmonic* but rather as an *arithmetic* mean, that is to say, by adding to a first extreme the same value that is subtracted from a second extreme. Thus, whereas the harmonic mean gives us $6 = 4 + 4/2 = 12 - 12/2$, the arithmetic mean gives us $6 = 4 + 2 = 8 - 2$. But, I am now convinced, it is awareness of the third (i.e., the *geometric*) mean that underlies the new turn that the discussion now takes, and precipitates us into the heart of what I understand to be the core concern of the *Theaetetus*: the possibility (and reality) of emergent generation.

As we have seen, the *kompsoteros* theory of emergent generation presupposes a twofold rational activity. This activity involves two phases: first, *separation,* according to which discreteness is introduced through (optional ways of) measuring off, or separating out, elements within an original continuum; and second, *combination,* through which, in interactive combination of selected elements, an emergent whole of parts is generated. As I read it, Socrates' introduction of the dice illustration is intended to highlight these points: the notion, first, of a continuum that precedes discreteness; second, the awareness that it is measure which, cutting the continuum, first yields discreteness, and thereby identity; and third, a recognition that the interactive combination of such elements can generate new entities in a new dimension. We can begin to see the significance of Socrates' question to Theaetetus, and the depth of wonder in his response.

For if one thinks of numbers first of all as entities in a number *series,* that is to say, if one thinks of number as consisting of a series of discrete units, then yes, the only way of effecting change will be simply by addition or subtraction. Put this way, Socrates' analogy becomes transparent. For so too in the case of sensible reality: if (like the uninitiated materialists they are about to exclude from the conversation: 155e2-6) one thinks of reality as consisting of pre-given discrete units or particles of matter, then the only way of things coming into being or passing out of being would be by addition or subtraction (conjunction or disjunction). I think Plato wants to make room for this as one very necessary operation, but at the same time to make it clear that it does not account for certain things coming newly into being; in other words, it is not a *generative* operation. What language should he use to communicate this thought as forcefully and as succinctly as possible to a mathematician?

The way Plato chooses is to have Socrates speak Theaetetus' own language, moving from their common understanding of the three Pythagorean means back into Theaetetus' own work in irrationals— exactly as he has described it earlier in the dialogue. Having introduced the quantity 6 as the harmonic mean between 4 and 12, Socrates now confronts Theaetetus with the following question (put into the mouth of those who, like Protagoras, insist on Man as the Measurer): Are these operations of increase by addition (and decrease by subtraction) the only ways of something's becoming more (or less) than it was—indeed, of something's coming into being at all?

> If Protagoras or anyone else should ask you, "Theaetetus, can anything become greater or more in any other way than by being increased?" what reply will you make? (154c7-9)

> And anything to which nothing is added and from which nothing is subtracted is neither increased nor diminished? (155a7-8)

At first, Theaetetus is happy enough with the statements, but now, as he considers again, he begins to realize the implications. Of course there is another way to generate that measurement marked by "6"—a way that grows out of the conception of magnitude as continuum and of number as measured intervals in that continuum, a way, moreover, for which we readers have also been carefully prepared by the dialogue's earlier report of Theaetetus' work with surds. For what Theaetetus described in his account of irrational roots was in fact the generation of number as a geometric mean between two extremes[4] —the distinction between rational and irrational roots resting on whether the generated geometric mean is or is not commensurable with the square measure of the original square and oblong figures. It thus seems that Socrates' question reminds Theaetetus, first, that "6" is the name of the determinate interval measured off within an original continuum of magnitude; second, that 6 may be variously measured off as the harmonic mean between 4 and 12, the arithmetic mean between 4 and 8, or the geometric mean between 4 and 9; and third, that (harking back to Theaetetus' determination of roots as geometric means) it is clearly not by any mere addition, but by interactive combination between the linear measure of the sides, that the generation of a new or second dimension is effected. Underlining this latter recognition,

Socrates is deliberately pointed in his choice of terminology, for in asking Theaetetus, "Can anything become greater or more in any other way than by being *increased*?" the term he selects is *auxēthen* (154c9), the very term that Plato uses of the peculiarly *generative* increase from the one-dimensionality that is the object of arithmetic, to the two-dimensionality that is the object of geometry, to the three-dimensionality that is the object of stereometry (e.g., *Rep.* VII, 528b2-3, d8; IX, 587d9; *Laws* X, 894a3; *Epin.* 990d6). Moreover, it is here, I believe, that Plato locates the source of Theaetetus' philosophic wonder—and this on two levels.

At a first level there is Theaetetus' obvious uncertainty as to how to answer Socrates' question about "increase"—such a simple question if taken at face value, such a subtle question if taken at the deeper level.[5] For, in response to the question as to whether anything can become greater than by being increased (which is then interpreted as increase through addition), Theaetetus is torn. At the level of common sense, he is naturally inclined to answer "no": there is no other way (154c10-d1). On the other hand, there is that earlier question as to whether the number 6 can be viewed in any other way than as a harmonic mean (154c4-5) and the implications recalled by the use of *auxēthen*. In light of this earlier question, which wrenches him back to his own work with irrationals, Theaetetus would have to say "yes," for not only are there, as we have seen, other means of increase (and decrease), but in his own work with surds he had himself been exploiting just such (nonadditive) means in his moves between dimensions—that is to say, his moves from the two-dimensionality of the original square and oblong figures to the one-dimensionality of linear magnitudes, then back to the second dimension, and finally his anticipation of an analogous move to a third dimension. This recognition rightly gives him pause: "If I consider the earlier question, I should say 'yes' for fear of contradicting myself" (154d1-2). It is this vacillation between the "no" dictated by an apparently commonsense view of reality already given as discrete, and the "yes" dictated by a view of reality as continuous wherein we ourselves must be responsible for the measuring, that accounts for the fact that "we find ourselves rather easily forced to make extraordinary and absurd statements, as Protagoras and everyone who agrees with him would say" (154b6-8). Moreover, once this basic antinomy is recognized and we become aware of the problem inherent in the notion of "measure"—whether it be the measuring which cuts the continuum of sound into determinate letters, or the measuring which cuts the continuum of the large and small into determinate quantities (155b6-c4)—then we will recognize the ubiquity of the problem (155c4-5). Specifically, Theaetetus finds himself trying to maintain three incompatible assumptions:

first, that nothing can ever become more or less in size or number, so long as it remains equal to itself...

secondly, that anything to which nothing is added and from which nothing is subtracted, is neither increased or diminished, but is always equal...

thirdly, that what was not previously could not afterwards be without becoming and having become. (155a3-b2)

As geometers who have been working with irrationals, however, both Theaetetus and Theodorus must recognize that not all these can be maintained in light of their own mathematical theory. Accordingly, as Plato reminds us in a different context, it is when we are confronted with contradiction that we are precipitated into reflection (*Rep*. VII, 523b9-524d5). So much for Theaetetus' first-level difficulty.

Having thus noted the extent of the problem raised by the dice, Socrates now goes on to suggest a deeper-level wonder. The dialogue continues with a strange little exchange:

Socrates: You follow me, I take it, Theaetetus, for I think you are not new at such things.
Theaetetus: By the gods, Socrates, I am lost in wonder [*thaumazō*] when I think of all these things, and sometimes when I regard them it really makes my head swim.
Socrates:...this feeling of wonder [*to thaumazein*] shows that you are a philosopher, since wonder is the only beginning of philosophy. (155c5-d4)

Failure to make sense of this exchange seems to me a weakness of the standard interpretations. On my reading, however, Socrates sees Theaetetus filled with wonder, not only at the non-additive power through which we generate successive dimensions in geometry (which he had discussed in his own account of surds), but also (as he had also noted in that same account) at our power to render successively rational what at each lower dimension is still irrational (*Theaet.* 148b1-2), thus bringing about ever more comprehensive rational order. As I understand Plato, this is genuinely cause for wonder:

To a man who can comprehend this assimilation to one another of numbers which are naturally dissimilar, as this is effected by reference to areas, it will be plain that this is no mere feat of human skill, but a miracle of God's contrivance...for those who hit on the discovery, and gaze on it, it is a device of God's contriving, which breeds amazement [*thaumaston*]. (*Epin.* 990d3-e2)

Theaetetus' amazement (Plato uses the same word, *to thaumazein*) is, moreover, recognized to be *philosophical* wonder because such reflection opens him up to the *philosophical* issues raised by the dice illustration, and thus by his own work with irrationals.

Bringing together these two levels of wonder, Socrates now suggests an analogy between his mathematical and philosophical problems. On the one hand, Theaetetus' vacillation between incompatible philosophical positions echoes the incompatibility of incommensurables:

> If you and I were clever and wise and had found out everything about the mind [things might be different]... But, as it is, we will want to look into the real essence of our thoughts, and see whether they harmonize with one another or not at all. (154d8-9, e3-5)

On the other hand, his success in resolving Theodorus' problem of incommensurability in geometry (by providing a comprehensive theory of successive dimensionality within which what is seen as irrational relative to one dimension may be brought into ratio in a higher dimension) now points the way to a comparable resolution of his problem of incommensurables in philosophy (by similarly providing a comprehensive theory of successive cognitive dimensionality within which what is seen as irrational relative to one dimension may be brought into ratio in a higher dimension):

> Do you begin to understand why these things are so, according to the doctrine we attribute to Protagoras?... And will you be grateful if I help you to search out the hidden truth... the mysteries of which I will reveal to you? (155d5-156a3)

On this interpretation, then, the discussion of the dice raises the absolutely pivotal question of how a thing comes to be more than it was, pointing to the peculiarly generative operation exhibited in Theaetetus' own exponential mathematics, in order to establish it as a model for what follows. Already broached as the secret doctrine of Protagoras (152c8-e8), what follows is the detailed and sophisticated version of this same "hidden" theory of emergent generation into which Theaetetus will now be initiated. In thus providing a link between Theaetetus' earlier account of his work with irrationals and the subsequent mysteries of the *kompsoteroi*, the dice illustration prepares the ground for Plato's far-reaching analogy between Theaetetus' work in mathematics and the *philosophical* quest of the dialogue.

This method of analyzing a problem by "modeling" it in terms of another that has been (or can be) solved, in order to facilitate a solution to the original problem, would have been familiar to Theaetetus. It seems to be what the mathematicians of the period called *apagōgē*, or "reduction," for, according to Proclus, "reduction [*apagōgē*] is a transition from one problem or theorem to another whose solution or proof makes manifest also that which is propounded."[6] According to my proposed interpretation, therefore, Theaetetus' account of his work with irrationals—deliberately recalled here in Socrates' dice illustration—turns out to embody a reductive solution to the epistemological and ontological problems of the dialogue. In finding a solution to problems of irrationality and emergent generation in the field of mathematics, he provides the model for a solution to problems of irrationality and emergent generation in the field of cognition.

III

This reading of the dice illustration is, I believe, superior to standard interpretations[7] for the following reasons:

(1) It explains why Theaetetus, with a mathematical mind of the first order, should find himself forced into a quandary by what otherwise seems a merely trivial question about an equally trivial play on words.

(2) It explains why, having on other occasions given thought to these matters, Theaetetus has been carried away by wonder and confusion at all that it might imply (155c8-10)—hence why Socrates can cover a great deal of ground in a few quick strides: "You follow me, I take it, Theaetetus, for I think you are not new at such things" (155c5-7).

(3) It explains why Socrates sees his wonder, not as a banal concern about the relative character of comparatives like *more* and *less* (i.e., as incomplete predicates), but as wonder about the fundamental nature of reality as the subject matter of mathematics and metaphysics, wonder about the nature of the rational enterprise, and therefore the kind of wonder that is the beginning of philosophy (155d2-4).

(4) It explains why the analogy with the dice is introduced here at this point in the dialogue: (a) to reveal the nature of the contradiction in our thinking about reality (154b6-7; 154e3-5; 155b4-5; 155c4-5) in order (b) to prepare the ground for a more subtle theory (both epistemological and ontological).

(5) It explains why, in the earlier part of the dialogue, Plato has gone out of his way to provide an account of Theaetetus' work with irrationals, in just sufficiently detailed outline to allow us to follow his reductive transition. (The conventional explanation of this section, which limits its function to its face-value introduction as providing an example of the sort of definition they seek, although of course true as far as it goes, nevertheless fails, I find, to account for the amount of detail provided.)

(6) It explains why the presence of Theaetetus, and, to a lesser extent perhaps, that of Theodorus, is absolutely crucial to the thought of the dialogue—why, in fact, it is so appropriate that Plato should have chosen to name it the *Theaetetus*.

APPENDIX B
EMERGENCE

The main thrust of theories of emergence in the twentieth century has been directed towards the evolution of the organic from the inorganic, the conscious from the non-conscious, and the mental from the physical. There have been arguments that develop analogies with chemical synthesis, as well as emergentist classifications that structure the universe from elementary particles to complex social systems. The appeal of emergence derives in part from the fact that it seems to offer an alternative to dualism;[1] but, as in the *Theaetetus*, controversy revolves around the relation between that which is said to emerge and that out of which it is said to emerge. For, whether the focus is on emergent entities (as, for example, in much of the discussion in the 1920s involving C. Lloyd Morgan: 1922, 1926; and A.O. Lovejoy: 1926), emergent properties (as, for example, in the work of C.D. Broad: 1925; P. Henle: 1942; and A. Pap: 1952), or emergent laws (as, for example, in the arguments of P. Meehl and W. Sellars: 1956; and P. Oppenheim and H. Putnam: 1958), an emergentist position characteristically stresses novelty as contrasted with that out of which the novel emerges. Confronted, however, with the task of clarifying this central concept, different positions offer different interpretations of what is implied by novelty in the context of explanation, causality, and predictability. This is, perhaps, where Plato's discussion of logos both touches, and departs from, contemporary approaches.

At one extreme, at least in this century, there have been those who, insisting on the inexplicability of emergence, resort to talk of uncertain or puzzling factors such as the "essence of entelechy"[2] or "the life and mind of a world organism."[3] A strong version of this approach finds expression in S. Alexander's claim that "the existence of emergent qualities is . . . to be accepted with the 'natural piety' of the investigator. It admits of no explanation."[4] Not surprisingly, this kind of attitude has been emphatically rejected by other emergentists, even by some who assert emergence at levels all the way from inorganic elements to complex social units. Thus W.M. Wheeler (1926) insists that "the organization is entirely the work of the components themselves and . . . is not initiated and directed by extra-spatial and extra-temporal 'entelechies' (Driesch), 'organizatory factors' (Eldridge), 'deity' (Alexander), or '*élan vital*' (Bergson)."⁵ It is on this issue of the explainability or nonexplainability in terms of its components that, for both Plato and ourselves, the question of emergent novelty seems ultimately to hang—and it is, perhaps, why Socrates' "dream" in the *Theaetetus* continues to tease and puzzle us: for the concept of emergence projects us swiftly into a discussion of the very nature of rational explanation, or logos.

Already back in the 1920s, A.O. Lovejoy, one of the most articulate of the proponents of emergence, was urging that the emergentist claim be set in the context of, and in contrast to, the medieval metaphysical principle of explanation: "there cannot be more in the effect than in the cause." Emergence, he suggested, should therefore be taken

> loosely to signify any augmentative or transmutative event, any process, in which there appear effects that in some one or more of several ways yet to be specified, fail to conform to the maxim that "there cannot be in the consequent anything more than, or different in nature from, that which was in the antecedent."⁶

The lines of battle seemed clearly drawn when, for example, A.E. Taylor (1926) accused emergentists of denying the principle *e nihilo nihil fit*, "which [he goes on to say] is *fundamental to all explanation*" (italics added).⁷ It is not, however, certain that the issue is quite so clear-cut. For, although one of the battles in the war of emergence has focused on this issue of causality versus noncausality, it becomes increasingly clear—both in discussion of the *Theaetetus*, and in the discussions of our own times—that the concept of causality is not itself without ambiguity.⁸ It is true that critics of the emergentist position sometimes pin a kind of radical indeterminism on the concept of emergence—as, for example, does C.R. Morris (1926), who, having attributed just such a view to the emergentists, goes on to find it "fantastic" that it should purport to be offering an intelligible explanation.⁹ It seems, however, more accurate to recognize—along with, say Meehl and Sellars (1956)¹⁰ or Nagel¹¹—that indeterminism is neither essential to, nor characteristic of, emergence. Of course, once the "supervenience" of emergent characteristics has become regular, it will on that score accommodate a Humean kind of causality, and with it a Humean type of predictability. What will prove to be crucial then is the case that initiates the regularity; hence the crux of the debate naturally shifts to that of causality-as-supporting-prior-predictability, for, as Henle notes, "it is because of the failure of one group of qualities to explain another that unpredictability in advance of the fact can be used as the criterion of emergence."[12] But here again, two difficulties arise to muddy the issue—each deriving in a different way from what might be termed the epistemological contingency of predictability.

The first, and weaker, form of objection dates back at least to the discussion of the 1920s. Proposing that "all the laws, emergent or other, are only provisional categories within the field of knowledge," W.L. MacKenzie (1926) therefore went on to conclude that "on the whole it seems to me that the best use of the term [i.e., *emergent*] is to name provisionally cases where causation is accepted as a fact, but where the steps of their production are not yet capable of scientific description".[13] Insofar as predictability is thus seen to reflect the historical state of knowledge, the very notion of emergent nonpredictability dissolves in simple relativity to the state of knowledge at a particular time—with the result that "nonpredictability...is, as it were, only a temporary disability".[14] It is this kind of approach which frames Oppenheim and Putnam's talk of the unity of science,[15] or Smart's talk of its being "in principle possible to deduce" so-called emergent properties.[16] There is, however, a second and stronger dimension of epistemological contingency which has become the focus of logical exploration and has led, interestingly enough, to a recognition of the theory-relative character of both emergent and non-emergent predictions alike.

Already in 1942, Henle had drawn attention to the relative character of predictability. The first step here involves recognition of the dependence of predictability upon evidence, for "predictability, far from being a mere predicate, is at least a tetradic relation and we must say, not that quality A is predictable, but rather that quality A is predictable by person B on evidence C with degree of assurance D." A second step establishes the dependence of evidence on theory, noting that

> prediction can be made...only when [data] are supplemented by hypothesis—and this applies equally to resultants and emergents. Thus the situation always involves a group of data, a, b, c, etc., a system of logic, L, a context of accepted theory, T, an hypothesis, H, and an occurrence of a characteristic, x, whose predictability is in question...In order for x to be predictable, it as well must be a consequence of a, b, c, H, and T.[17]

The upshot is that no characteristic—emergent or non-emergent—is per se either predictable or unpredictable, but may be said to be either only relative to some system. There is, consequently, a shift in the interpretation of emergence, which now is seen to represent anomaly in terms of the theory and so to call for radical redescription. As a result, we are led to identify an emergent as "a characteristic whose appearance calls for a revision of this all-embracing system."[18] In 1952, this relativity to theory was carried one step further when Arthur Pap argued that in those cases in which a predicate is definable exclusively by ostension, a law correlating the quality so defined with causal conditions of its occurrences may "without obscurantism" be characterized as *a priori unpredictable,* and so to this extent, we should therefore understand that "absolute emergence...is relative to a system of semantic rules."[19] In a similar vein, Nagel (1961) locates the issue on the level of logic and language, maintaining that "to say of a given property that it is an 'emergent' is to attribute to it a character which the property may possess relative to one theory and body of assumptions, but may not possess relative to some other theory.[20] Hence, in line with an instrumentalist stance on theory, the doctrine of emergence in the sense of the nonpredictability of certain properties must properly be understood as "stating certain *logical* facts about formal relations between statements rather than any experimental or even 'metaphysical' facts about some allegedly 'inherent' traits of *properties* of objects."[21]

The response from the side of the scientific realist is to press for criteria that would justify the preference for "one theory or body of assumptions" over another, even perhaps at the cost of making "metaphysical" claims.[22] Having done that, one can go on to insist that whether or not there are emergents is actually an empirical question.[23] And this is, I think, where we return to Plato. As I read him, he is offering a theory which in terms of internal coherence is theoretically simple, and in terms of accommodating the data within lawlike structure seeks to be comprehensively fruitful. Within that theory, however, emergence is no longer anomalous; it is seen rather as marking a relation between a whole and its parts, where material causality is to be asserted, but functional reducibility denied.[24] It is not, however, the functional differentiation of every complex in contrast to its components that indiscriminately constitutes for Plato a case of emergence. Thus, to take Wilfred Sellars' example: it is, of course, true that a system of pieces can be a ladder although none of its parts is a ladder; in other words, the complex of rungs and verticals (but not the parts, either separately or together) has the property of being climbable. At an overly simple glance, this might seem to be analogous to the cases identified as emergent; but, as Sellars goes on to note, "There is no trouble about systems having properties which the parts do not have *if these properties are a matter of the parts having such and such qualities and being related in such and such ways.*"[25] For Sellars, as for Plato, the real question arises where there is an ontological difference between the parts and the whole. For Sellars, this is the problem of inter-image reducibility, which for him is paradigmatically exhibited in the case of physical objects interpreted as systems of imperceptible/theoretical particles. Thus Plato too—although in some ways his answer is similar to, and in some ways the exact opposite of Sellars'[26]—concentrates on inter-level emergence, which for him is also paradigmatically exhibited in the case of physical objects, these now seen, however, as systematic wholes which are both analyzable into the sensible properties that, as it were, constitute the "parts," yet ontologically not reducible to those "parts." As I understand him, the *Theaetetus* is an exploration into this concept of emergence in the context of rational explanation, or logos.

NOTES

PROLOGUE

1. As there are different ways to separate the fleece for spinning and weaving, and correspondingly different ways to fashion the shuttle (*Crat.*, 389b8-c1), so there are different ways to structure and interpret a text. In each case the operation is teleological, with different starting points and different criteria yielding different divisions and consequently different identifications. Here the goal is an interpretation of the *Theaetetus* that will be at once coherent and comprehensive. Only in light of such an interpretative structure will we be able to assess a claim like Paul Shorey's that "it is arguable that the *Theaetetus* is the richest in thought of all the Platonic dialogues" (Paul Shorey, *What Plato Said* [Chicago: University of Chicago Press, 1933], p. 269).

2. W.K.C. Guthrie, "Twentieth-Century Approaches to Plato," *Lectures in Memory of Louise Taft Semple* (University of Cincinnati Classical Studies, Princeton, 1967), pp. 1-2; see also his *History of Greek Philosophy*, vol. 4: *Plato* (Cambridge: Cambridge University Press, 1975), pp. 43-44.

INTRODUCTION

1. The best-known occurrence of this metaphor is probably in the *Republic*, where Socrates' response to the threat of being engulfed by three successive "waves" culminates in the introduction of the notion of the philosopher-king (*Rep.* IV, 473c6-e4), but the mythology of salvation from the turmoil of the sea of argument runs deep throughout the dialogues (e.g., *Lach.* 194c2-5; *Protag.* 338a5-6; *Rep.* V, 453d9-11; *Theaet.* 177b8-c1; *Parm.* 137a5-6).

2. One thinks not only of the challenge posed from the standpoint of the social sciences (like that of Levy Strauss, Peter Winch, or even Michel Foucault), but especially of the clever attacks mounted from within the perspective of philosophy itself (like Jacques Derrida's criticism of what he calls the "logocentrism" of the tradition, or Richard Rorty's of what he takes to be philosophy's misguided effort to mirror nature). This critique of reason is honed to razor edge in the articulate rejection by so many intelligent women, both within and without philosophy, of a dangerously cerebral and impoverished concept of rationality which is held largely responsible for the long history of male and Western domination.

3. The line between historical accuracy and imaginative creation in the dialogues is difficult to draw; in the case of the *Theaetetus*, however, Plato does

make a point of having Eucleides insist that Socrates himself vouched for the report of the conversation (*Theaet.* 142c8-143a5).

A correspondingly difficult line to draw is that between views merely attributed to various characters, on the one hand, and those that represent the position of Plato himself, on the other. Since in the dialogues Plato does not speak in his own voice but—if at all—only through the personae of his characters, there must be questions raised about any suggestion that there are nevertheless to be found in the dialogues philosophical statements or doctrines attributable to Plato himself. Since, at certain points, I will in fact be making such a claim, certain observations seem to be in order here by way of justification.

First of all, when one finds a characteristic pattern of argument repeated in dialogue after dialogue, from early through middle to late periods, it seems to me more likely than not to reflect the approach of the author himself. Second point: the opinions expressed by various participants do very often contain insights which are not only not disproved, but actually (even if sometimes indirectly) defended; the problem is that they need to be subjected to the purification of cross-examination, in order to discard the worse and retain the better interpretations (*Soph.* 226d5-10). When these purified insights are seen to be not only consistent across the dialogues, but even sustained as mutually complementary so that their integration yields a coherent philosophical position, then I think we can seriously entertain the hypothesis that this represents Plato's own thought. Third point: when such philosophical doctrines do, moreover, find independent confirmation from outside the dialogues—as, for example, in the *Seventh Epistle* (even if it is not actually Plato's own) or in Aristotle's reports, then there seems to me to be reasonable support for believing that these doctrines do in fact represent Plato's own position.

4. *Logos* is one of those tricky words that do not translate easily, because to translate it is to do just what this dialogue will warn us against; that is, the Englishing of it tends to reduce it to just one of its aspects. For *logos* in Greek captures the comprehensive sense of rational structure as it applies either to product (hence can mean speech, a statement, a definition, a rational account or explanation, an argument, or simply discourse as such), or to the power of reason which produces the structure. Unfortunately, there is no obvious counterpart in English, so in order to preserve the comprehensive sense of the Greek (which I understand to be crucial to the argument of the dialogue) I shall often simply use the word *logos* and try to associate it with the English equivalent appropriate to the context.

5. Not surprisingly, the interpretation of *epistēmē*, meaning "knowledge," will turn out to be crucial—and tricky. In contrast to the situation with logos, where the problem is that we have many different English words for the one Greek word, here the difficulty is rather that Greek has many different words for what in English we uniformly translate as "knowledge." For this reason, some of the important distinctions that the dialogue later draws between various forms of knowledge are difficult to capture with only one English word at our disposal. For this reason I shall sometimes follow Plato in using *epistēmē* for the particular kind of knowledge they are seeking.

6. In this study generally, the argument is not affected by disagreements

between Professor Owen's earlier dating of the *Timaeus* and traditional interpretations that read it as one of the later dialogues. See G.E.L. Owen, "The Place of the *Timaeus* in Plato's Dialogues." *Classical Quarterly, n.s. 3 (1953), reprinted in R.E. Allen, ed., Studies in Plato's Metaphysics (Routledge and Kegan Paul, 1965),* pp. 313-338.

7. Pursuing (the philosopher's) true and (the sophist's) false claims to knowledge, discussion in the *Sophist* leads logically to the inner inquiry into the meaning of falseness as such (false speech, false opinion, and finally the sophist as false philosopher). This in turn projects us into the central discussion of the dialogue, the inquiry into being as object of philosophic knowledge; for it is only in light of that account that we finally come to understand the core notions of true and false—and therefore, both the philosopher and his mimic, the sophist.

8. It will be remembered that the theory of recollection is introduced at this point in the dialogue to persuade Meno that inquiry is possible and worthwhile. Having achieved this purpose, Socrates pauses before going on, in order to warn Meno: "Most of the points I have made in support of my argument are not such as I can confidently assert; but that the belief in the duty of inquiring after what we do not know will make us better. . . this is a point for which I am determined to do battle" (*Meno* 86b6-c2).

9. That the *Meno's* link between "remembering" and "dreaming" might be deliberately echoed here in the *Theaetetus* would fit well with the fact that numerous other parallels between the *Meno* and the *Theaetetus* have been noted by scholars (e.g., F.M. Cornford, *Plato's Theory of Knowledge: The Theaetetus and Sophist of Plato,* translated with a running commentary [London: Kegan Paul, 1935], p. 27; M.S. Brown, "*Theaetetus,* Knowledge, as Continued Learning," *Journal of the History of Philosophy,* 7 [1969]: p. 360).

In the context of *aporia,* there is an amusing parallel between the two dialogues with respect to people's reactions to the challenge of perplexity. In the *Meno,* we hear poor Meno's frustration as he turns on Socrates, accusing him of so bewitching and benumbing people that he is dangerously like the torpedo fish, and warning him that if he doesn't look out, those who don't know him might try to arrest him as a wizard (*Meno* 80a2-b7). In the *Theaetetus,* Socrates himself admits that people find him "a most eccentric person, who drives them to distraction," so much so that some are "actually ready to bite me" (*Theaet.* 149a8-9; 151c5-7).

10. For reactions to this riddling character of the *Theaetetus,* see, for example, K.M. Sayre, *Plato's Analytic Method* (Chicago: University of Chicago Press, 1969), pp. 120-123; G.R. Morrow, "Plato and the Mathematicians: An Interpretation of Socrates' Dream in the *Theaetetus* (201e-206c)," *Philosophical Review,* 79 (1970): 309-311; compare J. Burnet, *Greek Philosophy, Thales to Plato* (London: Macmillan and Company, 1914, 1950), pp. 251-252; and A.E. Taylor, *Plato: The Man and His Work* (London: Methuen, 1926; 7th. ed. 1960), p. 346.

11. One might add others—for example, Critias' understanding of the Delphic inscription "Know thyself" (*Charm.* 164d6-165b3, et seq.), or the contrast between Socrates' interpretation of Anaximander's "mind rules the universe" (*Phil.* 30d8) and the inadequate interpretation of which Socrates complains in the *Phaedo* (97b8-98c2). So too, in the *Theaetetus* itself, as I shall

argue later, Protagoras' "Man is the measure of all things" and Heracleitus' affirmation of flux are likewise subjected to cross-examination to purify them of false interpretations, and at the same time to expose the truth they embody.

12. See my "Why Dialogues? Plato's Serious Play," in *Platonic Writings/ Platonic Readings*, ed. Charles Griswold (New York: Routledge and Kegan Paul, 1988).

13. To Ludwig Edelstein, Plato's strictures against writing seem "un-Platonic," and it is this supposedly unPlatonic character of the *Seventh Epistle* that constitutes his main objection to the authenticity of the letter (e.g., *Plato's Seventh Letter*, Philosophia antigua XIV [Leiden: E.J. Brill, 1966], pp. 80-82). But Professor Edelstein makes equally little sense of the similar remarks in the *Phaedrus*, finding that "the passages in the *Phaedrus* raise a real problem. They make it hard to understand that Plato, holding the beliefs he propounds there, should have bothered to write at all" (p. 84).

14. For example, L. Campbell, ed., *The Theaetetus of Plato* (Oxford: Clarendon Press, 2nd. ed., 1883), p. 228; W. Lutoslawski, *The Origin and Growth of Plato's Logic* (London: Longmans Green and Company, 1897, 1905), p. 376; P. Shorey, *The Unity of Plato's Thought* (Chicago: University of Chicago Press, 1903, 1960; Archon Books, 1968), p. 71; Burnet, *Greek Philosophy*, pp. 251-252; Taylor, *Plato: The Man and His Work*, p. 346; Cornford, *Plato's Theory of Knowledge*, pp. 146-154; C. Mugler, *Platon et la recherche mathématique de son époque* (Strasbourg: Editions P.H. Heitz, 1948), p. 206; P. Kucharski, *Les chemins du savoir dans les derniers dialogues de Platon* (Paris: Presses Universitaires de France, 1949), pp. 232-234—who claims that after the initial plausibility, Socrates' critique exposes "l'inanité" of the dream; R.S. Bluck, "*Logos* and Forms in Plato," *Mind*, 65 (1956), reprinted in Allen, *Studies in Plato's Metaphysics*, p. 39; P. Friedländer, *Plato*, trans. H. Meyerhoff (New York: Pantheon Books, 1958-1969, vol. 3, pp. 185-186; N. Gulley, *Plato's Theory of Knowledge* (London: Methuen, 1962), pp. 99-100; W.G. Runciman, *Plato's Later Epistemology* (Cambridge: Cambridge University Press, 1962), p. 40; I.M. Crombie, *An Examination of Plato's Doctrines* (New York: Humanities Press, 1963), vol. 2, pp. 115-117; Sayre, *Plato's Analytic Method*, pp. 126-130; J.H. Lesher, "*Gnōsis* and *Epistēmē* in Socrates' Dream in the *Theaetetus*," *Journal of Hellenic Studies*, 89 (1969): 73-75; Morrow, "Plato and the Mathematicians," pp. 310-311; M.F. Burnyeat, "The Material and Sources of Plato's Dream," *Phronesis*, 15 (1970): 122; D. Wiggins, "Sentence Meaning, Negation, and Plato's Problem of Non-Being," in *Plato: A Collection of Essays*, ed. Gregory Vlastos (Garden City: Anchor Doubleday, 1971), p. 285; A.O. Rorty, "A Speculative Note on Some Dramatic Elements in the *Theaetetus*," *Phronesis*, 17 (1972): 235-237; J. McDowell, *Plato: Theaetetus* (Oxford: Clarendon Press, 1973), pp. 240-250; N.P. White, *Plato on Knowledge and Reality* (Indianapolis: Hackett, 1976), pp. 178-179; J. Klein, *Plato's Trilogy: The Theaetetus, the Sophist, and the Statesman* (Chicago and London: University of Chicago Press, 1977), p. 139; H. Teloh, *The Development of Plato's Metaphysics* (University Park, Pa.: Pennsylvania State University Press, 1981), p. 207; and E.S. Haring, "The *Theaetetus* Ends Well," *Review of Metaphysics*, 35 (1982)—the latter finding it "wildly wrongheaded" (p. 513, n. 10), "a child's version of epistēmē" (n. 11).

15. Cornford, *Plato's Theory of Knowledge*, p. 143.

16. Aristotle, *Met.* H, 1043b23-1044a9.

17. Campbell, *Theaetetus,* p. xxix.

18. Burnet, *Greek Philosophy,* p. 252, especially footnote 2; Taylor, *Plato: The Man and His Work,* p. 346, and footnote 2.

19. Cornford, *Plato's Theory of Knowledge,* p. 144.

20. Ibid.

21. J. Stenzel, *Plato's Method of Dialectic,* trans. D.J. Allen (Oxford: Clarendon Press, 1940), pp. 63-64: "I have no hesitation in saying that the doctrine of recollection is never referred to in the *Theaetetus* and that the general tone of the dialogue is rather against it"; cf. R. Robinson, "Forms and Error in Plato's *Theaetetus,*" *Philosophical Review,* 59 (1950): 3-4. See also R.H. Hackforth, "Notes on Plato's *Theaetetus,* 145d-201d," *Mnemosyne,* ser. 4, 10 (1957): 140. L. Robin proposes that the role played by recollection in the *Meno* is in the *Theaetetus* played by the notion of pregnancy and midwifery; in both cases it is insisted that ultimately we must do it ourselves, and the most Socrates can do is to *help* (*Platon* [Paris: Librairie Felix Alcan, 1935], pp. 72-73).

22. Crombie, *Examination of Plato's Doctrines,* vol. 2, p. 109.

23. Thus B. Jowett, *Dialogues of Plato* (Oxford: Clarendon Press, 4th. ed., 1953, vol. 3, p. 191), talks of "the vain search, the negative conclusion" (p. 223); for Lutoslawski, "the question of 'what is knowledge?' [is] raised in the *Theaetetus* and left unanswered" (*Origin and Growth of Plato's Logic,* p. 406); G. Grote elaborates a little further: "After a long debate, set forth with all the charm of Plato's style, no result is attained. Three different explanations of knowledge have been rejected as untenable. No others can be found; nor is there any suggestion offered, showing us in what quarter we are to look for the true one" (*Plato and the Other Companions of Socrates* [London: John Murray, 1865], vol. 2, p. 387). And so with Campbell, *Theaetetus,* pp. lvi, lxxi, 238; A. Diès ed., *Platon: Oeuvres complètes* (Paris: Société d' édition "Les belles lettres," 1924), vol. 8, p. 147; Shorey, *Unity of Plato's Thought,* pp. 50, 66; Shorey, *What Plato Said,* pp. 285-286; Burnet, *Greek Philosophy,* pp. 236, 237, 253; Taylor, *Plato: The Man and His Work,* pp. 347-348; Robin, *Platon,* p. 64; Stenzel, *Plato's Method of Dialectic,* pp. 66, 72; Cornford, *Plato's Theory of Knowledge,* pp. 151, 154; H.F. Cherniss, "The Philosophical Economy of the Theory of Ideas," *American Journal of Philology,* (1936), reprinted in Allen, *Studies in Plato's Metaphysics,* pp. 6-7; Friedländer, *Plato,* vol. 3, pp. 152, 154; A. Koyré, *Introduction à* la Lecture de Platon (New York: Brentano's, 1945), p. 88; A.J.M. Festugière, *Contemplation et la vie contemplative selon Platon* (Paris: Librairie philosophique J. Vrin, 2nd. ed., 1950), p. 408; Robinson, "Forms and Error," pp. 4, 14-15; W. Hicken, "Knowledge and Forms in Plato's *Theaetetus,*" *Journal of Hellenic Studies,* 77 (1957), reprinted in Allen, *Studies in Plato's Metaphysics,* p. 185; Gulley, *Plato's Theory of Knowledge,* pp. 101, 103; Runciman, *Plato's Later Epistemology,* p. 40; Crombie, *Examination of Plato's Doctrines,* vol. 2, pp. 105-106; E. W. Schipper, *Forms in Plato's Later Dialogues* (The Hague: Nijhoff, 1965), p. 28; Sayre, *Plato's Analytic Method,* pp. 133, 137; Lesher, "*Gnōsis* and *Epistēmē,*" p. 78; Morrow, "Plato and the Mathematicians," pp. 309, 313; J. Annas, "Knowledge and Language in the *Theaetetus* and *Cratylus,*" in *Language and Logos: Studies in Ancient Greek Philosophy presented to G.E.L. Owen,* ed. M. Schofield and M.C. Nussbaum (Cambridge: Cambridge University Press, 1982), pp. 112-114; and S.R. Benardete, *The Being of the Beautiful: Plato's Theaetetus, Sophist, and Statesman,* trans. and with commentary (Chicago and London:

University of Chicago Press, 1984), vol. 1, p. 182. A notable exception to this consensus is to be found in Haring's "The *Theaetetus* Ends Well," which proposes that Theaetetus' theoretical "grounding" of Theodorus' opinion about the particular surds provides the needed model for an analogously "grounding" interpretation of logos at the end, so that the final definition would be able to stand (pp. 523-527).

24. Not only does he believe that "the conclusion is an avowal of Socratic ignorance"; it also reflects Platonic ignorance, or at least Platonic perplexity (Shorey, *Unity of Plato's Thought*, p. 50; cf. p. 66). So too Hicken finds that "the dialogue reflects a genuine state of *aporia*" ("Knowledge and Forms," p. 187). According to Crombie, "Plato has come to have various more or less specific doubts and reservations about his earlier accounts of knowledge" (*Examination of Plato's Doctrines*, vol. 2, p. 106). Compare Robinson's suggestion that Plato is indeed confused, although apparently not aware of his own confusion: despite the searching critique to which the dialogue subjects his earlier account of knowledge as involving true opinion and logos, Plato nevertheless continues (one assumes uncritically) to subscribe to the earlier account ("Forms and Error," p. 16).

25. Lutoslawski, *Origin and Growth of Plato's Logic*, pp. 382, 385. Actually, he is even more enthusiastic: "This new development beginning here—with the substitution of categories for ideas, of the individual soul for the supercelestial space, of analysis and synthesis for poetical vision, of activity and passivity for immutable identity, of critical cautiousness for poetical eloquence—is a momentous step in the history of thought, and would have required another thinker than the author of the *Republic* and *Phaedrus* were he not of such an immense intellectual power, and had he not lived so long as to initiate a new philosophical movement after the age of fifty" (pp. 384-385).

26. Burnet finds that

it is improbable that he had a definite original philosophy of his own by the time the *Republic* was written...it is quite different from anything Aristotle ever ascribes to Plato himself. If Plato had originally taught this system [he is talking here chiefly of the soul and what he calls Plato's theory of goodness; but we know from the setting of the discussion (p. 174) that "this theory of goodness and the good is the exact counterpart of the theory of knowledge and reality which Plato ascribes to Socrates"]...we may be sure we should have heard something about this remarkable change of opinion, if the doctrine Aristotle ascribed to him was only a development of his later years. As it is, there is no hint anywhere in Aristotle that Plato ever taught anything else than what he regards as the genuine Platonic doctrine.

Again: "Aristotle knows of but one Platonic philosophy, that which identified the forms with numbers. He never indicates that this system had taken place of an earlier system in which the forms were not identified with numbers, or that he knew of any change or modification introduced into his philosophy by Plato in his old age" (Burnet, *Greek Philosophy*, pp. 178, 313).

27. Ibid., p. 213

28. Ibid., pp. 24, 283.

29. Ibid., p. 237; cf. p. 253.

30. Ibid., p. 253.

31. He stresses the shift, for example, from "participation" in the *Phaedo*, which is concerned with the relation of the particular things of sense to the forms, to "participation" in the *Sophist* (based on *ta koina* of the *Theaetetus*), which is concerned with the relation of the forms or kinds with each other (*Greek Philosophy*, p. 283).

32. As Taylor puts it, "Plato is now raising a different issue. We are to see that forms *as such* can 'combine' so that you can predicate one 'universal' of another, and it is the special function of the new science Plato is contemplating to specify the lines on which such combination is possible" (*Plato: The Man and His Work*, p. 388).

33. Ibid., p. 348.

34. Stenzel writes: "When he wrote the *Theaetetus*, he had...already obtained a clear grasp of the conception of knowledge which we find in the *Parmenides* and *Sophist*, in its essential outlines. That is to say, Dialectic had been completely freed from dependence on the Idea of the Good, which had been its essence in the *Republic*, and had become a logic which, if not purely formal, was at least free from a specifically moral content" (*Plato's Method of Dialectic*, pp. 66-67). Again: "We saw [earlier] how *logismos aitias* in his earlier system would lead ultimately to the Idea of the Good....But Plato's attitude has changed; he is interested in mere knowledge and definition; and he has turned to objects which it would, on the face of it, be meaningless and unnecessary to bring into a teleological connection with the Good—even the Good in its function as the cornerstone of rational knowledge...the Good falls into the background" (ibid., p. 72). Contrast Bluck's contention that Plato's conception of *epistēmē*, even in the *Theaetetus*, is (by analogy with spiritual or theological knowledge of the Good) still primarily teleological ("*Logos* and the Forms," pp. 40-45).

35. For Stenzel, the method of the later dialogues consists in definition achieved through division by classes; he sees the *Theaetetus* as marking—in anticipation—the introduction of this method:

> What is Plato's new method? It was not yet mentioned in the *Theaetetus*, but all the problems of this dialogue converged towards it, and Plato did not fail to give a clear indication of his future course. He raised a significant question: what is the *essential formula* which can raise right opinion to the plane of knowledge? Now it is the science of definition which gives such a formula. Definitions are the subject of the *Sophist* and *Statesman*; and the "philosophical" scholars are quite right in saying that method, and again method, is the content of both dialogues. From the first word of his argument in the *Sophist* to the last word of the *Statesman*, Plato leaves us in no doubt what *is* his method (*Soph.* 218c, d; *Statesman*, 287a); it is that analysis of class-concepts, *diairesis*, which leads in every case to a definition. (*Plato's Method of Dialectic*, p. 78; cf. pp. 85, 107-108)

36. As Campbell points out, "The whole spirit of Socrates, with his common instances and his resolute preference for human questions...pointed

in this direction," for "the truth is that Plato is perpetually striving to reconcile thought with reality . . . and continually acknowledges in practice that while all things are to be tested by logic, the conclusions of logic must be tested again by fact." Thus, while Campbell cites from the *Theaetetus* many direct appeals to "experience," he points at the same time to similar tendencies in the *Republic*, and even the *Phaedrus* (*Theaetetus*, pp. lii-liii).

37. Burnet, *Greek Philosophy*, p. 235.

38. Ibid., p. 248.

39. Stenzel, *Plato's Method of Dialectic*, p. 64. He goes on to observe that "whilst Plato's first interest was the moral one, he was primarily concerned with objects which could be understood *a priori;* later when he came to deal with empirical objects, he had to reconstruct his method." Robin notes that, although the *Theaetetus* is characterized by an emphasis on Becoming, it is not forgetful of the unity and unchangingness of Being (as implied not only by the respect accorded Parmenides and Melissus at 183d et seq., but also in the choice of Eucleides as narrator) (*Platon*, p. 119).

40. Brown, "*Theaetetus*," pp. 360-361, 377. Brown has a very carefully worked out argument to support his position—based on a fairly close analogy between procedure in the dialogue and the method of mathematical solution to problems of incommensurability as initiated by Theodorus and Theaetetus.

41. Robinson, "Forms and Error," p. 5.

42. Lutoslawski finds that "it is very surprising that among the possible meanings of *logos* enumerated, precisely that meaning which this word appears to have in connection with knowledge for Plato (*aitia*)is omitted, except in one passage in the familiar phase, *dounai te kai dexasthai logon:* 202c, in which *logos* is identified with sufficient reason, as in similar passages of the *Cratylus* (426a), *Phaedo* (76b, 95a), and *Republic* (531e)" (*Origin and Growth of Plato's Logic*, p. 378).

43. Thus Crombie suggests that the fact that they "almost ostentatiously ignore" a consideration of *logos* in the sense of the *Meno's logismos aitias* indicates the absence of any serious attempt to defend the final definition (*Examination of Plato's Doctrines*, vol. 2, p. 105). Likewise for Sayre, the omitting of any consideration of the "quite common use of the term . . . according to which *logos* means *ground*" convinces him that shades of meaning within that range might have been "highly suggestive in a serious attempt to make the third hypothesis work as an analysis of knowledge." It is his conviction that "Plato's procedure in ignoring these uses most certainly was deliberate. Yet if he had considered these senses, the dialogue could not have ended on the entirely negative note for which it has become famous" (*Plato's Analytic Method*, p. 133; cf. Schipper, *Forms in Plato's Later Dialogues*, p. 29).

44. In distinguishing between true opinion and knowledge, A.J. Ayer, for example, sought to develop the notion of "the right to be sure," without becoming involved in psychology (*The Problem of Knowledge* [London: Macmillan, 1956], pp. 28-34). Shorey, by contrast, understands the *Theaetetus'* effort to define knowledge over and against mere true opinion to be properly psychological, and is convinced that for Plato "no definition of knowledge that goes beyond a tautological formula can be given apart from a complete and definitive psychology" (*What Plato Said*, pp. 269, 286). Taylor, however, finds that "it has been at least forcibly suggested by the tenor of the whole argument

that all the proposed definitions have failed precisely because each of them has attempted to provide a *psychological* criterion of knowledge, and no such psychological criterion is possible" (*Plato: The Man and His Work,* p. 347).

45. Thus Crombie suggests that perhaps Plato now feels that his earlier conception of knowledge as *connaître* is now giving way to a recognition of the necessity for *savoir* (*Examination of Plato's Doctrines,* vol. 2, pp. 106-107). But his further argument that Plato's distinction between a correct account in terms of propositions, on the one hand, and direct acquaintance, on the other, is a more important distinction than that between a priori and empirical knowledge (ibid., p. 128; cf. p. 121) does seem rather far-fetched—on which point, see the review of Crombie's book by N. Gulley (*Philosophical Quarterly,* 15 (1965): 359).

46. For example, Bluck proposes that "some sort of personal acquaintance is the mark of knowledge...the outcome of the discussion of complexes no more suggests that knowledge is in fact of complexes than that it is of simples...It looks, then, as though *epistēmē* may be knowledge by acquaintance with Forms" ("'Knowledge by Acquaintance' in Plato's *Theaetetus,*" *Mind,* n.s. 72 (1963): 260-261). Compare, however, R.C. Cross's argument against such an interpretation ("*Logos* and the Forms in Plato," *Mind,* n.s. 63 (1954), and reprinted in Allen, *Studies in Plato's Metaphysics,* p. 24, and passim), which concludes that "in the end...forms are logical predicates displayed in *logoi,* and not simple nameables known by acquaintance" (ibid., p. 29). Bluck's rejoinder to Cross, "*Logos* and the Forms in Plato," appeared in *Mind,* n.s. 65 (1956), and is reprinted also in Allen's *Studies in Plato's Metaphysics.* Runciman interprets the conclusion of the *Theaetetus* as the assertion that "knowledge cannot be of complexes" (*Plato's Later Epistemology,* pp. 48, 129); rather, he maintains, it is "a sort of mental seeing or touching" (ibid., p. 52). (The supposed dilemma of whether Plato viewed the forms as simple or composite was the subject of a paper by Henry Teloh at the twenty-fifth annual meeting of the Metaphysical Society of America, in Boston, March 1975.)

47. According to James Lesher, the dialogue ends in failure because Theaetetus still believes that *gnōsis* is somehow the same as *epistēmē.* In contrast to his earlier inconsistency of usage (e.g., *Rep.* 477a-480), Lesher argues,

> these passages in the *Theaetetus* reveal that part of Plato's critical undertaking is to distinguish senses of "knowing" which had either been unknown or ignored in his earlier epistemology. It is a measure of his philosophical acumen that by the time of the *Sophist* Plato was no longer content to characterize knowledge of the forms as simple acquaintance with a supreme and simple entity, but as knowledge *that* certain Forms combined with others to make complex Forms...The distinction between *gnōsis* and *epistēmē* promoted in the refutation of Socrates' dream in the *Theaetetus* marks the beginning of this important development in Plato's later epistemology. ("*Gnōsis and Epistēmē,*" p. 78)

48. Runciman, *Plato's Later Epistemology,* pp. 17, 29, 34; cf. 13, 16.

49. Of the failure of the *Theaetetus,* Cornford observes: "The Platonist will draw the necessary inference. True knowledge has for its object things of a different order—not sensible things, but intelligible Forms and truths about

them... The *Theaetetus* leads to this old conclusion by demonstrating the failure of all attempts to extract knowledge from sensible objects" (*Plato's Theory of Knowledge*, pp. 162-163; cf. p. 151).

50. According to Cherniss, "The attempt of the *Theaetetus* to define knowledge fails, and this failure demonstrates that the logos, the essential characteristic of knowledge, cannot be explained by any theory which takes phenomena to be the object of intellection... The *Theaetetus*, then, is an attempt to prove that the theory of ideas is a necessary hypothesis for the solution of the problems of epistemology" (Philosophical Economy," p. 7).

51. R.H. Hackfort, "Platonic Forms in the *Theaetetus*," *Classical Quarterly*, n.s. 7 (1957): 53-58.

52. Shorey, unlike Cornford, finds that "although the ideas are not often or very explicitly mentioned, there is enough to show the presence of the doctrine in its normal form. The *agathon* and *kalon*, claimed for being as against becoming in 157d, is almost technical for the affirmation of the ideas. The *paradeigmata* of 176e can hardly refer to anything else. And the close parallel between 186ab and *Republic* 523, 524, admits no other interpretation" (*Unity of Plato's Thought*, p. 33).

53. For Burnet, the theory of forms or ideas represents "Socratic" thinking (deriving from Pythagorean influence), and therefore for the most part does not figure in the later "Platonic" dialogues (e.g., *Platonism* [Berkeley, Calif.: University of California Press, 1928], p. 46; *Greek Philosophy*, p. 235).

54. Talking of the absence of the forms from most of the later dialogues, Taylor comments:

> I do not see how to account for these facts on the view that Plato had himself originated the doctrine and regarded it as his special contribution to philosophy... the silence about the forms in the *Theaetetus* may mean either that when he wrote that dialogue he was feeling the necessity for a "Platonic" doctrine which had not yet been definitely worked out, or else that he *had* already arrived at the results Aristotle always assumes to be the Platonic teaching, and felt that they were so definitely his own that dramatic verisimilitude would be outraged by putting them into the mouth of Socrates (*Plato: The Man and His Work*, p. 348)

55. Shorey, *Unity of Plato's Thought*, p. 34.

56. H. Jackson, "Plato's Later Theory of Ideas IV, The *Theaetetus*," *Journal of Philology*, 13 (1885): 266. He goes on to associate the theory of ideas he finds implied in the *Theaetetus*, not so much with the ideas of the *Phaedo* period, but rather with those of the *Parmenides* (ibid., pp. 267-268). Sir David Ross finds the doctrine of forms implicitly present because of the sharp distinction between sensation and knowledge (*Plato's Theory of Ideas* [Oxford: Clarendon Press, 1951], p. 103), and a more recent commentator goes further, denying any final rejection of the last definition for just the same reasons as Cornford: the object of knowledge is the Forms (S. Wheeler, "The Conclusion of the *Theaetetus*," *History of Philosophy Quarterly*, 1 [1984]: 365).

57. Robinson points out that "Cornford's interpretation tends to imply that the *Theaetetus* regards the difference [between knowledge and true

opinion] as lying only in their objects. He writes as if, once we admit that the object of knowledge is the Forms, we know what knowledge is. He does not contemplate the view that, however much we know that knowledge is of the Forms, we do not thereby know what knowledge is . . . I think that at no time of Plato's life would he ever have regarded the statement that knowledge is about the Forms as the complete answer to the question 'what knowledge is' ("Forms and Error," p. 17). Glenn Morrow agrees that "it would be hasty to assume that all was clear sailing for Plato from this point onward . . . Unlike some of his modern followers, Plato was not so naive as to believe that an appeal to the doctrine of Forms was sufficient to settle all difficulties" ("Plato and the Mathematicians," p. 312).

58. As Robinson reads the dialogue, he finds that Plato "seems to imply in the *Theaetetus* that some knowable things have no logos at all. For the examination of the three senses of 'logos' is immediately preceded by a discussion of uncompounded elements, the tendency of which is to conclude that, if elements are unknowable because they have no logos, everything is unknowable, from which anyone who thought that knowledge does occur would have to conclude that a thing's being alogon does not make it unknowable" ("Forms and Error," p. 15).

59. Cross quotes from a paper read to the Oxford Philological Society by Professor Ryle (*"Logos* and the Forms," p. 14).

60. Cross points to the similarity of language at *Theaetetus* 202c and *Republic* 531e, where he is setting forth his earlier philosophical views (*"Logos* and the Forms," pl. 15). Lesher goes even further to point out that the elements, which are unknowable, are like the Forms in being *auto kath'hauto* (completely separate), *asyntheton* (simple), and *monoeides* (uniform). He then reminds us that at *Phaedo* 78 and 80 the forms are said to be *monoeides* and *asyntheton;* at *Symposium* 211b, Beauty itself is represented as *auto kath'hauto meth'houtou monoeides;* and finally, in the *Sophist* and *Statesman,* division is into classes which are simple and apart from every other class (*adiaireton, atmēton, atopon*). Lesher concludes that "far from showing the necessity for Forms as objects of knowledge, the dream theory points to a fundamental difficulty in Plato's earlier accounts of these lofty and eminent nameables" (*"Gnōsis* and *Epistēmē,"* p. 74). This point has been reiterated more recently by H. Teloh. Noting this "striking resemblance" between the description of the "dream" elements and Plato's middle-period Forms (which, he finds, renders them similarly unknowable), Teloh sees the *Theaetetus* as the occasion for Plato's rethinking his understanding of Forms: since the earlier "atomistic" interpretation of Forms is now seen to be "incompatible with the definitional enterprise," Plato begins instead to connect the Forms in a network whereby they lose their isolation, single-formedness, and eventually their separateness, and become the "kinds" of the *Philebus* and *Sophist* (*Development of Plato's Metaphysics,* pp. 208-209). It seems to me, however, that, although echoes of language prior to the *Theaetetus* obviously strengthen the theory of self-criticism, nevertheless the later use of similar language (as noted above by Lesher in the context of both the *Sophist* and the *Statesman*) would seem to raise serious doubts about the negative intention of the supposed criticism.

61. According to Shorey, there are two reasons the dialogue had to fail: (1)

the formal quest for an absolute definition always fails in Plato; (2) it is not possible to define knowledge, or explain error. The most we can do is describe and classify different stages of cognition and various forms of error (*Unity of Plato's Thought*, p. 66). In short, the force of the *Theaetetus* is to recognize that knowledge is ultimately "a mystery" not susceptible of explanation (*What Plato Said*, p. 284).

62. Festugière, *Contemplation*, p. 408.

63. Morrow points to the reader's surprise, not only at the rejection of the final definition, which embodies an apparently Platonic doctrine, but particularly at "the perfunctory character of the examination given it," and then goes on to observe that "Socrates' bland assumption that he has exhausted the possibilities and thereby refuted Theaetetus' proposal is enough to put us on our guard against taking too seriously the apparent frustration with which the dialogue ends" ("Plato and the Mathematicians," pp. 309-310).

64. Ibid., p. 311.

CHAPTER 1:
AMBIGUITY

1. The significance of the introductory section of the dialogue will become clear only gradually. Discussion here will therefore begin directly with the efforts to define knowledge, returning in context to review the opening exchange.

2. As I shall argue, the recurrence of assertions involving this idea of something being "nothing other than" something else (*ouk allo ti...ē...*) is at various points in the dialogues deliberate. Thus we find the following:

Knowledge is nothing other than perception (*Theaet.* 151e2-3).

The universe is nothing other than motion (*Theaet.* 156a5).

Much of the universe is nothing other than space (*Crat.* 412d2-3).

Being is nothing other than power (*Soph.* 247e3-4).

In exactly what sense might any of these assertions be defended? Does the claim that "*a* is nothing other than *b*" permit the reduction of *a* to *b*? As I read it, this is one of the overarching questions that is opened up here in the *Theaetetus*.

3. It is possible (though not, it seems to me, necessary) to read Professor McDowell this way when he translates *hos epistēmē ousa* (152c5-6) not as "since it is knowledge" or "as being knowledge" (as do Campbell, Fowler, Cornford, etc.), but rather as " 'as if it's knowledge'...understand[ing] the force of the words as something like 'This is what one would expect if it were correct that perception is knowledge,' " for he then goes on explicitly to propose the following: "In that case the point being made is that the veridicality of perception, derived not from the equation of knowledge with perception but from Protagoras' thesis, affords an argument in favour of the equation of knowledge with perception" (McDowell, *Plato: Theaetetus*, note on 151b1-c7, comment under (b), pp. 120-121).

4. Cornford likewise recognizes two distinct characteristics here (*Plato's Theory of Knowledge*, p. 32).

5. Cornford discusses two possible interpretations of "the wind itself" as understood by Protagoras—the one according to which the wind itself is both warm and cold, the other according to which the wind itself is neither warm nor cold. He believes Protagoras to have held the first, but that the second is a construction Plato will put on it as preparatory to the theory he will develop (Cornford, *Plato's Theory of Knowledge*, pp. 33-36). In contrast to commentators like Cornford who have speculated about what sort of conception of "the wind itself" is to be imputed to Protagoras, McDowell seems to be more faithful to the argument here when he claims that "such speculation seems pointless. It seems obvious that, at least as Plato interprets him, Protagoras refuses to make sense of questions about what the wind is like in itself, as distinct from questions about what it is like for one person or another (152b5-7)" (McDowell, *Plato: Theaetetus*, p. 119).

6. An extreme form of relativism, carried to the point of denying a common real world, as proposed, for example, by Taylor (*Plato: The Man and His Work*, p. 326), is rejected by Cornford as "much too advanced for Protagoras' date" (Cornford, *Plato's Theory of Knowledge*, p. 34). McDowell seems to follow Cornford in this weaker reading, suggesting that even at 152c5 we should add "for one" at the end, since "Plato is not always strict about these qualifying phrases" (*Plato: Theaetetus*, p. 120). It seems to me, however, that Campbell's insight here is sounder when he points up the radical step from "relative being. . . to 'being'" (*Theaetetus*, p. 39).

7. Socrates limits the claim here to strictly perceptual reality, that is, to "matters of warmth and everything of that sort" (152c1-2).

8. Thus, if one were to spell it out, Socrates' argument would, I suppose, go something like the following:

Argument from Protagoras' logos

If X feels the wind as cold,* then the wind is cold for him (152b6-7).
If X feels the wind as cold, then the wind seems cold to him (152b9).
If the wind seems cold to X, then X perceives the wind as cold (152b11).
If X perceives the wind as cold, then the wind is cold for him.
If X perceives $w\theta$, then $w\theta$ is the case for X (152c2-3) [since the only plausible reading of "to be the case" is "to be the case for X" (see McDowell's point, note 5 above)].
Therefore if X perceives $w\theta$, then $w\theta$ is (infallibly?) the case (152c5).**

*Literally: if the wind is blowing (152b2) and one feels shivering cold (152b3).
**Campbell draws attention to the radical character of this move (*Theaetetus*, p. 39).

Argument from Theaetetus' logos

If X perceives $w\theta$, then X knows $w\theta$ (Theaetetus' definition: 152c5-6).
If X knows $w\theta$, then $w\theta$ is (infallibly) the case (knowledge is infallible: 152c5-6).
Therefore if X perceives $w\theta$, then $w\theta$ is (infallibly) the case (152c5).

9. As noted above, Cornford distinguishes between the reality of what is apprehended, on the one hand, and the infallibility of the apprehension, on the

other, as "the two marks of knowledge, which any candidate to the title must possess" (*Plato's Theory of Knowledge*, p. 32).

    10. Thus:

Argument from Protagoras' logos

Perception is apprehension of what exists.
Apprehension of what exists cannot be false.
Therefore perception cannot be false (152c5-6).

Argument from Theaetetus' logos

Perception is knowledge [reading Theaetetus' definition as identity].
Knowledge cannot be false.
Therefore perception cannot be false (152c6).

In reading the *hos epistēmē ousa* as a deliberate restatement of Theaetetus' premiss in order to line up the two arguments, I am disagreeing with McDowell (see above, note 3) but following Campbell, who, translating the phrase as "in accordance with your theory," finds this reading required in order to "bring 'the wheel full circle' and to complete the identification of Protagoras' theory with that of Theaetetus" (*Theaetetus*, p. 39).

    11. Again, Socrates' argument might be (somewhat laboriously) spelled out as follows:

Ontological thesis implied by Protagorean doctrine
Either things are of themselves some one thing, or it is not the case that things are of themselves some one thing.

Either (w is of itself θ) or -(w is of itself θ).
  If w is of itself θ, then w is θ for every perceiver (at time t).
    If X perceives $w\theta$, then $w\theta$ is the case for X (at time t).
      If $w\theta$ is the case for X (at time t), then $w\theta$ is the case (at time t).
      If Y perceives $w-\theta$, then $w-\theta$ is the case for Y (at time t).
        If $w-\theta$ is the case for Y (at time t), then $w-\theta$ is the case (at time t).

    Therefore $w\theta$ is the case and $w-\theta$ is the case (at time t).
    Therefore -(w is θ) for every perceiver (at time t) (152b2-c3).
    Therefore -(w is of itself θ) (152d2-6).
Therefore it is not the case that things are of themselves some one thing (152d3).

Argument by *reductio* was a common form of argument (cf. Aristotle's account of the proof of the irrationality of $\sqrt{2}$ (*Prior An.* i 23, 41a26-27), the form of which is believed to be Pythagorean (H. Heath, *A History of Greek Mathematics* [Oxford: Clarendon Press, 1921], vol. 1, p. 157). It is likewise the form underlying Zeno's paradoxes.

    12. To find this hint merely in the irony of this passage would surely be far-fetched, but it seems to be carried through in the later cross-examination of Protagoras (see below, chapter 5).

    13. Although this ontological theory, according to which it is asserted that "everything is in motion, flowing like streams" (160d7-8), is associated no less

with Homer than with Heracleitus (e.g., 160d7, 179e3; cf. *Crat.* 402a4-b5), it is nevertheless convenient and, on the whole, consistent (e.g., *Crat.* 401d4-5; 402c2-3; 440c1-2) to refer to it as "Heracleitean."

14. This is the interpretation Cornford attributes to "this rather bare and obscure statement" as it occurs at 153e4-5, as also at 156e8 and 157a8, although here at 152d3 he takes it to mean simply that "no quality (contrary) exists *without its contrary*" (*Plato's Theory of Knowledge*, pp. 39-40, ftn3).

15. This reading of 152d3-153a3—according to which Plato is seen as leading us to successively stronger interpretations of "nothing is of itself any one thing"—differs quite radically from that of Professor McDowell.

In contrast to Campbell, who has nothing special to say about this formula, or Cornford—whose relatively brief discussion interprets it as "the doctrine that all sensible objects are perpetually changing" in contrast to "the real being of intelligible objects [which] is always the same, never admitting any kind of modification" (*Plato's Theory of Knowledge*, pp. 36, 39)—McDowell devotes seven pages to the analysis of this section. Translating *hen men auto kath' hauto ouden estin* as "nothing is one thing just by itself," he himself finds the expression ambiguous, but seems not to see Plato as aware of this ambiguity, and certainly does not consider the possibility that Plato might be deliberately playing on a studied ambiguity. Thus he proposes "two possible interpretations of these words: (a) Nothing is one thing without also being something else...incompatible with the first thing...; (b) Nothing is, on its own, any one thing—heavy, say—as opposed to being, e.g., heavy in relation to something else (in this case a perceiver)" (*Plato: Theaetetus*, p. 122). These two interpretations correspond, as far as I can see, to (a) a weak form of what I am calling interpretation 2, and (b) the straightforward form of what I am calling interpretation 1. What I am calling interpretation 3 he seems deliberately to exclude (see under his point [2], p. 122). As far as "the point of the secret doctrine" is concerned (ibid., p. 123), McDowell himself prefers to interpret the formula as expressing a linguistic concern "which centres on the rejection of 'be' in favour of 'come to be'" (ibid., p. 124). The difficulty of reconciling this with the text seems to me, however, to militate quite strongly against such an interpretation. There are several specific difficulties with McDowell's interpretation, which I shall try to note.

(1) Basing his argument on one version of Parmenidean logic, he goes on to attribute to Plato acceptance of a principle

A': "In the case of that which in any way is not f, it is not the case, strictly speaking, that it in any way is f"

—from which in turn he concludes that "if a thing is not big, say, for you, then...it cannot be strictly accurate to say that it is big in any way, e.g., for me." He concludes that this supposed acceptance of A' "indicates lack of enlightenment about the logic of of what may be called incomplete predicates" (ibid., p. 126). Two remarks seem to be to be in order. First, principle A' seems to me to be a strange assertion to attribute to Plato; after all, the entire passage which elaborates the formula (153d8-157c2) defends it as a thesis which, if true, would mean that the only accurate way of talking about perceptual qualities at all would be to admit that what is not f (e.g., not big) in some way (e.g., for you) will also be f (e.g., big) in some way (e.g., for me). Second, I should rather have thought Plato's position to be responding to the following question:

> What must be the case in order for us to maintain—as we do for any perceptual predicate—the following principle:

>> A'': In the case of that which in any way (e.g., for you) is not f, it will always be, strictly speaking, equally accurate to say that it in some other way (e.g., for me) is f.

In other words: *given* the logic of incomplete predicates required by Plato's relativization of all perceptual predicates, what must be the case for the referents of such predicates? (McDowell will shortly [i.e., in the case of the dice analogy at 154c1-5] make the same criticism about Plato's failure to grasp the logic of incomplete predicates; my longer discussion about the dice illustration in appendix A will, I hope, satisfactorily meet that second statement of his objection.)

(2) McDowell next proposes that further reflection on Parmenides' argument that "what is cannot come to be" might have suggested to Plato a distinction between "two sorts of subject matter: (a) that which is, statements about which can be generally described...using 'is'; and (b) that which comes to be, *for which 'comes to be' might be pressed into the same service.*" Although he finds nothing here in the *Theaetetus* to justify such a distinction—even to the point of admitting that "indeed, the secret doctrine is so stated as to imply that (a) is empty (152e1: 'nothing ever is')"—he nevertheless concludes, somewhat surprisingly, that "that need not, I think, damage the above account of how the secret doctrine is arrived at" (ibid., pl. 127).

(3) It is in connection with the dialogue's "nothing whatever is one, *either a particular thing* or of a particular quality" (152d6)—which constitutes the second part of the secret doctrine—that McDowell admits the greatest difficulty in defending his interpretation of that doctrine as a recommendation about linguistic usage. At this point, McDowell follows two somewhat different—but, to me, equally odd—lines of observation.

(a) He suggests that one way of handling the difficulty might be to interpret the formula's being applied to *things* as merely "a way of denying that things persist through time." His argument for this interpretation, however, depends on his claim that "the thesis that things are qualitatively unstable...Plato *apparently takes to be a consequence* of the rejection of 'be' in favour of 'come to be' in the case of statements purporting to say how things are qualified" (my italics) (ibid., p. 128). This strikes me as a strange claim in view of what the text is arguing. It is, I suppose, in a kind of a way understandable that he should tend to give logical primacy to his own linguistic emphasis rather than see the question of linguistic usage as a consequence of something prior; but even in his own translation, the two passages in question seem to acknowledge a reverse order of implication:

> Nothing is one thing just by itself, and you can't correctly speak of anything either as some thing or as qualified in some way... *since* nothing

is one—either one thing or qualified in one way. (My italics)
The fact is that, as a result of movement, change, and mixture with one
another, all the things which we say are—which is not the right way to
speak of them—are coming to be; *because* nothing ever is, but things are
always coming to be. (My italics) (McDowell's translation of 152d2-e1)

Actually, Burnet's Oxford Classical text, which is what McDowell is using (see
his Preface) seems to me to lean even more heavily towards reversing the order
of implication (152d7-e1). The Loeb translation done by H.N. Fowler thus
seems better to capture the sense of the passage:

It is out of movement and motion and mixture with one another that all
those things become which we wrongly say are—wrongly *because* nothing
ever is, but is always becoming. (My italics) (152d7-e1)

The difference between the translations hinges on the interpretation of what it
is that is being explained by the phrase *esti men gar oudepot' ouden aei de gignetai*
(152e1). Fowler (rightly, I think) takes it as explaining what immediately
precedes it, that is, the fact that we wrongly say things "are" (152d8-e1)—
which makes obvious good sense when paraphrased: "If things never are but
are always becoming, then it would follow that our saying they 'are' would be
wrong." McDowell's translation, on the other hand, takes the phrase in
question as explaining, not the immediately preceding fact that we use
language wrongly, but the earlier fact that things come to be as a result of
movement, change and mixture with one another (152d7-e1). It is harder to see
how this explanation would work with a paraphrase: "If things never are but
are always becoming, then it would follow that as a result of movement,
change, and mixture with one another, all the things which we say are...are
always coming to be." From McDowell's point of view, the trouble with the
Fowler kind of translation (and with the text itself, I venture to suggest) is that
is does not support his overall interpretation that the crux of the secret
doctrine "centres on the rejection of 'be' in favor of 'come to be'" (ibid., p. 124).
(b) McDowell's other remark about the difficulty of defending his proposed
interpretation in face of the second part of the secret doctrine is simply to
suggest that "perhaps it need not greatly concern us at this point. For [Plato]
may not have thought out fully the more general argument which this passage
seems to promise" (ibid., p. 128). This remark seems to me even more surprising
than the other—so carefully does it seem to me that Plato has thought out and
developed the more general argument which this passage does indeed
promise.
    The advantages of my proposed interpretation of this section over those of
McDowell's reading of a program of linguistic reform seem to me to be, first,
that it is consistent with the text; second, that it makes sense of the text; and
third, that it accords (as I shall now argue) with Plato's next moves as he leads
us, step by step, from acceptance of the weaker, to commitment to the stronger,
doctrine.
    16. Recall that what Socrates is offering here is a preliminary account of his

earlier statement that "all things are the offspring of flow and motion" (152e8);
the "sophisticated" account is yet to come.

17. My understanding of the argument here is shown in figure 8.

Figure 8.
Argument for Interpretation 2 of the Heracleitean logos:

In the case of things perceived as of a certain quality:
  either a: things of themselves really are of some quality
    or b: it is not the case that things of themselves really are of some quality

If a: then either (1) the object itself really is of that quality
          or (2) the subject itself really is of that quality

    If (1): w is itself really $\emptyset$
        then either (a) w is $\emptyset$ for X — i.e., if X perceives w
                              then X perceives w as $\emptyset$
                     and w is $\emptyset$ for Y — i.e., if Y perceives w
                              then Y perceives w as $\emptyset$
                     etc.
        or (b) w has changed.
        it is not the case that (b) w has changed;
        therefore (a) w is $\emptyset$ for X, and w is $\emptyset$ for Y, etc.
        But it is not the case that (a) w is $\emptyset$ for X...for Y, etc.
        Therefore it is not the case that (1) w is itself really $\emptyset$ (154b1-3)

    If (2): X is itself really $\emptyset$ (where X is the perceiving sense organ)
        then either (c) w is $\emptyset$ for X — i.e., if X perceives w
                              then X perceives w as $\emptyset$ at time t
                     and z is $\emptyset$ for X — i.e., if X perceives z
                              then X perceives z as $\emptyset$ at time t
                     etc.
        or (d) X has been affected.
        it is not the case that (d) X has been affected;
        therefore (c) w is $\emptyset$ for X, and z is $\emptyset$ for X, etc.
        But it is not the case that (c) w...z, etc., are $\emptyset$ for X
        Therefore it is not the case that (2) X is itself really $\emptyset$ (154b3-6)

Therefore not-a: it is not the case that either
                (1) the object is itself really $\emptyset$, or
                (2) the subject is itself really $\emptyset$

Therefore b: it is not the case that things of themselves really are of some quality.

Therefore in the case of things perceived as of a certain quality, it is not
        the case that things of themselves really are of some quality.

Thus, "nothing is of itself any one thing" under interpretation 2 — meaning nothing
        is of itself of any particular quality.

18. It could of course be argued that all he has shown is that of *things that
are perceived* nothing is of any particular quality; it says nothing of *things that are
not perceived*. True, it could conceivably be held that things that are *not* perceived
are really of some particular quality—but this totally untestable thesis Plato

ignores, and concludes that nothing ("nothing perceived" in the tenseless sense that covers "nothing perceived at any time by any perceiver") is of itself of any particular quality.

19. There are two (not unrelated) senses in which these layers of interpretation are to be understood as successively "sophisticated." First, there is the sense of "sophisticated" according to which Plato offers us interpretation 1 as the common and public one, interpretation 2 as the hidden doctrine taught in secret to an inner circle of (presumably more mature or better-trained) disciples, and interpretation 3 as what he calls the doctrine of "the sophisticates." Second, there is the sense of "sophisticated" according to which each subsequent interpretation is more philosophically sophisticated in that each offers a more comprehensive philosophical statement from which the less sophisticated interpretation will follow. This parallels that usage of "weak-strong" where the strong implies the weaker, but not vice versa.

20. Critical questions about the ensuing theory have been recently raised by Miles Burnyeat, who reads it as representing an unacceptably Heracleitean theory of perception ("Plato on the Grammar of Perceiving," *Classical Quarterly*, 26 [1976]: 29-51). With Burnyeat, I find this account "a superbly elaborate argument designed to unravel the implications and commitments of Theaetetus' definition of knowledge as perception" (Burnyeat, "Idealism and Greek Philosophy," *Philosophy Review*, 90 [1982]:5). Where I part company, however, is in the final assessment of the theory, for Burnyeat reads it as refuted and rejected, whereas I (as will become increasingly evident) see it as defended and maintained. In this respect, I join Burnet, Cornford, Jackson, Ritter, Stenzel, McDowell, and many other commentators, who have taken the theory here developed to be Plato's own. See references, G. Nakhnikian, "Plato's Theory of Sensation," part 2, *Review of Metaphysics*, 10 (1956): 306.

CHAPTER 2:
***KOMPSOTEROS* THEORY OF GENERATION**

1. One commentator who also finds it natural to talk of this as the theory of the *kompsoteroi* is Henry Jackson. Believing that the theory "originated with Plato himself," Jackson proposes that "he is indeed a better Heracleitean than Heracleitus himself, as appears when the theory of sensation passes from the *amuētoi* [uninitiated] to the *kompsoteroi;*" he argues that "in one stage of its development the Platonic system found a place, not only for the doctrine of flux, but also for its corollary, the 'mystical' theory of sensation...The 'mysteries' of the *kompsoteroi*...cannot be assigned to any of Plato's predecessors...he must therefore be held responsible for this speculation" (Jackson, "Plato's Later Theory," pp. 256, 265, 268).

2. It is illuminating to compare this interpretation with passages in another dialogue that also deal with the theme of generation and perception. (Later there will be opportunity to compare other aspects of the theory with approaches found in dialogues like the *Republic, Cratylus,* and *Philebus*). The dialogue I am thinking of is the *Timaeus*. Although Jackson finds this *kompsoteros* teaching of the *Theaetetus* to be incompatible with that of both the *Phaedo* and

the *Republic,* he does nevertheless see it as "not merely consistent with that of the *Timaeus,* but even necessary to its completion"; he concludes that "the two dialogues belong to the same period, and further that they are intended to supplement one another" ("Plato's Later Theory," pp. 269-270). Although my argument in no way depends on Jackson's earlier dating of the *Timaeus,* it does seem to me that Jackson is right in finding a striking consistency between the two dialogues. Thus, the *Timaeus* is equally insistent that the originally differentiated units constitute no elemental "given"; on the contrary, they are the created products of the Demiurge, or *nous,* and only later products at that; for "fire and the rest of the elements. . . cannot reasonably be compared by a man of any sense to. . . the first compounds" (*Tim.* 48b7-c2).

3. Thus, again, the account in the *Timaeus,* continuing to push the inquiry back beyond any differentiation into distinct elements, proceeds to derive those elements from more primitive *archai* defined in terms of mathematically ordered spatial relationships—but even these are to be understood not as "given," but as the work of divine structuring intelligence: "These we lay down as the *archai* of fire and all the other bodies. . . but the *archai* which are still higher than these are known only to God and the man who is dear to God" (*Tim.* 53b4-d7).

4. Once again, this would be consonant with the *Timaeus'* suggestion that "before the universe was organized and generated, all these things were in a state devoid of reason or measure" (*Tim.* 53a8), "moving in an irregular and disorderly fashion" (*Tim.* 30a4-5).

5. The view of quantity as continuous flow seems at times to be reflected in Euclid's language, for example, in the postulate, "to produce a finite straight line continuously in a straight line" (*Elements,* Postulate 2), and in his dealing with proportionality in terms of magnitudes (*megetha*) rather than units (*Elements* v. definitions). Later, in the same tradition, Nicomachus defines number not only in terms of units, but as "a flow [*chuma*]. . . of units" (*Introduction to Arithmetic,* i, 7, *Greek Mathematical Works,* tr. I. Thomas [Cambridge, Mass.: Harvard University Press, Loeb ed., 1939] vol. 1, pp. 72/73). See discussion below, under Mathematical Interlude: *Kompsoteros* Method and "Playing the Geometer."

For important work interpreting Plato's mathematical symbolism, see, for example, R.S. Brumbaugh, *Plato's Mathematical Imagination* (Bloomington, Ind.: Indiana University Press, 1954), and E.G. McClain, *the Myth of Invariance: the Origin of the Gods, Mathematics, and Music, from the Rg Veda to Plato* (New York: Nicholas Hays, 1976). McClain not only reveals significant links between mathematical, musical, political, and mytho-religious dimensions in Greek society, but shows how parallel structures and connections are to be found in other ancient world cultures.

6. In the language of other dialogues, this is to say that the ontological "given" is "this material element. . . inherent in the primeval nature, infected with great disorder" (*Stat.* 273b4-6); it is *alogos* (irrational, incoherent), *ametros* (unmeasured, unstructured), *anous* (irrational, mind-less) (*Tim.* 53a8; cf. 44a7-b1).

7. My understanding of 155e4-5 is as follows: In contrast to the true doctrine that "nothing is except motion" (156a4-5), the uninitiated hold that "nothing is except what they can grasp firmly with their hands" (155e4-5).

Now if it is graspable (in contrast to sheer motion, which is not), it would seem to be touch-resistent, space-occupying matter. In that case, then, they might see it as *either* (a) nondiscrete, that is, continuously solid matter—but in that case it would not be graspable; *or* (b) discrete or particulate matter, in which case to talk about it as "graspable" would offer a fairly accurate account from the point of view of people so uncultivated. I have therefore taken the point of view of the uninitiated to be a view of reality as consisting of discrete, and to that extent determinate, material particles. (This reading is, I believe, confirmed by the account of the materialist position in similar terms at *Sophist* 246a7-b3).

8. This second stage, involving division by means of measure, corresponds again to the pattern of organization in the *Timaeus* where, faced with the original state of irrational disorder, "God began by first marking it out into shapes by means of forms and numbers" (*Tim.* 53b4-5).

As suggested by Theaetetus' account of surds, no less than by Socrates' exchange with Meno's slave boy, one of geometry's advantages over arithmetic is that it makes possible the handling of irrational quantities. Since the linear continuum can be cut at any point, by which cutting either rational or irrational quantities may be measured off, Theaetetus is able to determine a line of irrational length as a mean proportional between two rational quantities (see appendix A). Sayre finds further evidence of this awareness at *Parmenides* 140c, noting that the close parallel between the definition of proportional magnitudes attributed to Eudoxus and incorporated into Euclid *Elements* V, and Dedekind's definition of irrational numbers, has been recognized by several historians of mathematics, and even by Dedekind himself (R. Dedekind, *Essays on the Theory of Numbers*, tr. W.W. Beman [Chicago: Open Court, 1901], pp. 39-40; see K.M. Sayre, *Plato's Late Ontology: A Riddle Resolved* [Princeton, N.J.: Princeton University Press, 1983], pp. 105-107).

9. This exhaustive division of reality into units exhibiting either an active or a passive power recalls the Stranger's suggestion in the *Sophist:* "I propose that everything which possesses any power [*dynamin*] of any kind, either to produce a change in anything of any nature or to be affected even in the least degree by the slightest cause...has real existence. For I set up as a mark characterizing being, that it is nothing other than power" (*Soph.* 247d8-e4).

10. This passage seems straightforward (e.g., Campbell, *Theaetetus,* p. 61; Cornford, *Plato's Theory of Knowledge,* p. 47; McDowell, *Plato: Theaetetus* , pp. 140-141). What I am pinpointing here, however, is that sense of "relative" which focuses on contrary "appearings" over and against some (supposed, but not actual) state of "really being." For this "appearing" (*anephanē*) in different contexts as active or passive (rather than "really being" one or the other, cf. McDowell, *Plato: Theaetetus*) echoes the slightly earlier passage which had highlighted the parallel contrast between qualities "appearing" over and against their "really being" (153e7; 154a3, b2, b4).

11. This seems to me the most reasonable and plausible reading of this condensed reference to the uninitiates' denial of "actions" (*praxeis*). After all, it seems unlikely that these unsophisticates would be denying actions in any of the ordinary senses of "doing" or "acting"; one is therefore forced to explore other possibilities of meaning that Socrates might conceivably intend. Given the context, one is led to expect reference to some positive act of mind over and

against a passive state in which one simply experiences reality as "given". But is there any specific justification in Platonic usage for reading *praxis* in this special sense of a positive act in contrast to a relatively passive condition in which one might receive external input? It seems to me that there is. Thus it seems to be just this awareness of an active, in contrast to a passive, state of reception or possession that we find in *Republic* IV, where passive possession and active doing are balanced off as *hexis te kai praxis (Rep.* IV, 433e12-434a1). Shorey, who translates *hexis* here as straight-forward "having," argues that *"hexis* is still fluid in Plato and has not yet taken the technical Aristotelian meaning of habit or state" (*Republic*, trans. Shorey, Loeb ed., vol. 2, p. 371, ftn. [d]). But Shorey makes no mention of the fact that by the time of the *Theaetetus*, *hexis* does indeed carry this meaning of condition, or habit, or state, for this is how it is used at *Theaet.* 153b5 and 153b9. Thus the preceding section of the *Theaetetus* itself would tend to support this reading of the traditional contrast between *praxis* as positive, active-voice action, over against a passive state of receptivity. The plausibility of reading *praxis* in this sense seems, if anything, even more clearly confirmed in the *Laws*, where *praxis* is used as deliberate contrast and foil for *pathos (Laws* IX, 876d4).

12. What we have so far are the determinate elements introduced at stage 2, through division, but as yet no sensible world of physical objects. Since such a description must seem puzzling, it might be fruitful to look at two analogies to help us understand what Socrates is saying about the situation so far. First, it seems to accord with a corresponding stage in his later illustrations from music and language in which, from an original indeterminate flow, sound is measured out into "intervals" in the one case and "letters" in the other —prior to the generation of music or language as such. Second, it seems to accord with the corresponding stage in the *Timaeus* in which (as we have just seen above), from an original indeterminate state, the Demiurge marks out shapes and relations prior to the generation of physical objects (*Tim.* 53b4-c7). In all these cases, there is on the one hand a recognition of the elements out of which music, language, *and physical reality* respectively *will arise,* and on the other a recognition that, as elements, these measured units *do not yet constitute* music, language, or *the world of physical objects as such.*

13. Plato's use of *dynamis* here apparently involves an adaptation of its traditional meaning in the context of geometry. Burnyeat has demonstrated that, according to ancient testimony, *dynamis* means "square." Citing Alexander of Aphrodisias' explanation that a square is called *"dynamis"* because it is *what the side is able to produce,* he shows that it is only in virtue of that meaning that Theaetetus can give it the new twist that refers to his line segments ("The Philosophical Sense of Theaetetus' Mathematics," *Isis,* 69 [1978]: 495-502). This explanation accords with Heath's parallel reminder that, while on the one hand *dynamis* means "square," on the other, a straight line is said to *dynasthai* a certain *area* by being *squared.* The substantive, *dynamis,* is usually used in the dative, as in *dynamei isē,* "equal in square." But it is clear in the context of *Theaetetus* 148b that it means what we call a "square root," that is, the equivalent in geometry of what in arithmetic we call a "surd" (T. Heath, *Mathematics in Aristotle* [Oxford: Clarendon Press, 1949], pp. 207-208).

14. One of the points one immediately notices in this account of sensation

in the *Theaetetus* is the apparent contradiction between this early presentation in which the sense organ is seen as active and the object as passive (154b1-3, 156b7-c3), and the later accounts in which the case is the reverse (159c8-9, 182a6-b2). The discrepancy is so glaring that it can hardly be read as inadvertent. I am more inclined to read it in light of the insistence that activity and passivity are mutually and radically relative in that any motion can appear as either active or passive (157a3-7), and therefore to take so-called objects as being in some sense passive and in another sense as acting on our organs of sense to generate sensation; likewise, the socalled organs can be seen as in some sense passive to the impact of objects and in another sense as acting upon those objects to generate sensible properties.

15. Translating this thought into the language of ordinary physical objects yields, of course, something like Cornford's translation, "As soon as an eye and something else whose structure is adjusted to the eye...," or Fowler's, "Now when the eye and some appropriate object..." Although McDowell in his translation gives us the phrase as Plato has it (i.e., "When an eye, then, and something else, one of the things commensurable with it..."), nevertheless in his note he explains that "commensurable with it" amounts to "perceptible by it" (*Plato: Theaetetus*, p. 138). There are, however, what seem to me compelling reasons for retaining Plato's own choice of *commensurable*. First, it picks up the original theme of commensurability as introduced by Theaetetus' work with surds. Second (as McDowell notes), it continues the allusion to "measure" in Protagoras' formula. Third, it offers, in terms of these successive *kompsoteros* stages, the most accurate capturing of that relationship between the "measured" elements of stage 2 which permits the move to stage 3. Each of these three considerations will in the long run prove to be significant.

16. Already, in the earlier account, Socrates seems to have anticipated this development, for there he had talked of the interaction between sensing subject and sensed object in terms of touch—with overtones (perhaps both literal and sexual) of "kindling" and "being kindled" (154b1, b4).

17. Again, it would seem that what these unsophisticates are denying must be generation (*genesis*) in a rather more subtle sense than the obvious coming-to-be and passing-away that even the uneducated would acknowledge.

18. *Emergence* is, of course, a term heavily laden with connotations deriving from twentieth-century discussions in the philosophy of science. To situate the present use of the term in the context of those discussions, see appendix B.

19. This point-by-point contrast with the views of the uninitiated seems designed to play a deliberate role in our coming to understand the position of the *kompsoteroi*. After all, for Plato, as well as for us, one of the most effective ways of clarifying any position is to explore the implications of its denial.

CHAPTER 3:
KOMPSOTEROS THEORY OF PERCEPTION

1. As the *Philebus* reminds us, although "some such change must always be taking place in us since everything is always flowing and shifting," it would be impossible that "we and all other living beings should be always conscious

of everything that happens to us" (*Phil.* 43a2-b6). For this reason, Socrates contrasts those sensations that do, and those that do not, reach to the level of consciousness—thereby distinguishing sensations that merit the name of perception from those innumerable disturbances of which we never become aware and which therefore remain on the level of sheer material impact. Thus we must "assume that some of the affections of our body are extinguished in the body before they reach the soul, leaving the soul unaffected, and that other affections permeate both body and soul and cause a vibration in both conjointly and in each individually"—and we should reserve for *conscious* sensation the term perception (*aisthēsis*) in its strict sense, so that "instead of saying that the soul forgets, when it is unaffected by the vibrations of the body, apply to them 'want of perception' " (*Phil.* 33d2-34a1).

2. Since there is controversy about how to interpret this theory, a word of explanation is in order. As I read it, Socrates distinguishes three levels here. (a) The original interacting motions are those with active and passive power (156a5-7)—although Socrates is quite insistent that even this distinction is not determinate, insofar as no motion is fixedly of either character; a motion becomes active or passive only in interaction relative to each other; and any motion can appear as either active or passive (157a3-7). These motions take place in space, are relatively stable, or "slow," and interact with any other similar motions within range (156c8-d1).

My understanding is that what Socrates is talking of at this level is what we think of as physical reality. It is conceived of as continuous motion, which, in its ebb and flow, moves in and out of becoming (and ceasing to be) what we come to think of as various kinds of physical objects. Such motions are slow relative to the next level; they occur in space, and mutually affect each other (e.g., holding back, or restraining [*ischei*] any other motion that comes within its range: 156c8-d1). These constantly shifting "motions" at one time actively affect others and at another are passively affected, becoming at times what we would describe as living matter with the physiological structure of sense organs, such as an eye, at others what we would describe as inanimate matter, such as sticks or stones (156a5-7, c8-d1, d3-4, e6; 157c1-2). Generative inter-action between these kinds of motions "begets" (156d1) those at the next level. (b) The "twins" which are "the offspring" of these physical-matter motions Socrates calls "swift motions". They have an effective range of operation not restricted by the same constraints of place as the physical-matter motions (156d1-3). These are apparently what we think of as subjective sensibility on the one hand (i.e., sensory powers that we "give names to, like sight and hearing": *opseis* and *akoai*), and as objective sensibility on the other (i.e., sensible properties that we give names to, like *whiteness* and *sounds: leukotēta* and *phōnai*) (156a7-c3, d1-5). Generative interaction between the subjective sensibility of the senses (e.g., the swift motion we call "sight") and objective sensibility (e.g., the swift motion we call "whiteness") produces the third level. (c) When a swift motion of sense (Socrates' example is "sight") and a swift motion of sensible property (his example is "whiteness"), being mutually "commensurable," do interact, then each "joins in giving birth" (*synapotiktontos*) to an act of sensation: a single occurrence in which are simultaneously born the products of the next generation—which Socrates emphatically distinguishes from senses and sensibles of level (b) "the eye becomes full of sight and so begins at that moment to see, and becomes, certainly not *sight,* but *a seeing eye;* and the object which joined in generating the color [*syggennēsan*] is filled with whiteness, and becomes in its turn, not *whiteness,* but *white"* (156d3-e5).

3. The *kompsoteros* account of perception is elaborated in some detail in the *Timaeus,* where *aisthēsis* is seen as arising in

> bodies subject to inflow and outflow...violently rolled along within a mighty river...in such a random way that progress was disorderly and irrational...The flood that foamed in and streamed out was immense... and the motions due to all these causes rushing through the body impinged upon the soul; and, for all these reasons, all such motions were then termed *aisthēsis* [apparently derived from *aissō* = dart, or rush]. (*Tim.* 43a5-c7)

4. Whatever the exact relation between mind (*nous*) and soul (*psychē*), it is clear that "wisdom and mind could never come into being without soul" (*Phil.* 30c9-10); or, as the *Timaeus* puts it, "*nous* cannot possibly belong to anything apart from soul. So, because of this reflection, God constructed *nous* within soul, and soul within body" (*Tim.* 30b3-5).

5. This point, too, is made in the *Timaeus:*

> In the beginning, all was in a state of disorder...nor was it possible to name anything worth mentioning, like fire or water...we must never describe fire as "this" but as "suchlike," nor should we ever call water "this" but "suchlike": nor should we describe any other element as though it possessed stability, nor, when we use terms like "this" and "that," should we suppose we are referring to something definite, for they are too volatile to be identified by "this" or "that" or by any other term that implies that they are stable. (*Tim.* 69b2-8, 49d5-e4)

6. It is not just that through language we mark difference and identify things (*Phil.* 25a2-4; *Stat.* 258c4-6). As the *Cratylus* puts it, a name is to be understood as "an instrument of teaching and of separating reality" (*diakritikon tēs ousias*) (*Crat.* 388b13-c1). Actually, the overlap between the *Theaetetus* and the *Cratylus* at this point is striking. For the *Cratylus* too sees language poised between what is given in nature on the one hand—nature for the most part being viewed in the same terms of flux that are echoed in the *Theaetetus:* "I seem to have a vision of Heracleitus saying some ancient words of wisdom as old as the reign of Cronos and Rhea, which Homer said too. Heracleitus says, you know, that all things move and nothing remains still, and he likens the universe to the current of a river" (*Crat.* 402a4-9)—and on the other, the deliberately imposed linguistic conventions of men (*Crat.* 434e4-7; 435b4-c6).

7. Compare Socrates' question to Hermogenes: "What do you think is the cause why anything is called by a name: Is it not...reason [*dianoia*] either of gods, or men, or both...works done by mind and reason [*nous te kai dianoia*]?" (*Crat.* 416c1-11).

8. At least, the subjective senses are referred to as "powers" (*dynameis*); on

the other hand, it is at the same time reiterated that the senses are relatively passive vis-a-vis objective sensibles—which evidently have power to "act on" subjective sensibility (*Theaet.* 159c4-6; cf. *Rep.* VI, 507c7-8; 507e6-508a1; 509b2-3; VII, 532a3).

CHAPTER 4:
KOMPSOTEROS METHOD

1. Aristotle's reports of Plato's philosophy are to be found especially in *Metaphysics* A, ch. 6, and M, ch. 4. Providing a detailed analysis and subtle interpretation of Aristotle's claims, Kenneth Sayre argues powerfully for the consistency between Aristotle's account and the ontology of the *Philebus* (*Plato's Late Ontology: a Riddle Resolved* [Princeton, N.J.: Princeton University Press, 1983]).

2. This talk of "hidden doctrine" and "initiation into mysteries" might be found to stir echoes of the long tradition of a Platonic "secret" or "esoteric doctrine."

Whether or not they should be linked to Aristoxenus' account of Plato's lecture on the Good, Aristotle's reports of Plato's later philosophy (at first sight so alien to that found in the dialogues) might be read as reinforcing his reference to "the so-called unwritten teachings" of Plato (*Phys.* 209b15). To many scholars, these ancient records have indeed suggested the existence of some secret body of Platonic doctrine, taught privately within the Academy, but not divulged in the written legacy of the dialogues. An eloquent defense of this position is to be found in the work of Tübingen scholars like H.J. Kramer and Konrad Gaiser, and in English, in John N. Findlay's *Plato, the Written and Unwritten Doctrines* (New York: Humanities Press, 1974); recent critical doubt stems largely from Harold Cherniss' *The Riddle of the Early Academy* (Berkeley: University of California Press, 1945). Two overviews of the controversy that I have found particularly helpful have been K. Gaiser's "Plato's Enigmatic Lecture 'On the Good,'" *Phronesis,* 25 [1980]: 5-37), and Sayre's *Plato's Late Ontology.*

The guiding principle in any interpretation of the problem should (I believe) be, as Hans-Georg Gadamer puts it, that "preference...unavoidably must be given to the literary dialogues over the doctrines constructed from the indirect tradition" ("Plato's Unwritten Dialectic," in *Dialogue and Dialectic* [New Haven: Yale University Press, 1980], p. 127), or as Sayre proposes: "What is written in the dialogues should guide our understanding of Aristotle's commentary rather than vice versa" (*Plato's Late Ontology,* p. 80). In keeping with this principle, Sayre argues—and as is evident from the present study, I agree with him—that in Plato's *Philebus* we find clear accord with Aristotle's account. Where I go further than Sayre is (1) in finding consonance between Aristotle's account and dialogues earlier than the *Philebus,* such as the *Theaetetus,* and (2) in finding the distinction between surface and deeper level, or "hidden," meaning to pervade the dialogues from beginning to end. Although not quite sure where this lands me in the overall scholarly controversy, I do thus find myself agreeing with an important assertion Gaiser makes in the name of the Tübingen school: "A theory of this kind, with a gradually increasing level of sophistication, seems to us to underlie all the dialogues, from the earliest ones on" ("Plato's Enigmatic Lecture," p. 8).

3. This "method" or "approach" is regarded as a "way" or "pathway." For example, in the *Philebus* Socrates assures us that "there certainly is no better road [*hodos*] nor can there ever be, than that which I have always loved" (*Phil.* 16b5-6); compare "the marvelous pathway" [*hodos*] of the *Seventh Epistle* (340c3). In the *Theaetetus*, this kind of movement between one and many is also talked of as "a road [*hodos*] to the whole through the elements" (208c6). At other times, it is "method" as a *meta hodos*, or *met'hodos* (e.g., *Stat.* 286d9; cf. 266d7; *Soph.* 227a8; 265a2).

4. *Phil.* 26e2-30c7. To use a term like *creative* does, I am afraid, lay me open to risk of misunderstanding. In using that term, I am, of course, not referring to creation ex nihilo (which for the Greeks does not occur), nor to production of the uniquely novel in the sense of the unpredictable. Rather, I am focusing on the activity in which we make, produce, create, generate, or bring into being; I am trying to translate terms like *poieō*: "make" or "produce" (e.g., *Phil.* 26e7; 27a5); *apergazomai*: "produce" or "create" (e.g., *Theaet.* 159d3; *Soph.* 262b7; *Stat.* 284b2); and *syntithēmi*: "construct so as to form a whole" (e.g., *Theaet.* 203c6; *Phil.* 30b3; *Crat.* 424e6-425a1, 427c9). My understanding of this usage is that to say something is produced or created is to say something is brought into being that is "new" in the sense that its present properties or power did not exist before: something is now present that was not so before. This is the kind of activity Plato's Stranger seems to have in mind when he says that "every power is productive [*poētikēn*] which causes things to come into being which did not exist before" (*Soph.* 265b8-10)—or which Socrates is thinking of when, in the *Philebus,* he reflects on their combining the appropriate elements to produce the good life and suggests that "if anyone were to say that we are like artists or artisans [*demiourgois*], with the materials before us from which to create our work [*demiourgein*], the simile would be a good one" (*Phil.* 59e1-3).

5. Hardly new, this assertion echoes points recently made in fresh contexts by Mitchell Miller and Richard Patterson. Miller, noting problems inherent in knowing how to make appropriate divisions, explains that "only if the form is *already present and providing guidance,* can the dialectician know that he is cutting 'according to forms' " (*Plato's Parmenides* [Princeton, N.J.: Princeton University Press, 1986], p. 182); Patterson points out that as model for sensible particulars, form "is roughly comparable to a final cause"; in other words, Plato's "is a teleological as well as an ontological theory of participation" (*Image and Reality in Plato's Metaphysics* [Indianapolis: Hackett, 1985], pp. 117, 135).

6. For now, the question is not, Who or what determines whether some combination of letters is or is not a genuine word? In a different context, that will lead to a consideration of "by nature" and "by convention." Here the question is rather, What makes it work or function as a word (whatever turns out to be the source of its determination)?

MATHEMATICAL INTERLUDE:
KOMPSOTEROS METHOD AND "PLAYING THE GEOMETER"

1. Plato is supposed to have said that "God is forever playing the geometer" (Plutarch, *Convivial Questions,* viii, 2. 1: *Greek Mathematical Works,* tr. I.

Thomas [Cambridge, Mass.: Harvard University Press, Loeb ed., 1939], vol. 1—hereafter referred to as GMW—p. 386/387). There is also a well-known legend that over the entrance to the Academy was engraved the following warning: "Let no one unversed in geometry enter through these doors" (Tzetzes, *Book of Histories,* 12th century A.D.: GMW, vol. 1, p. 386/387).

2. Theodorus was a pupil of Protagoras, who soon turned to mathematics (*Theaet.* 165a1-2). It seems he was the teacher, not only of Theaetetus (according to this dialogue), but, to some degree, of Plato himself. At least we are told that when Plato was twenty-eight years of age, after he had been associated both with those who professed Heracleitean doctrine and with those who followed Parmenides, he went to Cyrene to visit Theodorus the mathematician, whose lectures he attended (Diogenes Laertius, *Lives of Eminent Philosophers,* III, 6; II, 103). In the somewhat meager literature about Theodorus, Mitchell Miller's analysis of his character is outstanding; not only penetrating, it is also the most revelatory about the reasons for his presence in the dialogue. Drawing on various references in the *Theaetetus* and *Statesman,* Miller highlights the tension in Theodorus' character between his ability as one of the greatest mathematicians (e.g., *Stat.* 257a7-8) on the one hand, and on the other his inability (and unwillingness) to be philosophically reflective. In his uneasiness in philosophical discussion (e.g. 168e4-169b4; 177c3-4; 183c5-7) and his withdrawal from philosophy because of its being too abstract (165a1-2), Theodorus represents (as Miller makes clear) a direct antithesis to the Platonic/Socratic view of the proper relation between geometry and philosophy. His suspicion of abstraction leaves him, therefore, vulnerable to what Miller calls "the non-philosophical hegemony" of opinion and sense perception (*The Philosopher in Plato's Statesman* [The Hague: Nijhoff, 1980], pp. 4-5). On the other hand, as Miller elsewhere argues, Theodorus shows himself both unwilling and unable to "transcend the ontological 'trust,' the immediate acceptance of the concrete particulars of experience as ontologically basic" (*Plato's Parmenides,* p. 23). From the point of view of this study, this unsophisticated stance clearly marks him as one of the uninitiated, thus making him an ideal foil in this particular inquiry.

Theaetetus was renowned not only for his achievements with irrationals (he worked out a theory of quadratic surds), but also for his work in solid geometry (the "stereometry" of which the *Epinomis* speaks: 990d8; cf. *Rep.* VII, 528d8-e1), and especially for completing the theory of the five regular solids (Euclid, *Elements* X, Scholium, lxii, GMW, vol. 1, p. 380/381; J. Burnet, *Platonism,* pp. 100-102). Burnet concludes that "it will be obvious that Theaetetus of Athens was the real founder of mathematics as we understand the word." (See also Heath, *History of Greek Mathematics,* pp. 209-212.) Mugler finds that Theaetetus' general interests and tendencies are so much in the spirit of Plato that it is probably the Platonic influence that is paramount (*Platon et la recherche mathématique,* pp. 220-221). In terms of the long-term quest for knowledge (see appendix A, note 5), the similarities between Theaetetus and Socrates—which, even at the physical level, are adverted to by Theodorus (143e8-9)—are sufficiently striking to warrant Theodorus' enthusiastic praise (143e4-144b7) and Socrates' prophetic expectation (142d1-3). In 369 B.C., at the time of the conversation that constitutes the dialogue itself, Theaetetus is "little more than a boy," but already shows himself a youth of extraordinary promise. The characteristics evident even in the dialogue (quickness of understanding, courage, modesty, and a gentle, friendly manner) were apparently borne out in his later life, so that, from the perspective of thirty years later, when Theaetetus is dying and the earlier conversation is being recalled, Eucleides can praise him not only as brave on the field of battle, but as totally *kalos te kai agathon* (142b7).

3. On the proposed reading, Theaetetus' report of his work with irrationals fulfills more than one function. First and most obviously (despite certain difficulties, see below chapter 7), it is of course introduced as a model for the proposed definition of knowledge. Thus, we are shown in some detail how Theaetetus and his friend Young Socrates take the plurality of particular examples (all established by Theodorus to be cases involving incommensurability) and develop a definition of irrationals in terms of a theoretical framework, proving in a general way the irrationality of every square root of an oblong number—thereby enabling them to determine and predict future cases, that is, "call all the roots" (147d8-e1). Obviously, Theaetetus is to do likewise: taking the plurality of examples of knowledge, to develop a definition in terms of a theoretic framework which will enable us in any particular case to identify whether the cognitive state in question is or is not knowledge. At a deeper level, so this study is arguing, what is being illustrated is the very process of rational ordering itself. Although this reading naturally overlaps at points with those of others, the proposed interpretation is not by and large that of other critics.

The problem is of course that, reading this relatively detailed account of Theaetetus' work with surds, "we are led to wonder what it is in the procedure that appears to Plato so exemplary for Socrates' present inquiry concerning knowledge, and indeed for every Socratic inquiry of this kind" (J. Klein, *Greek Mathematical Thought and the Origin of Algebra* [Cambridge, Mass.: MIT Press, 1968], p. 55). Although many commentators focus on Plato's taking the occasion to honor the achievements of Theaetetus, Burnyeat rightly seeks to shift that focus from the historical to the philosophical, noting that the *philosophical* relevance of the mathematical episode within the context of the dialogue's inquiry into knowledge has not received the careful attention it deserves ("Philosophical Sense," p. 509; see also p. 491). Even one who normally does take seriously the mathematical element in the dialogues—like R. Brumbaugh—tends, however, in the case of Theaetetus' surds to discount the significance of its mathematical character, taking it simply at face value as an example of the kind of definition Socrates is seeking. Thus, Brumbaugh is convinced that "its relevance to the dialogue itself is only that of the other mathematical examples introduced as paradigms of definition in the *Meno* and the *Euthyphro* (*Plato's Mathematical Imagination* [Bloomington, Ind.: Indiana University Press, 1954], p. 40); as a result, he does not recognize what seems to me to be Plato's intended paradigm, and contrary to the interpretation suggested in this study, goes on to conclude that "Theaetetus can in no way explain knowledge to Socrates by following the method previously used in defining roots and magnitudes" (p. 269). If, however, its role as model for definition were all that Plato had in mind, then why so much detail? After all, if there is no further purpose than simply as model for definition, then the details of Theaetetus' report do indeed seem "dragged in" (van der Vaerden, *Science*

Awakening [Gronigen, Holland: P. Noordhoff, 1954] pp. 142, 166). On the other hand, since it turns out that Theaetetus actually worked on irrationals at a more complex level than indicated here (Burnyeat, "Philosophical Sense," p. 507), why does Plato stop short, giving the reader just this much of the account? Burnyeat himself, stressing the contrast between Theodorus' *examples* and the character of Theaetetus' *general* answer (pp. 501-505), sees the significance of the paradigm as pointing forward, and that in two parallel senses. On the one hand, for students in the Academy, here was "the birth of a fruitful idea, a youthful beginning" of what would prove to be a far-reaching study, but a study whose full significance would not emerge until its later fulfillment in Euclid. Analoguously, Burnyeat holds, the kind of cross-examination of an initial definition that constitutes Socrates dialectic is often also but a fruitful beginning which similarly points towards the future, requiring the kind of rigorous working out that will eventually yield real philosophical results (p. 511). Warning against would-be connections between Theaetetus' account of surds and other parts of the dialogue—for example, between Theaetetus' irrational *dynameis* (powers) and the subsequent *dynameis* in Socrates' account of sensation, or between Theaetetus' irrationals and the subsequent irrationals of Socrates' "dream"—Burnyeat would, I think, have to be critical of my effort to integrate into the *philosophical* purpose of the dialogue this very aspect that he discounts as "purely literary, symbolic connection." He seems in fact to be quite matter of fact about ruling out the kind of approach pursued in this study: "Now certainly, Plato is well able to enjoy a structural correspondence of this kind. But it would be uncharacteristic of him to let it become a substitute for serious philosophical content. Whatever the symbolic connections, we need a moral of greater consequence if we are really to integrate Theaetetus' story into the philosophical discussion" (pp. 509-510). That "moral of greater consequence" is of course what I am trying to develop.

4. This characteristic seems to me to be significant for understanding much of Socrates' conversation with Theaetetus. To justify this claim requires, however, not only an argument showing the connection between geometry and the substance of the *Theaetetus* (this I try to do throughout the present inquiry), but also some evidence that Theaetetus was in fact dealing with geometry in terms of continuous magnitude (this I shall now try to do in this note). What I hope to do is to establish, first, that the Euclidean view is not alien to that of Theaetetus, and second, that, according to the Euclidean view, geometry deals with quantity in terms of continuous magnitude.

First, the link between Theaetetus and Euclid. According to Proclus' *Summary,* what Euclid did in putting together the *Elements* was to "arrange in order many of Eudoxus' theorems, perfecting many of Theaetetus'" (GMW, vol. 1, p. 154/155). Heath points out that "there is . . . probably little in the whole compass of the *Elements* of Euclid, except the new theory of proportion due to Eudoxus and its consequences, which was not in substance included in the recognized content of geometry and arithmetic by Plato's time" (Heath, *History of Greek Mathematics,* p. 217). And, according to the commentary on Euclid X attributed to Pappus, the ground was prepared by Theaetetus' work, especially in the areas of irrationals and the five regular solids (Pappus' commentary quoted in Heath, *History of Greek Mathematics,* p. 209).

The second point involves the interpretation of Euclidean geometry itself. Euclid draws a distinction between arithmetic as the science of non-continuous, and geometry as the study of continuous, magnitude. In the tradition of Pythagorean mathematics there were, apparently, two different ways of representing number—one using dots or "alphas" for the units (e.g., Aristotle, *Physics* III, 4, 203a10-15; a puzzling application of this method seems to be reflected in the accounts of Eurytus' pebble shapes: Aristotle, *Met.*, N, 1092b10-13), and a second, that used here in the *Theaetetus* and also later by Euclid, according to which number was presented by straight lines proportional in length to the numbers they represented (see GMW, vol. 1, p. 86, ftn. a). These two different approaches seem to account for two correspondingly different definitions of number. The first is attributed by Iamblichus to Thales, who, "following the Egyptian view" (for an example of limitations in Egyptian mathematics, see I.E. Miller, *The Significance of the Mathematical Element in the Philosophy of Plato* [Chicago: Chicago University Press, 1904], p. 18), defined it as "a collection of units" (*monadōn systēma*) (Heath, GMW, vol. 1, pp. 69-70); it is a definition apparently echoed in one of Euclid's definitions in *Elements* VII, which defines number as "a multitude composed of units" (*monadōn*) and again later in Nicomachus' definition as "a determinate multitude or collection of units" (*plēthos orismenon ē monadōn systēma*). On the other hand, a different approach seems to be suggested when Nichomachus gives us the definition of number as "a flow of quantity made up of units" (*posotos chuma ek monadōn sygkeimenon*) (Nicomachus, *Introduction to Arithmetic*, quoted in GMW, vol. 1, p. 72/73). This latter approach is perhaps also reflected in another definition of Euclid's which occurs in a context reminiscent of this section of the *Theaetetus*, a definition this time in terms of "magnitudes" (*megetha*) (*Elements* V definitions)—the concept of magnitude essentially involving infinite divisibility and incommensurability (Heath, *History of Greek Mathematics*, p. 154). This latter approach, moreover, seems to accord with the Pythagorean view of points as boundaries (*horoi*) of spatial magnitudes (Aristotle, *Met.* N, 1092b9-10), as also with a Pythagorean definition of the unit which dates from the Platonic period, according to which a unit is understood as simply "limiting quantity" (*perainousa posotes*) (Heath, *History of Greek Mathematics*, p. 69).

5. One of the major instruments in the geometrical algebra of the Greeks was a device known as the Application of Areas. As Ivor Thomas explains: "One of the greatest Pythagorean discoveries was the method known as the application of areas, which became a powerful engine in the hands of successive Greek geometers...It is a vital part of the 'geometrical algebra' of the Greeks, who dealt in figures as familiarly as we do in symbols. This method was the foundation of Euclid's theory of irrationals..." (GMW, vol. 1, p. 186/187). Plutarch maintains that the discovery of this powerful mathematical instrument was more significant than the discovery of the so-called Pythagorean theorem (which is only one instantiation of its application): "Among the most geometrical theorems, or rather problems, is this: given two figures, to apply a third equal to the one and similar to the other; it was in virtue of this discovery they say Pythagoras sacrificed" (*Convivial Questions* viii, 24, 720A: GMW, vol. 1, p. 176/177). Interestingly enough, Mugler attributes its invention very largely to Plato himself—at least insofar as its first clear evidence seems to

be found in Plato's expression *isos kai homoios* ("equal and similar") (Mugler, *Platon et la recherche mathématique*, pp. 65-66). It is, of course, this same principle, or procedure, that Theaetetus is drawing on in his solution to the problem of surds: Given two figure, a square and an oblong, to apply a third that will be equal (i.e., in square measure) to the oblong, and similar (i.e., in shape) to the square (*Theaet.* 147d3-148b2).

6. There are times when Aristotle seems to insist, against Plato, that there is no way to generate numbers except by the addition (*prostithemi*) of units (*monades*) (*Met.*, M, vii, 1081b12-18)—which similar thought might underlie his apparent uneasiness at the notion that some numbers might not be commensurable (*ibid.*, e.g., 1081a17-20)?

7. e.g. Euclid, *Elements*, I, Postulate 2: "To produce (*ekbalein*) a finite straight line continuously in a straight line." It has been pointed out that the chief purpose here is "to delineate Euclidean space...as continuous (not discrete) and infinite (not limited)" (Thomas, GMW, vol. 1, p. 442, ftn.a). In view of the way in which Plato constantly links the *kompsoteros* theory of emergent generation back both to Theaetetus' work in generating surd lines, and to Socrates' midwifery with those pregnant, it becomes especially interesting to note that this word, *ekbalein*, used of producing lines, is also used of women bringing to birth.

8. "Flow": "*rhuen...rhueisan*": Sextus, *Adversus Mathematicos* (*Sextus Empiricus*, tr. R.G. Bury, Cambridge, Mass.: Harvard University Press (Loeb edition), 1949, vol. IV *Against the Professors*, Book iii *Against the Geometers*, 77, p. 282/283; cf., 29, p. 258/259. Sextus is of course disputing the claim.) Compare Aristotle, who refers to the generation from point to line to surface to solid as being through "movement" (*kinedeisan*) (*De An.*, A 4, 409a4)—although I am not sure how this relates to his comments above in note 6.

9. For detailed discussion of this issue and its relevance to the dialogue, see appendix A.

10. Compare Theon of Smyrna: "...numbers are invested with power (*dynamei*) to make triangles, squares, pentagons, and other figures..." (GMW, vol. 1, p. 132/133).

11. This feature of geometry is clearly of the greatest significance for Plato. Even apart from the specific reference to this same fact in the *Epinomis*, which talks of "assimilating dissimilar numbers, effected through reference to areas" (*Epin.*, 990d1-4); or the observation in *Greater Hippias* that "irrational quantities may be either irrational or, if taken together, rational" (303b7-c1), there is further explicit reference in the *Laws* to the general and shameful ignorance of the Greeks who are apparently unaware of commensurability and incommensurability in the context of lines, surfaces, and solids; the Athenian goes on to stress the consequent need for the freeborn to study "problems concerning the essential nature of the commensurable and incommensurable" (*Laws* 819d1-820c5). Theon of Smyrna, in the second century A.D., talks of "ratios (*logous*) appearing in numbers in accordance with the generative principles (*kata tous spermatikous logous*) for it is these which give harmony to the figures" (GMW, vol. 1, p. 132/133). Although many commentators register this fact in discussing Theaetetus' mathematical achievements, van der Waerden's reaction seems to me to be one of the most perceptive when he maintains, "In my

opinion, the merit of Theaetetus lies...not in his contribution to the theory of numbers, but in his study of incommensurable line segments which produce commensurable squares" (*Science Awakening*, p. 168). He does not, however, go on to explain just why this is so significant, either in itself, or in this dialogue. (By contrast, Burnyeat thinks this recognition is not central to Theaetetus' achievement: "The Philosophical Sense of Theaetetus' Mathematics," p. 501).

12. When, in the *Epinomis*, in the discussion of education in wisdom and piety, the Athenian leads the discussion to the special role of mathematics, he proposes as its goal "the revelation of a single bond of natural interconnection between all these problems" (*Epin.* 991e5-992a1).

CHAPTER 5:
"KNOWLEDGE IS...PERCEPTION"

1. The goal of cross-examination is not rejection, but interpretation. The *Sophist* describes elenchus as a process of discarding the worse in order to retain the better—a purification to which even the noblest must be subjected, whether the Great King or the god of Delphi himself (*Soph.* 226d5-7; 230b4-e3; *Apol.* 21b3-9).

2. Perhaps this is what Plato has in mind when he says that " 'it seems' is a mixture of sensation and speech" (*Soph.* 264b1-2). A similar point has been made by contemporary critics of hard empiricism, for example, by Wilfrid Sellars, "Empiricism and the Philosophy of Mind," in *Science Perception and Reality* (London: Routledge and Kegan Paul, 1963), pp. 127-132.

3. The term for "become more" which Socrates uses here in this discussion is relatively rare in Greek; it is *auxanō*, which means literally "increase in power." What is interesting is that this is the technical mathematical term Plato uses for a move to a higher dimension (e.g., *Rep.* VII, 528b2-3, d8; IX, 587d9; *Epin.* 990d6), thus specifically linking *kompsoteros* discussion of generation with Theaetetus' account of generating higher dimensions in geometry—which is, of course, just what I need for my claim that this is the point of the dice illustration (see appendix A).

4. The context of Socrates' remarks (about not staying for the mysteries) is Meno's failure to understand the superiority of defining 'figure' as "the limit [*peras*] of solid" (76a7, e3-9). Interestingly enough, this seems to be a definition within the framework of geometry conceived of as continuous magnitude, so that, like the *kompsoteros* "mysteries," it too is premissed on the notion of an original continuum divided, or bounded, by limit (see above, Mathematical Interlude, n. 4, and chapter 4). Associated by both Pythagoreans and Aristotle with color (itself inseparable from the notion of *peras*), 'figure' in Euclid comes to be that which is contained by one or more boundaries (*horos* or *peras*) (see discussion in Heath, *History of Greek Mathematics*, p. 293). The metaphor of "containing within boundaries" effectively calls up an image of something in liquid state which otherwise would flow indeterminately.

5. Although Burnyeat is, of course, right in identifying the structure of 179c-183c as a reductio ad absurdum, I will be departing from his straightforward conclusion that the argument is therefore "a proof that if the theory

were correct it would make language impossible" ("Idealism," p. 6).

6. This argument elaborates the one already suggested in the original introduction of *kompsoteros* theory. According to that earlier argument, we were similarly confronted with a dilemma: *either* language reflects reality "by nature" (157b6), that is to say, reality in its natural indeterminacy, *or* language reflects reality "by convention" (157b2), that is to say, reality as though it were discretely determinate. If the first disjunct holds, then we have a problem, because in order to have language at all, we "must" thus talk as though reality were discrete and stable; so, if we insist on reflecting reality as totally indeterminate, then we will have no language at all. If the second disjunct holds, then we have a problem, because in thus representing a determinate world (i.e., "making things stand still"), we are easily refuted—as in the case of the wind which is both warm and cold, the wine which is both sweet and sour, etc.

7. Theodorus is scathing in his reference to such disciples of Heracleitus, accusing them of being, like their universe, "in perpetual motion" (179d7-180c5). (The *Cratylus* similarly talks of such people as "having fallen into a kind of vortex, and being whirled about": *Crat.* 439c5). One of the ironies of the situation is that Theodorus, although a friend of Protagoras (e.g., 162a4; 164e4-5; 168e6-169a1), does not recognize the affinity between the Protagorean doctrine (which he seems to espouse) and the Heracleitean doctrine which undergirds it (and which he deplores).

8. On this question of judgment and perception, I am belatedly joining an ongoing dialogue that was sparked anew by a 1970 article by John Cooper. See J. Cooper, "Plato on Sense Perception and Knowledge: *Theaetetus* 184-186," *Phronesis*, 15 (1970) : 123-146; Burnyeat, "Plato on the Grammer" (1976); D.K. Modrak, "Perception and Judgment in the *Theaetetus*," *Phronesis*, 26 (1981) : 35-54; and J. Shea, "Judgment and Perception in *Theaetetus* 184-186," *Journal of the History of Philosophy*, 23 (1985) :1-14.

Since the argument that distinguishes opinion from perception (*Theaet.* 184b8-186e5) hinges on the former's but not the latter's apprehension of "truth" about "being," the question arises as to whether judgment does or does not also characterize perception. Cooper finds the dialogue unclear as to whether perception is to be understood as mere sensory awareness without any application of concepts, or whether there is some restricted use of concepts involved in labeling colors, sounds, etc., with their names. The problem is of course that the latter interpretation implies some independent action of mind, and to that extent would seem to undermine the contrast between perception and opinion (Cooper, "Plato on Sense Perception," pp. 130-131). In short, we seem to be faced with a dilemma. If, on the one hand, judgment is included in perception, then how is it different from judgments of opinion that deal with "being" and "truth"? If, on the other hand, judgment is excluded from perception, then in what does perception consist?

Cooper, Burnyeat, and Modrak each opt for some kind of judgment in perception; otherwise, as Burnyeat puts it, "Take away judgment and all that is left to perception is to be an unarticulated encounter with sensible things" ("Plato on the Grammer," p. 36). Cooper distinguishes the kind of minimal judgment in perceptual awareness that explicitly labels "sense contents" from the kind of reflective judgment about the deliverances of the senses (especially more than one sense) that characterizes opinion (Cooper, "Plato on Sense Perception," pp. 123, 131, 144). As I understand him this corresponds to what I have talked of as a bringing of the sensory experience to conscious awareness through "naming." With Modrak, I too see a need to situate the 184-186 discussion of perception in the context of the secret doctrine of 156-157 (Modrak, "Perception and Judgment," p. 35); with her also, I distinguish judgments of opinion from simple perceptual judgments; with her, I hold that prior learning is the necessary condition for making any such judgment (p. 44). Where I depart from her interpretation is in her seeing such perceptual judgments as having existential import, that is, as being "a judgment about objects in the world" (p. 48), for on my reading it is precisely this character that distinguishes judgments of *opinion* from the merely "naming" identifications of *perception*. Having as it were forfeited this disjunction, Modrak must find another and so goes on to differentiate these judgments of perception from those of knowledge in terms of the latter's actually encompassing the implications of our perceptual judgments (pp. 48-51).

By contrast, Shea wants to eliminate all judgment from perception while yet retaining a perceptual "sorting (or labeling) according to innate concepts" ("Judgment and Perception," p. 13). Accusing Cooper (and by implication Burnyeat and Modrak) of "straying from the text" and thereby of confusing labeling and judgment, he claims that judgment requires predication, which in turn requires a *koinon* such as existence, whereas "to perceive is to look at the world under certain stipulated conditions . . . To put it crudely, Plato holds that to perceive *x* as *k* does not require the judgment that *x* is a *k*" (Shea, "Judgment and Perception," pp. 13-14).

It seems to me that the dispute hinges on one's interpretation of the ambiguous term *judgment.* Whatever the vocabulary used, however, all insist (rightly, I believe) on a distinction between the simple labeling or naming operation that characterizes perception, and the full-scale judgment which, using *ta koina* (especially existence), characterizes opinion. Along with these scholars, I too want to make room for a perceptual operation between the unarticulated encounter of mere sensation and the properly so-called judgments of opinion. This is the conscious awareness of perceptual experience under a label (or "name": *Theaet.* 156b2-7) that permits us to identify and register the experience in the sense that I can say I am having a "red," or a "salty," or whatever, perception.

9. My interpretation of this section, identifying a single agency that perceives through the senses as instruments—"whether we should call it soul or something else" (184d1-5, though at 185e6 and 186c1-2 he does quite simply call it "soul")—obviously runs counter to the kind of interpretation proposed by Burnyeat, who sets this assertion in critical opposition to the account that I am calling "*kompsoteros* doctrine" and that he is calling the "Heracleitean theory of perception" ("Plato on the Grammar," pp. 30-46). In contrast to his position, I am reading this assertion as actually *required* by *kompsoteros* theory.

If I am right in taking *kompsoteros* theory in the *Theaetetus* to correspond closely to what, in the *Philebus*, Socrates describes as his beloved method (16b5-6), then it is only to be expected that at important junctures we should find correspondence between the two accounts. (For example, Socrates' clarification for Theaetetus that perception (*aisthēsis*) concerns "sensations which reach the soul through the body" (186c1-2) parallels his corresponding clarification for Protarchus that, strictly speaking, *aisthēsis* refers to just those sensations which "penetrate from the body through to soul" (*Phil.* 33c9-34a8). Now, in the *Theaetetus'* identification of the agency of soul, Socrates seems to be giving us another example of correspondence. After all, the *kompsoteros* account has provided us with the first three of the *Philebus'* four features of the universe: first, the infinite, or unlimited; second, limit, through which measure is introduced into the unlimited; and third, the generated product of the combination of these two, which both dialogues talk of in terms of a child born of intercourse. On my interpretation, what is now required by the *kompsoteros* account is an explicit reference to the *Philebus'* fourth factor: soul or mind as agent (maker or cause), for "wisdom and *nous* cannot come into existence without soul" (*Phil.* 26e1-30c10). Before we leave this analysis of perception in terms of Socrates' beloved method, the discussion therefore demands that some account be taken of soul as primary and causal agent. (It is true that throughout my earlier discussions of *kompsoteros* method I already made reference to the agency of rational soul; this is because it seems to me already implicit there in that account [as it was similarly anticipated in the *Philebus*] long before we come to its explicit recognition at 184d1-5).

10. On making claims about Plato's own philosophical position, see above, Introduction, note 3.

11. Obviously, not all language is ambiguous. As Socrates explains to Phaedrus: "When one says 'iron,' or 'silver,' we all understand the same thing, don't we? But what if one says 'justice,' or 'goodness'? . . . Let us call the latter 'those in which we wander' [i.e., among meanings]" (*Phaedr.* 263a2-b9).

CHAPTER 6:
"KNOWLEDGE IS TRUE OPINION"

1. It has become customary to interpret this section of the *Theaetetus* as correcting Plato's earlier supposition that it is the senses themselves that perceive (e.g., *Rep.* VII, 523c-524b; V, 479a; X, 602c-603a), whereas now for the first time he makes it clear that it is really the subject that perceives *through* the senses as its instruments (e.g., Cooper, "Plato on Sense Perception," p. 125; Burnyeat, "Plato on the Grammar," pp. 33-35; McDowell, *Plato: Theaetetus*, pp. 185-186). My reading of this section of the *Phaedo* is obviously questioning such a change of mind on Plato's part, at least between the time of the *Phaedo* and the *Theaetetus*. I therefore find myself persuaded by A.J. Holland's argument that there is on the contrary a parallel between this claim in the *Theaetetus* and the assertion, for example, in the *Republic* that since sight and the other senses give us inadequate reports of opposite qualities, it is mind by itself which has to recognize the opposites as distinct, for "such differences as there are between the two arguments are differences of presentation rather than substance" (A.J. Holland, "An Argument in Plato's *Theaetetus*: 184-186," *Philosophical Quarterly*, 23 (1973): 115). Holland thinks the point an important one to make because it

contradicts a now common view of Plato's development (originated very largely by Ryle and Robinson in opposition to Cornford), according to which the *Theaetetus* represents a very different outlook from that of the *Republic* (Holland, "An Argument," p. 112).

2. It actually turns out to be a biconditional, since he shortly adds, "Each, since it has a different *dynamis*, is related to a different object...of necessity" (*Rep.* V, 478a3-4). The same point is made in the *Timaeus:* 51d3-7.

3. It is, of course, precisely because opinion and knowledge are alike in this respect, and do *not* come by nature, that the *Meno* has to ask that central question of how they may be acquired, "since neither of these two things— knowledge and opinion—is a natural property of mankind, being acquired" (*Meno* 98c10-d1).

4. This point has been noted by a number of commentators, for example, Taylor, *Plato: The Man and His Work*, pp. 344-345; Morrow, "Plato and the Mathematicians," p. 309; and Rorty, "Speculative Note," p. 231.

5. On examination, the perceptions that constitute the "elements" of physical objects are seen to fulfill the conditions listed above (see chapter 4). (1) They are *similar* in that all are simple perceptual impressions—fleeting, but nameable, occurrences. (2) They are *dissimilar*, first in the noninterchangeability of the interacting sense (sight helping to produce the occurrence of white; taste, that of sweet; and so on), and second, in presenting different (even contradictory) appearances from moment to moment depending on the changing conditions of subject and object. (3) The various perceptions are *mutually relative* in the sense, first, that, for example, seeing color is to be understood simply as one kind of sense experience relative to other kinds, and second, that any particular color, for example, is simply one determinate within a determinable range of color and so relative to every other color. (4) In isolation, any perception is useless or powerless to become anything more than a mere momentary perceiving because belief in the existence of an object requires the comparison and calculation of perceptions (in the plural) through *syllogismos*. (5) By contrast, in proper interaction with other elements, each perception exhibits a kind of "power," or *dynamis*. (This seems to be similar to the meaning of "power" as Theaetetus uses it of the "roots" [literally, "powers"] from which a square is generated, for according to *kompsoteros* theory, the perceptions are likewise the "powers" from which an object is generated.)

6. There is a difficulty about opinion, and the objects of opinion, that needs to be raised here because it is a standard source of puzzlement, and it bears on the interpretation being advocated here. But perhaps we should first look at what sometimes appears to be a problem but I think is really not. This relates to the fact that, on the one hand (as in the *Gorgias, Timaeus,* and Books V-VII of the *Republic,* Plato is at pains to identify the object of opinion as "the many" of the visible world; on the other (as for example in the *Sophist,* and perhaps the *Meno* and the *Philebus*), the object of opinion seems to be propositional truth. I do not believe that of itself this is a problem here, since opinion is being interpreted as beliefs *about* objects and events, such beliefs being expressible *in* statements, which in turn represent judgments reached either with intuitive spontaneity or achieved as the conclusion of a thought

process. Thus, "thought is conversation of the soul with itself, and opinion is the final result of thought" (*Soph.* 264a8-b1), for

> soul, when it thinks, is merely conversing with itself, asking itself questions and answering, affirming and denying. When it has arrived at a decision, whether slowly or with a sudden bound, and is at last agreed, and is not in doubt, we call that its opinion (*Theaet.* 189e8-190a4)
> and if someone is with him, he might repeat aloud to his companions what he had said to himself, and thus that which we called an opinion now becomes a statement. (*Phil.* 38e1-4)

Opinion, thus understood, happily enough includes not only the *Republic's* classic case of belief in the many beautiful and just things (*Rep.* V, 476c2; 479a3, e1-3), but it also includes the specific cases that Plato himself actually produces as examples of opinion—for example, identifying the diagonal of the square (*Meno* 85b1-7), pointing out the road to Larissa (*Meno* 97a9-b3), judging which letters go to make up a name (*Theaet.* 207e7-208b2), identifying the person in the distance (*Theaet.* 191b2-6), identifying the object under the tree (*Phil.* 38c5-d7), and judging Theaetetus to be sitting rather than flying (*Soph.* 262e8-263b5). It also clearly includes the ostensive level of all those dialogues (from the *Euthyphro* to the *Sophist*) where an introductory phase cites instances of whatever it is that is the subject of the inquiry. So far so good. In making the move from subjective perception to objective judgment (whether right or wrong), we are still clearly in that realm of spatiotemporal becoming between nonbeing and being. Now we come to the real difficulty.

The problem actually arises in the very place Plato is making his original point. For right in the middle of the *Republic's* discussion of belief in the many, the object of opinion seems suddenly to be extended to include traditional views, *nomima*, no longer only about "the many," but also about "justice," "beauty," etc. (*Rep.* V, 479d3-5). It might be argued that in this context Plato is still referring to conventional judgments about the many and various *cases*— since *nomima* is fluid enough, with its suggestion of customs and practical conventions, to be stretched in that direction. But the question cannot really be sidestepped in that way, because it in fact refers to the familiar stage of a dialogue in which the respondent proposes some traditional saying—as, for example, Charmides' citing of the dictum that *sōphrosyne* is "minding one's own business" (*Charm.* 161b5-6), Meno's citing of the poet's description of virtue (*Meno* 77b2-5), or Polemarchus' citing of the poet Simonides' account of justice (*Rep.* I, 331e3-4). In all these cases, we get what looks not so much like a belief about "the many" (i.e., actual persons, actions, etc., that may be judged to be just or what not), but rather a belief about "the one" (i.e., justice, or virtue itself in the realm of abstract entities beyond that of spatiotemporal opinion).

Perhaps the first thing to be said is that it does seem clear that, for Plato, these kinds of citations of traditional formulae are introduced, not as cases of actual reasoning about those concepts, but rather as cases of opinion in the sense that they have been adopted—like the aviary birds, transferred or handed over (*paradoton paralēpton: cf. Meno* 93b4-5) for "possession" (*ktēsamenos* ...*kektēsthai: Theaet.* 197e4; 198b5)—without real understanding. In other words, just as opinion can point out or produce the actual letters needed to spell a name, so it seems that one can point out or produce a formulaic, or conventional, account of justice, virtue, etc.—and what is more, just as with the letters of Socrates' name, or the road to Larissa, the person may actually be right. I think the point Plato is making, in each of these discussions where he is contrasting opinion with knowledge, is that although the opinion may in fact be true, it is at most belief or conviction *that,* without the theoretical reasoning *why.* This distinction would account for Socrates' pursuit of elenchus, introduced in order to show one respondent after another that, so long as one cannot defend a logos from misinterpretation—that is, from its "being tumbled about" (*Rep.* V, 479d4-5) and "wandering" (*Rep.* V, 479d9) like the statues of Daedalus (*Euth.* 11b9-e1; 15b7-10; *Meno* 97d6-10)—then, even though the opinion itself may in fact be true, one still lacks the conceptual understanding required to explain *why* it is true, and in what sense it "holds." The task therefore becomes that of cutting through the ambiguity of any mere formula which has been pointed out in the uncritical conviction that it is the traditional (and, as it turns out, right) definition. This in turn is effected through the very cross-examination that we see Socrates undertaking with a view to anchoring that true opinion with reasoning. As I understand it, this is why, in both the *Meno* and *Theaetetus,* the discussion of opinion, along with the insistence on its quite radical differentiation from knowledge (e.g., *Meno* 98b1-5; *Theaet.* 201c4-7), leads in both cases directly into reflection on true opinion's natural complement, reasoning. Thus Theaetetus' move to the final definition, "knowledge is true opinion with logos" (201c9-d1), will properly echo the *Meno's* explanation that

> true opinions, so long as they stay with us, are a fine possession...but they do not care to stay for long, and run away out of the human soul, and thus are of no great value until one makes them fast with causal reasoning [*aitias logismō*]...But when once they are fastened, in the first place they turn into knowledge, and in the second are abiding. And this is why knowledge is more prized than right opinion: the one transcends the other by its bonding [*desmō*]. (*Meno* 97e6-98a8)

7. *Analogismata.* I am translating *analogizomai* as "reckon up," "list," or "take account of," as for example at *Rep.* I, 330e5, or *Protag.* 332d1. In the *Cratylus,* Socrates echoes the same distinction drawn here in the *Theaetetus* between animals who do not, and men who do, reflect on sensation (*Theaet.* 186c1-3), when he contrasts the response of an animal who does not "examine and *analogizetai*" what it senses with that of a man who does (*Crat.* 399c2-4).

8. *Syllogismos,* from the root "collect," seems to cover various kinds of rational "bringing together," ranging from putting together observed facts to form a conclusion (as at *Crat.* 412a5-6, and perhaps *Charm.* 160d8), to actual ratiocination and inference (as at *Phil.* 41c9).

9. It is because of this character of judgment that can attain to "truth" with respect to "being" that Plato sometimes assimilates opinion to logos and knowledge (e.g. *Rep.* IX, 585b14; *Phil.* 66b8-9; *Tim.* 77b5)—although at other times he will sharply differentiate it from both (e.g., *Meno* 98b2; *Phaedo* 84a7-b1;

Rep. V, 477b7-8; *Phaedr.* 262c1-2; *Tim.* 37b6-8; 52a7; *Phil.* 58e5-59a9).

10. So the *Sophist,* echoing the same notion of inner dialogue that culminates in judgment, points out that "in logos we know there is just affirmation and negation...Now when this arises in the soul silently by way of thought, can you give it any other name than opinion?" (*Soph.* 263e10-264a2).

11. Gail Fine also draws attention to the fact that Theaetetus' definition of knowledge as true opinion rests on this dichotomy—and that Plato's rejection of the dichotomy goes hand in hand with the refutation of that definition ("False Belief in the *Theaetetus,*" *Phronesis,* 24 [1979], e.g., p. 77).

12. Knowing the elements, but being ignorant of how they best fit together as a whole, would I believe account for most false opinion—whether empirical (by wrongly combining perceptions), or abstract (by wrongly combining, say, 7 and 5), or mixed (by wrongly combining, say, scientific data to yield a theory that ultimately proves false because it fails to cohere with further data).

13. Related to this contrast between initiates and uninitiates, dialectic and eristic, is Socrates' contrast between the freeborn philosopher and the servile word mongerer in his famous "digression" on the philosopher. Although Socrates himself calls it a "digression" (and McDowell views it as "serv[ing] a purpose which, in a modern book, might be served by footnotes or an appendix" [McDowell, *Plato: Theaetetus,* p. 174]), Festugière is probably closer to the mark in seeking a middle way between what he finds to be Wilamowitz' relegation of the section to the periphery of the dialogue, and Diès' location of it at the central core (Festugière, *Contemplation,* pp. 409-411). Cornford, preoccupied with the silent presence of the Forms, sees it as "studded with allusions to the *Republic,* and in the course of it the moral Forms are plainly, though unobtrusively, mentioned" (*Plato's Theory of Knowledge,* p. 83; see also p. 89).

Although my understanding of the role of the "digression" is at this point far from subtle, I nevertheless wonder whether Socrates might not be presenting us here once more with an all-or-nothing dichotomy. Read this way, the portrait of the would-be philosopher is offering us yet another variation on the "knowledge versus no-knowledge" disjunction, and on the equally false disjunction between extreme relativism and some kind of extreme absolutism. As in every other case, despite the initial plausibility, we are (I believe) led to see the inadequacy of each disjunct. At the very least, the sketch of the philosopher is bafflingly unlike the philosopher the dialogues give us, either in ideal or in the character of Socrates himself. As commonly noted, the "philosopher" that is portrayed, caught up as he apparently is in abstraction from spatiotemporal human experience, is ultimately no more satisfying than his opposite. Kucharski is emphatic when he insists that "the least one can say is that the philosopher sketched here is certainly not qualified to be a guardian in terms of the *Republic's* demand for involvement" (*Les chemins du savoir,* p. 366). Others note how far short the would-be philosopher of the digression falls from the Socrates of the dialogues, who, contrary to the description here, certainly does "know his way to the marketplace." Meanwhile, Benardete's critical assessment is sharper still: "The philosopher's ignorance of the all-too-human is total, for he does not even know that he does not know...[By contrast], it is Socrates who knows the name, reputation, and wealth of

Theaetetus' father, and cares more for potential philosophers in Athens than in Cyrene" (*Being of the Beautiful,* pp. 131-132). Read in light of the interpretation being proposed here, the digression's false dichotomy between abstract reflection and withdrawal on the one hand, and the involvement of experience on the other, harks back to Theaetetus' original recognition that, whatever one's final identification of knowledge, it must include *both* abstract and concrete, or theoretic and practical forms (*Theaet.* 146c8-d2); on the other hand, it looks forward to the final demand that knowledge will encompass *both* true opinion in the realm of practical experience, and logos in the realm of the theoretical. The burden of the inquiry is to insist on an ultimate wholeness in which, as mutually opposed but "fitting" elements, the practical and theoretic will constitute a unity that qualifies as genuine knowledge. If this proposed interpretation has anything right about it, then this digression too tugs at a thread that runs from beginning to end of the dialogue, gently replacing the dichotomies of eristic with a reconciliation of opposites. Drawing attention to the digression's insistence on just such a mutuality (even between good and evil), W.J.W. Koster suggests that what we actually have here is the principle of the connection of contraries, which—like so much else in the *Theaetetus*—is naturally reminiscent of Heracleitus (*Le mythe de Platon, de Zarathoustre et des Chaldéens* [Lugduni Batavorum: E.J. Brill, 1951], pp. 36-37).

14. As the *Cratylus* suggests, it all depends on the goal (*Crat.* 389b8-d2). Just as from the same fleece differently spun thread and differently woven fabric will be appropriate depending on whether we want a veil or a rug, so from the same linguistic font we can generate language that is either humane and healing or tyrannical and humanly impoverishing. Against the perverse, or even merely clumsy, hacking of eristic, Socrates sets the subtle surgery of dialectic (cf. *Phaedr.* 265e1-3); against a goal of domination (whether in argument as with a sophist or in politics as with a demagogue), Socrates will constantly set a goal of individual and social health. As I understand it, this is why it is the dialectician who must ultimately judge of the fitness of linguistic distinctions (*Crat.* 390c2-11).

15. The significance of ambiguity, which seems to me to be played on through out this discussion (as well as through the dialogue as a whole), is apparently not something that has impressed most other commentators. In fact, Ackrill seems to suggest the opposite:

> The idea we would like to see developed here is the idea that the same item can be referred to in different ways, and that the principle that to understand an expression involves knowing what it stands for is ambiguous and misleading. But there is no trace of this line of thought in Plato's discussion, except perhaps for the final remark [i.e., that we need to understand knowledge in order to come to understand false opinion]." (J. L. Ackrill, "Plato on False Belief: *Theaetetus* 186-200," *Monist,* [1966]: 402)

16. On this point, Cornford wonders if Plato "overlooked" the inclusion of complex pieces of knowledge such as "the sum of 7 and 5," since he believed that would account for false judgment as a wrong putting together of two pieces of knowledge along the lines of the wax block's comparison of

impressions and imprints (*Plato's Theory of Knowledge*, pp. 137-138). But Ackrill (rightly, I think) is critical, for not only is it difficult to see how Cornford's suggestion would explain the possibility of thinking "the sum of 7 and 5" to be "11," but also it is difficult to see how it explains the possibility of thinking "the sum of 7 and 5" to be "12" either—since they would then be two different birds (Ackrill, "False Belief," p. 399). Frank Lewis proposes to meet this difficulty with an ingenious solution, suggesting that although there is but one and the same bird, there are actually two hunts; in other words, although the numbers represented by the two beliefs are identical, there are nevertheless two beliefs (F.A. Lewis, "Foul Play in Plato's Aviary," in *Exegesis and Argument: Studies in Greek Philosophy*, ed. E.N. Lee, A.P.D. Mourelatos, and R.M. Rorty [Assen, Netherlands: Van Gorcum, 1973], pp. 278-279). For the reasons already suggested, I do not believe that this is the point Plato is making.

17. It is disconcerting to discover that what seems to me to be the quite brilliant relevance of this discussion to the pursuit of knowledge as a whole is often seen by commentators as irrelevant. Although Ackrill points out that any interpretation of the parts of the discussion of true opinion has to make sense in terms of what follows ("False Belief," p. 391), Fine is one of the few critics who spell out some of these connections (e.g., "False Belief," pp. 77-78).

18. On this point, Cornford and McDowell offer different interpretations. McDowell sees the aviary account as offering a criticism of the theory of recollection as this was presented in the *Meno* (*Plato: Theaetetus*, pp. 222-223); Cornford argues that the theory being presented in the aviary model is not Plato's theory of recollection at all (*Plato's Theory of Knowledge*, pp. 135-136). According to the approach being advocated in this study, both Cornford and McDowell are on to something—Cornford, because it *is* a deliberately inadequate interpretation of *a* recollection theory; McDowell, because it is indeed coming under attack.

19. Although Plato himself might not have recognized empiricism as such (Holland, "An Argument," p. 99), it is (I believe) helpful for *us* to see his moves in those terms.

20. The majority of commentators whom I have read (Fine's "False Belief" is a notable exception) interpret this section on false opinion as though Plato himself were stymied. Sometimes Plato's supposed confusion is attributed to his own view of knowledge (purportedly a kind of acquaintance) (e.g., Runciman, *Plato's Later Epistemololgy*, pp. 17, 29, 34; cf. Lesher, *Gnōsis* and *Epistēmē*" p. 78). C.J.F. Williams ingeniously interprets Plato's position as caught in the ambiguity of what Quine came to distinguish as opaque and transparent readings of belief reports; he excuses Plato as being in the position of someone who had read the "Reference and Modality" of the early Quine, but not his later *Word and Object* ("Referential Opacity and False Belief in the *Theaetetus*," *Philosophy Quarterly*, 22 [1972], e.g., pp. 289, 302). Ackrill, who finds Plato confused on the issue of false opinion, comments in a footnote: "Plato might of course be letting Socrates commit this mistake precisely in order to make us see that it is a mistake. Such is the beautiful flexibility of the dialogue form. But I do not think that this way out is necessary." He himself tends to come down on the side of those who see Plato as responsible for Socrates' committing "a very gross mistake" ("False Belief," p. 389). Perhaps the point of view furthest from my own is that expressed by Richard Robinson:

Is it necessary to suppose that Plato meant us to infer *anything* from his discussion of error in the *Theaetetus*?... But, if Plato *was* thinking of any ulterior effect on his reader... he probably said to himself something like this: "Of course it is quite obvious that error *does* occur, and therefore it is quite certain that there is something wrong with every argument that offers to prove that error *cannot* occur, and therefore I am giving to philosophers the delightful task of finding out what is wrong with these arguments."... But error is just believing a false proposition... [Robinson concludes] the correct solution of the problem of error is merely to show what is wrong with any proffered argument for the conclusion that error cannot occur. ("Forms and Error," pp. 13, 24, 25)

CHAPTER 7:
"...AND LOGOS"

1. The point is that, when appropriately combined (i.e., according to the stipulations of any particular language: e.g., *Crat.* 389d8-390a7), meaningless letters can become meaningful. In this context, therefore, *syllabē*, as a first unit of meaning, would seem to be ideally translated as "morpheme," or better still, "semanteme." This, at least, is what I understand to be the point both of the discussion of elements in the *Cratylus* (422aff.), and of letters and syllables in the *Theaetetus* (203a3-b9). As the complex of letters which constitutes the first unit of meaning, the syllable is thus a genuinely emergent entity.

2. This is reflected in the *Cratylus'* assertion that the truth of a logos depends on true reference in its constituent elements, for "logoi are a combination [*synthesis*] of verbs and nouns" (*Crat.* 431b1-c1). It is also why, unless they are simply nonsense, sentences—but not the verbs or nouns in isolation—*say something* (*Soph.* 261d8-262e1).

3. Following the same pattern, the generative combination of elements once again yields a new whole. As the *syllogismos* of perceptions generates opinion (*Theaet.* 186d3), and as *synthesis* of verbs and nouns generates sentences (*Crat.* 431b1-c1), so propositions now functioning in turn as higher-level "elements" (*stoicheia*) (cf. Aristotle, *Met.* B, 3, 998a25-27, and Heath, *Mathematics in Aristotle*, p. 205), will generate argument as a higher-level *syllogismos* (e.g., *Phil.* 41c9).

4. In its examination of logos, the *Theaetetus* will again remind the reader of its quite special ties back to the *Meno* and forward to the *Sophist*. From different angles all three dialogues direct our attention to logos as definition; moreover, in doing so all three make a particular point of providing actual examples of the kind of definition sought (i.e., a theoretic definition, which, when needed, can be defended in argument). Thus the definition of figure (and subsequently of color) illustrates what Socrates wants by way of a definition of virtue in the *Meno*; the definition of the angler serves in the *Sophist* as paradigm for the later definition of the sophist.

5. It might be interesting to try to line up earlier model and later account—that is, the definition of surd proposed as a model at the beginning of the dialogue, and the effort at definition of logos that is rejected at the end. It might go something like figure 9.

Figure 9.
Comparison between (approved) definition of surd
and (rejected) definition of logos

Definition of surd endorsed as Model of logos (147d3-148b2)	Definition of logos apparently rejected as Account of logos (206c7-208e6)
(1) Theatetus provides a verbal account in the course of which terms like *square, multiply, line,* etc., freely occur to represent or image his opinion.	(1) The first meaning proposed is simply "making one's own thought clear through speech, by means of verbs and nouns, imaging one's opinion in the stream that flows through the lips" (206d1-4).
(2) The model points to (enumerates) measure (size) and shape as key elements in linear and plane relations — distinguishing square numbers (as products of equal rational factors) from oblong (products of unequal rational factors).	(2) The second interpretation of logos at the end of the dialogue involves "an enumeration of elements...an orderly description in terms of its elements" (207b4-5, c6-7).
(3) The model proposes a unique differentiation of surds from all other (i.e., rational) roots: x is a root of y if (i) $y = ab$; and (ii) $a{:}x :: x{:}b$; but x is *irrational* only if, for a given y, a and b are always unequal.	(3) The third interpretation of logos at the end of the dialogue focuses on "the ability to tell some characteristic by which the object in question differs from all others" (208c7-8).

6. One of the questions sometimes raised by commentators on this passage is: Why does Plato have Theodorus stop at 17 square feet? (for example, Mugler, *Platon et la recherche mathématique,* pp. 202-203; H. Cherniss, "Plato as Mathematician," *Review of Metaphysics,* 4 [1950-51] :411). Although it is true that he had to stop somewhere—so why not at 17?—it is nevertheless an intriguing fact that a Pythagorean theorem, closely touching the *Meno's* point about side and diagonal, generates a series of numbers that stops (according to the version that has come down to us via Theon of Smyrna) precisely at the number 17 (Theon of Smyrna, ed. Hiller, 42. 10-44. 17, GMW, vol. 1, pp. 132/133-136/137).

What would first of all be interesting about even an oblique reference to that theorem at just this point is that, like Theaetetus' response to Theodorus' question, it likewise constitutes an effort to provide a handle on irrationals. In other words, this side-and-diagonal theorem indicates one way in which irrationals may be approached in terms of rationals alone; Theaetetus' theory of surds offers another way of viewing incommensurables through commensurables.

It is a beautiful theorem which hinges on the fact that, given a series of squares that starts with one of side 1 and diagonal 1, and where each successive square is determined by adding one diagonal to a side and to the diagonal two sides, it is not the proportion between side and diagonal that remains invariant, but rather the difference between the square on the diagonal and the sum of the squares on the sides. Thus:

side 1 diagonal 1	:	the square on the diagonal (i.e., 1)	=	the sum of the squares on the sides (i.e., 2) *minus one*
side 2 diagonal 3	:	the square on the diagonal (i.e., 9)	=	the sum of the squares on the sides (i.e., 8) *plus one*
side 5 diagonal 7	:	the square on the diagonal (i.e., 49)	=	the sum of the squares on the sides (i.e., 50) *minus one*
side 12 diagonal 17	:	the square on the diagonal (i.e., 289)	=	the sum of the squares on the sides (i.e., 288) *plus one*

It is evident that to continue (since the next step gives us 1682 *minus one*) begins to be unwieldy. Might $\sqrt{17}$ have come to be an accepted stopping point, indicating "and so on"? Mugler points out that the area of figures whose square measure is 5, 10, and 17 can in each case be expressed in the form, $a^2 + 1$, but that this does not hold for 18 [nor, in fact for subsequent numbers until 26, then 37, 50, etc.] (*Platon et la recherche mathématique*, pp. 202-203).

A second point of interest notes that this same series of ordered pairs—i.e., 1/1, 3/2, 7/5, 17/12, constitutes an ever closer approximation to $\sqrt{2}$ (see I. Thomas' discussion of this point, GMW, vol. 1, p. 137, footnote (a))—the irrationality of which was apparently known. (It is generally believed that the Pythagoreans were aware of the irrationality of $\sqrt{2}$, and that in his *Prior Analytics* Aristotle indicated the method by which they proved it (*Pr. An.*, i, 23, 41a26-27). If the reference to the side-and-diagonal theorem is deliberate, it would account for the fact that Theodorus begins, not with $\sqrt{2}$ as one might otherwise expect, but rather with $\sqrt{3}$—the problem then being to distinguish irrational from rational roots in cases greater than $\sqrt{2}$ through a formula which would cover or account for the "apparently infinite number" of irrational square roots; in other words, Theaetetus and Young Socrates sought to arrive at a formula through which any and all such irrationals could be identified or "called" (*Theaet.* 147d8-e1).

7. Clearly, to be able to "call" the roots is not just a question of finding a name for these irrational numbers, since Theodorus has already called them "incommensurable," but rather a question of providing a single definition in terms of which any future quantity can be identified or "called" (*prosagoreusomen*) as rational or irrational. If this were not the case, the episode could hardly function as a model (148d4-7) for finding a definition of "knowledge"— the name of which causes no difficulty.

8. For example, Aristotle, *History of Animals*, 582a19; *Generation of Animals*, 727b8.

9. Like its English counterpart, *con-ception*, so *syl-labē* means literally to be "held together," "collected," and so becomes an apt metaphor not only for the conception of a child, but for any emergent "holding together" of elements. Thus, in tandem with the extension of *stoicheion* from "letter" in the linguistic

sense to "element" in general, "*syllabē*" is extended from "syllable" in the linguistic sense to "complex" in general.

10. Diès notes that the interpretations of logos explored here at the end of the dialogue do not include the one Plato himself often used, "raison causale, c'est à dire reminiscence"; he then concludes that this leaves the field open to a Platonic explanation of *epistēmē* after all—interpreting such a definition to involve reference to "its proper object," that is, intelligible being (Diès, *Platon: Oeuvres complètes*, vol. 8, p. 153).

On my reading of the dialogue, causal reasoning in the sense in which I understand it in the *Meno* is also notably present in the *Theaetetus*. Thus, there is a sharp parallel between the slave boy's identification of the diagonal (which is a judgment of true opinion based on Socrates' demonstration in this particular case), and Theodorus' identification of the irrationals up to $\sqrt{17}$ (which are also judgments of true opinion based on his demonstration in each particular case). What Meno's slave boy needs for his true opinion to be transformed into knowledge is the kind of theoretical grasp that explains *why* this is so, that is, by subsuming that particular case under a general law (in this case the theorem named after Pythagoras, which demonstrates that in every case the square on the diagonal will be equal to the sum of the squares on the other two sides). What Theodorus likewise needs for his true opinion to be transformed into knowledge is an analogous kind of theoretical grasp that explains *why* this is so, that is, by similarly subsuming those particular cases under a general law (in this case provided by the theorem Theaetetus develops, which enables them to identify in every case whether or not the side will be incommensurable in length with the unit of area measurement). For this reason, I think Haring is right in reminding us that this earlier discussion of surds already provides a clue for what she calls "a non-defective sense of logos," because there we see Theaetetus *grounding* Theodorus' true opinion, and thus transforming it ("*Theaetetus* Ends Well," pp. 523-527). See also Aristotle, *De An. II* 2, 413a4-21.

11. On this reading, Benardete is right in noting that this second interpretation of logos involves division, whereas the third will point rather to addition—although it should be clear that on my reading we would have to say, not "addition," but "combination" (*Being of the Beautiful*, p. 180).

12. It seems to me that this point is not always properly understood, so that what Plato sees as a necessary move *through* but eventually *beyond* the listing of particulars is sometimes misread as "rejection" or "rebuke" and even as "contempt" for the empirical, as though Plato did not recognize it as "the necessary starting point of the inquiry" (e.g., J. Beverslius, "Socratic Definition," *American Philosophical Quarterly*, 11 [1974]: 331-336; Beverslius goes on to attribute to Socrates the "incoherence" expressed in Meno's paradox: on the one hand, we need to scrutinize known instances of *x* in order to discover the *eidos*/definition common to them; on the other, one cannot recognize something as an instance unless one already knows the *eidos*/definition [p. 334]. For discussion of this paradox, see above, chapter 5).

This criticism is of course familiar from Wittgenstein's vehement stance: "I cannot characterize my standpoint better than by saying that it is opposed to that which Socrates represents in the Platonic dialogues. For, if asked what knowledge is, I would list examples of knowledge and add the words, 'and the like.' No common element is to be found in them all" (MS #302, 14, quoted by G. Hallett, *A Companion to Wittgenstein's Philosophical Investigations* [Ithaca: Cornell University Press, 1977], p. 33). The same point, is echoed by P. Geach ("Plato's *Euthyphro:* An Analysis and Commentary," *Monist,* 50 [1966]: 372).

13. As an example of one effort to show the real conclusiveness beneath apparent inconclusiveness, see my "Knowledge and Virtue: Paradox in Plato's *Meno,*" *Review of Metaphysics,* 39 (1985): 261-281.

14. It seems natural to relate *logos (or logismos)* and *dianoia,* as Plato himself frequently does (e.g., *Phaedo* 65e6-66a2; 79a3; *Rep.* VII, 529d4-5; *Theaet.* 206d1; *Soph.* 260c4; 263e3). Although the meanings of each do in fact tend to overlap (thus *dianoia,* as discursive thought or reasoning, gets extended to the notion of thought expressed; and *logos,* as verbal expression, gets extended to abstract reasoning), perhaps it makes most sense to take *logos* here in its meanings of "statement," "proposition," "hypothesis," "thesis," etc., as both starting point and conclusion of *dianoia.*

15. The ability "to give (and receive) an account," which figures so prominently in the *Republic* (e.g., VII, 531e4-5; 534b3-6), and the *Phaedo* (e.g., 95d7) is equally insisted on here in the *Theaetetus* (e.g., 202c2-3)—as also in the *Statesman* (e.g., 286a4-5). It would therefore seem to represent an abiding concern on Plato's part, through both middle and late periods.

16. This is not a conventional reading. For the weight of scholarship against me at this point, see Introduction, notes 11-20.

17. As examples of puzzled response, let me quote from two distinguished critics. Kenneth Sayre has noted that, more than any other passage in the *Theaetetus,* recent philosophers have been intrigued by "the mysterious Dream Theory," for "there is the tantalizing question why Plato introduced the 'dream theory' into the dialogue in the first place." "What is not clear is why Plato depicted Socrates as being reminded of this theory at all, and why at this particular stage in the dialogue." Again:

> Nothing is said explicitly in the dialogue to prepare the reader for those details of the theory...and Plato himself offers no clue regarding its sponsorship or why he is particularly concerned to refute it. The theory, in short, seems at first to be without connecting links, either historical or systematic, to any other theory or philosophic viewpoint treated in the dialogue. And if so, one can only wonder what Plato's reasons were for introducing it at this crucial point, and why he takes such great care to show that the theory is self-defeating. (*Plato's Analytic Method,* pp. 120-121, 122-123, and note 58)

A no less puzzled attitude is expressed by Glenn Morrow:

> A...puzzling feature is the fact that [the] refutation is introduced by a passage in which Socrates recounts a curious dream [which]...appears to prepare the way for the refutation of the later interpretation of logos as meaning an enumeration of constituent parts; but when this meaning of logos is taken up later, the characteristic feature of the dream—namely the contention that the parts are unknowable—is quietly dropped. It is

obvious that Plato thought the dream was relevant to the proposal of Theaetetus, but just how is it so? Its position shows that it is of fundamental importance, but with respect to what problem? ("Plato and the Mathematicians," pp. 310-311)

J. Annas neatly puts the question for all of us: "What is the dream theory *doing* in the *Theaetetus*?" (She goes on to argue its relevance in light of the *Cratylus'* [unwitting] recognition that logos understood as analysis cannot regress infinitely; what Plato needs is some version of Aristotle's insight that *kinds* of explanation and justification are "ineliminably plural" ("Knowledge and Language in the *Theaetetus* and the *Cratylus*," *Language and Logos*, ed. M. Schofield and M. Nussbaum [Cambridge: Cambridge University Press, 1982]).

18. This point is made—though with rather different implications—by both Miles Burnyeat ("Material and Sources," pp. 103-105) and Amélie Rorty ("Speculative Note," pp. 229-230). There is an important piece by David Gallop which explores both negative and positive aspects of dreams in the dialogues; it is a perceptive and wide-ranging article which recognizes the significance of dreams ("Dreaming and Waking in Plato," in *Essays in Ancient Greek Philosophy*, ed. J.P. Anton and G.L. Kustas [Albany, N.Y.: State University of New York Press, 1971], pp. 187-201).

19. Others have also noted this need for cross-examination. Thus Burnyeat points out that sometimes (as at *Crat.* 439c-440d) the framework of "dreaming" suggests "a refusal to take a firm stand for or against a view that keeps suggesting itself as worthy of attention, but which needs a hard examination before one can commit oneself to its truth" ("Material and Sources," p. 104). So too, Rorty, insisting that "if an unexpected phrase is used repetitively [as is "dream" at 201d8 and 202c5], there is probably a reason for it," points out that dreams, though prophetic, require careful interpretation ("Speculative Note," pp. 229-230). Gallop is even more explicit, noting that "the dreamer's vision is significant, even if opaque... The dream requires interpretation, but the dreamer himself cannot provide it" ("Dreaming and Waking," p. 188).

20. In the *Philebus*, the discussion is introduced via the same issue of unity and plurality, and leads similarly into the account of compounds in terms of "mixture" and "combination"—*ta koinon* (31c2); cf. *koinos genomenos* (22a2); *meignus* (25e3; 63e7); *meikton* (27d1); *meixis* (27b9; 59e1; 64d3); *symmeixis* (23d7; 64c5); *meixis kai krasis* (63e9-64a1); *sygkrasis* (61c2; 64d10). The components are, correspondingly, *ta kerannumena* (64d11).

21. In thus taking seriously the framework of the "dream," I am in obvious disagreement with those who tie the dream reference to Socratic-Platonic chronolgy. Thus, Cornford reads it as an oblique way of telling us that the theory was advanced after Socrates' death (*Plato's Theory of Knowledge*, p. 144); according to Crombie, Plato's calling it a "dream" indicates that "it is a post-Socratic theory, and Plato's historical conscience is pricking him" (*Examination of Plato's Doctrines*, p. 109). Compare Taylor (*Plato: The Man and His Work*, p. 346) and Rorty ("Speculative Note," p. 236). With Burnyeat, I find this implausible—although Burnyeat's own suggestion that it is "just a literary device to call attention to the theory's importance without violating the canons of Socratic midwifery" seems to me (as he himself acknowledges) to leave much to be

explained ("Material and Sources," p. 105). By contrast, my interpretation follows a number of suggestions made by Gallop in his illuminating article ("Dreaming and Waking," see above).

CHAPTER 8:
"...WHAT KNOWLEDGE REALLY IS"

1. The source of Socrates' "dream" has been the occasion of much speculation (see discussion in Introduction). This ranges all the way from those who, like A Koyré, think "the 'someone' of the dream...is probably Socrates himself," offering a genuine Platonic definition—though Theaetetus' account is likely to be a garbled version (*Introduction à la lecture de Platon*, pp. 84-85)—to those who, like Robin, see it as so remote from Platonic thinking that he warns us, "Whatever the historical interest of the 'dream,' conjectures about it in no way help understand Plato's own thought" (*Platon*, p. 61). According to Diès we can imagine Theaetetus smiling pointedly at Socrates the way Charmides had smiled at Critias, to indicate sly recognition of the source (Diès, *Platon: Oeuvres complètes*, vol. 8, p. 144); others, however, find that, at the least, it is "exceedingly unlike" anything in the *Phaedo, Republic,* and other earlier dialogues (e.g., Haring, "*Theaetetus* Ends Well" p. 512, ftn. 7).

2. There are not many commentators who find positive value in the "dream" version of the final definition, but there are a few who do insist that the dream is not fully refuted. The problem is, however, that interpretations of what constitutes its core of truth vary greatly. Thus, Koyré insists that we at least should realize that all along we have been using terms like *knowledge* and *to know* as if we already knew their meaning; we should therefore anticipate Theaetetus' ending up with a circular definition. Theaetetus' failure lies then in not realizing that this is inevitable, not understanding that the necessary circularity of *any* definition of knowledge reveals the preeminent character of that notion. Knowledge, he insists, is nothing other than possession of the truth, and it is the way to truth via reasoning that Socrates here opens up—though as to exactly how the dialogue actually leads to truth he is less explicit (Koyré, *Introduction*, pp. 92-93). D.W. Hamlyn points out that at the conclusion of the refutation Socrates says the elements are more *gnōstos* than complexes, not more *epistētos*, which leads him to conclude that there is no reason to reject the view that there are simples of which we have *gnōsis,* that is to say, direct acquaintance ("Forms and Knowledge in Plato's *Theaetetus*: A Reply to Mr. Bluck," *Mind,* 66 [1957]: 547); M. Yoh agrees with the latter point, arguing that in Plato's view, simples are not necessarily *alogon,* and hence are knowable, as the "dream" theory holds ("On the Third Attempted Definition of Knowledge: *Theaetetus* 201c-210b," *Dialogue* (Canada), 14 [1975]: 429). For Haring, after the dream theory has been "purged," there remains "an approvable remnant...the possibility that explanation concerns letter-like elements, as they are now understood to be—not as the dream theory described them"; but again, she is not as explicit as one would wish about how this actually resolves the problem of the dialogue ("*Theaetetus* Ends Well," p. 518).

3. Although Yoh believes Plato does not mean anything particular by his letters and syllables (Yoh, "Third Attempted Definition," p. 426, ftn. 9), Burnyeat suggests that the "dream" theory relies heavily "for its plausibility, and even its intelligibility, on the letter-syllable model in terms of which it is stated" ("Material and Sources," p. 119). But as this study has argued, although it may be true that its original intelligibility is enhanced by the model, there is throughout the dialogue much other evidence for its plausibility. Shorey's interpretation of the letter-syllable model recognizes that Plato's "main purpose" is to address the metaphysical question: Is the whole the sum of its parts except in mathematics? Can the world be explained as a mechanical summation of elements? He too finds Plato stressing the whole as "a new emergent form and distinct idea...not the composition of its elements but a new emergent idea" (Shorey, *Unity of Plato's Thought*, p. 71; *What Plato Said*, p. 285).

4. This contrast between those who have been initiated into the mysteries of generation and those who have not runs right through the dialogue, culminating, as it were, in this final section. E. Des Places believes that the reiterated contrast between initiated and uninitiated, in this and other dialogues (like *Gorgias* 493a1-c3; *Phaedo* 69c4-6; 81a7-8) reflects Plato's serious interest in the Mysteries ("Platon et la langue des mystères," in *Études Platoniciennes* [Leiden: E.J. Brill, 1981], p. 88).

5. The dilemma is brought to explicit focus when Theaetetus sees the impossibility of interpreting "whole" as *either* different from "all the parts" *or* as the same as "all the parts" (204a8-205a9). Sometimes the discussion of "the all" and "the whole" at 203e-205c leads a reader to suppose that Theaetetus might be ready to recognize genuine wholeness in contrast to a mere either-or. By contrast, McDowell maintains that "the dream theory, like the argument against it, envisages no possibility other than, on the one hand, being simple and hence having no parts, and on the other, being identical with a number of parts." He further notes that Theaetetus' moves here "reflect the mistaken view about the relation between a whole and its parts which is attacked at *Parmenides* 157c4-e2" (*Plato: Theaetetus*, pp. 244-245). By contrast, Haring is critical of the way Socrates "discredits" Theaetetus' effort to find an inter-mediate position involving a whole-with-parts (204a-b); she is convinced that he is trying to articulate a view closer to the kind of wholeness that I see the dialogue endorsing (Haring, "*Theaetetus* Ends Well," pp. 515-516).

6. One of the tantalizing features of Socrates' "dream" is that he seems here at the end of the dialogue to be picking up again the issue of irrationals that was introduced at the beginning by Theaetetus. The question is, is this deliberate?, and if so, then to what point? Critics' responses to this question—as to so many others in the *Theaetetus*—offer amazing variety. Where Diès wants to take seriously the reintroduction of irrationals, finding that "il serait bien étrange que Platon n'eut pas vu et n'eut pas voulu ces correspondences" (Diès, *Platon: Oeuvres complètes*, vol. 8, p. 128), Burnyeat, by contrast, rather discounts it: "That there should be a certain resemblance between Socrates' restriction of logos to the level of syllables and Theaetetus' account of certain irrationals as lines commensurable in square only (147d-148b) is something Plato is, I think, capable of enjoying for its own sake, without necessarily wanting to press the

point very far" ("Material and Sources," p. 106). Where H. Meyerhoff believes
Plato wants us to think back to earlier passages in the dialogue where he was
also concerned with the simplest elements of perceptual experience ("Socrates'
'Dream' in the *Theaetetus*," *Classical Quarterly*, n.s. 8 [1958]: 131-138), Benardete
sees the "impasse" at the end of the dialogue pointing rather to the fact that
"the soul and its experiences cannot be understood mathematically" (*Being of
the Beautiful*, p. 183).

   On this point, one of the most intriguing and challenging lines of
interpretation that I know comes from Diès and Mugler. Diès, who links the
Theaetetus in interesting ways with both the *Parmenides* and the *Sophist*, finds an
echo of Socrates' "dream" in the *Sophists'* attribution of irrationality (alogon) to
nonbeing, for he reads the dream as maintaining that what is *alogon* and
unknowable is the "fond de la réalité. . . le mystérieux et nécessaire élément"
(Diès, *Platon: Oeuvres complètes*, vol. 8, p. 128). Mugler carries the point a step
further. The discovery of irrationality was, he believed, "comme une révélation"
for Plato. Being forced to confront the reality of irrationals—which in their
indeterminate character seem to reflect the indeterminate flux of Heracleitus—
he found himself correspondingly forced to confront the reality of the world of
becoming, thus reinforcing the tie between mathematical discovery and
Platonic metaphysics. In other words, Mugler finds the tardy recognition of the
reality of irrationals paralleled by the tardy recognition of nonbeing, so much
so that he sees the "parricide" of the *Sophist* as really the metaphysical
expression of the work of mathematicians from Pythagoras to Theodorus. All
this he finds, moreover, to be anticipated in Socrates' "dream," for there,
although irrational and unknowable, the elements are nevertheless apprehended by perception. Following Diès, Mugler sees Plato drawing a parallel
between Theodorus' irrationals, which, although defying grasp in arithmetic,
can yet be constructed, and the world of becoming, which, although defying
grasp in knowledge, can yet be apprehended by the senses. This, he believes,
demands a rethinking of the limits of reason as Plato saw them in the *Republic*
(Mugler, *Platon et la recherche mathématique*, pp. 195, 203-206). The latter point has
been reiterated by critics representing quite different approaches (for example,
Brown, "*Theaetetus*," pp. 359-379; J. Novak, "Plato and the Irrationals," *Apeiron*,
16 [1982]: 71-85; 17 [1983]: 14-27); Annas, "Knowledge and Language" pp.
101-114).

   7. It is in these terms that I understand the reiterated distinction between
the plurality of constituent elements as matter of a thing on the one hand, and
the unity of form as *idea* on the other (e.g., 203c5-6; 204a1; 205c2, d5).

   8. This passage in the *Parmenides* is followed up by the well-known
discussion of parts and wholes, where it is affirmed that "the whole must be
one composed of many . . . the part is a part, not of the many nor of the all, but of
a single concept which we call a whole, a perfect unity created out of all" (*Parm.*
157c6, d7-e2). McDowell recognizes a possible problem implied by what he
sees as a discrepancy between this sophisticated handling of wholeness in the
Parmenides and the apparently unsophisticated handling here in the *Theaetetus*
(*Plato: Theaetetus*, pp. 243-247). This apparent contrast creates a problem,
however, only if the refutation of the "dream" is taken at face value; when read
in the way here proposed, then the *Theaetetus* and the *Parmenides* are in complete

agreement. This still leaves open, however, the question of how we are to understand this reference to "a single form and a single concept which we call a whole" (H.N. Fowler's translation, in the Loeb edition, of *mias tinos ideas kai henos tinos: Parm.* 157d8-e1). As Patterson points out, forms are not in an obvious sense wholes of parts; for example, Justice itself is not a whole consisting of well-ordered parts like the just soul or just city of the *Republic* (*Image and Reality,* p. 88). On the other hand, Klein seems to find some such complexity of form to be relatively unproblematic, for "as the elementary form of the problem of the 'one and the many' is to the dianoetic *methexis* problem, so is the latter to the ontological problem of the 'community of ideas' " (*Greek Mathematical Thought,* p. 80). But the sense in which form may be viewed as a whole of parts is, as Miller points out, tricky (Miller, *Plato's Parmenides,* pp. 176-183). The principal difficulty, he finds, is that, on the one hand, we have Plato's various well-known assertions attributing unity and simplicity to the forms (especially in the *Parmenides'* insistence on the simplicity of partlessness), and on the other, the *Sophist's* talk (and, as we have just seen, the *Parmenides'* talk as well) of their being wholes and parts. Miller points out that once it is clear that we have moved from a physical to a conceptual, or eidetic, relation of inclusion and subsumption, then the conception of the form as composite or complex ceases to be problematic, and forms can be interpreted as wholes of parts. But, as he notes, this does not yet explain just how the two sets of claims can be reconciled. Miller explores two possible ways of harmonizing the statements about simplicity on the one hand and wholeness on the other. According to his first interpretation, it is the original conversion of the soul from concern with materiality to awareness of immateriality that requires the insistence on partlessness and simplicity, but once that conversion has been achieved, the practice of dialectic via collection and division now requires the "new notion of logical complexity," thereby allowing the former stress on simplicity to drop from view. The second possibility that Miller considers relates back to the *Theaetetus,* and to my reading of Socrates' "dream." If it is correct to read the *Theaetetus* as attributing to the objects of knowledge *both* simplicity *and* complexity, then one might distinguish between a preanalytic insight or intuition which in recollection apprehends the form as *simple,* and a dialectical analysis which through collection and division apprehends the form as *complex.* Although I do not want to limit the object of knowledge to forms in this purely conceptual sense, I find truth in both of Miller's proposals, especially in his making room for two distinct modes of apprehension as ingredients in knowledge—although I take these modes to be opinion on the one hand and dianoetic reasoning as logos on the other, with what he is calling insight or intuition operating at *each* successive level of the cognitive process. There is another point of divergence between us which invites reflection, for in linking this discussion of the problem of the one and the many to that in the *Philebus,* Miller goes on to talk of collection and division as showing the form to be "one, determinately many, and unlimitedly many" (Miller, *Plato's Parmenides,* p. 277). Evidently he is offering a reading of this passage that differs from mine (see above, chapter 4).

9. Here I am clearly departing from the position of those who take the conclusion at face value, a position significantly represented by Wittgenstein's

exclamation: "Reading the Platonic dialogues, one has the feeling: what a frightful waste of time! What's the point of these arguments that prove nothing and clarify nothing?" (*Culture and Value*, ed. P. Winch [Chicago: University of Chicago Press, 1980, 1931], p. 14). By contrast, the tension I am emphasizing between what is being said and what is actually meant would seem to constitute a classic case of *irony*. It is, however, easier to refer to Socratic irony than to pin down just what constitutes it. Is Socrates deceiving Theaetetus? Is Plato deceiving the reader? Is it "irony" at all? A fruitful way to consider this problem would be to set it within the framework of the distinctions drawn by G. Vlastos ("Socratic Irony," *Classical Quarterly*, 37 [1987]: 79-96). According to Vlastos' approach, the tension I am arguing for might best be understood as what he calls "complex irony" in which "what is said both is and isn't what is meant" (p. 86). Within this category Vlastos locates Socrates' disavowals both of knowledge and of teaching, since the irony rests on the ambiguities involved in interpreting both "knowledge" and "teaching" (pp. 86, 92). Behind such irony Vlastos finds a purpose so little noticed that there is no name for it; it involves, in effect, propounding a kind of riddle which is then left to be solved by the hearer—along with the risks of being misunderstood (p. 79). What Vlastos recognizes in Plato's presentation of Socratic irony is this riddling ambiguity in which it is left to the reader to interpret the meaning. It turns out that my reading of the "ironic" conclusion of the dialogue is consonant, not only with Vlastos' complex analysis of irony, but also with C. Griswold's interpretation: "There is tension in the dialogues between the surface of the text and its context, a tension that points to an underlying meaning. In general, Platonic irony . . . depends on the difference between the dialogue that the reader conducts with Plato's text and the dialogue that is conducted by the interlocutors within the text" (*Self Knowledge in Plato's Phaedrus* [New Haven: Yale University Press, 1986], pp. 12-13j).

10. For a warning about my use of a term like *creative intelligence* see above, chapter 4, note 4.

CONCLUSION

1. Diogenes Laertius tells us that the followers of Eucleides (with whom Plato and other Socratics sought refuge and solace after the death of Socrates), originally known simply as "Megarians," came to be called "Eristics" (although later again his followers were also called "dialecticians" because of the question-and-answer form of their arguments). He cites Timon's report of "wrangling Eucleides [*eridanteo Eukleideo*] who inspired the Megarians with a frenzied love of eristic controversy [*erismou*]" (Diogenes Laertius, *Lives of Eminent Philosophers, Eucleides of Megara* II, 106-108).

2. Diogenes Laertius has preserved Eucleides' argument against analogy, which is cast in just that form that we have identified as "eristic": "He rejected the argument from analogy, declaring that it must be taken either from similars or from dissimilars. If it were drawn from similars, it is with these and not their analogies that their arguments should deal; if from dissimilars, it is gratuitous to set them side by side" (*Lives*, II, 107).

EPILOGUE:
THE MATHEMATICAL PARADIGM

1. Although I believe the actual phrase *logō te. . . kai ergō* occurs only once in the *Theaetetus* (173a2-3), it riddles the dialogues generally; for example: *Prot.* 325d2; *Rep.* II, 382a1-2, e8-9; VI, 492d5; 498e4; VII, 534d3-4; *Tim.* 19e1; *Laws* 647d6; 769e5-6; 885b2.

2. Iamblichus, *On Nichomachus' Introduction to Arithmetic,* quoted in GMW, vol. 1, pp. 110/111-112/113; Archytas (responsible for renaming the subcontrary "harmonic"), is cited by Porphyry in his *Commentary on Ptolemy's Harmonics,* GMW vol. 1, pp. 112/113-114/115.

3. Theon (ed. Hiller, 106 15-20) reporting Adrastus (GMW vol. 1, p. 125, ftn. a).

4. Although the following actually duplicates some material in the Mathematical Interlude, it is sufficiently relevant to the argument here to warrant repetition. The three means may be seen in a nutshell:

(1) The *arithmetic* mean b between two extremes, a and c, is determined as
$$a + x = c - x = b$$
thus, for example, the arithmetic mean between 4 and 12 is: $4 + 4 = 12 - 4 = 8$ —determination of the mean having been effected by addition and subtraction.

(2) The *harmonic* mean b between two extremes, a and c, is determined as
$$a + \frac{a}{x} = c - \frac{c}{x} = b$$
thus, the harmonic mean between 4 and 12 is: $4 + 4/2 = 12 - 12/2 = 6$— determination of the mean having been effected by division as well as by addition and subtraction.

(3) The *geometric* mean between two extremes, a and c, is determined as
$$a : b = b : c, \text{ or } ac = b^2$$
thus the geometric mean between 4 and 12 is $\sqrt{48}$—determination of the mean in this case having involved generation of a different dimension.

5. As Theaetetus anticipates (148b2), the same device would permit the generation of cube roots. (Thus, a solid of, say, sides 2, 4, 8, and therefore of volume 64, would be in cubic measure the equivalent of a cube of side 4—and so for any cube roots, either rational or irrational.) But the Application of Solids, where a solid of given measure and shape could be "applied" to a different shape with the same measure, was still a puzzle (as is evident in the problem of the doubling of the Cube)—although they did apparently realize that whereas the generation of square roots required only one geometric mean, that of cube roots required two (*Tim.* 32a7-b8).

6. As examples, let me cite just two critics. For A. Wedburg, the equality of the two central sections "is obviously an unintended feature of the mathematical symbolism, to which no particular significance should be attached" (*Plato's Philosophy of Mathematics* [Stockholm: Almquist and Wiksell, 1955], p. 103). Faced with the same problem, Brumbaugh introduces—albeit with "some reluctance"—a theory which he calls "interference of metaphor" to get around

what he regards as, if not an oversight, then at least an unfortunate feature of the diagram. Determined to make all four sections of the line unequal, Brumbaugh exclaims, "The figure referred to here has proportions which cannot be combined by any geometrical construction" (Brumbaugh, *Plato's Mathematical Imagination*, p. 98; see his discussion, pp. 91-100).

7. We should perhaps have been alerted to the relevance of dimensionality from the very beginning. After all, Socrates does reiterate the two-dimensionality of *eikasia's* images at the first cognitive level—comparing them to "shadows and reflections in water and on smooth surfaces" (*Rep.* VI, 510a1-2), and then again as shadows on the wall of the cave (*Rep.* VII, 515a6-8).

8. That this is what Plato has in mind seems further suggested by a strange passage at *Republic* IX, 587c3-588a2. There Plato calculates the measure by which the pleasure of the king (at the highest of the four levels) exceeds that of the tyrant (at the lowest, where he enjoys only the phantom appearance of pleasure). What is interesting is that he proceeds first to represent the tyrant's pleasure by 9 ("3 times 3, to yield a plane number measured "longitudinally": 587d3-7—a "plane number" perhaps representing the two-dimensionality of the tyrant's phantom, or shadowy, pleasure); then "by a process of squaring and cubing" (587d9) he concludes that the pleasure of the king is represented by 729 relative to that of the tyrant. It would seem that what he has done is, by successive squaring and cubing, to take us from the original level 9 of the tyrant, through the other three levels, that is:

$$9 : 81 = 81 : 729$$

—which would corresponds to the formula we have just identified for the Divided Line of the *Republic*:

$$a : a^2 = a^2 : a^3.$$

9. As is clear (both from this discussion and from chapter 8 above), this study does not agree with the kind of interpretation of the Divided Line that one finds, for example, in I.E. Miller. Although he argues for there being, on the side of the knower, the four familiar divisions (*eikasia, pistis, dianoia, and nous*), he maintains that, on the side of the object—that is, with respect to the discussion Socrates postpones as requiring too much time (*Rep.* VII, 534a5-8)—if there is any distinction between objects on the third and fourth levels, then it is but "formal and apparent, rather than real in the mind of Plato" (*Significance of Mathematical Element*, pp. 45-46). (Many critics sound as though they would agree with him). By contrast, Mugler offers an original and challenging proposal about the levels in Plato's ontology. Recognizing the role of dimensionality in Plato's philosophy, Mugler argues for a series of ontological levels corresponding to the series of dimensions he believes Plato is envisaging—from the two-dimensionality of the cave shadows, through the three-dimensionality that Plato calls *hē bathous auxē* and *hē tritē auxē* (*Rep.* VII.528b2-3, d8), or simply *to bathos* (as at *Theaet.* 194d, e) to a final conception of time itself as a fourth dimension analogous to the move from becoming to being, and expressed in the "true astronomy" (*Rep.* VII, 529d1-530c1). It is an intriguing

proposal, especially when linked, through astronomy, with time. With Cherniss, however, I wonder if Mugler's suggestion that Plato already had the concept of time as a fourth dimension might not rather be closer to a thought-provoking leap of imagination (Cherniss, "Plato as Mathematician," p. 398).

10. Proclus, *On Euclid*, GMW, vol. I p. 252/253.

11. Theon of Smyrna, quoting Erastosthenes, *Platonicus*, GMW vol. 1, pp. 256/257. Even after Hippocrates effected the reduction of the problem, reformulating it in terms of a double geometric proportion, it remained a puzzle since the two mean proportionals prove to be irrational. According to the accounts, the best minds of the time set themselves to devising ways of determining them (e.g., GMW, vol. 1, pp. 260/261-308/309).

12. Even one who normally does—like Brumbaugh—tends, however, in the case of Theaetetus' surds, to discount the significance of the mathematical paradigm, taking it simply at face value as an example of the kind of definition Socrates is seeking (*Plato's Mathematical Imagination*, pp. 40, 269).

13. See discussion of this point by Brown, "*Theaetetus*," p. 363.

14. Diogenes Laertius, *Lives of Eminent Philosophers*, III, 6.

15. Robin finds that the *Theaetetus'* obvious focus on becoming is countered, or balanced, by the fact that it is Eucleides, leader of the Eleatic school of Megara, who narrates the conversation (*Platon*, p. 119).

16. Diogenes Laestius, *Lives*, II, 107.

APPENDIX A:
SOCRATES' DICE ILLUSTRATION

1. The harmonic mean is "that which exceeds the one term and is itself exceeded by the other by the same fraction of the respective terms" (*Epin.* 991a6-7; compare Archytas' discussion of Means, cited by Porphyry in his *Commentary on Ptolemy's Harmonics*, and Ivor Thomas' compact translation: "*b* is the harmonic mean between *a* and *c* if

$$\frac{a - b}{a} = \frac{b - c}{c}$$

(GMW, vol. I, p. 112/113, and ftn. (a), p. 114). What we have here in the dice illustration is

$$\frac{12 - 6}{12} = \frac{6 - 4}{4}$$

—which in turn equals one-half, that is, that ratio of 4 by which 6 exceeds 4 and is also that ratio of 12 by which 6 is less than 12. It thus constitutes a classic case of a harmonic mean. (Theaetetus might even be alerted here by Socrates' choice of numbers, since the harmonic mean between the extremes of 6 and 12—i.e., a variation on the numbers Socrates is working with—was regarded as of special significance: *Epin.* 991a6-b4).

2. Nicomachus, *Introduction to Arithmetic,* GMW, vol. 1, pp. 118/119-120/121.

3. Iamblichus, *On Nicomachus' Introduction to Arithmetic,* GMW, vol. 1, pp. 110/111-112/113.

4. Thus, for example, to use Socrates' familiar example from the *Meno,* the surd which measures the side of the sought-for square (whose area was to be the equivalent of two squares of side 2, i.e., of an oblong 2 x 4) will, in Theaetetus' account, be identified as $2:x=x:4$, or $\sqrt{8}$. A. Wasserstein makes an interesting connection from mathematics to music, pointing out that the interval of a full tone cannot be divided into exact semitones, but needs the geometric mean to make the division (which will yield two irrationals) ("Theaetetus and the History of the Theory of Numbers," *Classical Quarterly,* n.s. 8 [1958]: 173).

5. Theaetetus' confusion at these apparently simple questions that lead into ever deeper questions about generation and existence echoes in striking fashion details of Socrates' own biography as he gives it to us in the *Phaedo.* For there too, having commonsensically supposed addition to be the obvious source of increase (*Phaed.* 96c3-d6), Socrates finds himself led through numerical problems as superficially naive as those about the dice (96d8-e4), finally to confront the central philosophical question of "how anything is generated or is destroyed or exists" (97b5-6). It seems that Theaetetus' likeness to Socrates (*Theaet.* 143e8-9) is more than merely physical.

6. Proclus, *On Euclid* i, GMW, vol. 1, p. 252/253.

7. Under "standard interpretations" I have in mind those, for example, of Campbell, Cornford, and McDowell, which have been considered above in some detail. It seems to me surprising that among both commentaries on the *Theaetetus* and studies of the significance of mathematics in the dialogues there should be so few who address this problem of Socrates' dice illustration.

Thus it seems of no particular significance even to discerning critics like Miller (*Significance of the Mathematical Element*), Cherniss ("Plato as Mathematician"), Brumbaugh (*Plato's Mathematical Imagination*), Klein (*Greek Mathematical Thought* and *Plato's Trilogy*), or Burnyeat ("Philosophical Sense"). Vlastos does at one point refer to "the six dice, which are supposed to be both numerous and not numerous, because they are more numerous than four dice and less numerous than twelve," but simply finds it "evident . . . that here Plato suffers from a certain confusion" ("Degrees of Reality in Plato,") in *New Essays on Plato and Aristotle,* ed. R. Bambrough [London and New York: Humanities Press, 1965], p. 14).

APPENDIX B:

EMERGENCE

1. Although the more obvious alternative to dualism is usually taken to be some form of reductionism, it has been argued that the plausibility of reductionism itself rests on a suppressed premiss of dualism. As A. O. Lovejoy put it in the earlier discussions of emergent evolution, the mechanistic

conception of preformation that underlies reductionism escapes the paradox of psychic emergence through its "association with some form of psycho-physical dualism," for, as he goes on to explain, "the eventual triumphs of that principle [i.e., reductionism] in modern science were made possible through the restriction of its literal application to the physical order, after that order had first been carefully purged of the classes of facts most recalcitrant to such application" (A.O. Lovejoy, "The Meanings of 'Emergence' and its Modes," in *Sixth International Congress of Philosophy, Proceedings* [New York]: Longmans Green and Company, 1926], p. 20).

A differently expressed, but basically similar, recognition of this aspect of the problem seems to underlie Meehl and Sellars' distinction between physical$_1$ and physical$_2$ in the context of emergence, and to prompt the later wry criticism of mind-brain identity theories. (To be "physical$_1$" is to belong to the space-time network; to be "physical$_2$" is to be definable in terms of theoretical primitives adequate to describe completely the actual states (though not necessarily the potentialities) of the universe before the appear-ance of life: P.E. Meehl and W. Sellars, "The Concept of Emergence," in *Minnesota Studies in the Philosophy of Science,* ed. H. Feigl and M. Scriven, [Minneapolis: University of Minnesota Press 1956], vol. 1, p. 252.) For either we read the reduction of raw feels to brain processes as a strong claim made in terms of "microtheory adequate to the explanation of inanimate physical objects"—in which case the claim is as yet unfounded and to that extent (at least at present) "very exciting, but false"—or we read it as a weak claim made in terms of "microtheory adequate to the explanation of any physical object, animate or inanimate," thereby enlarging the scope of the physical to include the neurophysiological processes of "core [i.e. defleshed] persons"—in which case the claim, "trivially...[and] almost undoubtedly true, is relatively non-controversial and unexciting." (W. Sellars, "The Identity Approach to the Mind-Body Problem," in *Philosophical Perspectives,* [Springfield, Ill.: Thomas, 1959, 1967], pp. 370, 381, 386).

2. H. Driesch, "Emergent Evolution," in *Sixth International Congress of Philosophy, Proceedings* (New York, 1926), p. 3f.

3. A.C. Garnett, "Scientific Method and the Concept of Emergence," *Journal of Philosophy,* 39 (1942): 485.

4. S. Alexander, *Space, Time and Deity,* Gifford Lectures, Glasgow, 1916-1918 (London: Macmillan), vol. 2, p. 46.

5. W.M. Wheeler, "Emergent Evolution of the Social," in *Sixth International Congress of Philosophy, Proceedings* (New York, 1926), p. 41. See also note on A. Lowry (note 24 below).

6. Lovejoy, "Meanings of 'Emergence,' " p. 22.

7. A.E. Taylor, *Evolution in the Light of Modern Knowledge* (1925), p. 460.

8. Plato's intention in the *Theaetetus* (at least as this study interprets it) is to confront us anew with what he sees as subtleties in the concept of causality. It might thus be argued that if one were to take causality in a sufficiently rich sense to include not only lower-level components in the sense of Plato's "elements" or Aristotle's material cause, but also to take serious account of form as causal, then theories of emergence would clearly not be a-causal. In fact, for C. Lloyd Morgan, the "new" that appears in emergent evolution is

chiefly a new sort of "relatedness" (*The Emergence of Novelty* [London: William and Norgate, 1933], p. 33) which, as Henle recognizes, is not a-causal, but it is rather the case that "emergent evolution has to do with a causal situation . . . i.e., something organic *brought into being by* inorganic processes, yet not explained by these" (italics added). This is why he can suggest that the most accurate way of presenting the notion of original novelty is in Aristotelian terms, according to which the novelty that is being asserted is not to be understood as simply a recent conjoining of form and matter to constitute this particular, but rather as a case where the form itself is new—or, in Platonic terms, that we have here a first appearance of the form in this world (P.M. Henle, "The Status of Emergence," *Journal of Philosophy*, 39 [1942]: 487).

9. C.R. Morris, "The Notion of Emergence," *PAS* Suppl., 6 (1926): 54.

10. Meehl and Sellars, "Concept of Emergence," pp. 240-241.

11. Nagel recognizes that the doctrine of emergent evolution is "entirely compatible with the belief in the universality of the causal principle, at any rate in the form that there are determinate conditions for the occurrence of all events" (E. Nagel, *The Structure of Science* [London: Routledge and Kegan Paul, 1961], p. 377).

12. Henle, "Status of Emergence," p. 488.

13. W.L. Mackenzie, "The Notion of Emergence," *PAS* Suppl., 6 (1926): 67-68.

14. Ibid., p. 60.

15. P. Oppenheim and H. Putman, "Unity of Science as a Working Hypothesis," *Minnesota Studies in the Philosophy of Science*, ed. H. Feigl, M. Scriven, and G. Maxwell (Minneapolis: University of Minnesota Press, 1958), vol. 2, p. 15 and passim.

16. J.J.C. Smart, *Philosophy and Scientific Realism* (London: Routledge and Kegan Paul, 1963), p. 51

17. Henle, "Status of Emergence,": p. 489-490.

18. Ibid., p. 491.

19. A. Pap, "The Concept of Emergence," *British Journal for the Philosophy of Science*, 2 (1952): 310. Pap's position is perhaps best seen in contrast to that of Mackenzie back in 1926, who, recognizing the appearance of secondary qualities as "one of the very best illustrations of the need for a term like emergent," had nevertheless gone on to assert universal predictability in principle, for "it does not here exclude the tracing after the fact of the steps through which the effect, say, of ammonia on the nostrils could, conceivably, be brought within some formula wide enough to include both the microscopic structure and the 'secondary quality' effect" ("Notion of Emergence," p. 65). Picking up the same illustration, Pap first of all discounts as "undeniable but irrelevant" the emergentist proposition that " 'this gas has smell S' cannot be logically deduced from the premise 'this gas has such a molecular structure' alone, without the use of an additional premise asserting the correlation between structure and secondary quality" (Pap, "Concept of emergence," p. 306). On this point Pap agrees with Mackenzie that the special composition law (i.e., NH_3 has the smell S) *could* have been predicted before someone smelled it—so long as original evidence for the general composition law (i.e., the law that whenever the two gases combine chemically in the volume proportion of

1:3, then the resulting compound has smell S) does not include ostensively definable properties of ammonia. But there's the rub; for if the ammonia-smelling predicate admits of only ostensive definition, then (Pap argues) the prediction would be impossible since one would not know what quality was being predicted. In short, Pap maintains, "a law correlating a quality Q with causal conditions of its occurrence can, without obscurantism, be argued to be *a priori unpredictable* if the predicate designator Q is only ostensively definable" (pp. 310-311).

Actually, there is a curious analogy here between Pap's line of argument and that of Socrates' "dream" before Pap veers off in a somewhat different direction. Both are trying to elucidate emergence in the context of explain-ability: for Pap the issue is approached in terms of that which is deducible or predictable versus that which is unpredictable; for Plato, the issue is approached in terms of that which is *logon* versus that which is *alogon*. Both assert complexity as a condition of explainability in their respective contexts; both maintain, however, that if there are complexes then there also are (ultimately?) simples as components. Both recognize that such simples will not be explainable: for Pap they will be a priori unpredictable; for Plato they admit of no logos.1 Both insist that although not susceptible of explanation, such simples do nevertheless admit of some kind of immediate identification: thus, Pap talks of their being understood through ostensive definition only; for Plato, they can only be named, for they have no definition but only a name. Both, finally, try to get a purchase on the problem by dealing with it on the level of language: thus, Pap explains that "the expression describing it [the complex] contains sub-designators (predicates and/or proper names) understood through ostensive definition only...If there are qualities which admit of *a priori* prediction there must also be qualities, less complex ones, which do not admit of *a priori* prediction" (p. 308); Plato, for his part, spells out the contrast in terms of the simples having only a name and the complex having a definition (logos) or expression (rhētas) made up of the combination of names (*Theaet.* 202a8-b7).

Although the argument of each is directed toward justification of the concept of emergence, they nevertheless differ in final emphasis and outcome. For Pap, the focus is on the emergence of ostensively definable secondary qualities that are on the one hand correlated with causal conditions of their occurrence, yet on the other hand a priori unpredictable on the basis of (and to that extent not fully explained by) those conditions. For Plato the parallel is clear: that which emerges is likewise to be understood on the one hand in terms of those factors which constitute causal components of its occurrence, but on the other hand the emergent defies full explainability in terms of those same constituent elements. A first major difference between the two is evident, however, in that Pap takes as paradigmatically emergent those qualities that are definable exclusively by ostension, whereas Plato takes as paradigmatically emergent the meaningful syllable which is contrasted with its nonmeaningful, but simply nameable, letters. In other words, for Pap, that which is nonexplain-able and nonpredictable but only ostensively definable is the emergent itself; for Plato that which is nonexplainable but only identifiable by name is that out of which emergence arises. Second, whereas Pap seems to limit emergence to just those cases of ostensively definable secondary qualities, Plato is proposing a more general theory of emergence of which secondary qualities are simply a special case. For Plato wants to make room for successive emergence at a series of levels; hence the complex and its elements will always be relative not only to each other but also to the level at which they occur.

20. Nagel, *Structure of Science*, p. 369.

21. Ibid. As I understand him, the approach tends to interpret emergence as primarily an epistemological concept in a sense analogous to the interpretation of scientific law as primarily an epistemological instrument.

22. A familiar tension between the epistemological and the metaphysical tends to surface in these discussions. Interpreting emergence as an epistemological concept always to be understood as logically relative to a particular system, Henle notes that the condition of its actually being a metaphysical concept would be that the logical simplicity of the hypotheses in question be ultimately justified ("Status of Emergence," p. 491). But for a scientific realist, this is the goal even if, as for Sellars, Completed Science functions regulatively like a Kantian Idea of Reason. This is why he can say the following:

> The question, "Does the world contain emergents?" requires to be answered in terms of a scientific account of observable phenomena, and although with reference to a given scientific picture of the world the question is a *logical* one which concerns the formal structure of this picture, taken absolutely, the question shares the inductive character, and hence corrigibility in principle, of the scientific enterprise. (Meehl and Sellars, "Concept of Emergence," p. 239)

23. Meehl and Sellars, "Concept of Emergence," p. 252.

24. Cf. Meehl and Sellars' reminder that even a "correct" theory (i.e., one formulating a lawful relation between values relating to theoretical entities and the values relating to observables) does not mean that the two entities are analyzable into each other—in other words, it demonstrates correlation, not identity (ibid.,) p. 251.

More recently, discussing emergence in the context of reducibility, A. Lowry has drawn a fine contrast between a thesis falsely imputed to emergentists (then attacked)—"full understanding of the parts does not suffice for an understanding of the whole"—and the thesis which more accurately captures the emergent position (and which is invulnerable to that attack)— "the parts cooperate to form the whole and, in so doing, are modified according to the plan of the whole. Understanding this cooperation, therefore, depends upon understanding the plan of the whole" ("A Note on Emergence," *Mind*, 83 [April 1974]" 276).

The term *function* as used here is intended to capture Plato's concept of the active and passive power of a thing (e.g., *Phaedr.* 270d2-5).

25. W.F. Sellars, "Philosophy and the Scientific Image of Man," *Science, Perception, and Reality* (London: Routledge and Kegan Paul, 1963), p. 26.

26. For Sellars, the three-dimensional world of physical objects is an appearance to us of the real world of theoretical entities as postulated by science ("Empiricism and the Philosophy of Mind," *Science, Perception, and*

Reality, p. 173; "Philosophy and the Scientific Image of Man," p. 27; "Scientific Realism and Irenic Instrumentalism," *Philosophical Perspectives*, pp. 338, 363, and passim). For Plato, to talk of "the real world" is a more complicated affair (see, for example, chapter 2 and Overview in chapter 8).

SELECT BIBLIOGRAPHY

Ackrill, John. "Plato on False Belief: *Theaetetus* 187-200," *Monist,* 50 (1966): 383-402.

Allen, Reginald E. "The Argument from Opposites in *Republic* V," *Review of Metaphysics,* 15 (1961): 325-335.

———(ed.). *Studies in Plato's Metaphysics.* New York: Routledge and Kegan Paul, 1965.

Annas, Julia. "Knowledge and Language in the *Theaetetus* and the *Cratylus,*" in *Language and Logos: Studies in Ancient Greek Philosophy presented to G.E.L. Owen,* ed. Malcolm Schofield and Martha C. Nussbaum. Cambridge: Cambridge University Press, 1982.

Bambrough, Renford (ed.). *New Essays on Plato and Aristotle.* New York: Humanities Press, 1965.

Benardete, Seth B. *The Being of the Beautiful: Plato's Theaetetus, Sophist, and Statesman.* Translated and with commentary. Vol. 1. Chicago and London: University of Chicago Press, 1984.

Beverslius, J. "Socratic Definition," *American Philosophical Quarterly,* 11 (1974): 331-336.

Bluck, R.S. "False Statement in the *Sophist,*" *Journal of Hellenic Studies,* 77, no. 2 (1957): 181-186.

———"'Knowledge by Acquaintance' in Plato's *Theaetetus,*" *Mind,* n.s. 72 (1963): 259-263.

———*"Logos* and Forms in Plato," first published in *Mind,* n.s. 65 (1956): 522-529; reprinted in *Studies in Plato's Metaphysics,* ed. R.E. Allen. New York: Routledge and Kegan Paul, 1965.

Bondeson, W.B. "Perception, True Opinion, and Knowledge in Plato's *Theaetetus,*" *Phronesis,* 14 (1969): 111-122.

Brown, Malcolm S. *"Theaetetus,* Knowledge as Continued Learning," *Journal of the History of Philosophy,* 7 (1969): 359-379.

Brumbaugh, Robert S. *Plato's Mathematical Imagination.* Bloomington, Ind.: Indiana University Press, 1954.

Burnet, John. *Greek Philosophy, Thales to Plato.* London: Macmillan and Company, 1914, 1950.

———*Platonism.* Berkeley, Calif.: University of California Press, 1928.

Burnyeat, Miles F. "Idealism and Greek Philosophy: What Descartes Saw and Berkeley Missed," *Philosophical Review,"* 90 (1982): 3-40.

———"The Material and Sources of Plato's Dream," *Phronesis,* 15 (1970): 101-122.

———"The Philosophical Sense of Theaetetus' Mathematics," *Isis,* 69 (1978): 489-513.

———"Plato on the Grammar of Perceiving," *Classical Quarterly,* 26 (1976): 29-51.

———"Protagoras and Self Refutation in Plato's *Theaetetus,"* *Philosophical Review,* 85 (1976): 172-195.

Bury, R.G. "*Dynamis* and *Physis* in Plato," *The Classical Review,* 8 (1894): 297-300.

Campbell, Lewis. *The Theaetetus of Plato.* Edited with introduction. 2nd ed. Oxford: Clarendon Press, 1883.

Cherniss, Harold F. "The Philosophical Economy of the Theory of Ideas," *American Journal of Philology,* 1936; reprinted in *Studies in Plato's Metaphysics,* ed. R.E. Allen, New York: Routledge and Kegan Paul, 1965.

———"Plato as Mathematician," *Review of Metaphysics,* 4 (1950-1951): 395-425.

Cole, A.T. "The Apology of Protagoras," *Yale Classical Studies,* 19 (1966): 101-118.

Cooper, J. "Plato on Sense Perception and Knowledge: *Theaetetus* 184-186," *Phronesis,* 15 (1970): 123-146.

Cornford, Francis M. "Mathematics and Dialectic in the *Republic* VI-VII," *Mind,* n.s. 41 (1932), Part 1: 37-52; Part 2: 173-190.

———*Plato's Theory of Knowledge. The Theaetetus and Sophist of Plato.* Translated with a running commentary. London: Kegan Paul, 1935.

Crombie, I.M. *An Examination of Plato's Doctrines,* vol. 2: *Plato on Knowledge and Reality.* International Library of Philosophy and Scientific Method. New York: Humanities Press, 1963.

Cross, R.C. "*Logos* and the Forms in Plato," *Mind*, 1954; reprinted in *Studies in Plato's Metaphysics*, ed. R.E. Allen. New York: Routledge and Kegan Paul, 1965.

Desjardins, Rosemary. "The Horns of Dilemma: Dreaming and Waking Vision in Plato's *Theaetetus*," *Ancient Philosophy*, 1 (1981): 109-126.

———"Knowledge and Virtue: Paradox in Plato's *Meno*," *Review of Metaphysics*, 39 (1985): 261-281.

———"Why Dialogues? Plato's Serious Play," in *Platonic Writings/ Platonic Readings*, ed. Charles Griswold. London and New York: Routledge and Kegan Paul, 1988.

Des Places, Edouard. *Etudes Platoniciennes*. Leiden: E.J. Brill, 1981.

Diès, August (ed.). *Platon: Oeuvres complètes*, vol. 8: *Théétète*. Paris: Société d'édition "Les belles lettres," Collection des Universités de France, publiée sous le patronage de l'Association Guillaume Budé, 1924.

Diogenes Laertius. *Lives of Eminent Philosophers*. With an English translation by R.D. Hicks. 2 vols. (Loeb Classical Library.) Cambridge, Mass., Harvard University Press, 1938.

Edelstein, L. *Plato's Seventh Letter*. Philosophia antiqua XIV. Leiden: E.J. Brill, 1966.

Festugière, André J.M. *Contemplation et la vie contemplative selon Platon*. Le Saulchoir bibliothèque de philosophie. 2e ed. Paris: Librairie philosophique J. Vrin, 1950.

Findlay, John N. *Plato, the Written and Unwritten Doctrines*. New York: Humanities Press, 1974.

Fine, Gail. "False Belief in the *Theaetetus*," *Phronesis*, 24 (1979): 70-80.

Friedländer, Paul. *Plato*. Vol. 3. Translated from the German by H. Meyerhoff. New York: Pantheon Books, 1969.

Gadamer, Hans-Georg, *Dialogue and Dialectic: Eight Hermeneutical Studies of Plato*. Translated and with an introduction by P. Christopher Smith. New Haven: Yale University Press, 1980.

Gaiser, Konrad. "Plato's Enigmatic Lecture 'On the Good'," *Phronesis*, 25 (1980): 5-37.

Gallop, David. "Dreaming and Waking in Plato," in *Essays in Ancient Greek Philosophy*, ed. J.P. Anton and G.L. Kustas. Albany, N.Y.: State University of New York Press, 1971.

———"Plato and the Alphabet," *Philosophical Review*, 72 (1963): 364-376.

Gargarin, M. "The Purpose of Plato's *Protagoras*," *Transactions and Proceedings of the American Philological Association* (1969): 133-164.

Gibson, A. Boyce. "Plato's Mathematical Imagination," *Review of Metaphysics*, 9 (1955): 57-70.

Gosling, J.C. "*Doxa* and *Dynamis* in Plato's *Republic*," *Phronesis*, 13 (1968): 119-130.

Greek Mathematical Works: Selections Illustrating the History of Greek Mathematics. With an English translation by Ivor Thomas. 2 vols. (Loeb edition). Cambridge, Mass.: Harvard University Press, 1939.

Griswold, Charles. *Self Knowledge in Plato's Phaedrus*. New Haven: Yale University Press, 1986.

Grote, George. *Plato and the Other Companions of Socrates*. 3 vols. London: John Murray, 1865.

Gulley, Norman. *Plato's Theory of Knowledge*. London: Methuen, 1962.

Guthrie, W.K.C. *Twentieth-Century Approaches to Plato:* Lectures in memory of Louise Taft Semple. University of Cincinnati Classical Studies 1. Princeton, 1967.

Hackforth, R.H. "Notes on Plato's *Theaetetus* 145d-201d," *Mnemosyne*, ser. 4, 10 (1957): 128-140.

————"Platonic Forms in the *Theaetetus*," *Classical Quarterly*, n.s. 7 (1957): 53-58.

Haden, J. "On Plato's Inconclusiveness," *Classical Journal* (Athens), 64 (1969): 219-224.

Hare, R.M. "Plato and the Mathematicians," in *New Essays on Plato and Aristotle*, ed. R. Bambrough. New York: Humanities Press, 1965.

Haring, Ellen S. "The *Theaetetus* Ends Well," *Review of Metaphysics*, 35 (1982): 509-528.

Heath, Thomas. *A History of Greek Mathematics*, vol. 1: *From Thales to Euclid*. Oxford: Clarendon Press, 1921.

————*Mathematics in Aristotle*. Oxford: Clarendon Press, 1949.

Heidel, W.A. "The Pythagoreans and Greek Mathematics," *American Journal of Philology*, 61 (1940): 1-33.

Hicken, Winifred. "The Character and Provenance of Socrates' Dream in the *Theaetetus*," *Phronesis*, 3 (1958): 126-145.

————"Knowledge and Forms in Plato's *Theaetetus*," *Journal of Hellenic*

Studies, 77 (1957), reprinted in *Studies in Plato's Metaphysics*, ed. R.E. Allen. New York: Humanities Press, 1965.

Holland, A.J. "An Argument in Plato's *Theaetetus*: 184-186," *Philosophical Quarterly*, 23 (1973): 97-116.

Jackson, Henry. "Plato's Later Theory of Ideas, IV: The *Theaetetus*," *Journal of Philology*, 13 (1885): 242-272.

Klein, Jacob. *Greek Mathematical Thought and the Origin of Algebra*. Cambridge, Mass.: MIT Press, 1968.

_____*Plato's Trilogy: The Theaetetus, the Sophist, and the Statesman*. Chicago and London: University of Chicago Press, 1977.

Koster, Willem J.W. *Le mythe de Platon, de Zarathoustre et des Chaldéens: Etude critique sur les relations intellectuelles entre Platon et l'Orient.* Lugduni Batavorum, E.J. Brill, 1951.

Koyré, Alexandre. *Introduction à la lecture de Platon*. New York: Brentano's, 1945.

Kucharski, Paul. *Les chemins du savoir dans les derniers dialogues de Platon*. Paris: Presses Universitaires de France, 1949.

Lesher, James H. "*Gnōsis* and *Epistēmē* in Socrates' Dream in the *Theaetetus*," *Journal of Hellenic Studies*, 89 (1969): 72-78.

Lewis, F.A. "Foul Play in Plato's Aviary," in *Exegesis and Argument: Studies in Greek Philosophy: Essays presented to Gregory Vlastos*, ed. E.N. Lee, A.P.D. Mourelatos, and R.M. Rorty. Assen, Netherlands: Van Gorcum, 1973.

Lutoslawski, Wincenty. *The Origin and Growth of Plato's Logic*. London: Longmans Green and Company, 1897, 1905.

McClain, Ernest G. *The Myth of Invariance: the Origin of the Gods, Mathematics and Music from the Rg Veda to Plato*. New York: Nicholas Hays, 1976.

_____"Plato's Musical Cosmology," *Main Currents in Modern Thought*, 30 (1973): 34-42.

McDowell, John. *Plato: Theaetetus*. Translated with notes. Oxford: Clarendon Press, 1973.

Matthen, Mohan, "Perception, Relativism, and Truth: Recollections on Plato's *Theaetetus* 152-160," *Dialogue* (Canada), 24 (1985): 33-58.

Meyerhoff, Hans. "Socrates' 'Dream' in the *Theaetetus*," *Classical Quarterly*, n.s. 8 (1958): 131-138.

Miller, Irving E. *The Significance of the Mathematical Element in the Philosophy of Plato.* Chicago: University of Chicago Press, 1904.

Miller, Mitchell, Jr. *The Philosopher in Plato's Statesman.* The Hague; Nijhoff, 1980.

_____*Plato's Parmenides: The Conversion of the Soul.* Princeton, N.J.: Princeton University Press, 1986.

Modrak, Deborah K. "Perception and Judgment in the *Theaetetus*," *Phronesis,* 26 (1981): 35-54.

Moravscik, Julius M.E. "*Symplokē Eidos* and the Genesis of *Logos*," *Archiv für Geschichte der Philosophie,* 42 (1960): 117-129.

Morrow, Glenn R. "Plato and the Mathematicians. An Interpretation of Socrates' Dream in the *Theaetetus* (201e-206c)," *Philosophical Review,* 79 (1970): 309-333.

Mugler, Charles. *Platon et la recherche mathématique de son époque.* Strasbourg: Editions P.H. Heitz, 1948.

Nakhnikian, G. "Plato's Theory of Sensation," *Review of Metaphysics,* 9 (1955): 129-148, 306-327; 10 (1956): 355-356.

Owen, G.E.L. "The Place of the *Timaeus* in Plato's Dialogues," *Classical Quarterly,* n.s. 3 (1953): 79-95, reprinted in Allen, R.E., ed., *Studies in Plato's Metaphysics.* New York: Routledge and Kegan Paul, 1965.

_____"Plato and Non-Being," in *Plato,* ed. G. Vlastos. Vol. 1. New York: Doubleday, 1971.

Parain, Brice. *Essai sur le logos platonicien.* Paris: Gallimard, 1942.

Patterson, Richard. *Image and Reality in Plato's Metaphysics.* Indianapolis: Hackett, 1985.

Polansky, R.M. Unpublished manuscript on the *Theaetetus.*

Robin, Leon. *Platon.* Paris: Librairie Felix Alcan, 1935.

Robinson, Richard. "Forms and Error in Plato's *Theaetetus*," *Philosophical Review,* 59 (1950): 3-30.

_____*Plato's Earlier Dialectic.* 2nd ed. Oxford: Clarendon Press, 1953.

Rorty, A.O. "A Speculative Note on Some Dramatic Elements in the *Theaetetus*," *Phronesis,* 17 (1972): 227-238.

Rose, L.E. "Plato's Divided Line," *Review of Metaphysics,* 17 (1964): 425-435.

Ross, W.D. *Plato's Theory of Ideas.* Oxford: Clarendon Press, 1951.

Runciman, Walter G. *Plato's Later Epistemology.* Cambridge, Cambridge University Press, 1962.

Ryle, G. "Letters and Syllables," *Philosophical Review,* 49 (1960): 431-451.

Sayre, Kenneth M. *Plato's Analytic Method.* Chicago: University of Chicago Press, 1969.

_____*Plato's Late Ontology: A Riddle Resolved.* Princeton, N.J.: Princeton University Press, 1983.

Schipper, E.W. *Forms in Plato's Later Dialogues.* The Hague: Nijhoff, 1965.

Shea, Joseph. "Judgment and Perception in *Theaetetus* 184-186," *Journal of the History of Philosophy,* 23 (1985): 1-14.

Shorey, Paul, *The Unity of Plato's Thought.* Chicago: University of Chicago Press, 1903, 1960; Archon Books, 1968.

_____*What Plato Said.* Chicago: University of Chicago Press, 1933.

Skemp, J.B. *The Theory of Motion in Plato's Later Dialogues.* Amsterdam: Hakkut, 1967.

Stenzel, Julius. *Plato's Method of Dialectic.* Translated by D.J. Allen. Oxford: Clarendon Press, 1940.

Taylor, A.E. "Continuity," in the *Encyclopedia of Religion and Ethics,* vol. 4, ed. J. Hastings. New York: Scribners, 1912.

_____*Plato: The Man and His Work.* (1926). 7th ed. London: Methuen, 1960.

Teloh, Henry. *The Development of Plato's Metaphysics.* University Park, Pa.: Pennsylvania State University Press, 1981.

Vlastos, Gregory. "Degrees of Reality in Plato," in *New Essays on Plato and Aristotle,* ed. R. Bambrough, London and New York: Humanities Press, 1965.

_____"Socratic Irony," *Classical Quarterly,* 37 (1987): 79-96.

Waerden, Bartel Leendert van der. *Science Awakening.* Gronigen, Holland: P. Noordhoff, 1954.

Wasserstein, A. "Theaetetus and the History of the Theory of Numbers," *Classical Quarterly,* n.s. 8 (1958): 165-179.

Wedburg, Anders. *Plato's Philosophy of Mathematics.* Stockholm: Almquist and Wiksell, 1955.

Weingartner, Rudolph H. *The Unity of the Platonic Dialogue: The Cratylus, the Protagoras, the Parmenides.* Indianapolis, Ind.: Bobbs-Merrill, 1973.

Wheeler, Samuel. "The Conclusion of the *Theaetetus*," *History of Philosophy Quarterly*, 1 (1984): 355-368.

White, N.P. *Plato on Knowledge and Reality*. Indianapolis, Ind.: Hackett, 1976.

Williams, C.J.F. "Referential Opacity and False Belief in the *Theaetetus*," *Philosophical Quarterly*, 22 (1972): 289-302.

Yoh, May. "On the Third Attempted Definition of Knowledge: *Theaetetus* 201c-210b," *Dialogue* (Canada), 14 (1975): 420-442.

Yolton, J.W. "The Ontological Status of Sense-Data in Plato's Theory of Perception," *Review of Metaphysics*, 3 (1949): 21-58.

INDEX

Ackrill, J., 239n.15, 240n.16, 240n.20
Addition, simple, 38, 40, 52, 79, 91, 138, 162-3, 167
aisthēsis. See Perception
Ambiguity, 15-28, 239n.15; and initiation, 29-30; and interpretation, 6-8, 41-42, 54, 100, 133, 137, 152, 171, 201-202n.11, 213n.15, 234n.11. *See also* Interpretation
Anaxagoras, 104
Anaximander, 201n.11
Annas, J., 203n.23, 246n.17, 249n6
Antisthenes, 8
apagogè, see Reduction (mathematics)
apeiron, see Continuum
Aporia: in the dialogues, 137, 201n.9, in the *Theaetetus,* 83, 126, role of, 2, 4-6, 100, 137
Application of areas, 229n.5, 252n.5
Aristotle, 128; his account of Plato's philosophy, 61, 200n.3, 204n.26
De Anima, 409a4, 230
Generation of Animals, 727b89, 243
History of Animals, 582a19, 243
Metaphysics, 998a25-27, 241; *1043b23-1044a9,* 202; *1048a86-88,* 39; *1092b10-13,* 229; *1081a17-20, b12-18,* 230
Physics, 203a10-15, 229; *209b15,* 224
Prior Analytics, 41a26-27, 212
Aviary model of mind, 83, 112, 120-121, 141, 236n.6, 240n.16

Benardete, S.R., 203n.23, 238n.13, 244n.10, 249n.6
Beverslius, J., 244n.12
Bluck, R.S., 202n.14, 207n.46
Bond *(desmon),* 172
Brown, M.S., 10, 201n.9, 206n.40, 249n.6, 254n.13
Brumbaugh, R.S., 218n.5, 227n.3, 252-253n.6, 254n.12

Burnet, J., 8, 9, 10, 11, 201n.10, 202n.14, 203n.18, 203n.23, 204n.26, 204n.27, 205n.28, 205n.29, 205n.30, 205n.31, 206n.37, 206n.38, 208n.53, 226n.2
Burnyeat, M.F., 202n.14, 220n.13, 227n.3, 231n.11, 231n.5, 232n.8, 233n.9, 246n.18, 246n.19, 248n.3, 248-249n.6, 255n.7

Campbell, L., 8, 10, 182, 202n.14, 203n17, 203n.23, 205-206n.36, 211n.6, 213n.15, 219n.10, 255n.7
Cave: of the *Republic,* 7, 39, 121
Cherniss, H., 11, 203n.23, 208n.50, 224n.2, 242n.6, 254n.9, 255n.7
Clay: definition of, 126-127
Collection. *See* Combination
Combination, 3, 69, 75; cause of, 69; dialectic as knowledge of, 70; epistemological, 52-53, 55, 60; in geometry, 34, 37-38; interpretation of, 153, 161-163; as mixture, 246n.20; in music and tragedy, 130; ontological, 37-40, 60, 63-65; successive, 149, 151; as *sygkritikē,* 71; as *syllabein,* 128, 243-244n.9; as *syllogismos,* 116, 128, 151, 237n.8, 241n.3; as *synthesis,* 241n.3. *See also* Addition, simple
Commensurability and incommensurability, 38, 149, 221n.15, 242n.6. *See also* Irrational(s)
Complex. *See* Whole of parts/elements
Continuum: in geometry, 34-35; in *kompsoteros* theory, 128-129; ontological 34-37, 60, 61-62, 64-65; perceptual, 47-49, 60
Convention: by convention, 223n.6, 225n.6, 232n.6
Cooper, J., 232n.8, 234n.1
Conford, F.M., 8, 11, 182-183, 201n.9,

269

of, 49-51, 123, 223n.6. *See also* Letters
and syllables
Lesher,J., 202n.14, 203n.23, 206n.47,
209n.60, 240n.20
Letters and syllables: as model for
emergent generation, 67, 75, 115, 124,
128, 153, 166, 225n.6, 241n.1, 243-244n.9,
248n.3; as model for separation and
combination, 65, 74, 77, 220n.12
Lewis, F., 240n.16
logon didonai. See logos
Logos: meaning and translation, 123,
200n.4, 245n.14, 245n.15; interpretation
of, 128-129, 130-134, 159-160, 164,
241n.4, 242n.5, 244n.10; as providing
grounds, 10-11; as rendering an
account *(logon didonai)*, 3, 128-130,
245n.15; role in knowledge, 3-4. *See also*
Definition
Lutoslawski, W., 8, 9, 10, 202n.14, 204n.25,
206n.42

Method, philosophical, 225n.3. *See also*
Dialectic, method of
McClain, E.G., 218n.5
McDowell, J., 111, 183-185, 202n.14,
210n.3, 211n.5, 211n.6, 213-215n.15,
219n.10, 221n.15, 234n.1, 238n.13,
240n.18, 248n.5, 249n.8, 255n.7
Mean (mathematics), 173-178, 185-187,
252n.4, 254n.1
Meno's paradox, 93-94, 118, 141, 244n.12
Meno: parallels with *Theaetetus,* 201n.9,
203n.21, 241n.4, 244n.10
Midwife: Socrates' role as, 37, 56, 59, 71,
83, 101, 158, 163, 169, 171, 203n.21
Miller, I.E., 229n.4, 253n.9, 255n.7
Miller, M., 225n.5, 226n.2, 250n.8
Mind: activity of, 34-35, 37, 49, 69, 74-75,
122, 128, 232n.8; relation to soul, 223n.4,
234n.9
Models of mind. *See* Waxblock model of
mind, Aviary model of mind
Modrak, D., 232n.8
Morrow, G., 12-13, 201n.10, 202n.14,
203n.23, 209n.57, 210n.63, 210n.64,
235n.4, 245n.17
Mugler, C., 202n.14, 226n.2, 229-230n.5,
242-243n.6, 249n.6, 253-254n.9
Music: as model for emergent generation,
64-65, 77, 129, 220n.12

Mysteries: and esoteric doctrine, 224n.2;
initiation of reader, 29, 42, 68, 71, 77,
116, 149; initiation of Theaetetus, 28, 29,
33-34, 42, 56-57, 66, 68, 100, 163, 169,
172; in the *Meno,* 231n.4; Plato's interest
in, 248n.4; Plato's own theory, 217n.1

Nature, by: *versus* by convention: 49,
223n.6, 225n.6, 232n.6, 235n.3
Nicomachus, 186, 229n.4, 255n.2
"nothing other than..." *(ouk allo
ti...e...),* 16, 41, 54, 103, 129, 210n.2
Novak, J., 249n.6

One-many structure, 65-66, 68, 128-130,
134, 143-144, 163, 177. *See also* Whole of
elements/parts
opinion: objects of, 235-237n.6; summary
account, 164; false opinion, 107-113,
117-118, 201n.7; knowledge as true
opinion, 103-122; true opinion and
recollection, 5-6; role of true opinion in
knowledge, 2-4. *See also* knowledge:
Definition as true opinion and logos
ouk allo ti...e... See "nothing other
than..."
Owen, G.E.L., 201n.6

Pappus, 228n.4, 230-231n.11
Patterson, R., 225n5, 250n.8
Perception: as contrasted with sensation,
45-46, 221-222n.1, 234n.1; *kompsoteros*
theory of, 45-57, 60, 80, 83-99, 164;
judgment in, 232-233n.8
Philosopher: "digression" on the, 238n.13
Plato: as Heracleitean, 217n.1; his
philosophy, 200n.3, 224n.1
Apology: 21b et seq., 7,146; *21b3-9,* 231, *21b4,*
7
Charmides: 160b9-d3, 140; *160d8,* 237;
161b5-6, 236; *161c9,* 7; *162a10,* 7; *162b4,* 7;
162e6 et seq., 6; *164d6-165b3,* 201; *166e5 et
seq.,* 7; *167d1-9,* 106; *168d3-e1,* 106;
173a3-174c3, 147;
Cratylus: 387a2-8, 164; *388b7-c1,* 164;
388b13-c1, 223; *389b1-3,* 76; *389b8-c1,*
199; *389d8-390a7,* 241; *390c2-11,* 239;
399c2-4, 237; *401d4-5,* 213; *402a4-9,* 223;
402a4-b5, 213; *402c2-3,* 213; *412a5-6,* 237;

State what kompsolm... is

Hunt 513-253-536

En Dayton
white Deera Bowl

On Infallibility 160 (7-9, 17'D1-

151 - on objects as complexes of perceptual images
15c - all are ambiguous becomes all dmt / fixfinkys

Cleet (S)

162 onk